being
sociological

DOING RESEARCH ▪ MODERNIZING

being

▪ STRATIFYING: CLASS ▪ GOVERNING

▪ SEXUALIZING ▪ BEING: IDENTITY ▪ F

socio

▪ EDUCATING ▪ STRAYING: DEVI

INFORMING: MEDIA ▪ RELATING: FAMILY

VORKING ■ CONSUMING ■ TRADING

OWER ■ RACIALIZING ■ GENDERING

NG: EMOTIONS ■ BELIEVING: RELIGION

E ■ MEDIATING: TECHNOLOGY ■

BELONGING: COMMUNITY ■ FINISHING

Edited by

**Steve Matthewman,
Catherine Lane West-Newman
and Bruce Curtis**

contents

First published 2007 by
PALGRAVE MACMILLAN
Houndmills, Basingstoke, Hampshire RG21 6XS and
175 Fifth Avenue, New York, N.Y. 10010
Companies and representatives throughout the world

PALGRAVE MACMILLAN is the global academic imprint of the Palgrave
Macmillan division of St. Martin's Press, LLC and of Palgrave Macmillan Ltd.
Macmillan® is a registered trademark in the United States, United Kingdom
and other countries. Palgrave is a registered trademark in the European
Union and other countries.

ISBN-13: 978-0-230-00522-8 hardback
ISBN-10: 0-230-00522-5 hardback
ISBN-13: 978-0-230-00523-5 paperback
ISBN-10: 0-230-00523-3 paperback

This book is printed on paper suitable for recycling and made from fully
managed and sustained forest sources.

A catalogue record for this book is available from the British Library.

Library of Congress Cataloging-in-Publication Data
Being sociological / [edited by] Steve Matthewman, Catherine Lane West-Newman,
    Bruce Curtis.
       p.cm.
    Includes bibliographical references and index.
    ISBN-13: 978-0-230-00522-8 (cloth)
    ISBN-10: 0-230-00522-5 (cloth)
    ISBN-13: 978-0-230-00523-5 (pbk.)
    ISBN-10: 0-230-00523-3 (pbk.)
       1. Sociology. I. Matthewman, Steve. II. West-Newman, Catherine Lane, 1942-
III. Curtis, Bruce, 1961-

    HM585.B45 2007
    301—dc22

                                                                    2006047143

10   9   8   7   6   5   4   3   2   1
16   15   14   13   12   11   10   09   08   07

Printed in China

list of tables

acknowledgements

The editors would like to thank Emily Salz, Commissioning Editor for Sociology, Media and Cultural Studies at Palgrave for her enthusiasm for, and support of, this project. We would also like to thank the International Advisory Board for their helpful commentary and support.

Every effort has been made to trace all the copyright holders but if any have been inadvertently overlooked, the publishers will be pleased to make the necessary arrangements at the first opportunity.

editorial board

notes on the contributors

David Bedggood, Senior Lecturer in Sociology, University of Auckland, Auckland, New Zealand.
dr.bedggood@auckland.ac.nz

Chris Brickell, Senior Lecturer in Gender and Women's Studies, University of Otago, Dunedin, New Zealand.
chris.brickell@stonebow.otago.ac.nz

Ian Carter, Professor in Sociology, University of Auckland, Auckland, New Zealand.
ir.carter@auckland.ac.nz

Bruce Curtis, Senior Lecturer in Sociology, University of Auckland, Auckland, New Zealand.
b.curtis@auckland.ac.nz

Roger Dale, Professor, Graduate School of Education, University of Bristol, Bristol, England.
R.Dale@bristol.ac.uk

Douglas Hoey, doctoral student, Department of Sociology, University of Auckland, Auckland, New Zealand.
d.hoey@auckland.ac.nz

Mike Lloyd, Senior Lecturer in Sociology, Victoria University of Wellington, Wellington, New Zealand.
Mike.Lloyd@vuw.ac.nz

Peter T. Manicas, Professor of Philosophy Emeritus, Queens College, CUNY, and Director, Interdisciplinary Studies, University of Hawai'i at Mānoa.
manicas@hawaii.edu

Steve Matthewman, Senior Lecturer in Sociology, University of Auckland, Auckland, New Zealand.
s.matthewman@auckland.ac.nz

Tracey McIntosh, Senior Lecturer in Sociology, University of Auckland, Auckland, New Zealand.
t.mcintosh@auckland.ac.nz

Aaron Norgrove, doctoral student, Department of Sociology, University of Auckland, Auckland, New Zealand.
aaronnorgrove@gmail.com

Rhonda Shaw, Lecturer in Sociology/Social Policy, Victoria University of Wellington, Wellington, New Zealand.
rhonda.shaw@vuw.ac.nz

Michael Stevens, doctoral student, Department of Sociology, University of Auckland, Auckland, New Zealand.
m.stevnz@yahoo.co.nz

Martin Sullivan, Senior Lecturer, School of Sociology, Social Policy and Social Work, Massey University, Palmerston North, New Zealand.
M.J.Sullivan@massey.ac.nz

Ivanica Vodanovich, Consultant Sociologist and Member of the New Zealand Human Rights Review Tribunal, Auckland, New Zealand.
i.vodanovich@auckland.ac.nz

Catherine Lane West-Newman, Senior Lecturer in Sociology, University of Auckland, New Zealand.
l.westnewman@auckland.ac.nz

introduction:
on being sociological

Reading this book

This book has an open and shameless purpose. We want to seduce you into the world of sociology where we, and you, can explore this curious thing – society – in which we all have a part. The 'social' is produced in and through humans doing things collectively. It is characterized by amazing richness, variety, complexity, puzzlement, and capacity to excite both pleasure and misery. That's a lot for one book to attempt, and so it's pretty obvious that our version of being sociological is just that. It is one set of descriptions and explanations among the many possible others and so we must begin by explaining why our version of the subject is shaped the way it is.

Seduction is not necessarily about sex (though it is often thought of and used in that context) or about 'leading astray'. But it is about being tempted and enticed. Some textbook writers are inhibited by the belief that all the ideas (sociological theories) that have been proposed by sociologists should, like competing candidates for election in a democratic state, be given equal time and attention. This is undoubtedly fair but it won't necessarily achieve our goal of tempting and luring you into wanting to know more. The project of seduction requires different strategies. So it is only proper that we begin by revealing the choices we made.

We set out to make a book that introduced some of the main ideas and issues in the contemporary world that are currently being explored in present-day sociology. Because sociology today rests on the work of earlier generations of sociologists, discussing the present also meant returning to the past and describing the platform of their ideas that grounds our present thinking. Our central purpose is to demonstrate the form and content of sociological analysis and argumentation. This is achieved through presentation of a range of social institutions – family, community, religion, education, work, for example – and sociological concepts such as class, ethnicity, gender, power and consumerism. Each chapter describes and illustrates the uses we make of theory and evidence within that particular context.

The first three chapters may be read as an extended introduction to what follows. 'On Being Sociological' introduces the idea that sociology exists to make sense of the many shapes and dimensions of social being. West-Newman and Matthewman describe the practice that we call 'being sociological' as a process which is also a perspective; a way of using evidence to see and understand, and very often to critique existing social arrangements. The structural, institutional and behavioural dimensions of society are seen as social processes through which we make and maintain our world. 'Doing Research' describes some of the ways in which sociologists collect and analyse the evidence that forms the basis of their research and theorizing. Curtis critiques the idea of a great conceptual divide between qualitative and quantitative methods and illustrates their reconciliation through the case study of Muhammad Ali's boxing fight record. 'Modernizing' takes the circumstances of colonization in one settler society as the starting point from which to describe the historical antecedents and theoretical foundations of sociology. Carter describes the relationship between modernity and the discipline of sociology through its founding fathers (Marx, Weber, Durkheim) to the present and traces modernity's positive and negative aspects. He argues that 'processes unleashed by the Enlightenment and the Dual Revolution remade, and still remake, the world, so nobody was or is untouched'.

Within this context 'Working' pays its respects to the founding fathers, especially Marx, and focuses on processes of control and resistance in the workplace. Drawing on contemporary accounts that prioritize the labour process, Curtis describes a range of conceptual understandings which have been developed over the past 25 years, including individualist practices in face of a triumphant managerialism, cyborg work, and tactics of consumption. 'Consuming' looks at what it means to live in a consumer society, where social status is equated with spending power and where constant desire exists for the new and fashionable; the chapter considers the implications of global inequalities in the ability to consume. 'Trading' introduces the social significance of market, money and trading and sets them in the context of a globalized world economic system. 'Stratifying: Class' introduces the concept of class through three empirical case studies – Aotearoa New Zealand (where class appears to be subordinated to ethnic and gender inequality); Argentina (where recent events suggest that class has given way to social movements of the unemployed); and Iraq (where categories of religion and nationality cut across those of class). Bedggood argues that class relations remain a fundamental feature of modern capitalist society and that other dimensions of social inequality such as race, gender and nationality are rendered more intelligible through an understanding of their relations to class. 'Governing: Power' then introduces some of the many sociological uses of the concept of power, including Weber's foundational connection between power as capacity and the mechanisms of political dominance, pluralist conceptions of power in democracy developed in mid-twentieth-century American political sociology, and Manuel Castells' more global perspective on poverty as an inequality of power. Finally there is a description of Foucault's conception of disciplinary power, its sources and effects.

The next four chapters are concerned with characteristics of social identity that are associated with collective and individual experiences of inequality. Each considers the extent to which such identities are socially constructed and determined and the role of ideology in privileging certain identities over others. In 'Racializing' Vodanovich traces the sometimes complex connections between 'race', ethnicity and nationalism both conceptually and in the everyday lives of people and notes some of the ideological and practical consequences of this mode of classifying human collectivities. 'Gendering' examines several perspectives on the social construction of gender – as difference, as division, and as performance – and describes some of the ways in which notions of femininity and masculinity are (re)produced alongside and against each other. In 'Sexualizing', Stevens is concerned with how the social patterning of sexual expression, desire and behaviour has been shaped and challenged since the advent of modernity. He describes how various societies at different times have allowed more or less freedom and tolerance of sexual difference; contemporary challenges to hetero-normativity; and the uses of state power to regulate human sexuality. 'Being: Identity' introduces the sociology of self through its conceptual origins in American social psychology, illustrates its sociological development in the work of Goffman, and sets those ideas into the context of contemporary disability rights activism. It then looks at recent developments that claim the arrival of post-modern fragmented identity.

So far, the chapters have fallen relatively easily into groupings. But, as is always the case with classifying anything, more than one method is possible and no scheme is perfect. So although we might pretend to have a strong reason for grouping the next chapters together, the truth is that they run in the order they do because that seemed as good as any other possibility. 'Feeling: Emotions' is about the social causes and consequences of emotional experience, which is a quite new field of sociological interest. Here West-Newman describes the links between biological and social constructionist explanations of emotions and looks at some social dimensions of love, revenge and grief.

The remaining chapters could be said all to be about social institutions in some way or another, although this is a category so broad it can hardly count as a meaningful classification. 'Believing: Religion' is about sociological understandings of spiritual beliefs, many of them religious, and about the social and political implications of such beliefs, when they are collectively held. McIntosh argues that as a tool for making sense of human consciousness and experience religion is a core element of social life and its significance should not be underestimated. In 'Educating' Dale considers education systems as a significant means by which societies seek to define and strengthen national distinctiveness, strengthen national economies, address social problems and in the process deeply affect the life chances of individuals. He argues that current processes of change in education, brought about through the global impact of neo-liberalism education, require new modes of envisioning and understanding.

The sociology of deviance, introduced in the chapter called 'Straying: Deviance', deals both with crime and with non-criminal behaviours that are said to violate social norms. The decision to call the chapter 'straying' rather than 'deviating' signals that not all apparent violations of social norms are either individually blameworthy or socially disruptive. By writing not about crime but about the experience of other forms of social deviance Lloyd offers a rather different way of beginning to think about what sociologists mean by 'deviance' and why the concept has been so widely used within the discipline.

'Mediating: Technology' begins from the acknowledgement that contemporary existence takes place within complex, yet vulnerable, socio-technical systems that inform everything that we do. Matthewman takes the automobile as his case study of technology's global impact and argues that technology and user are engaged in a relationship that is sometimes enabling and sometimes constraining and either way is fully implicated in social life. 'Informing: the Media' introduces the sociology of the media through a focus on three significant research areas: media effects on audiences, the production of meaning through mediated signs, and the political economy of the media. Finally, there are two chapters on areas of active social interaction and participation. In the first of these, 'Relating: Family', Shaw examines the significant changes in the sociology of the family since the foundational work by Talcott Parsons on the American nuclear family in the 1950s. She describes the diverse and complex forms taken by current family formations and draws on actual examples of family practices and types to illustrate the cultural and situational diversity of family life. Discussion of new trends in family formation includes changing patterns of intimacy and care, same-sex and elective families, changes to marriage and fertility patterns, and the impact of the latter on reconstituted, blended and sole-parent families. In 'Belonging: Communities', the concept of community is taken back to its late nineteenth-century formulation by Tönnies and its subsequent uses in sociology, taken through to its present contemporary appearance in the context of social groupings that have grown up around the internet and made 'virtual' communities of their own.

Many of these chapters cover a variety of theoretical approaches and examples from diverse places. But some do not. This is because we wanted to demonstrate the range and variety of sociological styles and subjects available when the sociological imagination is at work. And so we have chapters that are unashamedly partial in both senses of the word. Their authors choose and write about the theories, issues and evidence that allow them to make a strong case for the position they favour. Now we need to explain what we mean by this phrase, 'the sociological imagination at work'.

Pleasure and play

> If I read this sentence, this story, or this word with pleasure, it is
> because they were written in pleasure.
>
> R. Barthes, *The Pleasure of the Text*, p. 4

Chances are you will not be reading this book because you have already decided to become a sociologist. Few of us have ever decided that in advance; mostly it happens by accident, a seduction of ideas and possibilities. However, there are reasons why some people take to this subject with enthusiasm; they do so because they have realized what might be discovered through being sociological. This is a subject with quite distinct pleasures and possibilities.

Probably the most significant characteristic of good sociology is that it understands what it is for – that it is above all 'an *attempt to understand*' (Berger, 1966, p. 15). Because curiosity is the key quality for sociological understanding we need to be deeply interested in the spectacular and mundane details of the lives of other people. What, we continually ask, is actually going on here? And we are not necessarily satisfied by the obvious answer because commonsense explanations are not always right. Sometimes what we take for granted about the way the world is may, in fact, be wrong. Human interaction in social situations is amazingly complex and diverse and the collective social arrangements that we construct and within which we live our individual lives are the result of choices among multiple possibilities. Because social arrangements are incredibly complex there is a very high probability that things won't always work in the ways they are supposed to. From the point of view of a politician or any authority given the task of managing segments of the society, this is an issue of working out why things go wrong and how they can be fixed – they look for, or are ambushed by, social problems. But for sociologists the really interesting questions are about the means by which society ever works at all and why, most of the time, it seems to be quite effective. Of course, there are societies that fall apart – usually under the stress of warfare, economic collapse, or biospherical disasters of famines, earthquakes and tsunamis – but when this happens it is perceived as a disaster and not as business as usual.

In the local butcher's shop on a Monday morning we discuss the weather – hot and sunny. He says one of the staff has not turned up today so everyone else has to do more work. I say that it is too hot to sit at my computer writing a book. He asks, 'What is it about?' I say 'Sociology'. His eyes glaze over and the conversation comes to a halt while he rather hopelessly waits for me to tell him what that is and I struggle to find the right short sentence. 'Exploring what people do together in society', I say feebly. What I might have said if the next customer had not been leaning over my shoulder was that sociology uses causal reasoning based on evidence to explain how society works. All of which makes the point that it is easier to say what sociology does than what it 'is' and that it might take more than one sentence to explain. Everything that happens in society – when people are making arrangements to achieve their particular purposes, managing their collective existence, doing things together – can be the source of that evidence. Almost everyone notices to some extent what is happening around them in the world (some with more care and enthusiasm than others) but being sociological means looking at the world *in a particular way*. Its distinctiveness comes from 'the habit of viewing human actions as *elements of wider figurations*: that is, of a non-random assembly of actors locked together in a web of *mutual dependency*' (Bauman, 1991, p. 7). This has been described as the sociological way of seeing and, if we take 'seeing' to mean much more than just gazing with our eyes, this idea makes sense. Sociological seeing is a particular way of finding meaning in what is there to be observed about the ways in which people live together in their world. What is too often left out of books that introduce sociology is precisely that sense of lateral thinking, of play, of humour, which more often than not characterizes the very best sociology. We need to recognize that we are dealing with the 'human comedy' of society because, Peter Berger points out, if we remain unaware of 'this comic dimension of social reality' we will miss some of its most essential features, for there are, in short, 'insights that one can obtain only while laughing' (1966, p.187).

In his *Invitation to Sociology* Peter Berger (1966, pp. 32–3) explained the pleasure of sociology as an 'excitement of discovery' not of finding out new and strange things but of encountering the familiar 'transformed in its meaning'. Sociology has a fascination, he said, which 'lies in the fact that its perspective makes us see in a new light the very world in which we have lived all our lives' (1966, p. 33). This matter of studying the world we live in has implications not only for those coming new to it but also for sociologists who must simultaneously live in the world and examine its workings. Our lives and our professional knowledge and practice inevitably become intertwined so that in the midst of even the most intense personal experience we may suddenly remember what sociological analysis says. Burying loved ones, losing one's job, falling in love, are all accompanied by recalled knowledge of theories, facts, and even figures about the social aspects of these experiences. Sometimes such knowledge, and the distance it brings to the experience, helps one to cope better; sometimes it does not. Ian Craib (2003), after a diagnosis of cancer and extended treatment, used his inside knowledge to write about fear of death, supposedly defeated for the time being by cocktails of dangerous drugs. But we read his reflections with the poignant knowledge that cancer returned, quite quickly, so that he died before the work appeared in print. Such knowledge inevitably shapes our engagement with his analysis, but does not alter the point that understanding the social conditions of his fear and offering insights to others in a similar situation seemed good to him, even though it did not alter the outcome. On a less profound level, what we choose to investigate, as sociologists, is inevitably shaped by our tastes, life experiences and perception of what is, and is not, important.

Some chapters in this book will undoubtedly interest you more than others; probably this will be related to your own life circumstances and experiences and also your hopes and intentions for the future. On the other hand, all good sociology has certain other characteristics which you may find less than appealing.

You might want to stop here

Who was it that said that the outskirts of every city should have a billboard which simply reads: 'I doubt it'? It's a very sociological sensibility.

There are two schools of thought: that knowledge is power and that ignorance is bliss. If you think the former, then sociology will serve you well. If you think the latter you might want to discontinue the journey. It is better that you do not proceed past this point. 'Little animals from cartoons, talking rabbits, doggies, squirrels, as well as ladybugs, bees, grasshoppers', Czesław Milosz tells us, 'have as much in common with real animals as our notions of the world have with the real world. Think of this, and tremble' (Milosz, 1998, p. 47). Indeed it can be terrifying: sociologists tell us that we may be at most risk from those we are most intimate with (Brownmiller, 1976), that the most ordinary people can do the most unspeakable things – torture, murder, even genocide (Arendt, 1963). There are comforts in delusions, in thinking that the world is as it should be. It is so much easier to believe that the unemployed are out of work because they are lazy, that the homeless live outside because they prefer fresh air, that prisons are full of bad people because there are no bad circumstances. It is much more troubling to think that the *system* itself is at fault, that structural inequalities are embedded within it, that some people do so well only because others do so very badly.

Precisely these points are captured in Richard Flanagan's (2001) novel *Gould's Book of Fish: A Novel in 12 Fish*, which begins with a central character who sells reproduction furniture to wealthy American cruise ship passengers. The chairs are surplus from a government office, but they are passed off as (American) Shaker furniture brought to Australia by Nantucket whalers. The passengers were not, the character says in his defence, buying furniture but buying stories – in this case, the most comforting that a wealthy American can, for these are tales of 'Us Finding Them Alive and Bringing Them Back Home' (Flanagan, 2001, p. 6). The tourists had money, something that the furniture sellers were short of. In return for their money:

> [T]hey only asked ... to be lied to and deceived and told that single most important thing, that they were safe, that their sense of security – national, individual, spiritual – wasn't a bad joke being played on them by a bored and capricious destiny. To be told that there was no connection between then and now, that they didn't need to wear a black armband or have a conscience about their power and their wealth and everybody else's lack of it; to feel rotten that no-one could or would explain why the wealth of a few seemed so curiously dependent on the misery of the many. (Flanagan, 2001, pp. 8–9)

To have illusions punctured can be unsettling and sociology does this. Our 'first wisdom' is that things are not necessarily as they appear (Berger, 1966, p. 34). It exposes connections and relationships; it renders visible the links between past and present, rich and poor. Sociology illuminates what the privileged and the powerful prefer to hide, but it may also show us things that will challenge our ontological security. So, before we proceed any further, some more words of caution: Warning: Sociology will corrupt your taken-for-granted world. You will never take anything at face value again.

If you lack inquisitiveness, avoid shock and never seek to be challenged; if you really take no pleasure in discovery and have no desire to see the world afresh; if you want to believe that things can only be how your teacher or preacher said they are; if you never say 'I doubt it', sociology is best avoided (Berger, 1966).

To be sociological is to come to the realization, as Italo Calvino (1995, pp. 9–10) does in 'The Flash', that things do not have to be as they are, that we do not simply have to accept present arrangements and that all of the mundane objects in our existence – traffic lights, cars and everything else besides – are not separate from the world. We can consider alternatives. It can be otherwise. Take the first things on Calvino's list: traffic lights and cars. Why lights instead of a roundabout? Why *that* number of colours? Who colour-coded social actions? Why must red mean stop, green go, and amber stop or go? Why drive on *that* side of the road? Why drive at all? Why cars instead of mass transit? Why not public as opposed to private transportation? Who decides? Who benefits? How does it all affect us?

How do the threads run? Sociology as critique

Reflecting on the place of C. Wright Mills, probably still America's most famous sociologist as social critic, Robert Merton saw that 'he reached out, crystallised, politicalised ... he represented a *social* protest, a social anger, and there was a good deal to rebel against' (quoted in Mullan, 1987, p. 287). Some claim that a critical position is inherent to sociology: 'I think the sociologist's question is always "it looks exactly like that, therefore it cannot possibly be – how is it really?" ... [S]ociology is by definition the critical edge, even to its own assumptions' (Stuart Hall quoted in Mullan, 1987, p. 249).

If so, then this positioning has a long and honourable history. For the young Karl Marx and his comrades, criticism – *Kritik* – functioned as rallying cry and as programme. Dogmatic assertions, prefabricated solutions and free-floating abstractions were dispensed with. The only way towards a future perfect world was by critiquing the one existing. Criticism clarifies and demystifies, if used to help explain social actions. In such a task nothing is to be spared. As Marx (1978, p. 13) wrote to Arnold Ruge: 'I am speaking of a *ruthless criticism of everything existing.*' Neither the conclusions derived from this process nor the powerbrokers that would oppose them should be feared. This is the essence of the sociological spirit, our approach to the world. No social formation is fixed and unchangeable; nothing is 'natural' and timeless; there are always alternatives. Marx makes this point in *The German Ideology*. 'As for that seemingly unalterable realm, supposedly not human, it is human in disguise. No countryside, no matter how bucolic, has meaning beyond its historical and social context' (Finkielkraut, 2001, p. 37). Where Ludwig Feuerbach saw 'true essences' and 'sensuous certainty', Marx saw the actions of commerce and industry. To Feuerbach the cherry tree was obviously part of nature. To Marx it was brought into this place at a specific time by specific people bent on agricultural exploitation. 'Beneath the sand, the cobblestones; beneath the appearance of what is given', then, 'the reality of conflict and of what has been constructed' (Finkielkraut, 2001, p. 37).

We find a similar exchange between two of the principal characters in Robert Musil's (1997) modern classic *The Man without Qualities*. Once more we see that human labour lies behind beautiful nature. The world was not always this way; it was made so. Passing through an enchanting valley, its hillsides paved with pines, Diotima heaps praise on the scenic splendour. To be sure, she is not so naïve as to see a pristine nature without a human presence; she can accept the hand of a planter. But what she is not able to see is an intensively managed plantation that exists solely for the purposes of profit. Ulrich, meanwhile, views this 'nature' as nothing more than raw material for primary industry. 'Who planted you, O lovely woods, so high up there above?' asks Diotima, echoing the lyrics of a song. Ulrich is quick to respond:

> The Landbank of Lower Austria. Don't you know, cousin, that all the forests hereabouts belong to the Landbank? The master you are about to praise in the next line is a forester on the bank's payroll. Nature in these parts is a planned product of the forestry industry, a storehouse of serried ranks of cellulose for the manufacturers, as you can see at a glance. (Musil, 1997, p. 302)

As in Marx and Feueurbach, here are two very different takes on how the world is as it is. To Diotima we attribute a commonsense view, while Ulrich seems fully possessed of the sociological imagination. Indeed, there is a long history of dominant groups using capital, equipment and skills to arrange nature into something of their liking (Williams, 1975, p. 123). Sociologists seek to uncover such actions. For us nothing is given, everything is constructed.

In any society or social formation some groups of people do better than others. Advantage and disadvantage are unevenly distributed, and often they fracture along lines of social class, age, gender, ethnicity and sexuality. Sociologists sometimes use the acronym CAGES to remind ourselves of these inequalities and their place in the constraints within which we all make our histories. 'Sociology', then, 'originated in the impulse to criticize the principles of the society with which it found itself confronted' (Adorno, 1981, p. 46). When Theodor Adorno (1981, pp. 37–46) inspected Karl Mannheim's sociology of knowledge he saw a scene that was altogether too benign: harmony and integration, life chances in the lap of objective forces, neutral laws and the lottery of personality. Against this Adorno draws our attention to the sort of questions sociologists *should* ask: who controls whom; the sources of social conflict; what is right and wrong; patterns of dependence, deprivation and sacrifice; the operations of social power and the conferment of privilege; economic and political control. Learning from Marx and Adorno, we can make an important point: first and foremost sociology is a critical discipline. Pierre Bourdieu would say that it is a discipline which makes trouble. Sociology is a problem because it 'reveals things that are hidden and sometimes *repressed*', because it speaks truth to power, because its 'objects are stakes in social struggles – things that people hide, that they censor, for which they are prepared to die' (Bourdieu, 1993, p. 9). Sociologists are troublesome because they do not stick to the official script, because they go beyond everyday understandings, because they are forever sceptical of the politics of naming. What separates a just war from an illegal occupation, a terrorist from a freedom fighter? Sociology interrogates those that decide and the mechanisms they employ to legitimate these judgements.

Ghosts and silences

Among the difficult questions sociologists may raise when they look beneath the surface of things present, and the past which made them so, are those that probe noteworthy silences and seek out ghosts. In an evocative exploration of such things Avery Gordon (1997, p. 7) explains their significance:

> Haunting is a constituent element of modern social life. It is neither pre-modern superstition nor individual psychosis; it is a generalizable social phenomenon of great import. To study social life one must confront the ghostly aspects of it. This confrontation requires (or produces) a fundamental change in the way we know and make knowledge, in our mode of production.

The traces of ghosts which appear to those sensitized to their existence, or at least willing to concede possible conditions for existence, mark injustices and injuries of the past, now passed into silence. Gordon's own examples of ghosts include the disappeared of Argentina and the slave ancestors of African Americans. Many others may also be identified – for example in the disturbing and uncomfortable remains of indigenous peoples colonized in 'the great European imperial adventures', which reshaped so much of the global configuration of peoples into modern nation states (see Chapter 2, 'Modernizing'). In contemporary societies the sociological imagination can allow us to see that 'that which appears not to be there is often a seething presence, acting on and often meddling with taken-for-granted realities'. This, Gordon argues, is the ghost – 'the sign or empirical evidence ... that tells you a haunting is taking place' (1997, p. 8).

Again the haunting theme returns us to the sociological necessity of critique that exposes both the violence of modernity and the mechanisms of its forms of domination. The transformative power of sociology, if indeed it is to have any, lies in the capacity to reveal what has been silenced and denied; but that same potential is constrained by disciplinary norms of evidence which are more appropriate to some sociological tasks than to others. In cases like these, literature may turn out to be more sociological in effect than sociology itself. Indeed Gordon (1997, p. 25) points out that the separation of story telling (as fiction) and social science (as fact) wrenches apart much that belongs together because good sociology is about 'both the production and the interpretation of stories of social and cultural life'. In this Introduction the imaginations of Musil and Sebald walk the boundaries of fact and fiction to show us new things about the sociality of life and the essential 'constructedness' of meaning. They engage 'a whole realm of experience and social practices that can barely be approached without a method attentive to what is elusive, fantastic, contingent and often barely there' (Gordon, 1997, p. 25).

Because they sit so comfortably with our own declared position on the possibilities of the sociological imagination, we've given considerable attention to Gordon's ideas. But they are by no means the only invocation of haunting in contemporary explorations of our globalized world. Sneja Gunew's (2004) work on multiculturalism in (former) British settler colonies likens them to 'haunted nations' entangled in their imperial past and points to the role of imagination as a 'social faculty' through which we see the world. Similarly, Jacqueline Rose (1996, pp. 4–5) seeks to understand the roots of Israeli–Palestinian relations in their bedrock of 'states of fantasy', arguing that 'political identities and destinies' can only be understood by 'letting fantasy into the frame' for it 'plays a central constitutive role in the modern world of states and nations' as it 'involves, alongside the attempt to arrest the present, a journey through the past'.

How do the threads run? Consciousness and connections

> I have kept asking myself ... what the invisible connections that determine our lives are, and how the threads run.
>
> W. G. Sebald, *Campo Santo*, pp. 200–1

Sociology is a form of consciousness, a way of thinking. Of particular concern are the often unarticulated or hidden connections within society, the figurations that help shape our fate. We may be unaware of invisible constraints, conducting our lives '[a]s if everything did not depend on who regulates whom' (Adorno, 1981, p. 37). It is the task of good sociology to reveal to us the unseen connections that determine our lives. Disciplined by history, anchored to persons and place, mindful of context and nuance, able to see the often unseen connections that are nonetheless there and that make a difference – this is precisely how all good sociology should proceed. *What are the unseen connections that determine our lives? How do the threads run?* These are amongst the most profound questions a sociologist can ask.

The microcosm of a rock pool seen through the eyes of a neurophysiologist's patient illustrates this theme (Broks, 2003). James was troubled by an encyclopaedia illustration of such a pool, most particularly by what he could not see in that picture but that was, for him, there. The scene was too benign – underneath was an unnamed thing that avoided categorization, beneath a brittle star, partially obscured by tangles of brown weed and shore crab claws, a spidery thing. But worst of all, it was the very same thing that inhabited his own brain. The peculiar anguish of this 'reality' is, of course, particular to James and his illness, but the perception of unseen connections is not. Sketched depictions do not capture all of real life and a rook pool, like a brain, can be a fraught place. James realized that there was more going on in this environment than the illustration allowed him to see. This supposedly authoritative version seemed to omit the most crucial elements. A fixed image can neither convey patterns of dependence and predation within the pool – the barnacle at risk from the dog whelk – nor 'the invisible alchemy of the seaweeds' as they absorb sunlight, and take nourishment from water and gas. Niches and networks, actions and processes – the very things of life itself – all lost in the frozen moment. This is the problem with still lives – life is not still. 'A rock pool is, in reality, a precarious place', notes Broks (2003, p. 81), '[t]o survive is to mesh with complex networks of behaviour and intricate patterns of physics and chemistry, all shaped minutely by the ebb and flow of the tides and the rotation of the Earth'. Biology, chemistry, physics; the microscopically small and the astronomically large; all of them have their place in the humble rock pool of life. What on the surface appears simple is in reality deeply complex. Budding sociologists can take lessons from this: what counts are the things we clearly see and the things we do not, things small, medium and large, and the dynamic ways in which they relate to and interact with each other. Good sociology will take cognizance of all of this: of structures, systems and forces in motion; of relationships, connections and forms of interaction; and of the meaning of individual and collective action.

W. G. Sebald (2003, pp. 12–13) gives us a sense of this complexity. Here is his answer to the causes of the post-war German economic miracle; it contains a mixture of the obvious, observable and mundane with things far less noticeable, much less named:

> The prerequisites ... were not only the enormous sums invested in the country under the Marshall Plan, the outbreak of the Cold War, and the scrapping of outdated industrial complexes – an operation performed with brutal efficiency by the bomber squadrons – but also something often less often acknowledged: the unquestioning work ethic learned in a totalitarian society, the logistical capacity for improvisation shown by an economy under constant threat, experience in the use of 'foreign labour forces', and the lifting of the heavy burden of history that went up in flames between 1942 and 1945 along with the centuries-old buildings accommodating homes and businesses. ... And in addition to these more or less identifiable factors in the genesis of the economic miracle, there was also a purely immaterial catalyst: the stream of psychic energy that has not dried up to this day, and which has its source in the well-kept secret of the corpses built on the foundations of our state, a secret that bound all Germans together in the post-war years, and indeed still binds them, more closely than any positive goal such as the realization of democracy ever could.

Modernity

Thus far we have discussed the pleasures of discovery, sociology's claims to novelty, our insistence on criticism, our quest to give voice to the marginalized, and the ways in which we try to render visible the habitually unseen. What we have yet to discuss are the reasons for sociology's being. In short, sociology came about to make sense of the 'great transformation' (Polanyi, 1957) from traditional to modern life. This includes a series of shifts: in cognitive and political authority from religion to science, church to state, monarchy to democracy, making citizens of subjects; in socio-economic organization from field to factory, guild to vocation, kin unity to bureaucracy; and in the location of social activity from country to city, region to nation. In sum, they profoundly alter the scope, scale and intensity of social life. Another way to think about modernity is through nouns of action: industrialization, urbanization, bureaucratization, rationalization, democratization, individualization, secularization, fragmentation. This draws our attention to the fact that we are dealing with processes of rendering, states of being, alterations and transformations, acts of conversion. Such processes are uneven and they meet resistance. They continue to happen, and they are yet to come.

Terry Eagleton (2004) once joked that no one knows which month the Dark Ages ended. A similar problem presents itself with what we call modernity. There is no single point at which modern times began. Writing in the European context, Jürgen Habermas (1981, p. 5) isolates three great cultural transformations that begin at the start of the sixteenth century: European discovery of the 'New World', the Renaissance, and the Reformation. For him, these are the events that delineate the modern world from the Middle Ages. Alex Callinicos (1999, pp. 14–15) also writes from a European perspective, but prefers to begin a century later, urging that the modern world begins with the peace that follows the Wars of Religion and the Thirty Years War (1618–48), the Scientific Revolution of the seventeenth century, and the European powers' global struggle for supremacy from the mid-eighteenth century. Also included are the French and Industrial Revolutions. Doubtless there are other factors, for this is a list which can never be complete. Marshall Berman (1982, p. 16) would certainly want us to be mindful of mass: demographic upheavals, the significance of communication systems, the effects of social movements, all undergirded by the ever-growing – but crisis-ridden – capitalist mode of production. Taken together, these processes make people think *in fundamentally different ways* about the world and their place in it.

The medium of film can help us make yet more sense of modernity. It is an interesting exercise to read Georg Simmel's (1964) 'Metropolis and Mental Life' and then watch Charlie Chaplin's (1936) *Modern Times*. If you did not 'get' modernity by reading about sensory overload or becoming a cog in the machine, you would certainly recognize it when you see it. Ron Fricke's (1992) documentary film *Baraka* is another way into the stuff of sociology. It is a meditation on human–environment relationships, ranging across six continents and 26 countries. While its entirety is recommended, we want to focus here on 14 minutes of it. They provide stunning visual imagery of the great transformation. For this short segment shows the move from hills to plains, forests to shanties, country to city; and nature's thorough domination by culture.

The process begins with the attack of rainforest by chainsaws and of mineral-rich land by high explosives. Ants scurry across the leaves as the saws buzz, a sign of things to come. Later we see the creation of a world that looks fit neither for animal nor human habitation. A young Kapayo gazes out from the foliage. The next time that we are shown children they stare through the cages that frame their slum windows. 'Free', so to speak (remember our CAGES). High-rise city apartments are shown, box on box, life on life. Then high-rise cemetery compartments, box on box, death on death. We have reached a threshold moment in our history: more people now live in urban areas than in rural. Henceforth global population growth will be in the cities. Most of this growth will be in the developing world, where 'only the slum remains as a fully franchised solution to the problem of warehousing the twenty-first century's surplus humanity' (Davis, 2004, p. 28). Cut to an Indonesian cigarette factory, where hundreds of women toil shoulder to shoulder. Their individual machines are made of wood. The film moves onwards, to the subways of Tokyo, then to São Paolo and Park Avenue, New York. A great mosque in the Middle East, then two train stations in two different countries: Shibuya and Grand Central. The camera fixates on the clock. Traditional societies worked on organic time; they needed to know when to sow and reap harvests, and when livestock would give birth. Ours is a world dominated by precise mechanical time; it synchronizes social actions and dominates our lives. Next we see a pair of factories devoted to high technology: one makes video recorders, the other computer keyboards. This time things are more recognizably modern: metals and plastics have replaced wood, the machines seem to be in charge now, and the pace of work is no longer controlled by the workers. The assembly line moves the components. Then escalators move commuters. Battery farms are shown. Subway gates control the flow of rush-hour workers; who goes where. Sorting gates in the factory farms do something similar, only this process sorts more fundamental destinations: life from death. The tempo quickens; the soundtrack and the images speed up. Eggs on conveyor belts, chicks on conveyor belts, and people on conveyor belts blend into one another to dizzying effect.

The film has no dialogue. The director has deliberately omitted signposts on this journey. He is not interested in us knowing where each scene is filmed. In a world of change we have no certainty. It could be a Brazilian gold mine – the Serra Pelada? Is the next mine Chuquicamata in Chile? The wetlands could be on any number of continents. The slums look as though they are Brazilian *favela*, but perhaps they are Bolivian, just as the later shots could be the *conventillos* of Quito or the *colonias populares* of Mexico City. The high-rise slums could be the old walled city of Kowloon or they could be in part of Manila. Is it the Grand Mosque in Mecca that is shown or the great mosque in Cairo? We can be reasonably sure that footage is taken in a JVC factory (in Yokosuka?), and the other factory is definitely producing keyboards, but its location is unclear. Thailand? The escalators could be anywhere in the urbanized world and the battery farms could be anywhere in the West. This uncertainty is not merely geographic, it is also existential. Where in the world are we? (We are, after all, dealing with global happenings.) How did we come to be here? And how are we to live our lives? These are questions that we all have to face.

We have just witnessed the spread of instrumental reason in the modern world. After all, the most rational way to house millions of people is on top of each other; likewise, the most rational way to get the maximum number of people from A to B is to stuff them together on mass transportation, just as production is most rationally organized by breaking down each task into its smallest possible component. But what is the human cost of all of this? The final scene contains a solitary figure (a Butoh dancer?). The person screams. In light of everything we have just witnessed, this is perhaps the most rational response. It appears that society rather than the person is sick. Sociology came about to make sense of the metropolitan experience, and in these scenes we see many of our greatest concerns: the irrationality of rationality, the double-edged sword that is progress, the significance of clock-time, the intensification of social life, and the fate of the individual in mass society. Though the person screams the scream is silent. It is the task of sociology to give voice to that scream.

Worrying for the world – ethics and social theory

Sociologists make social theory 'in order to try to understand the world better', or so Howard Becker (quoted in Mullan, 1987, p. 121) says, and, as one of the more durable and respected of United States sociologists, we see no reason to disbelieve him. What Becker is actually getting at here is an explanation of sociology's need for theorizing. The word itself has a particular meaning for us in this book. Each chapter begins with a gerund – identifying, feeling, stratifying, gendering – the form of a verb that acts as a noun while retaining the verb's capacity to signal activity, process, movement, happening. This is because we want most strongly to signal two things. First, that understanding how societies work and making theory are ongoing processes, always necessarily under construction. And second, that while sociology cannot do its work without theory – some kind of abstracted generalizing about why things are the way they are – that theory should be always subservient to understanding, prized for its practical capacity not as an end in itself. Theory exists not to be understood but to help us to understand.

If our processes of generalizing from evidence and extrapolating from what we know to what we do not generates plausible theory then we have established a baseline to argue that some social arrangements and effects are desirable and life-enhancing but others damage lives, destroy human potential, and generate suffering to the extent that they deserve rejection and replacement. We need, therefore to theorize so that we may understand the operation and consequences of capitalism, the subjugation of women, imperialism, environmental degradation and the mechanisms through which social inequalities are created and sustained.

Ghassan Hage lives in Australia and holds up a mirror to the local paranoia of 'white nationalism' and Australian dilemmas of living in a multicultural society constituted through indigenous Aboriginal people, British settlers, and waves of European and, more recently, global migration. In particular he unwraps the problems of racism in societies where anti-intellectualism is a respectable social and moral position. His granny in Bathurst cared for the nation in a quite particular way – by worrying about it. She 'worried about Australia, she worried about Catholics in Lebanon, she worried about my marriage and she worried about me driving on the highway to Bathurst'. In short, she did what people do when 'worrying is the last available strategy for staying in control of social processes over which they no longer have much control' (1998, pp. 10–11). It is also what people do when they do not understand the social processes around them that are changing their world and the way they can live within it. Frameworks of ideas for comprehending our social world and its tendency to reconfiguration and change do not, of course, give individuals the power to reverse such things. But they may, nevertheless, provide the somewhat uncertain but better-than-nothing comforts of explanation and perhaps even strategies to minimize personal fall-out.

It is at this point, of course, that the question of ethical positioning in the sociological project becomes most acute. Since its earliest days many, though not all, sociologists have conceived the practice of sociology to be a moral project. This is true both of those included in the official canon (more or less affectionately known as the dead white men) and those less visible who are themselves still ghostly presences – a haunting on the perimeter of the discipline. Two kinds of disappearance have taken place. Sociology as a moral project was diminished and blurred, perhaps more in America than elsewhere, as practitioners succumbed to the lure of scientific respectability and 'pure reason'. More importantly, though, were the individuals whose voices were silenced and lost because their social location placed them outside the 'charmed circle' of professional academic sociology. Charles Lemert names three figures – Anna Julia Cooper (a black woman), W. E. B. Du Bois (a black man) and Charlotte Perkins Gilman (a white woman) – whose work was profoundly sociological and might easily be regarded as foundational if they had been socially relevant and acceptable within the academic world of their time. This is, then, a matter of inclusion and exclusion, of recognized and unrecognized capacity to generate knowledge. Lemert remarks the irony that they were, as part of their society's many 'repressed and ignored public intellectuals ... either scrupulously excluded or not plainly visible from within the culture sociology meant to explain and save' (2004, p. xxx). In a sense he sees this as an inevitable consequence of sociology's dual positioning as '*both* a prophetic voice criticizing modern society *and* a believing adherent to the promise of modern culture' (2004, p. xxxi).

C. Wright Mills, writing in the 1950s, used the term 'post-modern' to refer to social conditions in the world of his own time. What he discerned in his own society led him also to argue for the necessity to reclaim for sociology a moral position through the contributions of its public intellectuals to that society. Those who responded to the call include women and members of racial and ethnic minorities, who appear from the 1970s and in ever-increasing strength are part of the resurgence. Making the invisible visible in themselves, they have prompted majority scholars to join the cause. Charles Lemert, Zygmunt Bauman, bell hooks, Avery Gordon – naming is invidious because there are so many. If you agree that being sociological is an ethical practice then these names are worth pursuing. Of course we hope that this all makes good sense to you, but you won't really know unless you give it a try. So now read on ...

Suggestions for further reading

Bauman, Z. (1991) *Thinking Sociologically* (Oxford: Blackwell).
Game, A. and A. Metcalfe (1996) *Passionate Sociology* (London: Sage).
Lemert, C. (2004) *Sociology After the Crisis*, 2nd edn (London: Pluto).
Mills, C. W. (1971/1959) *The Sociological Imagination* (Harmondsworth: Penguin).

Bibliography

Adorno, T. W. (1981/1967) *Prisms*, trans. Samuel and Sherry Weber (Cambridge, MA: MIT Press).
Anderson, R. J., J. A. Hughes and W. W. Sharrock (1985) *The Game: An Introduction to Sociological Reasoning* (London and New York: Longman).
Arendt, H. (1994/1963) *Eichmann in Jerusalem: A Report on the Banality of Evil* (New York: Penguin).
Barthes, R. (1975) *The Pleasure of the Text* (New York: Hill and Wang).
Bauman, Z. (1991) *Thinking Sociologically* (Oxford: Blackwell).
Berger, P. L. (1966) *Invitation to Sociology: A Humanistic Perspective* (Harmondsworth: Penguin).

Berman, M. (1982) *All That is Solid Melts into Air: The Experience of Modernity*, 1st edn (New York: Simon and Schuster).

Berman, M. (1988) *All That is Solid Melts into Air: The Experience of Modernity*, 2nd edn (New York: Penguin).

Bourdieu, P. (1993) 'A Science that Makes Trouble', *Sociology in Question* (London and Thousand Oaks, CA: Sage), pp. 8–19.

Broks, P. (2003) *Into the Silent Land: Travels in Neuropsychology* (London: Atlantic Books).

Brownmiller, S. (1976) *Against Our Will: Men, Women and Rape* (Harmondsworth: Penguin).

Callinicos, A. (1999) *Social Theory: A Historical Introduction* (Oxford: Polity Press).

Calvino, I. (1995) 'The Flash', *Numbers in the Dark and Other Stories* (New York: Pantheon), pp. 9–10.

Craib, I. (2003) 'Fear, Death and Sociology', *Mortality* 8(3), pp. 285–95.

Davis, M. (2004) 'Planet of Slums', *New Left Review* 26 (March/April), pp. 5–34.

Durkheim, E. (1951/1897) *Suicide: A Study in Sociology*, trans. John A. Spaulding and George Simpson, ed. George Simpson (Glencoe, IL: Free Press).

Eagleton, T. (2004) 'The Anatomy of Fascism', *The New Statesman*. Available: http://www.newstatesman.com/Bookshop/300000082709 [accessed 9/6/2004].

Finkielkraut, A. (2001) *In the Name of Humanity: Reflections on the Twentieth Century* (London: Pimlico).

Flanagan, R. (2001) *Gould's Book of Fish: A Novel in 12 Fish* (Sydney: Picador).

Gordon, A. F. (1997) *Ghostly Matters: Haunting and the Sociological Imagination* (Minneapolis and London: University of Minnesota Press)

Gunew, S. M. (2004) *Haunted Nations: The Colonial Dimensions of Multiculturalisms* (New York: Routledge).

Habermas, J. (1981) 'Modernity versus Postmodernity', *New German Critique* 22, pp. 3–14.

Hage, G. (1998) *White Nation: Fantasies of White Supremacy in a Multicultural Society* (Annandale, NSW: Pluto Press).

Lemert, C. (2004) *Sociology after the Crisis*, 2nd edn (Boulder, CO: Paradigm; London: Pluto).

Marx, K. (1978/1843) 'Letter to Arnold Ruge', in R. C. Tucker (ed.), *The Marx–Engels Reader*, 2nd edn (New York: W. W. Norton), pp. 12–15.

Mills, C. W. (1971/1959) *The Sociological Imagination* (Harmondsworth: Penguin).

Milosz, C. (1998) 'A Warning', *Road-side Dog* (New York: Farrar, Straus and Giroux), p. 47.

Mullan, B. (ed.) (1987) *Sociologists on Sociology* (London: Croom Helm).

Musil, R. (1997/1978) *The Man without Qualities*, trans. Sophie Wilkins (London: Picador).

Polanyi, K. (1957) *The Great Transformation* (Boston, MA: Beacon).

Rose, J. (1996) *States of Fantasy* (Oxford: Clarendon Press).

Sebald, W. G. (2003) 'Air War and Literature: Zürich Lectures', *On the Natural History of Destruction*, trans. Anthea Bell (London: Hamish Hamilton), pp. 1–105.

Sebald, W. G. (2005) *Campo Santo* (New York: Random House).

Simmel, G. (1964/1903) 'The Metropolis and Mental Life', in Kurt Wolff (ed. and trans.), *The Sociology of Georg Simmel* (New York: The Free Press), pp. 409–24.

Williams, R. (1975) *The Country and the City* (New York: Oxford University Press).

① doing research

Bruce Curtis

KEY
POINTS
- Research can be explored through a number of binaries, of which quantitative and qualitative are the most significant.

- Ragin (1987, 1994) recasts this distinction in terms of the process of developing categories for cases and variables. He also offers insight into the matching of research and the goals of sociological inquiry.

- This approach to understanding differences between quantitative and qualitative research downplays claims about epistemology (Blaikie, 1993; Crotty, 1998) and the technical elements of practice or methods. Rather it allows a political appreciation of forms of research and goals of sociological inquiry that echo C. Wright Mills (1959).

Introduction: beyond words and numbers

Sociology is a broad church encompassing the study of all facets of contemporary society. The homepage of the International Sociological Association (http://www.ucm.es/info/isa) currently lists 59 transnational research committees, working groups and thematic clusters each dealing with different specialties of sociological inquiry; and more are added each year. Despite this universe of choice the research that enables meaningful sociological inquiry is routinely divided into just two types or methodologies: quantitative and qualitative. Furthermore the majority of sociological inquiry – or at least its public and published outputs – is sustained by a relatively narrow clustering of research practices or methods, mainly distributed across this qualitative–quantitative divide. There are, of course, exceptions. Webb et al. (1966) and Kellehear (1993) suggest that the study of material traces and use of unobtrusive methods lie outside these axes, and the archival work of social historians is also somewhat problematic to the formulation.

This division of research into quantitative and qualitative groupings is an example of what Ludwig Wittgenstein (1958, p. 17) has called 'our craving for generality'. A similar division has been posited between male and female perspectives. What have been described as the 'first feminist social science texts' (Oakley 2000, p. 32) appeared in the 1970s to challenge the existing dominance of male perspectives – in choice of subject matter and in ways of knowing. Their authors, explicitly or implicitly, claimed that male dominance and quantitative methods existed in what Ann Oakley (2000, p. 33), herself a pioneer and pivotal figure in this field, describes as 'a (more or less) unconscious conspiratorial alliance'. In a movement of simple (and sometimes simplistic) reversal, objectivity was dramatically rejected by anti-positivist feminists and its previous epistemological status claimed instead for personal subjective experience. The resulting objectivity/subjectivity paradigm wars are now history but their useful legacy is our recognition that social knowledge and experience are intrinsically gendered. This is now integral to what we know as being sociological (see Chapter 9, 'Gendering').

Oakley is undoubtedly accurate in her contention that understanding qualitative and quantitative research as a dichotomy, as an either/or choice, is ultimately a social and historical construct. However, her support for the notion that 'in most social science research projects the terms "quantitative" and "qualitative" neither add insight nor credibility, and nothing would be lost by their omission' (Oakley, 1998, p. 724) misses the possibilities for useful categorization on the basis of overlapping and criss-crossing similarities which Wittgenstein has called 'family resemblances' (Wittgenstein, 1953, pp. 31e–32e). The approach to the quantitative and qualitative divide used in this chapter adopts the modest proposal suggested by Wittgenstein. Quantitative and qualitative are used as descriptors of similar existing practices on the part of sociologists rather than as any broader epistemological claim.

Qualitative research is most closely associated with participant observation and other less interactive forms of fieldwork (Crotty, 1998). Similarly, the collation of data within this methodology is usually achieved by the methods of interviews, logs and personal journals (Adler and Adler, 1994). The varied foci and findings of qualitative research are published in an equally wide variety of forms and styles. In contrast to this eclecticism, quantitative research is dominated by a particular methodology and method: the survey and questionnaire, respectively (De Vaus, 2002). Thus survey data are typically collected through questionnaires, which are delivered to respondents using face-to-face techniques, mail, telephone and the internet (Dillman, 2000). The survey involves the use of statistical analysis and now almost inevitably uses dedicated software packages. The findings of quantitative research also tend to have a more standardized format, which focuses on issues of sampling, margins of error and the reliability and validity of the questionnaire (i.e., the survey instrument).

The readily observed difference between numbers and words is important to the quantitative–qualitative binary. From this commonsense perspective, quantitative research generates data and analyses that are numerical in form, including counts, distributions, correlations, etc.; whereas qualitative research centres on words, including stories, life histories, descriptions, etc. (Denzin and Lincoln, 1994, pp. 1–17). The decision to opt for numbers or words is therefore a strategic choice for researchers. In other words, numbers and words do very different things for researchers. Numbers are most commonly associated with the capacity to *condense* data, insofar as a number can represent almost anything amenable to sociological inquiry: an average, a rating, a correlation, etc. Words or writing, on the other hand, are prized for an opposite property, the capacity to detail and to *extend*. One example will suffice. Haralambos and Holborn (1991, p. 707) present an important position within the discipline of sociology (although arguably not within the broader social sciences) when they claim that: 'compared to quantitative data, qualitative data are usually seen as richer, more vital, as having greater depth and as more likely to present a true picture of a way of life, of people's experiences, attitudes and beliefs'.

It is important to mention that most subjects of sociological inquiry can be explored through the use of either numbers or words, albeit not with equal efficiency. In this sense numbers and words represent opposite ends of a representational and analytical continuum. In practice the two mechanisms of communication are interlinked. All quantitative research requires qualitative judgement. Collecting data in a quantitative form, as numbers, inevitably requires opinion on the part of the respondent and/or the researcher. For example, rating the clarity of lectures in a course survey, where 1 = excellent, 2 = good, 3 = average, 4 = below average, 5 = poor, produces numbers and possibly a class average which are in turn based on non-numerical decision making or opinions. Equally, all qualitative judgements can be represented quantitatively (they can be coded). However, the enduring difficulty in interpreting codes centres on understanding the assumptions and rules used in creating them.

Quantitative and qualitative research can also be understood in terms of what sociologists like to do. They can be characterized as fascinations by researchers with generating forms of numbers or words. It is therefore fairly unsurprising that there is not a great deal of movement between the two methodologies, research types, insofar as they require somewhat different skill sets. Proof of the reluctance of many sociologists to move between quantitative and qualitative research can be found in the publication of textbooks on research and methodology. While there are masses of textbooks on qualitative research, and probably an equal number on quantitative research, there are relatively few on both. Unfortunately the justifications for undertaking quantitative versus qualitative research and vice versa often appear as defensive positioning rather than as rational debate in sociology. For example, the statement by Haralambos and Holborn is correct only insofar as it downplays the efficient matching of research methodologies with the goals of sociological inquiry (Ragin, 1994). It is not too much of an exaggeration to think that a one-sided appreciation of qualitative research might also reflect a growing prejudice in sociology wherein students and established practitioners are drawn to words partly because of an aversion to mathematics and statistics. In this respect sociology is both the critical voice of the social sciences, of what C. Wright Mills called 'the sociological imagination' (Mills, 1959) *and* unfortunately becoming the natural home for social scientists who can't do maths!

The balance of this chapter focuses on the logic of research and the differences and similarities between its quantitative and qualitative types. The main elements of discussion are those of *categorization* – developing cases and variables, framing the research in terms of the interaction of theory and data, and the matching of forms of research with specific goals of sociological inquiry.

Cases and variables

Ragin (1987, 1994) has written on the linkage of qualitative and quantitative research with the specific goals of sociological inquiry. He recasts the numbers versus words debate in terms of the elemental categories of research: *cases* and *variables*. These categories are the building blocks of sociological inquiry. Indeed, the choice between numbers and words is a secondary one that more or less follows from a primary decision about these categories. Quantitative research tends to focus on large numbers of cases and relatively few variables. The capacity for numbers to condense data is most useful in this context. Qualitative research tends to focus on few or singular cases and many variables. The capacity for words to enhance data is most useful in this context. The use of cases and variables in research can be illuminated, without recourse to frightening statistical formulae or philosophizing on understanding reality (i.e., epistemology) (Blaikie, 1993, pp. 201–16), by looking at a famous moment in sporting history – the night Muhammad Ali knocked out George Foreman to regain the World Heavyweight Boxing Title.

The relevant entry on Muhammad Ali's boxing record for the fight reads: '30 Oct 1974 George Foreman Kinshasa KO8 Won World Heavyweight Title'. This entry is an example of a case. The 57 alphanumeric characters (excluding blanks) making up the case profiles the fight across five variables. The five variables are: 'Date', 'Opponent', 'Venue', 'Result', 'Title'. These variables can be unpackaged somewhat. The fight took place on 30 October 1974 in Kinshasa, Zaire. The fight began in the early hours of the morning because it was to be televised via satellite to viewers in Britain and the USA, which was an innovation at the time. Because the World Heavyweight Title was at stake the fight was scheduled for 15 rounds, each of 3 minutes. Ali's opponent was George Foreman. Foreman was the title holder and then regarded as unbeatable by most boxing commentators. Muhammad Ali knocked out (KO'ed) George Foreman in the eighth round of the fight. The World Heavyweight Title passed to Ali, who became only the second boxer ever to regain the title.

Clearly a single case with five variables can only convey a limited amount of information to the reader/researcher. However, multiple cases can be illuminating, even with few variables. For example, Muhammad

FEELING: EMOTIONS • BELIEVING: RELIGION • EDUCATING • STRAYING: DEVIANCE • MEDIATING: TECHNOLOGY • INFORMING: MEDIA • RELATING: FAMILY • BELONGING: COMMUNITY • FINISHING

29

Ali's boxing record can be presented as 61 cases (fights) and the same five variables as used above (see Table 1). The resulting 2,700 alphanumeric characters (excluding blanks) provide an overview of the rise and fall of a boxer whom many still regard as 'The Greatest' (Hauser, 1992). The use of multiple cases with uniform variables allows the researcher to observe variation of those variables across the cases. What is important is how the variables change in relation to each other. In this example as few as five variables ('Date', 'Opponent', 'Venue', 'Result', 'Title') provide a lot of information.

Table 1 **Muhammad Ali's boxing record**

Date	Opponent	Venue	Result	Title
29 Oct 1960	Tunney Hunsaker	Louisville, KY	W6	
27 Dec 1960	Herb Siler	Miami Beach, FL	KO4	
17 Jan 1961	Tony Esperti	Miami Beach, FL	KO3	
7 Feb 1961	Jim Robinson	Miami Beach, FL	KO1	
21 Feb 1961	Donnie Fleeman	Miami Beach, FL	KO7	
19 Apr 1961	Lamar Clark	Louisville, KY	KO2	
26 Jun 1961	Duke Sabedong	Las Vegas, NV	W10	
22 Jul 1961	Alonzo Johnson	Louisville, KY	W10	
7 Oct 1961	Alex Miteff	Louisville, KY	KO6	
29 Nov 1961	Willi Besmanoff	Louisville, KY	KO7	
19 Feb 1962	Sonny Banks	New York, NY	KO4	
28 Mar 1962	Don Warner	Miami Beach, FL	KO4	
23 Apr 1962	George Logan	Los Angeles, CA	KO6	
19 May 1962	Billy Daniels	New York, NY	KO7	
20 Jul 1962	Alejandro Lavorante	Los Angeles, CA	KO5	
15 Nov 1962	Archie Moore	Los Angeles, CA	KO4	
24 Jan 1963	Charlie Powell	Pittsburgh, PA	KO3	
13 Mar 1963	Doug Jones	New York, NY	W10	

Date	Opponent	Venue	Result	Title
18 Jun 1963	Henry Cooper	London	KO5	
25 Feb 1964	Sonny Liston	Miami Beach, FL	TKO7	Won World Heavyweight Title
25 May 1965	Sonny Liston	Lewiston, ME	KO1	Kept World Heavyweight Title
22 Nov 1965	Floyd Patterson	Las Vegas, NV	KO12	Kept World Heavyweight Title
29 Mar 1966	George Chuvalo	Toronto	W15	Kept World Heavyweight Title
21 May 1966	Henry Cooper	London	KO6	Kept World Heavyweight Title
6 Aug 1966	Brian London	London	KO3	Kept World Heavyweight Title
10 Sep 1966	Karl Mildenberger	Frankfurt	KO12	Kept World Heavyweight Title
14 Nov 1966	Cleveland Williams	Houston, TX	KO3	Kept World Heavyweight Title
6 Feb 1967	Ernie Terrell	Houston, TX	W15	Kept World Heavyweight Title
22 Mar 1967	Zora Folley	New York, NY	KO7	Kept World Heavyweight Title
26 Oct 1970	Jerry Quarry	Atlanta, GA	KO3	
7 Dec 1970	Oscar Bonavena	New York, NY	TK15	
8 Mar 1971	Joe Frazier	New York, NY	L15	For World Heavyweight Title
26 Jul 1971	Jimmy Ellis	Houston, TX	KO12	
17 Nov 1971	Buster Mathis	Houston, TX	W12	
26 Dec 1971	Jurgen Blin	Zurich	KO7	
1 Apr 1972	Mac Foster	Tokyo	W15	
1 May 1972	George Chuvalo	Vancouver	W12	
29 Jun 1972	Jerry Quarry	Las Vegas, NV	KO7	
19 Jul 1972	Al Lewis	Dublin	KO11	
20 Sept 1972	Floyd Patterson	New York	KO7	
21 Nov 1972	Bob Foster	Stateline, NV	KO8	
14 Feb 1973	Joe Bugner	Las Vegas, NV	W12	
31 Mar 1973	Ken Norton	San Diego	L12	
10 Sep 1973	Ken Norton	Los Angeles	W12	
21 Oct 1973	Rudi Lubbers	Jakarta	W12	

FEELING: EMOTIONS • BELIEVING: RELIGION • EDUCATING • STRAYING: DEVIANCE • MEDIATING: TECHNOLOGY • INFORMING: MEDIA • RELATING: FAMILY • BELONGING: COMMUNITY • FINISHING

31

Date	Opponent	Venue	Result	Title
28 Jan 1974	Joe Frazier	New York, NY	W12	
30 Oct 1974	George Foreman	Kinshasa	KO8	Won World Heavyweight Title
24 Mar 1975	Chuck Wepner	Cleveland, OH	KO15	Kept World Heavyweight Title
16 May 1975	Ron Lyle	Las Vegas, NV	KO11	Kept World Heavyweight Title
30 Jun 1975	Joe Bugner	Kuala Lumpur	W15	Kept World Heavyweight Title
1 Oct 1975	Joe Frazier	Manila	KO14	Kept World Heavyweight Title
20 Feb 1976	Jean Pierre Coopman	San Juan	KO5	Kept World Heavyweight Title
30 Apr 1976	Jimmy Young	Landover, MD	W15	Kept World Heavyweight Title
24 May 1976	Richard Dunn	Munich	KO5	Kept World Heavyweight Title
28 Sep 1976	Ken Norton	New York, NY	W15	Kept World Heavyweight Title
16 May 1977	Alfredo Evangelista	Landover, MD	W15	Kept World Heavyweight Title
29 Sep 1977	Earnie Shavers	New York, NY	W 15	Kept World Heavyweight Title
15 Feb 1978	Leon Spinks	Las Vegas, NV	L15	Lost World Heavyweight Title
15 Sep 1978	Leon Spinks	New Orleans, LA	W15	Won World Heavyweight Title
2 Oct 1980	Larry Holmes	Las Vegas, NV	LTK11	For World Heavyweight Title
11 Dec 1981	Trevor Berbick	Nassau, Bahamas	L10	

The variations of 'Date', 'Opponent', 'Venue', 'Result' and 'Title' outline the trajectory of Ali's career. 'Date' and 'Venue' chart the rise of a local boxer (born Louisville, Kentucky) into an international superstar fighting across the USA and in Britain, Germany and more remote locales like Indonesia and Zaire. 'Date' and 'Result' demonstrate the longevity of Ali's career and his amazing capacity to bounce back from defeat and adversity. A check with 'Title' shows he won the World Heavyweight Title three times and was defeated in his second to last fight challenging again for the title. Indeed, Ali was unbeaten between 29 October 1960 and 8 March 1971. His record to this point is 29 wins to 0 losses. In subsequent fights his record is 27 wins to 5 losses.

A closer examination of 'Date' highlights a three-year gap in his record, from 22 March 1967 to 26 October 1970. A check with 'Title' shows that in the earlier fight he 'Kept World Heavyweight Title'; the later fight was not a title one and yet his first loss (on 8 March 1971) was 'For World Heavyweight Title'. In short, Ali did not lose his title in the ring. On 28 April 1967 Ali refused induction into the US Army on religious grounds. He was a minister in the Nation of Islam. US boxing authorities subsequently stripped him of his licence to box and the US Government confiscated his passport while it prosecuted him under the Universal Military Training and Service Act. Ali won this lawsuit when on 28 June 1970 the US Supreme Court reversed Ali's draft evasion conviction. Ali was then able to return to boxing. While Ali was unbeaten in the 1960s, the variables underscore his comeback as being more problematic. 'Date' and 'Result' show that after his comeback he challenged for the title after only two fights; in the 1960s he had challenged for the title after 19 fights. This title fight was his first loss. A comparison of Ali's win–loss record between his first and second careers is not the only evidence of his decline. Prior to his enforced break he won 22 of 29 fights by knockout; later he won 13 of 32 by knockout. This suggests differences between the 'young Ali' and the 'old Ali'. Ali's first career was characterized by his devastating hand speed and the inability of his opponents to hit him. His second career was marked by an ability to absorb punishment and to win by what the experts call 'ring craft'. 'Result' confirms that Ali was never knocked out.

Including 'Opponent' in the assessment of variation across variables outlines some of the reasons for Ali becoming a sentimental favourite despite his refusal to fight in Vietnam and membership of the Nation of Islam. First, he fought regularly and against the best available opponents. Second, it is an adage in boxing that fighters are remembered because of their opponents. Ali had several memorable opponents and campaigns, winning the title from Sonny Liston (and winning the rematch), beating Joe Frasier (the first man to defeat him) 2–1, and most famously beating George Foreman to regain the title. Third, Ali's losses are also part of his legacy. His defeat to Joe Frazier (on 8 March 1971) in what was billed as 'The Fight of the Century' delayed but did not derail his comeback. He later twice defeated Frazier. Similar was the unexpected loss to Ken Norton, and this was also twice avenged. By the time of his shock defeat to Leon Spinks, Ali was in boxing terms a veteran. Reversing the loss allowed Ali to become the first boxer to win a title three times. His last hurrahs (coming out of retirement) against Larry Holmes and Trevor Berbick did nothing to diminish his record (as in both cases he was overmatched and suffering from the onset of Parkinson's Disease).

Muhammad Ali's boxing record is, of course, a slight example of a case and variable dataset. Indeed, 61 cases x 5 variables is insignificant compared to the size of even a modest survey. For example, a small telephone survey exploring alcohol use or holiday destinations or some such would rarely generate less than 500 cases and 20 variables. The resulting dataset would be about 30 times larger than Ali's boxing record and far more amenable to statistical analysis of the variation of variables, so that closer attention could be paid to the relationships between them (for example, between gender and excessive drinking, or educational attainment and enjoyment of opera). Large surveys have thousands of cases and hundreds of variables. As noted, Ali's boxing record is a tiny dataset of 2,700 alphanumeric characters structured by 61 cases x 5 variables. Despite its small size the dataset provides an entrée to analysing the career of a famous boxer in terms of the variation of five variables. This type of analysis is the crux of quantitative research. A similar-sized dataset – 1,800 characters (excluding blanks), 437 words – is presented below to introduce qualitative research.

In 1975 Norman Mailer wrote *The Fight*, a book about the World Heavyweight Title match between Ali and Foreman. Foreman had enormous punching power and had knocked out a series of opponents on his way to the championship, including Joe Frazier who had defeated Ali. Mailer attended the fight in Zaire and was there in the weeks leading up to the fight. The following extract from his book looks at the last 18 seconds of the fight (Foreman was knocked down and counted out at 2:58 of round 8). The extract comes from the closing passages of three chapters dedicated to describing the fight. Previously, Mailer describes the rounds where Ali had lain against the ring ropes while Foreman threw a barrage of punches. By the eighth round Ali was fresher than Foreman:

> With twenty seconds left to the round, Ali attacked. By his own measure, by the measure of twenty years of boxing, with the knowledge of all he had learned of what could be and could not be done at any instant in the ring, he chose this as the occasion and lying on the ropes, he hit Foreman with a left and a right. Into this last right hand he put his glove and his forearm again, a head-stupefying punch that sent Foreman reeling forward. As he went by, Ali hit him on the side of the jaw with a right, and darted away from the ropes in such a way as to put Foreman next to them. For the first time in the entire fight he had cut off the ring on Foreman. Now Ali struck him a combination of punches as fast as the punches of the first round, but harder and more consecutive, three capital rights in a row struck Foreman, then a left, and for an instant on Foreman's face appeared the knowledge that he was in danger and must start to look to his last protection. His opponent was attacking, and there were no ropes behind the opponent. What a dislocation: the axis of his existence was reversed. He was the man on the ropes! Then a big projectile exactly the size of a fist in a glove drove into the middle of Foreman's mind, the best punch of the startled night, the blow Ali saved for a career. Foreman's arms flew out to the side like a man with a parachute jumping out of a plane, and in this doubled-over position he tried to wander out to the center of the ring. All the while his eyes were on Ali and he looked up with no anger as if Ali, indeed, was the man he knew best in the world and would see him on his dying day. Vertigo took George Foreman and revolved him. Still bowing from the waist in this uncomprehending position, eyes on Muhammad Ali all the way, he started to tumble and topple and fall even as he did not wish to go down. His mind was held with magnets high as his championship and his body was seeking the ground. He went over like a sixty-year-old butler who has just heard tragic news, yes, fell over all of a long collapsing two seconds, down came the Champion in sections and Ali revolved with him in a lose circle, hand primed to hit him one more time, and never the need, a wholly intimate escort to the floor. (Mailer, 1975, pp. 207–8)

Qualitative research tends to focus on few or singular cases and many variables. In the above example the case is of a single fight (the equivalent of a single entry on Ali's boxing record). The variables are multiple and not precisely defined. From the extract above we can observe at least eight: the use of bodies, tactics and strategy, the character of Ali, the character of Foreman, an aesthetic of combat, analysis of defeat and victory. There are undoubtedly more. The variables in combination profile the case in considerable depth and the capacity for words to *enhance* data is demonstrated insofar as it takes longer to read the passage than for the events (over 18 seconds) to occur. We should also recall the opening statement by Haralambos and Holborn to the effect that qualitative data, using words, is richer, more vital and provides greater depth than quantitative data (using numbers). Indeed a distinction between depth (using words, exploring qualities) and breadth (using numbers, quantifying variations) is another way of thinking about differences between research with few or singular cases and many variables and research with a large number of cases and relatively few variables. This distinction emphasizes the scope of research as much as its ethos. Before examining the important issue of efficiently matching types of research with the goals of sociological inquiry, it is useful to examine the framing of research.

Framing research

The discussions above of the two datasets (Ali's boxing record and the extract from *The Fight*) required considerable parenthetic statement (the comments in brackets). Parenthetic statements are used to amplify and to clarify. In the two examples above these statements demonstrate a dilemma in research. It is impossible to start researching/understanding something without first knowing at least a little about it. Textbooks often present research as involving inductive or deductive strategies or a combination of both (Blaikie, 1993, pp. 131–61). Blaikie notes that an inductive research strategy: 'corresponds to a popular conception of the activities of scientists, i.e. of persons who make careful observations, conduct experiments, rigorously analyse the data obtained and hence produce new discoveries or new theories' (ibid., p. 133). A deductive research strategy: 'begins with a question or a problem that needs to be understood or explained. Instead of starting with observation, the first stage is to produce a possible answer to the question, or explanation for the problem' (ibid., p. 144). In very simple terms, the inductive strategy starts with data and no theory, while the deductive strategy does the opposite – it starts with theory and no data. These are extremely abstract terms, of greater interest to philosophers than sociologists and social scientists in general. The most important feature of this debate is that for practical purposes it is necessary to know a little about the problem or issue being explored and the relevant theory *before* beginning research.

Needing to know a little before you can begin research and how best to build an explanation is the constraint of framing. Framing represents an *interaction* on the part of the researcher between the body of sociological theory and the problem or issue he or she is interested in. The result is that research is always a process involving the interaction of data and theory and vice versa. In the terms used by Ragin (1987, 1994), this process involves the development of categories, most notably those of *cases* and *variables*. It is a moving approximation for building categories and identifying cases and variables. Indeed the starting point for research is always either a case or a variable (though knowing which may not be apparent at the beginning). Regardless of the subject matter, the experiences, attitudes, beliefs under scrutiny can be categorized in generating a dataset as either a case (example, instance, type, etc.) or a variable (aspect, dimension, feature, etc.). For example, the French sociologist Loïc Wacquant enrolled in a boxing gym in Chicago in order to move beyond the stereotypical representations of black ghettos and of boxing. Wacquant trained and fought in the gym for more than three years and socialized with his fellow boxers. In doing so he generated 2,300 pages of notes on his observations on the case. He describes his engagement in the process of framing this research as an attempt to overcome various stereotypes and, in particular:

> [T]o avoid the excess knowledge of spontaneous sociology that the evocation of fights never fails to conjure, one must not step into the ring by proxy with the extra-ordinary figure of the 'champ' but 'hit the bags' alongside anonymous boxers in their habitual setting of the gym. (Wacquant, 2004, p. 6)

Ragin goes on to note that the framing of quantitative and qualitative research are somewhat different. He describes quantitative framing in terms of 'fixed framing'. Quantitative research tends to focus on large numbers of cases and relatively few variables. In this respect the most important categorization is of the variables and their measurement. Of central importance is the capacity for the researcher to observe variation in variables across the cases. For example, the explanatory power of a survey is not much affected by the addition or removal of a few cases. There is no difference in the statistical value of a survey with 1,000 cases and one with 1,050. Even the addition or removal of several hundred cases will have only a minor effect on the 'margin of error'. Thus, the most important task for a researcher conducting a quantitative investigation is to determine the variables to describe the cases. It is variation in these variables *across* cases that is crucial. Finding sufficient numbers of cases to make the observation from is a secondary problem. Think of Muhammad Ali's boxing record. The variables 'Date', 'Opponent', 'Venue', 'Result' and 'Title' provide the basis of analysis much more so than the number of cases. It would be of little significance if Ali had had a few more fights at the beginning or the end of his career. Further, the five variables used in Ali's record can be applied to all of his opponents, or even to all the recorded fights of all boxers. The latter would produce an enormous dataset: millions of cases (fights) x the same 5 variables. Analysis of such a dataset could answer myriad of questions.

Quantitative research has a fixed framing insofar as decisions made around the character of variables determine its success or failure. While the categorization of variables can be fine-tuned or even piloted prior to fieldwork, once these variables are applied to cases there is no – or only limited – scope to revise them. For example, if a questionnaire is mailed out to 1,000 addresses (cases) and a typo is discovered in one of the questions (variables), there is very little that can be done to rectify the mistake. In contrast, qualitative research enjoys a 'fluid framing'. Qualitative research tends to focus on few cases and many variables. Of central importance is the capacity for the researcher to develop a rich appreciation of the case(s). For example, Norman Mailer wrote an entire book on a single fight. This emphasis on few cases provides greater scope for interaction between theory and data in the process of categorization. Becker describes this process of interaction between theory and data, of building categories, as follows:

> you develop and test your theory case by case. You formulate an explanation for the first case as soon as you have gathered data on it. You apply that theory to the second case when you get data on it. If the theory explains that case adequately, thus confirming the theory, no problem; you go to the third case. When you hit a

'negative case,' one your explanatory hypothesis doesn't explain, you change the explanation of what you are trying to explain, by incorporating into it whatever new elements the facts of this troublesome case suggest to you, or you change the definition of what you're going to explain so as to exclude the recalcitrant case from the universe of things to be explained. (Becker, 1998, p. 195)

Goals of sociological inquiry

Ragin identifies distinct goals of sociological inquiry and matches these to quantitative and qualitative research. Six of these goals are presented in Table 2.[1] This typology is informed by the differing focus on cases or variables and the interaction of researchers between the body of sociological theory and the social issues they address.

Table 2 **Quantitative and qualitative research and goals of inquiry**

Goal of inquiry	Quantitative research	Qualitative research
1. Identifying patterns	Used mainly	Used rarely
2. Making predictions	Used mainly	Used rarely
3. Testing theories	Used mainly	Used occasionally
4. Developing theories	Used occasionally	Used mainly
5. Interpreting events	Used rarely	Used mainly
6. Giving voice	Used rarely	Used mainly

Source: Ragin (1994, pp. 32–3).

The first goal, identifying patterns, involves research where the aim is to measure the significance of social relations or phenomena. This form of research tends to focus on the behaviours, attitudes and beliefs of the general population or some designated sub-group. Such research is commonly undertaken at the behest of agencies of government or corporate sponsors (e.g., surveying alcohol usage, or modes of travelling to work). The second goal, making predictions, is closely linked to the

---

1 It should be noted that Ragin argues for a third research methodology, the comparative approach, applicable to social inquiry with moderate numbers of cases *and* variables. This shares elements of qualitative and quantitative research and is best understood in terms of the triangulation of research (Ragin, 1987, 1994).

first and involves the extrapolation of identified trends (e.g., predicting the winner of an election, or the uptake of subsidized medical care). The first and second goals of social inquiry use the information generated by research in the realm of practice – that is, the results of user surveys, opinion polls and even market research are used to inform the policy and practice of their sponsoring organizations. The third goal, testing theories, relates to the body of sociological theory. This testing of theory centres on versions of hypothesis testing (e.g., the hypothesis that increased subsidies on visits to doctors will result in better health care, or that decriminalizing marijuana will result in reduced crime). The impact of theory testing is typically incremental to the body of sociological theory. This type of 'experimentation' usually results in gradual changes to prevailing paradigms, although they may stimulate very sudden reversals in policies and practices by the sponsors of research.

The first set of three goals of sociological inquiry (identifying patterns, making predictions, testing theories) cluster in the realm of quantitative research. They are most readily achieved through quantitative approaches (many cases, relatively few variables). Similarly, they are amenable to a fixed framing insofar as they tend to operationalize or test from what is considered by researchers to be a fairly accurate body of knowledge (e.g., theories and broad assumptions about people's experiences, attitudes and beliefs). In other words, the process of categorization is well advanced in terms of building key *variables*, the devices used to measure experiences, attitudes and beliefs, etc. There are broad associations here with *deductive* strategies, in that research starts with a developed theory and possibly even many variables, but no data (cases).

The second set of three goals of sociological inquiry cluster in the realm of qualitative research. The first of this set – the fourth goal, developing theories – moves beyond the more conservative conventions of testing theory. This goal centres on challenging the existing body of sociological theory and on advancing alternative perspectives (e.g., the notion that some powerful transnational corporations have a vested interest in poverty, disease and world hunger, or that 'txting' is a new language of the digital age). This type of research is precisely about the categorization of variables through *inductive* strategies or what Becker calls *analytical induction*. One of the weaknesses of quantitative research, with its predetermined variables and fixed framing, is that it is difficult to ask questions about things that the researcher doesn't already know about. Imagine developing a questionnaire on the subject of a topic you know nothing about! As a result, the classical survey can only confirm or confound the existing body of theory. Qualitative research has a far greater potential to reveal the unexpected and to begin a process of building new variables and *new* theory. Glasser and Strauss (1967) called this capacity 'grounded theory'. Of course, the downside of qualitative research is that because of the limited number of cases it can say little about the broader social context (i.e., needing many cases). As a result, challenging or radical findings drawn from qualitative research often require 'triangulation' – combining several approaches to confirm results – before they are accepted.

The fifth goal is interpreting events, including those of particular social or cultural significance (e.g., the experiences of soldiers in war or the bombing of the World Trade Center). Just as testing theory (goal 3) and developing theory (goal 4) differ, in that the latter has a greater potential to reveal new perspectives, a focus on interpreting events moves beyond simply identifying patterns (goal 1). Identifying patterns – quantitative research in general – is above all good at classifying what is typical and normal. Interpreting events tends to focus on happenings or sets of behaviours that are not assumed to be normal and may indeed be atypical. The sixth goal, giving voice, moves even further from the normative assumptions underlying quantitative research and includes the task of advocacy. This task of representing the margins of society and of taking the part of outsiders or excluded groups is an important *political* aspect of sociology (Mills, 1959) (see Introduction, 'On Being Sociological').

Qualitative research involves the in-depth examination of instances of the social world that are not necessarily considered to be typical, normal or even desirable by the mainstream. The key aspect of categorization in this form is case-centric: to identify the main features of cases, to provide holistic accounts, to explore the essential qualities of a limited number of cases. Qualitative research enjoys a fluid framing insofar as it is possible to interrogate the categories of case and variable used at the same time as illuminating the case. In contrast, quantitative research is variable-centric and emphasizes parsimony: the fewest variables possible are used to represent multiple cases.

FEELING: EMOTIONS • BELIEVING: RELIGION • EDUCATING • STRAYING: DEVIANCE •
MEDIATING: TECHNOLOGY • INFORMING: MEDIA • RELATING: FAMILY • BELONGING: COMMUNITY • FINISHING

41

Some of the main differences between quantitative and qualitative research are shown in Table 3.

Table 3 *Differences between quantitative and qualitative research*

	Quantitative research	Qualitative research
1. Cases and variables	Many cases, few variables	Few cases, many variables
2. Categorization	Variable-centric; building variables	Case-centric; building cases
3. Framing	Fixed; variables determined	Fluid; variables interrogated
4. Words and numbers	Numbers, to condense	Words, to enhance
5. Scope of research	Breadth, shallow	Depth, narrow
6. Start point of research	Somewhat deductive; theory	Somewhat inductive; data
7. Goals of inquiry	Identifying patterns; making predictions; testing theories	Interpreting events; giving voice; advancing theories
8. Political stance	Tending conservative	Tending radical

Conclusion

This chapter has used a somewhat trivial example, in the boxing record of Muhammad Ali, to unpackage some of the main differences between quantitative and qualitative research. Like much research, this topic is meaningful to the researcher in ways that are not always made obvious to the reader. For sociologists biography – or, as Bourdieu (1977) would term it, *habitus* – is a crucial resource. How that resource is utilized, whether in sentimental or analytical form, for example, is not given. In this case, the author acknowledges Ali as a boyhood hero, and the consequence is the combination of sentimental and analytical forms of writing in this chapter. C. Wright Mills presented this tension as an imperative for research combining personal troubles and public issues.

Mills concluded his famous primer *The Sociological Imagination* thus:

> It is the political task of the social scientist – as of any liberal educator – continually to translate personal troubles into public issues, and public issues into the terms of their human meaning for a variety of individuals. It is his task to display in his work

> – and, as an educator, in his life as well – this kind of sociological imagination. And it is his purpose to cultivate such habits of mind among the men and women who are publicly exposed to him. To secure these ends is to secure reason and individuality, and to make these the predominant values of a democratic society. (1959, p. 187)

Mills was writing at a time when sociological research was dominated by forms of quantitative research (he called this abstracted empiricism) and writing that was largely disconnected from genuine research or empirical work (he called this grand theory). This was a politically and academically conservative period, and the bulk of sociological research was implicated in various Cold War agendas.

Mills offered a call to arms which sought to strengthen the liberal elements of American society and in particular the discipline of sociology. In terms of the latter he argued that the sociological imagination involved the capacity to bridge the gulf between personal troubles and public issues. In the context of the day this has to be understood as a *rebalancing* of research agendas and a greater use of qualitative approaches in giving voice, interpreting events and advancing theories. Mills helped to inspire at least a generation of sociologists, to revitalize qualitative research and to enhance sociology. Quantitative approaches are enjoying a resurgence – which in itself is no bad thing – but the challenge of Mills to sociologists and researchers remains.

Suggestions for further reading

Becker, H. (1998) *Tricks of the Trade: How to Think about Your Research While You're Doing It* (Chicago, IL: University of Chicago Press).

De Vaus, D. (2002) *Surveys in Social Research*, 5th edn (London: Routledge).

Webb, E. J., D. T. Campbell, R. D. Schwartz and L. Sechrest (1966) *Unobtrusive Measures – Nonreactive Research in the Social Sciences* (Chicago, IL: Rand McNally).

FEELING: EMOTIONS • BELIEVING: RELIGION • EDUCATING • STRAYING: DEVIANCE • MEDIATING: TECHNOLOGY • INFORMING: MEDIA • RELATING: FAMILY • BELONGING: COMMUNITY • FINISHING

43

Bibliography

Adler, P. A. and P. Adler (1994) 'Observational Techniques', in *Handbook of Qualitative Research*, ed. N. Denzin and Y. S. Lincoln (Newbury Park, CA: Sage), pp. 377–92.

Becker, H. (1998) *Tricks of the Trade: How to Think about Your Research While You're Doing It* (Chicago, IL: University of Chicago Press).

Blaikie, N. (1993) *Approaches to Social Inquiry* (Cambridge: Polity Press).

Bourdieu, E. (1977) *Outline of the Theory of Practice* (Cambridge: Cambridge University Press).

Crotty, M. (1998) *The Foundations of Social Research: Meaning and Perspective in the Research Process* (London: Sage).

Denzin, N. K. and Y. S. Lincoln (1994) 'Entering the Field of Qualitative Research', in *Handbook of Qualitative Research*, ed. N. K. Denzin and Y. S. Lincoln (Newbury Park, CA: Sage), pp. 1–17.

De Vaus, D. (2002) *Surveys in Social Research*, 5th edn (London: Routledge).

Dillman, D. (2000) *Mail and Internet Surveys: The Tailored Design Method*, 2nd edn (New York: Wiley).

Glasser, B. G. and A. L. Strauss (1967) *The Discovery of Grounded Theory* (Chicago, IL: Aldine).

Haralambos, M. and M. Holborn (1991) *Sociology, Themes and Perspectives*, 3rd edn (London: HarperCollins).

Hauser, T. (1992) *Muhammad Ali: His Life and Times* (New York: Touchstone).

Kellehear, A. (1993) *The Unobtrusive Researcher: A Guide to Methods* (St Leonards, Australia: Allen and Unwin).

Mailer, N. (1975) *The Fight* (Boston, MA: Little Brown).

Mills, C. W. (1959) *The Sociological Imagination* (New York: Oxford University Press).

Oakley, A. (1998) 'Gender, Methodology and People's Ways of Knowing: Some Problems with Feminism and the Paradigm Debate in Social Science', *Sociology* 32(4), pp. 707–31.

Oakley, A. (2000) *Experiments in Knowing: Gender and Method in the Social Sciences* (Cambridge: Polity Press).

Ragin, C. (1987) *The Comparative Method: Moving Beyond Qualitative and Quantitative Strategies* (Berkeley, CA: University of California Press).

Ragin, C. (1994) *Constructing Social Research: The Unity and Diversity of Method* (Thousand Oaks, CA: Pine Forge Press).

Strathmore, W. (2003) *Muhammad Ali: The Unseen Archive* (London: Paragon).

44

DOING RESEARCH · MODERNIZING · WORKING · CONSUMING · TRADING · STRATIFYING: CLASS · GOVERNING: POWER · RACIALIZING · GENDERING · SEXUALIZING · BEING: IDENTITY ·

Wacquant, L. (2004) *Body and Soul: Notebooks of an Apprentice Boxer* (Oxford: Oxford University Press).

Webb, E. J., D. T. Campbell, R. D. Schwartz and L. Sechrest (1966) *Unobtrusive Measures: Nonreactive Research in the Social Sciences* (Chicago, IL: Rand McNally).

Wittgenstein, L. (1953) *Philosophical Investigations*, trans. G. E. M. Anscombe (Oxford: Basil Blackwell).

Wittgenstein, L. (1958) *Preliminary Studies for the 'Philosophical Investigations', Generally Known as the Blue and Brown Books* (Oxford: Basil Blackwell).

FEELING: EMOTIONS • BELIEVING: RELIGION • EDUCATING • STRAYING: DEVIANCE •
MEDIATING: TECHNOLOGY • INFORMING: MEDIA • RELATING: FAMILY • BELONGING: COMMUNITY • FINISHING

45

2 modernizing

Ian Carter

KEY
POINTS
- Sociology is a European invention. Its name was coined in the 1830s by Auguste Comte.

- It is the academic discipline that specializes in understanding group life in modern society.

- The origins of what we call modernity lie in the Dual Revolution: the Industrial Revolution and the French Revolution.

- The Industrial Revolution transformed economic life; the French Revolution invented modern political life – active citizenship replaced traditional patterns of kinship and monarchy.

- Early sociology was influenced by thinkers of the Enlightenment. They celebrated progress – the expansion of human control over the natural world.

- Positive aspects of modernity include improvements in human health and life span, widespread access to consumer goods, and the freedoms of democratic citizenship.

- Negative aspects include industrialized death for soldiers and civilians in major wars and extermination camps, depletion and pollution of natural resources, and the injuries of colonization to indigenous peoples.

In the beginning: two worlds?

People, Karl Marx said in *The Eighteenth Brumaire of Louis Bonaparte* (1852), make their own history – but not under conditions of their own choosing. At its best, sociology explores this mixture of constraint and possibility that faces each of us every day. Thus sociology fills the space, C.Wright Mills insisted, where biography meets history; where individuals' private troubles collide with much larger public issues. Good sociology unsettles our mundane lives, makes us realize how many ways there are – or have been – to live as humans. We can make this point more concrete by a thought experiment, taking our minds far away and long ago from southern England, where this book is published. We must imagine ourselves in a bay at the top end of New Zealand's South Island in 1642, as local people saw a new and terrifying sight: 'floating islands' crammed with 'goblins from the sea' moving inexorably towards the land. We know, though local people did not, that Abel Tasman's Dutch exploration fleet was busy discovering a new-found land.

This first contact – to the best of our current knowledge – between European and Maori people collided different socially shared senses of what it is to be human. All peoples use foundation myths to explain who they are, and how they come to be where they are. Maori foundation myths tell of a world born from copulation between Ranginui, the sky, and Papatuanuku, the earth; of Maui, who sailed from ancestral Hawaiiki to fish up Te Wai Pounamu – which today we call the South Island – with Te Ika A Maui, New Zealand's North Island; and of the seven *waka* in that Great Fleet which carried different *iwi* (tribes) from Hawaiiki. European myths among Tasman's crew harked back to God's six days' hard labour spent creating the universe from a void, that process recounted in Genesis 1:1. More modestly than these, late Victorian British Pakeha (people without Maori ancestry) looked back to mid-nineteenth-century planned settlements; and to earlier visits by European explorers – the Dutchman Abel Tasman in 1642, the Englishman James Cook in 1769, the Frenchmen Surville in 1769 and de Fresne in 1772. Odd voyages of discovery these, of course, since Maori knew where Aotearoa (the modern Maori name for New Zealand) lay all the time.

Anne Salmond's book *Two Worlds* (1991) explores first contact between Europeans and Maori, two groups of people holding world-views invigorated by strikingly parallel myths about God and Ranginui/Papatuanuku. But why *two* worlds? For Salmond, a professor of Maori Studies, the answer is obvious. Enshrined in Te Tiriti o Waitangi (an important 1840 treaty between the British Crown and some local tribal chiefs), biculturalism must be the leading social dimension of New Zealand society today; Maori face Pakeha (non-Maori). But as sociologists (or, indeed, as citizens), might we not wish to break down this grab-bag Pakeha category, exploring foundation myths and lived experience among ethnic groups who arrived here on a wide variety of *waka* (canoes), from sailing brigs through steamers to Boeing 747s? What about Chinese people arriving in New Zealand as indentured gold-field labourers in the mid-nineteenth century, as economic migrants and students in the late twentieth century? What about Croatian immigrants to Northland gum-fields; or people from different Pacific islands enticed to the industrializing cities to ease factory labour shortages in the mid-twentieth century; or Indo-Fijian migrants fleeing racist Fijian nationalism in the 1980s, and continental Europeans fleeing Hitler's racism in the 1930s; or Dutch settlers quitting decolonized Indonesia in the late 1940s, and Afrikaans- or British-descended settlers quitting decolonized southern Africa in the 1990s? How can these peoples' particular and varied experiences be captured in a crude division between Maori and Pakeha? Like all social theories, biculturalism acts as a spotlight. Those things that it illuminates – notably, the disgraceful history of resource expropriation from, and cultural imperialism towards, indigenous people – are thrown into high relief. But like any searchlight, biculturalism throws things that lie outside its bright, narrow beam into darker shadow, making them more difficult to see.

The title *Two Worlds* can tempt us into a second difficulty, thinking that relations between Maori and Pakeha today resemble what they looked like in 1642. They do not. Even within bicultural discourse we must recognize four worlds, not two. Maori live today in a radically different social world from that inhabited by their pre-contact ancestors: predominantly urban dwelling rather than wholly rural; living in a fully monetized economy; in a society centred on citizenship in a (waning) welfare state, not distinct, if shifting, *iwi* (tribes); in a society based on written transmission rather than oral; in a world built around private property rights rather than communal use-rights; in an English-speaking society rather than one which speaks Maori. We could go on. But some among these differences also tell us that the world that early European visitors left behind when they set sail for Aotearoa has changed no less radically than the social world that they found. Those two early worlds held more in common than we now find it easy to recognize. Technology provides one touchstone (see Chapter 16, 'Mediating'). It is much too simple to list things that pre-contact Maori lacked – the wheel, metal tools, gunpowder – and to assume that when Abel Tasman anchored in Taitapu (Golden Bay) an 'advanced' society touched a 'primitive' society for the first time. But if larger Maori watercraft could not run as close to the wind as European square-riggers, then the speed of local paddled canoes astounded and frightened Dutch, French and British explorers – as did local people's stature: Maori warriors seemed huge and hulking to European sailors, weedy heirs to malnourished generations. Nor was Aotearoa the only place where European visitors stood toe to toe with local people. In the eighteenth century, outcaste agricultural labourers in Madras (in southern India) enjoyed better real incomes than English farm labourers; and ordinary Chinese people enjoyed higher standards of consumption than most Europeans. In 1900, by contrast, British working-class household incomes stood 21 times higher than those enjoyed – or suffered – by Madras labouring households (Davis, 2001, pp. 292–3). What caused the change?

Made in Europe

No less than three-masted square-rigged sailing brigs, sociology is a European invention: the very name was not coined until the 1830s, by the Frenchman Auguste Comte. The first university chair in sociology was not established until 1900, its first occupant another Frenchman, Émile Durkheim. That is not to say that things resembling sociology did not exist earlier than that, of course; one of the last social sciences to take its modern form, these events simply mark our subject's *institutionalization* as an academic discipline. Let me illustrate this with an anecdote from my own experience. My first university teaching job was in the University of Aberdeen, founded in 1495. Much oddness still hung around this place when I arrived in 1968. Though my wife was a physicist, Aberdeen University held no physics department. Instead, this subject was taught as 'natural philosophy'. And first-year Arts students were compelled, most resentfully, to take and pass a paper in moral philosophy (or, in a feeble concession wrung from moral philosophers, in logic). These oddities harked back to the eighteenth century, when moral philosophy – which, at that time, still encompassed physics among so much else – was the organizing principle underlying Scottish university education. Today we use modern categories to describe Scottish Enlightenment luminaries, contrasting the economist Adam Smith with the philosopher David Hume and the sociologist Adam Ferguson: but all these men earned their professorial crusts as moral philosophers. Over the next two centuries a new intellectual *division of labour* (a key sociological concept coined by Smith, Ferguson and others) blew apart the older organization of university teaching and learning. In my students' jaundiced accounts at least, in 1968 Aberdeen's moral philosophers still clung grimly to their jobs by forcing students to study a trivial subject obsessed with what one should do if one saw somebody else fall in a canal. As Table 4 shows, by this year the interesting bits from two centuries earlier had long migrated elsewhere, to new and more specialized disciplines.

Table 4 **The social sciences**

Subject	Object
History	Time
Geography	Space
Economics	Resource allocation under conditions of scarcity
Politics	Power
Psychology	Individual mental processes
Anthropology	Group life in primitive societies
Sociology	Group life in modern societies

As we see here, *structural differentiation* blew Scottish moral philosophy apart, generating a range of more effective and more efficient social science disciplines in this new intellectual *division of labour*. To the last discipline to crystallize – sociology – went the important task of understanding social life after the Dual Revolution that made the modern world which we still inhabit: the 1789 French Revolution and Britain's eighteenth-century Industrial Revolution.

Two revolutions

Adam Ferguson coined the phrase 'division of labour', but the term's most celebrated early example appears in the first chapter of Adam Smith's *The*

FEELING: EMOTIONS • BELIEVING: RELIGION • EDUCATING • STRAYING: DEVIANCE •
MEDIATING: TECHNOLOGY • INFORMING: MEDIA • RELATING: FAMILY • BELONGING: COMMUNITY • FINISHING

2   51

Wealth of Nations (published in 1763). Since many people take this book to be the pioneer economics text, we might expect to find there what we find in the first chapter of a modern economics primer: a dreary, fake-mathematical analysis of demand and supply functions. Not so. Smith's first chapter is about how to make pins. It tells the story of how few pins any workman could make in a day when he had to perform each task in turn (cut a piece of wire to the correct length, sharpen one end, solder on the pin head, polish the finished product, pack pins in boxes), when compared with the vastly greater scale of production available from a group of workers when each man performed one specialized task in that new and radical social institution, the *factory*. The factory was the key early novelty in that Industrial Revolution which started in eighteenth-century Britain, before spreading round the world. Adam Smith was right to be dazzled by industrialization's promise: it was this phenomenon's effects that pulled European living standards so far ahead of Chinese and Indian by 1900. At the broadest scale, only two really Big Things have ever happened in human history (Diamond, 1997). The first was the domestication of plants and animals in a range of temperate locations round the world, some 10,000 to 15,000 years ago. Domestication allowed settled agriculture and pastoralism to develop. This permitted the invention of cities, of occupational specialization, of social stratification. The second really Big Thing to happen in human history – what Karl Polanyi (1957) called 'the Great Transformation' – was industrialization, breaking humankind's dependence on organic (plant and animal) resources. This second watershed marked humankind's entry to the modern world. 'To modernise is to industrialise', Krishnan Kumar (1988, p. 4) tells us – and, as we saw in Table 4, to sociology went the task of understanding modernity. As industrialization's ferment transformed economic life first in Britain, then in France, Germany and the United States, then in Japan, then in so many other places, intellectuals struggled to understand what was making the world around them turn upside down. Confusion deepened when, from 1789, the French Revolution invented our modern political life, centred on active individual citizenship rather than on traditional patterns of kinship and kingship.

The men who today we think of as sociology's 'founding fathers' (we still have not recognized our founding mothers, but see McDonald, 1994) all were obsessed with understanding European people's transition to modernity through the Dual Revolution. Each man's particular theoretical scheme reflected his ideas' precise form but, as Table 5 shows, all produced some version of a two-box model contrasting premodern social, economic and political arrangements with modern life: *the traditional/modern dichotomy*.

Table 5 **Classical sociologists' variants on the traditional/modern dichotomy**

	Traditional	Modern
Karl Marx (1818–1883)	Feudalism	Capitalism
Émile Durkheim (1858–1917)	Mechanical solidarity	Organic solidarity
Max Weber (1864–1920)	Traditional domination	Legal–rational domination
Ferdinand Tönnies (1855–1936)	Natural will	Rational will

Of course, as these founding fathers sought to understand and explain what made modern society qualitatively different from what had gone before, all brought inherited ideas to bear on the world around them. Published in 1867, the first volume in Karl Marx's *Capital*, that notorious masterpiece, contains a double argument. The first explores in minute detail how, in 'the classic case' (England), economic resources were broken out from their premodern feudal form so that they might be reconstructed in a modern capitalist formation. On this groundwork he built his second argument, about how drivers impelling this process would continue to operate, pushing human progress onwards from capitalism to socialism and then to full communism. Émile Durkheim's first book, *The Division of Labour in Society* (1893), compared forms of social order in traditional societies and modern societies. Arguing that strong pressures towards individualism (political from the French Revolution, economic from capitalist industrialization) imperilled social order, Durkheim urged the need to find new forms of social integration for modernity's new times. Comparing forms of domination, Max Weber distinguished traditional authority in premodern societies, where followers accept leaders' legitimacy because those leaders' rule is hallowed by belief in gods (or, perhaps, just by brute custom), from legal–rational authority in modern societies, where codified legal procedures legitimize rule (Parkin, 1982, pp. 80–3, 87–9) (see Chapter 7, 'Governing'). Though Weber took the closest

FEELING: EMOTIONS • BELIEVING: RELIGION • EDUCATING • STRAYING: DEVIANCE • MEDIATING: TECHNOLOGY • INFORMING: MEDIA • RELATING: FAMILY • BELONGING: COMMUNITY • FINISHING

2   53

interest in careful comparison between different societies at different times, he was no less fearful for modernity's future than was Durkheim. Rigid rule following in bureaucratically organized capitalist society would lead humanity inexorably, he thought, to a new iron cage, as inhuman and disenchanted *rationalization* trundled onwards like a battlefield tank. Finally, *Community and Association* (1877), Ferdinand Tönnies' hugely ambitious attempt to summarize modernity's distinguishing features, rooted difference in a profound split between nature and culture. An interesting terminus this, for like Marx, Durkheim and Weber, Tönnies' ideas had their own genealogy. In every case, searching for these ideas' ancestry whisks us straight back to the Enlightenment.

Enlightenment

Adam Smith, David Hume and Adam Ferguson were all Scottish Enlightenment luminaries. But what *was* the Enlightenment? In Roy Porter's (1990) influential formulation, this was a broad movement of seventeenth- and eighteenth-century progressive and liberal intellectuals, scattered widely from Germany through France and Britain to the United States. Different contexts produced rather different emphases in these intellectuals' work – on the pressing need for political freedom in pre-revolutionary France, for instance, against an emphasis on removing barriers to commercial freedom in post-revolutionary England and Scotland – but several broad principles were widely shared. All Enlightenment *philosophes* (a French term which many commentators urge would be better rendered in English today as 'sociologists' rather than 'philosophers') celebrated *progress* – the expansion of human control over the natural world, of culture over nature. *Science* was progress's motor. Building on Isaac Newton's tremendous success in unravelling physical laws governing mechanics and gravitation, Enlightenment writers proposed wheeling empirical science, Newton's key method, into new areas. Since these new areas included social life, the search for *laws of social development* was on. This search had to be intellectually fearless, risking political unpopularity (questioning existing churches' and priests' privileged position, for instance) by disregarding conventional pieties. That things happened to be organized in any particular way at any particular time was no strong reason why this should continue. When investigating social life or the natural world, disciplined *reason* winnowed good arguments from bad, no matter how time-hallowed bad arguments might prove. In seeking laws of social development one must always *compare*, and one must always be *critical*. As the very word 'enlightenment' suggests, these thinkers assumed that applying scientific reason to human affairs would lead people steadily from darkness to light, freeing humankind from pre-modern ignorance and religious superstition. It all sounds wonderful; but problems soon began to emerge. First, while Enlightenment writers (almost) all stood for liberty, they tended to generalize rather quickly from their own experience when deciding what that word meant. Educated men could be enlightened, but could women, servants or slaves? Scientific reason bumped up against a second difficulty when shifted into the social sphere, tending to assume that logic – when properly applied – would always produce a single solution to any problem. As we shall see, these difficulties still cause problems today.

As an intellectual discipline, sociology still bears forceps marks from its Enlightenment birth (Hamilton, 1996). Some of us may have decided that, in a strict sense at least, laws of social development do not exist (or even, like Michel Foucault, that if they did exist then they would impede our search for individual and social freedom, a competing Enlightenment virtue) but all sociologists are committed to comparison and critique (see the Introduction, 'On Being Sociological'). Refusing to venerate existing social arrangements tends to make us a radical bunch, unpopular with conservative politicians. Though it is possible to be a politically conservative sociologist, not many of us (outside Germany, interestingly) manage that task. To use Max Weber's term, sociology has an *elective affinity* for radicalism. Of course this leaves open the question whether political radicals find sociology congenial, or whether studying sociology turns people into radicals by forcing them to question major features of the society into which they were born (see the Introduction, 'On Being Sociological').

Two roads

To repeat, sociology is the academic discipline specialized in understanding group life in modern society. But what, today, do we do with this topic? Many things, of course. Contributors to one text (Hall et al., 1996) used the notion of modernity to introduce students to a huge range of sociological issues, from politics and class to culture and gender, in past, present and near future societies. That made sense for, broadly speaking, no sociology can exist which is not about modernity (unless scholars choose to use sociological ideas to explore pre-modern social worlds, of course.) But we can distinguish two tendencies within sociological work on modernity. Each takes a different attitude to ancient Scottish moral philosophy. One seeks to connect sociology (and sociological theory in particular) with that residual philosophy left behind by crystallizing social sciences. The starting point here is *Community and Association* (1877). In this book Ferdinand Tönnies erected a theory of modern society by combining ideas drawn from a wide range of previous social critics' work. The American sociologist Talcott Parsons copied this pattern in *The Structure of Social Action* (1937), blending Max Weber's ideas with Émile Durkheim's. Trained first in economics, Parsons erected his own vast theoretical model, best approached through a couple of short late books (1966, 1971): these share the virtue, unusually for this writer, of having being edited into fairly lucid English. Starting with Weber's ideas on *Verstehensoziologie* (a sociology concerned to understand how people make sense of their own experience, and how social interaction between individuals builds into larger social structures), he developed a theory of social structure infused by *the problem of order*, by Durkheim's haunted sense that a fragile society always needs maintenance if it is to hold together. Parsons's mature theory is a remarkable intellectual achievement, elegantly constructed and with coherent relations holding among teeming internal elements at levels from each individual's interior life to ultimate values. Its difficulty lies not in logical inconsistency but in abstraction, in its extreme remoteness from the world we all inhabit. Talcott Parsons made important contributions to some empirical areas in sociology (notably those pertaining to medicine and to organizations) but his essays in these domains maintain little connection with his general social theory. Much the same holds true for some sociological theorists who have surfed in Parsons's wake: the British sociologist Anthony Giddens is an obvious example.

The big problem with social theory content to trail along in philosophy's wake is that it finds itself discommoded so frequently by history. One spectacular recent example of this has to do with post-modernity. Broadly contemplating most advanced economies' shift from making things to shuffling paper and digital data, from manufacturing to services as the leading economic sector, the last two decades have seen a rush (not including Anthony Giddens) of social theorists who urged that humankind had crossed a world-historical divide comparable with domestication and industrialization. In these people's view we were about to quit modernity for a post-modern world. Waxing lyrical over this new world's glories (a realm of surfaces rather than depth, of consumption rather than production, of irony rather than seriousness, of multi-occupations rather than modernity's boring single career), these intellectuals urged us that since we could not change the world we should just lie back and enjoy it. So what if hordes of people lost their jobs through deindustrialization? So what if welfare provisions wrung from dominant social groups through class action over many generations fell to bits? An industrial working class and a welfare state had been no more than transient triumphs, detritus from an 'Enlightenment project' which social theory now declared always to have been a delusion. Today all this stuff looks dated.

Observing some social theorists' contortions, we might be tempted to say, 'To hell with it: let's just use common sense to understand the modern world.' Sadly, this will not work: we need theory to organize our understanding, to transform the welter of sense-impressions which batter us each day into evidence for coherent analysis. If a philosophy-focused social theory does not help us very much in this task, then where else might we turn? Let us return to eighteenth-century Scottish moral philosophy in order to find another way forward. What if we chose to ignore the division of intellectual labour that destroyed pre-modern moral philosophy as a viable activity? The European nineteenth century's new intellectual division of labour worked moderately well in its time and place, but now it gets in the way. For pay and rations reasons scholars in universities are still labelled 'sociologist', 'psychologist', 'geographer' or whatever; but the range of research and teaching interest within each discipline now greatly exceeds the difference marking its distance from other specialisms. Much of today's most interesting intellectual work goes on in the spaces between disciplines, not within them. Sometimes this new work crystallizes in new academic units – women's or gender studies; development studies; science, technology and society studies; cultural studies – but often scholars work as sociologists (for example) while researching and teaching well beyond this discipline's conventional nineteenth-century boundary.

So it is with modernity, sociology's central theoretical interest. The historical accident that saw critics in a range of humanistic disciplines – art history, musicology, literary criticism, architecture – all happening to choose 'modernism' as the overarching term to describe a range of styles in early twentieth-century cultural production has generated fruitful confusion among three terms: *modernism* as a set of artistic practices, *modernization* as a sociological category concerned with the process of becoming modern, and *modernity* as the key sociological category used to describe the condition of being modern. A rich and fascinating literature has grown up around this confusion. Some material was written by humanists working into sociological territory: the art critic T. J. Clark's (1999) book on Paris as the birthplace of pictorial modernism is a good example here, as is the German literary critic Walter Benjamin's meditation on Paris as the capital of the nineteenth century in his extraordinary *The Arcades Project* (1999). From the other side, building on the sociologist Georg Simmel's earlier contemplation of the manner in which living in new industrial cities transformed the way people made sense of their social worlds, Wolfgang Schivelbusch wrote three classic books about how modernity changed human consciousness. The first of these three, *The Railway Journey* (1986), focused on modern means of travel; the second, *Disenchanted Night* (1988), on forms of artificial lighting. The third book, *Tastes of Paradise* (1993), cut a longer passage through time, exploring how the act of ingesting 'substances of pleasure' – from spices to sugar; from tea, coffee and chocolate to alcohol and other mind-altering drugs – changed Europeans' consciousness. But perhaps the best example of this whole fruitful endeavour is Marshall Berman's *All That is Solid Melts into Air: The Experience of Modernity* (1982). Taken from Marx and Engels' *The Communist Manifesto* (1848), Berman's main title insists that this is a piece of sociological writing. But he then launches on an exhilarating voyage of discovery into realms far removed from sociology's conventional boundaries: to Goethe's *Faust* as a textual embodiment of unevenly modernizing processes in early nineteenth-century German states; to Baudelaire's poetry and *feuilletons* (prose poems) expressing what it felt like to live in a Paris demolished and reconstructed – for military and public health reasons – by Baron Haussman in the 1850s and 1860s; to nineteenth-century Russian creative writers from Pushkin to Dostoevsky as they responded critically to an eighteenth-century St Petersburg ruthlessly created from nothing by Tsar Peter I, at uncounted human cost, as he sought to modernize Russia technically without changing her political structures; to a sharply pointed critique of the planner Robert Moses' drive to smash expressways through late twentieth-century New York. Here the sociological idea of modernity lives and breathes in time and place, energizing our understanding and engaging our imagination. This is all very far removed from Talcott Parsons's arid abstractions – and none the worse for that.

Back to the beginning

Where does all this leave us? Does sociology's fascination with modernity still matter in the early twenty-first century? The answer to that question must be 'yes'. For good or ill we still live in a modern world.

For good or ill: this story is not unmixed. Constructing a profit and loss ledger, we find some hefty entries in the profit column. 'What earlier century,' Marx and Engels asked in 1848, 'had even a presentiment that such productive forces slumbered in the lap of social labour?' (Tucker, 1978, pp. 477). Capitalist industrialization had exploited that social labour for more than a century when these words were written; and it has continued on its rampaging way ever since, piling up heaps of wealth unparalleled in human history. This wealth has not been shared equally within or between nation states, but there can be no doubt that capitalist modernity's broad effect has been for good. Today, people are taller and healthier than ever before, and they live longer. Capitalist agriculture has lifted the spectre of hunger – our species' haunting shadow through the ages – from ever-larger proportions of the world's population. Thus over the last couple of generations public health concerns in industrialized countries have shifted from finding ways to eke out inadequate food supplies to persuading people to eat less: obesity, not malnutrition, now tops the policy agenda. We can trace how, over the last hundred years, telephones, radio sets, electric and gas stoves, private cars, refrigerators, television sets, personal computers – even the mobile phone – have turned from luxury objects into staples of mundane existence in industrialized countries. Today we all own far more *stuff* than did our grandparents, and we pay (or, often, owe) through seductive credit arrangements that would have appalled our thrifty ancestors. In consumer goods as in food, modernity has placed things that only the richest few in any society could have hoped to own 200 (or 50, or 10) years ago within the average Joe's and Josephine's reach. The French Revolution's democratic impulsion lives and prospers widely in modern society, in realms far removed from the narrowly political. The American composer Aaron Copeland did well to celebrate modernity in his 'Fanfare for the Common Man'.

In sketch form, those are our ledger's positive entries; and an impressive list they make. But its negative column also contains some weighty items. First comes the matter of modernity's underside. Intellectuals promoted the Enlightenment as a road map for humanity's journey to individual and human freedom, but Max Weber's morbid fears about rationalization's iron cage proved prescient. Since in material terms most of us are freer from want and poverty than were our parents and grandparents, why do we not *feel* free? Modern medical science has trounced pre-modern shamanism: so why do alternative therapies still prosper so? And why are British water supplies detectably contaminated with antidepressant drug residues? We are much richer than our grandparents were: but (as Buddhists might suggest) do our mounting heaps of *stuff* simply burden our souls? Consumerism is a great thing for manufacturers, but have they conned us into thinking trivial possessions are essential for modern living? (see Chapter 4, 'Consuming'). Beyond all this, the blood-soaked twentieth century saw applied science industrialize death in war both for soldiers (think – if you dare – of Passchendaele and Verdun in the First World War) and for civilians (nuclear bombs dropped from American aircraft on Hiroshima and Nagasaki, Agent Orange and napalm dropped from American aircraft on Vietnam). And Nazi technocrats needed no more than bog-standard factory production methods to turn millions of fellow human beings to ashes in Second World War extermination camps, twentieth-century Europe's abiding horror (Bauman, 1989).

The second debit item in this ledger concerns whether modernity can persist in anything like its current form. Ripping wealth from Nature's womb was a triumphant vindication of Enlightenment intellectuals' call for culture (in the guise of applied science) to expand at the expense of untamed nature. This has all proved a rip-roaring success; but in their different registers scientists and Greens join today in urging that hindsight makes this process look more like rape than seduction. Though contention still swirls around issues like global warming, there can be no doubt that rapid resource depletion and rising pollution levels insinuate that industrialization cannot continue as before. Changes in the international division of labour reinforce this message. As we saw at the beginning of this chapter, when European explorers first visited New Zealand, average living standards for indigenes there (or in India, or in China) compared well with those in western Europe; yet by 1900 average British standards stood 20 times higher than in India. Today, much evidence suggests that parts of India are following eastern China (and before that, south-east Asian 'tiger economies') into full industrialization. Since this will lift living standards for a huge chunk of humanity we must welcome that; but rising consumption expectations in the world's two most populous nations will dramatically rack up the looming global resource/pollution crisis. But can we cavil at other people seeking social and economic improvement, when our own economies have largely quitted manufacturing for the service sector?

The third item in modernity's debit column is more directly social. Many recent critics have pointed out that Enlightenment intellectuals were European men in wigs. Generalizing from their own experience, they assumed that progress could be measured by benefits accruing to people just like themselves. Thus Voltaire, the premier eighteenth-century social critic, declared that enlightened Man no longer needed organized religion's fairy tales; but he conceded that weaker vessels – women and servants – might need a 'rational religion' to provide psychic support. Though this struggle seems no less remote today than Father Christmas, more-or-less organized working-class action over two centuries forced a modestly fairer distribution of modernity's fruits between rich and poor (Thompson, 1963). With parallel logic, feminist critics point out how, since women were identified with nature and men with culture, the Enlightenment's project to expand the cultural realm at the expense of nature necessarily demeaned rather more than half of those who hold up the sky (Lloyd, 1984). The Dual

Revolution changed rather than cured this myopia, since new gendered divisions of labour developed. Men occupied a prestigious public sphere centred on waged work and political life, while married women increasingly found themselves forced into a private world of unwaged domestic labour (see Chapter 9, 'Gendering'). Modern total wars allowed some women brief respite from this private sphere until demobilized men reclaimed 'their' jobs. Only in the last three decades have we seen this pattern break, as deindustrialization destroyed full-time blue-collar male waged jobs on a massive a scale, replacing them (initially at least) with part-time female waged work in manufacturing and services.

The final debit item in modernity's ledger is cultural. Those men in wigs were all Europeans, or of European extraction. Expanded international divisions of labour imposed ideas born in one place and time on many other places around the world. Missionaries' and traders' rhetoric spoke about 'opening up' new worlds and enlightening people previously hidden in darkness; but from the other end this meant massive disruption to existing patterns of exchange and understanding. As the most distant parts of the globe became embroiled in intricate trading networks, immensely remote Aotearoa became New Zealand, 'the farthest Promised Land' (Arnold, 1981), for many rural working-class Britons extruded from their native land by transformed tenure arrangements in a new capitalist agriculture. To provide land to settle these migrants in their new promised land, sharks like John Logan Campbell, 'the Father of Auckland', played tribe against tribe, chief against chief. (No less acutely, some chiefs played land shark against land shark, of course.) When voluntary land sales by Maori failed to meet settlers' surging demands, provincial, national and imperial governments weighed in with sequestration measures ranging from the principled to the piratical; and if all 'legal' measures failed then British military force lay close at hand, ready to help. With most land soon fully converted to a fully commercialized commodity, the Enlightenment project – *progress* – could roll forward in New Zealand. To a degree unparalleled on any other part of the globe's surface, exotic animals (sheep, cattle, deer, cats, dogs, rabbits, Norway rats, stoats, possums) and plants (grasses, wheat, oats, turnips) terraformed that country, making it a land fit for European migrants. Though located half a world away, Aotearoa became Britain's Farm in the South Seas. In boom periods many New Zealanders did rather well out of this – for some years this nation's inhabitants enjoyed the world's highest average living standards. Largely because they presented such a formidable military challenge to early settlers, many Maori fared less badly than indigenes in other colonized territories; but even here basic cultural understandings were disrupted either through conscious policy (in education, in religion) or through the mundane application of European ideas to non-European peoples. Yet even here modernity's ambiguity remains. Though today's Maori live shorter lives, have lower average educational qualifications, earn less, have higher unemployment rates and are over-represented in prison populations when compared with New Zealanders of European ancestry, yet modern Maori live longer, eat better and have wider opportunities than their ancestors enjoyed three centuries ago. As processes unleashed by the Enlightenment and the Dual Revolution remade, and still remake, the world, so nobody was or is untouched. At western Europe's antipode, modernity still rules the roost.

Suggestions for further reading

Bauman, Z. (1989) *Modernity and the Holocaust* (Cambridge: Polity Press).

Bauman, Z. (2000) *Liquid Modernity* (Cambridge: Polity Press).

Berman, M. (1982) *All That is Solid Melts into Air: The Experience of Modernity* (New York: Simon and Schuster).

Davis, M. (2001) *Late Victorian Holocausts: El Niño, Famines and the Making of the Third World* (London and New York: Verso).

Hall, S., D. Held and D. McGrew (1992) *Modernity and Its Futures* (Cambridge: Polity Press in association with the Open University).

Bibliography

Arnold, R. (1981) *The Farthest Promised Land* (Wellington: Victoria University Press).

Bauman, Z. (1989) *Modernity and the Holocaust* (Cambridge: Polity Press).

Bauman, Z. (1992) *Intimations of Postmodernity* (London: Routledge).

Benjamin, W. (1999) *The Arcades Project*, trans. Howard Eiland and Kevin McLaughlin (Cambridge, MA: Belknap Press).

FEELING: EMOTIONS • BELIEVING: RELIGION • EDUCATING • STRAYING: DEVIANCE •
MEDIATING: TECHNOLOGY • INFORMING: MEDIA • RELATING: FAMILY • BELONGING: COMMUNITY • FINISHING

2   63

Berman, M. (1982) *All That is Solid Melts into Air: The Experience of Modernity* (New York: Simon and Schuster).

Clark, T. J. (1999) *The Painting of Modern Life: Paris in the Art of Manet and His Followers*, rev. edn (London: Thames & Hudson).

Davis, M. (2001) *Late Victorian Holocausts: El Niño, Famines and the Making of the Third World* (London: Verso).

Diamond, J. (1997) *Guns, Germs and Steel: The Fates of Human Societies* (London: Jonathan Cape).

Durkheim, E. (1893/1964) *The Division of Labour in Society*, trans. W. D. Halls (New York: Free Press).

Giddens, A. (1973) *The Class Structures of the Advanced Societies* (London: Hutchinson).

Giddens, A. (1984) *The Constitution of Society: Outline of the Theory of Structuration* (Cambridge: Polity Press).

Giddens, A. (1990) *The Consequences of Modernity* (Cambridge: Polity Press).

Giddens, A. (1997) *Sociology*, 3rd edn (Cambridge: Polity Press).

Hall, S., D. Held, D. Hubert and K. Thompson (eds) (1996) *Modernity: An Introduction to Modern Societies* (Oxford: Blackwell).

Hamilton, P. (1996) 'The Enlightenment and the Birth of Social Science', in *Modernity: An Introduction to Modern Societies*, ed. S. Hall, D. Held, D. Hubert and K. Thompson (Oxford: Blackwell), pp. 19–54.

Hobsbawm, E. (1962) *The Age of Revolution: Europe, 1789–1848* (London: Weidenfeld & Nicolson).

Kumar, K. (1988) *The Rise of Modern Society* (Oxford: Blackwell).

Lloyd, G. (1984) *The Man of Reason: 'Male' and 'Female' in Western Philosophy* (London: Methuen).

Lyotard, J. F. (1984) *The Postmodern Condition: A Report on Knowledge*, trans. G. Bennington and B. Massumi (Manchester: Manchester University Press).

McDonald, L. (1994) *The Women Founders of the Social Sciences* (Ottawa: Carleton University Press).

Marx, K. (1867/1976) *Capital*, vol. 1, trans. Ben Fowkes (Harmondsworth: Penguin).

Marx, K. and F. Engels (1967) *The Communist Manifesto* (Harmondsworth: Penguin).

Parkin, F. (1982) *Max Weber* (Chichester: Ellis Horwood).

Parsons, T. (1937) *The Structure of Social Action: A Study in Social Theory with Special Reference to a Group of Recent European Writers* (New York: McGraw-Hill).

Parsons, T. (1966) *Societies: Evolutionary and Comparative Perspectives* (Englewood Cliffs, NJ: Prentice-Hall).

Parsons, T. (1971) *The System of Modern Societies* (Englewood Cliffs, NJ: Prentice-Hall).

Polanyi, K. (1957) *The Great Transformation* (Boston, MA: Beacon).

Porter, R. (1990) *The Enlightenment* (Basingstoke: Macmillan).

Salmond, A. (1991) *Two Worlds: First Meetings between Maori and Europeans, 1642–1772* (Auckland: Viking).

Schivelbusch, W. (1986) *The Railway Journey: The Industrialisation of Time and Space in the Nineteenth Century* (Berkeley, CA: University of California Press).

Schivelbusch, W. (1988) *Disenchanted Night: The Industrialisation of Light in the Nineteenth Century*, trans. A. Davies (Berkeley, CA: University of California Press).

Schivelbusch, W. (1993) *Tastes of Paradise: A Social History of Spices, and Intoxicants*, trans. David Jacobson (New York: Vintage).

Thompson, E. P. (1963) *The Making of the English Working Class* (London: Gollancz).

Tönnies, F. (1877/1955) *Community and Association*, trans. C. P. Loomis (London: Routledge and Kegan Paul).

Tucker, R. C. (ed.) (1978) *The Marx–Engels Reader*, 2nd edn (New York: W. W. Norton).

FEELING: EMOTIONS • BELIEVING: RELIGION • EDUCATING • STRAYING: DEVIANCE • MEDIATING: TECHNOLOGY • INFORMING: MEDIA • RELATING: FAMILY • BELONGING: COMMUNITY • FINISHING

2   65

working

Bruce Curtis

KEY
POINTS

- The founding fathers of sociology, notably Karl Marx and Max Weber, focused on paid work as an important driver of innovation and change in society.

- Paid work produces all the commodities – in the form of goods and services – in society and is the source for all profits and, hence, capitalist accumulation.

- The sociology of work has tended to focus on efforts at managerial control over work and workers' resistance to these initiatives.

- The 'recalcitrant worker' is the centrepiece of much of the sociology of work.

- Fordism and McDonaldization are important moments in the struggle for control over work. Fordism involved the introduction of the assembly line into work and heralded mass production. McDonaldization extends these principles into the realm of service work and consumption.

- Bauman argues that capitalist societies are experiencing a shift from a 'work ethic' to an 'aesthetic of consumption'. This mirrors the rise of consumer society.

- The development of a consumer society is also associated with 'disenchantment' of both workers and consumers. On the one hand, workers are in more and more ways constrained in the forms of resistance available to them. On the other, consumers confront a crass commercialism and seek forms of authenticity.

- There are some possibilities for resistance and re-enchantment in workers and consumers becoming ironic and subversive agents.

Introduction: work and the material world

Work is – perhaps unfortunately – the single activity that most of us will spend most of our lives doing. It is a doubly important aspect of life, in that it is of overriding importance to us as individuals and to society in general. For individuals work – or, more precisely, paid work – is the basis of livelihood. The vast majority of individuals must work for a living or rely on pensions and other benefits that are a redistribution of other people's wages collected as taxes. Work also provides a measure of worth well beyond wages and the lifestyles they allow. Individuals are so categorized, assessed, ranked and rewarded because of their work status. One hundred years ago, Max Weber, who was one of sociology's founding fathers, argued that the 'spirit of capitalism' was a commitment to the accumulation of wealth that was not found in other societies (Weber, 1970). This commitment was expressed through a work ethic (Weber used the term 'Protestant ethic') that was ascetic in nature and thus fostered savings and accumulation. However, Zygmunt Bauman (1998) is just one of the present-day sociologists who argue that the work ethic is in decline in the modern-day world and is in the process of being replaced by an aesthetic of consumption. While this claim will be discussed in more depth later on, it is certainly also true that the work ethic retains a powerful legacy. This is visible in the ways that people who are not in paid employment may be stigmatized with disapproving epithets.

Work is central to society because it is the mechanism by which the overwhelming majority of things are produced. The buildings, fixtures, books, cars, roads, clothes, watches, jewellery and other goods (and services) that surround us are all the products of work. Work and production are inextricably interlinked. In a contemporary capitalist society, where things are produced primarily as commodities to be sold and livelihoods are based on waged labour, work and production are more-or-less synonyms. Work also infiltrates non-work, in that when we are enjoying leisure (and, in capitalist societies, this inevitably means consuming commodities) we are gaining pleasure from the fruits of (someone else's) work. In the midst of leisure there is work. Similarly, consumption is predicated on production. Indeed, work links production and consumption in at least three other ways. While it is obvious that production and consumption are linked in terms of the demand and supply of commodities, these other aspects of work tend to be obscured by the everyday world. The other (invisible, immaterial) things that work produces are profits, classes and aspirations (see Chapter 4, 'Consuming').

Nevertheless, it is important to note the distinction between work constituted as paid work, and unpaid work or labour. Marx and Engels, as well as Weber, focused on paid work as a main driver of capitalist societies. Unpaid work or labour was regarded by these founding fathers as a residual category that takes place in the domestic sphere. Such marginalization has raised the ire of feminists since at least the late nineteenth century, who have argued that capitalist societies are sustained as much by the realm of unpaid work and *domestic* labour as by paid work. The difference, they have argued, is that domestic labour is perceived as belonging to the realm of women and therefore of little interest to the founding *fathers* of sociology. Indeed, many feminists argue that men have a collective interest in marginalizing the domestic labour of women precisely because they benefit from its unpaid nature (Waring, 1996). Feminist accounts assume that divisions between men and women are of central importance in capitalist societies and tend to downplay the commonalities between the genders, especially in terms of paid work. At the same time, the domestic sphere is increasingly penetrated by forms of paid work (for example, take-away meals, house cleaning services, child care facilities, legalized prostitution, couples counselling), and the significance of unpaid work is arguably in decline (see Chapter 9, 'Gendering').

First, and most significantly, paid work is the place where things (commodities in the form of goods and services) are made and where profits are generated. The *fundamental* driver of capitalist society is the accumulation of capital (i.e., money in its liquid form). The origin of all capital is profit. Profit is the sum of money capitalists gain when the costs of production (raw materials, rents, plant and premises, etc.) and wages are subtracted from the value of the commodities produced at work. One of the great contradictions of capitalism is that while workers produce all the value of society, they receive only a portion of this value as wages from the sale of commodities. Furthermore, there is an inverse relationship between wages and profits. An increase in wages, among other things, results in a reduction in profits. This produces politics of the nil-sum.

FEELING: EMOTIONS • BELIEVING: RELIGION • EDUCATING • STRAYING: DEVIANCE •
MEDIATING: TECHNOLOGY • INFORMING: MEDIA • RELATING: FAMILY • BELONGING: COMMUNITY • FINISHING

3   69

Second, work is also the place where the two great classes of capitalism are forged: the bourgeoisie and the proletariat. The term 'bourgeoisie' describes the class of modern capitalists who are owners of the means of production and employers of wage labour. 'Proletariat' is the name given to the class of modern wage labourers who, having no means of production of their own, are reduced to selling their labour power in order to live. The terms 'capitalists' and 'workers' are synonyms for bourgeoisie and proletariat, respectively (see Chapter 6, 'Stratifying: Class').

Finally, work is the place where aspirations are generated. Production/work is where all the possible things the people might find useful are given physical form (as commodities). However, the selection of commodities produced does not float free from the broader struggle between capitalists and workers. While the law of demand and supply operates it always does so in terms of class interest. Because capitalists rather than workers determine what is to be produced, the range of commodities available always reflects what capitalists consider to be proper and useful.

Thus, paid work (which in Marx and Engels' terminology is called 'production') is also the source of innovation in society. The incessant drive on the part of capitalists to increase profits and to accumulate capital imparts a permanent impermanence to society. The life cycle of both commodities and ideas, the movement from their innovation to obsolescence, is constantly shortened. Or, in Marx and Engels' phrasing:

> The bourgeoisie cannot exist without constantly revolutionizing the instruments of production, and thereby the relations of production, and with them the whole relations of society. Conservation of the old modes of production in unaltered form, was, on the contrary, the first condition of existence for all earlier industrial classes. Constant revolutionizing of production, uninterrupted disturbance of all social conditions, everlasting uncertainty and agitation distinguish the bourgeois epoch from all earlier ones. All fixed, fast frozen relations, with their train of ancient and venerable prejudices and opinions, are swept away, all new-formed ones become antiquated before they can ossify. All that is solid melts into air, all that is holy is profaned, and man is at last compelled to face with sober senses his real condition of life and his relations with his kind. (Marx and Engels, 2004, p. 7)

Control and resistance

Marx and Engels offer commentary on a world where the two great classes of capitalism confront each other; bourgeoisie and proletariat. They are convinced that the 'laws of motion' of capitalism will result in the impoverishment of the toiling masses and realization that their interest can only be served by communist revolution: 'Let the ruling classes tremble at a communistic revolution. The proletarians have nothing to lose but their chains. They have a world to win. Working men of all countries, unite!' (Marx and Engels, 2004, p. 52). The sociology of work has a more unassuming agenda. In part, this reflects the fact that work and the 'relations of production' found in work situations only very rarely involve a direct confrontation between bourgeoisie and proletariat. Rather, the bourgeoisie (capitalist owners) involve themselves in the day-to-day affairs of work in only the very smallest of capitalist enterprises or businesses. Mid- and large-scale businesses are constituted very differently to forms of such simple or immediate control (Edwards, 1979). Inevitably, the owners of businesses employ agents or managers to manage work and workers. Such managers – formally, the agents of capitalist owners – range from the CEO to front-line supervisors. The political ramifications of management are not considered by Marx and Engels.

In addition, there are the effects of subjectivity. In *The Communist Manifesto* (1848) Marx and Engels sketch: how capitalism has supplanted feudalism, the dynamics of modern industry, the contradictions of capitalism, and also a programme for the Communist Party. All this, it must be noted, is covered in only a few dozen pages. Indeed, Karl Marx would spend much of the rest of his life researching and analysing the laws of motion of capitalism. Only the first volume of his findings, *Capital*, was published before his death. His friend and comrade, Frederick Engels (who died in 1895), edited and published volumes two and three in 1885 and 1894, respectively. This enormous body of work analyses capitalism through objective categories. That is, membership of the 'category' bourgeoisie or proletariat is treated as the result of rational and measurable criteria (i.e., ownership or not of the means of production) and in no way involves subjective aspects like belief, opinion or attitudes. However, as the early American sociologist W. I. Thomas noted: 'If men define situations

FEELING: EMOTIONS • BELIEVING: RELIGION • EDUCATING • STRAYING: DEVIANCE • MEDIATING: TECHNOLOGY • INFORMING: MEDIA • RELATING: FAMILY • BELONGING: COMMUNITY • FINISHING

3   71

as real, they are real in their consequences' (Thomas and Thomas, 1928). In other words, subjective factors lead people to define situations and to take action. And, as a host of sociologists have discovered (Goldthorpe, 1969), the majority of the proletariat do not readily define themselves as such. This gives rise to the so-called 'embourgeoisement thesis' as an explanation for declining working-class solidarity and adoption of middle-class values.

The sociology of work, which is a scholarly rather than a revolutionary discourse, addresses these 'deficiencies' in Marxism. This is not to say that sociologists are disconnected from the playing-out of class struggle. Indeed, Thompson and Ackroyd (1995) contend that sociological interest in work ebbs and flows as a function of worker militancy and industrial unrest. Where workers are troublesome, organized in strong unions, demanding high wages and strike-prone then the sociology of work is sure to follow. Certainly, the focus of sociology of work is the 'recalcitrant worker'. The core of this sociology can be said to be about issues of control and resistance (that is, efforts at managerial control and worker resistance). Worker resistance returns after each new managerial initiative.

> Whether it be the establishment of Taylorism, bureaucracy, human relations, or new technology, extravagant claims as to the rationality and effectiveness were made by managerial advocates and too often believed by academics. We know now that workers learned to bend the bars in these particular iron cages. Why should the current crop of new management practices be any different? (Thompson and Ackroyd, 1995, p. 629)

Control represents managerial efforts to get the most out of workers across a number of dimensions that operate in both the formal and informal spheres of work. The formal aspects include: documented contracts and collective agreements, rates of pay, bonus schedules, procedures and protocols. The informal aspects include everything else at work: tricks, short cuts, oversights, illegal practices, restrictions and the like. Typically, but by no means always, the informal sphere of work tends to undermine the formal. For example, plagiarism is an informal practice used by students to complete work in contradiction to the formal guidelines issued by universities.

Control and managerial effort focuses on five dimensions. These centre on constraining workers and securing the process of production for management. First, there is a focus on productivity. This involves efforts at maximizing the output of workers. Second, there is a focus on efficiency, which has as its goal minimizing wastage by workers in the process of production. Third, is compliance, or ensuring that workers comply with the rules of management. Fourth, is subordination. This relates to all the efforts by management to ensure workers are passive in work and, in particular, not resistant to change. Fifth, is the goal of flexibility or ensuring that workers are accommodating to change.

Workers resist managerial control across all of the above five dimensions and in each case formal and informal measures are adopted. Formal and informal examples of worker resistance are countless but are clustered around three main areas. Bargaining involves the collective or individual negotiation of awards and contracts that cover work. The effort bargain is the often informal practices determining how much work is actually done. In the last recourse absenteeism (withdrawal from work) and sabotage (the disruption of work) are also effective mechanisms of resistance.

Management has a long history of trying to secure control at work. Frederick Taylor (1865–1915), author of *Principles of Scientific Management* and *Shop Management*, was a champion of what he called 'scientific management'. Scientific management aimed to eliminate workers' efforts to restrict output through innovations in the design of work. The approach used stopwatches, detailed observation and documentation to break work down into its smallest component parts and to reassemble the design of work to the greatest benefit of management. Scientific management had ideological aspects that were at least as important as its insights into the design of work. Firstly, were its claims to science. By claiming that his management techniques were scientific, Taylor sought to legitimate his approach as objectively true. Secondly, scientific management privileged the managerial view of work and the worker. Thus, work was regarded as useful only insofar as it generated profits. Further, workers were regarded as inherently opposed to management and at the same time as incapable of operating efficiently without management. These ideological aspects are found in all contemporary management systems.

More recently, the focus on control and resistance at work has its origins in the work of Harry Braverman (1974). Braverman's *Labor and Monopoly Capital: The Degradation of Work in the Twentieth Century* drew attention to the labour process; that is, the process of production in which labour power is applied to raw materials and machinery to produce commodities. Braverman was concerned with the loss of craft skills in the modern/ industrial organization of work. He identified the process of deskilling as central to control:

1. Deskilling involves the separation of mental work and manual work (the separation of hand and brain, of conception and execution, of direct and indirect labour).
2. Deskilling is the objective of scientific management. It is a means of securing managerial control over the labour process.
3. Deskilling removes the skills, knowledge and science of the labour process and transfers these to management. At the same time deskilling pits manual and mental workers against each other.
4. Deskilling facilitates the dispersal of the labour process across sites and time (its decomposition across place and time).
5. Deskilling increases the capacity of capitalists to exploit workers and simultaneously reduces the capacity of workers to resist managerial control.

Deskilling reaches its zenith in the design of work called Fordism (named after Henry Ford, founder of the Ford Motor Company). Ford, who was the greatest practitioner of scientific management as it was then understood, is famous for his mass production of the Model T car. He achieved this phenomenal output and became one of the first billionaires by transforming the ways in which cars were made. The key to this redesign of work was the introduction of the assembly line into his factories. The assembly line allowed Ford to determine the pace and order of work, to drastically deskill the work involved in making cars and to hire the cheapest labour needed to complete the range of tasks. Arguably, he put machines in charge of the process. Lewis Mumford describes this 'technic' of mass production as: 'The tendency in mass production is to transfer initiative and significance from the worker who once operated the machine to the machine that operates the worker' (Mumford, 1973, p. 287) (see Chapter 5, 'Trading').

Littler (1985) argues that mass production or Fordism includes four main aspects. Firstly, and most apparent, is the assembly line. The assembly line is continuous as well as paced and ordered by management.

Secondly, the use of highly specialized (i.e., one use only) machine tools. These replaced the general-purpose tools (lathes, etc.) that dominated earlier workshops and required highly skilled workers. Thirdly, standardized products: the assembly line could make only one or very few products without retooling by management. Fourthly, the use of scientific management in the surveillance of work and job design.

Of course, deskilling and Fordism are not limited to the production of cars and heavy machinery. George Ritzer suggests that the success of the fast-food company McDonalds is the result of the dissemination of Fordist principles and deskilling. In this sense, a McDonalds outlet is one big assembly line, used to deliver a range of pre-assembled food. The workers at McDonalds are deskilled to the extreme and rely on highly specialized machines (grillers, warmers, electronic tills, etc.) to complete each order in a minimum of time. So successful is this advance in managerial control that Ritzer has coined the term 'McDonaldization': 'the process by which the principles of the fast-food restaurant are coming to dominate more and more sectors of American society as well as of the rest of the world' (Ritzer, 1996, p. 1).

The McDonaldization thesis is interesting for two reasons. (1) It identifies the process of 'McJobs'. McJobs are the low-paid, low-interest, dead-end positions into which increasingly large numbers of young people are channelled. They epitomize deskilling and the exercise of managerial control. They are predicated on the implementation of scientific management (Fordism, McDonaldization) and on the use of new technologies of control. (2) McDonaldization is particularly reliant on new technologies of surveillance that transform places of work into a 'Panopticon'. Originally proposed by Jeremy Bentham, the Panopticon was a design of prison created to allow permanent observation of the inmates at all times. Michel Foucault argues:

> The perfect disciplinary apparatus would make it possible for a single gaze to see every thing constantly. A central point would be both the source of light illuminating everything, and a locus of convergence for everything that must be known: a perfect eye that nothing would escape and a centre towards which all gazes would be turned. (Foucault, 1979, p. 173)

Sewell and Wilkinson describe the application of the Panopticon in work like this:

> The Panopticon should facilitate the collection and storage of (useful) information, provide the means of supervision (through instructions or physical architecture) and monitor behaviour and compliance with instructions. The Panopticon does this by providing a physical superstructure of control based on visibility. Meanwhile, compliance of the subject population is achieved via economic, coercive or normative sanctions. A well-developed system of surveillance at once increases the capacity to identify any breach of rule deserving sanction, and reduces the likelihood of the necessity to invoke the sanction. (Sewell and Wilkinson, 1992, p. 274)

The inmates of a Panopticon (whether it be a prison, factory, McDonalds outlet, bank or other place of work) are potentially under constant surveillance. Sewell and Wilkinson (1992) suggest that new technologies now decisively favour management in the struggle for control at work. These technologies include those tracking individuals (CCTV, face-recognition software, swipe cards, computer logins and passwords); tracking things, including inventory and stock (barcodes, integrated alarms); recording activity (sales, monitoring of phone calls); as well as the redesign of entire organizations to eliminate the need of inventories and warehouses full of stock (these are typically called Just-In-Time systems). In the face of these developments the recalcitrant worker is in more and more ways constrained in the forms of resistance available to them. Because they do not know when they are free from surveillance there is a tendency for self-discipline.

Gabriel (1999) lists the new managerial controls that putatively eliminate the recalcitrant worker. This list makes depressing reading. It includes changes to organizations – in particular: flatter hierarchies (fewer middle managers); flexible working practices (often teamwork); continuous measurement and scrutiny in benchmarking and comparison of work. Alongside these organizational shifts are the new management systems, which operate to eliminate all slack from the production process by removing inventories, spare parts, warehousing, etc. This approach to work design is coupled with electronic surveillance, including cameras, performance monitoring, electronic tagging, and the resulting individualization of performance. Perhaps more insidious is the new managerial/corporatist ethos: this pervasive culture stresses loyalty, teamwork and confession over all forms of collectivity and resistance.

Arlie Hochschild (1983) argues in *The Managed Heart: The Commercialization of Human Feeling* that management is now able to demand forms of emotional labour from their employees. Her case study was of cabin crews working for Delta Airlines who were required to smile and be charming in the face of abusive language, sexual advances, and sometimes physical injuries like the deliberate pouring of hot coffee over them. Emotional labour is now a central element of much work, especially that involving interaction between workers and customers (notably in retailing and service work). Indeed, highly McDonaldized jobs are often those with the greatest demands on employees for emotional labour. For example, staff are required to learn and to adhere to predetermined scripts in their dealings with customers (how to answer a phone, how to offer an upsized portion, how to refuse a legal request for a refund). The key to such emotional labour is that the employee is expected to offer much more than just the form of words. The employee is expected to simulate the appropriate emotions which are those predetermined by management. Arguably such emotional labour generates its own version of repetitive strain injury, in the form of a blurring of what are authentic emotions and what are manufactured or managed as part of a job (see Chapter 12, 'Feeling: Emotions').

Nevertheless, Michael Burawoy contends in *Manufacturing Consent: Changes in the Labor Process under Monopoly Capitalism* (1979) that Braverman overstates deskilling in securing control. Burawoy argues that Braverman (like Marx and Engels before him) ignores the subjective realm and definition of the situation.

> In identifying the separation of conception and execution, the expropriation of skill, or narrowing of the scope of discretion as the broad tendency in the development of the capitalist labour process, Harry Braverman missed the equally important parallel tendency toward the expansion of choices within those ever narrower limits. It is the latter tendency that constitutes a basis of consent and allows the degradation of work to pursue its course without continuing crisis. Thus, we have seen that more reliable machines, easier rates, the possibility of chiseling, and so forth, all increase the options open to the operator in making out. (Burawoy, 1979, p. 94)

FEELING: EMOTIONS • BELIEVING: RELIGION • EDUCATING • STRAYING: DEVIANCE •
MEDIATING: TECHNOLOGY • INFORMING: MEDIA • RELATING: FAMILY • BELONGING: COMMUNITY • FINISHING

3   77

'Making out' is the process of defining the situation and finding meaning in work. Burawoy's main contribution to the control and resistance debate was to reimagine the labour process as a game in which the struggle for control takes unexpected turns. Making out operates almost exclusively in the informal sphere, is frequently individualistic and offers the threat of subversion of managerial control. Nevertheless, the invisibility of seeming resistance should not be confused with its absence. Indeed given the new technologies of control and the decline of collective bargaining the only viable forms of resistance are now invisible. These new forms of resistance include a failure to act, acting ritualistically, leaking information, rumour-mongering, whistle blowing. There are 'sins' of omission. Sins of commission remain and centre on the pilfering of non-material resources (e.g., ideas, computer time, protocols) and the dissemination of anti-corporatist counter-ideologies.

Paul Du Gay in *Consumption and Identity at Work* (1996) has extended the notion of the labour process as game with particular emphasis on counter-ideologies. He uses the concept of *la perruque* – the work of appearing to work. Du Gay draws on Michel de Certeau's work:

> La perruque is the worker's own work disguised as work for his employer. It differs from pilfering in that nothing of material value is stolen. It differs from absenteeism in that the worker is officially on the job. La perruque may be as simple a matter as a secretary's writing a love letter on 'company time' or as complex as a cabinetmaker's 'borrowing' a lathe to make a piece of furniture for his living room ... Accused of stealing or turning material to his own ends and using the machines for his own profit, the worker who indulges in la perruque actually diverts time from the factory for work. (Du Gay, 1996, p. 147)

More broadly, Du Gay suggests that new tactics of resistance are at play. Interestingly, these challenges to managerial norms are played out as tactics of consumption at work. These are the tactics of otherwise powerless individuals and are often highly symbolic. They include challenging forms and styles of uniforms and all efforts at enforced uniformity at work. They also involve being cynical in the face of managerial/corporate enforced cheeriness, challenging manufactured egalitarianism at work, being resigned in the acceptance of policies and change, the subversion of meetings, and the inappropriate use of space and time wherever possible.

Similarly, Gabriel concludes that the recalcitrant worker deserves greater attention. He suggests that 'recalcitrant identities can also be pursued in other ways'. For example, researchers do not seriously look at 'material and symbolic contests over the physical spaces of organizations'. They could explore contests over:

> size, location, and quality of physical premises, equipment, and furniture, the personalization of individual and group workspaces (and the countertendency to reappropriate this space from employees through hotdesking and teleworking), and the creation of no-go areas for superiors through a variety of subordinate strategies. (Gabriel, 1999, p. 200)

Recalcitrant identities could also be explored through contrasting employees' consumption patterns within their organizations with consumption in their private lives. This might include how they spend their 'lunch hour', use (and abuse) of 'company accounts, corporate hospitality and business travel', and kinds of clothing worn to work. Gabriel points out that 'these may seem marginal terrains within organizations – yet, it is their very marginality that renders them less accessible to the controlling gaze' (Gabriel, 1999, p. 200).

From work ethic to aesthetic of consumption

Zygmunt Bauman (1998) suggests that developments in the contemporary world constitute a shift from producer society to consumer society. The shift is associated with the rise of service work, as well as new technologies of production and consumption. It involves the abandonment of the norms of a work ethic for those of an aesthetic of consumption. The majority of members of a producer society are primarily engaged as producers (workers). As a result, society is shaped by the needs of its members to play the role of producers. The norms of such a society are productivist: they encourage work and the work ethic. In contrast, the majority of members of a consumer society are primarily consumers. This society is shaped by the needs of its members to play the role of consumers. Norms are consumerist: there is an aesthetic of consumption. Further, Bauman argues that the characteristics of the virtuous citizen differ greatly between producer and consumer societies. The ideal citizen in a producer society is, in effect, the same as those of the bourgeois society decried by Marx and Engels and idealized by Weber. However, the ideal citizen of a consumer society is the near opposite of this sober individual. Some important oppositions between the two forms of 'ideal' citizens are shown in Table 6.

Table 6 **Ideal citizens in producer and consumer societies**

Ideal citizen in producer society	Ideal citizen in consumer society
Endures monotony	Seeks pleasure
Is habituated to routine	Looks for difference
Defers gratification	Advances gratification
Is deliberate	Is compulsive
Respects tradition	Is eager for experience
Is loyal	Is fickle
Is readily satisfied	Is insatiable

In producer society, surveillance and discipline (Bauman uses the notion of drills) are the foundations of control. Compulsory schooling, compulsory military training, apprenticeships, careers and religion all underpin versions of the work ethic. In consumer society different technologies of control are required. These are emergent and not readily documented. Clearly, surveillance and discipline are not abandoned; rather they become a necessary component for seduction (Bogard, 1996). Accordingly, consumers – especially youthful consumers – are urged to construct lifestyles from high-end commodities.

A shift from a producer to a consumer society involves much more than a simple break. To a certain extent both forms coexist, while the marginal elements of the former develop in the latter. Insofar as this process is underway (and it certainly seems to account for the different perspectives of younger and older members of society), it generates problems for the articulation of work and leisure, production and consumption. In short, the old techniques of control of work and labour markets (Edwards, 1979) appear increasingly dated and ineffective. This is ultimately the result of the reconstitution of citizens from workers to consumers. Such reconstitution, Rob Shields (1992, pp. 1–20) suggests, may require a new 'aesthetic of self'. As a result, there is undoubtedly a new tension between the demands of production (and work) and of consumption (and leisure).

In the realm of leisure, shopping is increasingly central and implicated in the values of consumer society:

> Shopping is not ... best understood as an individualistic or individualizing act related to the subjectivity of the shopper. Rather the act of buying goods is mainly directed at two forms of 'otherness'. The first of these expresses a relationship between the shopper and a particular other individual such as a child or partner, either present in the household, desired or imagined. The second of these is a relationship to a more general goal which transcends any immediate utility and is best understood as cosmological in that it takes the form of neither subject nor object but of the values to which people wish to dedicate themselves. (Miller, 1998, p. 12)

Thus, Miller suggests that shopping is as much about care for the other as it is about self-gratification. The cosmological elements of this process surely confirm that work is no longer the only place where aspirations are generated and fulfilled.

In absolute contrast, in the realm of work – and again, especially for young people – hyper-deskilled McJobs are increasingly the norm. McJobs offer almost no scope for the fulfilment of aspirations. They are, by definition, low-paid, boring, and rely on burn-out and high turnover of staff. Similarly, Du Gay (1996) emphasizes how the creation of the enterprising customer (consumer) has contradictory and negative results for workers. The most interesting tasks are transferred from worker to the customer: self-service is the mechanism of this transference. Hence, expertise, skill and esteem are transferred from worker to the customer. As a result workers are compromised by the demands of customers and the protocols of management.

In *The Simulation of Surveillance: Hypercontrol in Telematic Societies* (1996) William Bogard suggests that the blurring of the work and leisure divide is one possible way forward for production in consumer society. He introduces the concept of cyborg work (see also Haraway, 1992). Cyborg work is the assemblage of human–machine in information-rich work. Most importantly, it involves the use of electronic prosthetics at work. Examples of these include: cell phone, laptop, personal pagers, wireless internet, headphones. Bogard argues that cyborg work allows the intensification of work at the same time as it blurs the boundaries between work and leisure. As a result, cyborg workers are simultaneously more productive than their counterparts, more interested in work and what it offers, and less concerned with bargaining and other forms of resistance.

Regardless of whether or not cyborg work – or some other accommodation with the aesthetic of consumption – is the way forward for production in consumer society, the new aesthetic poses a problem for contemporary social theory: whether it be versions of the 'embourgeoisement thesis' or the struggle for socialism. This is largely because contemporary consumers appear decidedly atomized compared to their productivist precursors. In this respect, Shields (1992) suggests that an episodic tribalism will displace the earlier certainties of class and community. This tribalism of consumption involves: the cross-cutting of class and community by lifestyles based on consumption alone; the recognition that lifestyle forms the basis of a tribalism that is institutionally unfixed, intense and unstable (the old certainties of community are supposedly rejected); and, whereas class and community are ascribed and passive, tribalism is achieved, active, reliant on self-monitoring, and, as a result, intrinsically short-lived.

Despite these efforts at categorization, the sorts of social relations that hyper-consumerism and lifestyle-based tribalism may engender are unclear. Part of the problem is what prosperity might look like in the future. Seduction, simulation, cyborg-work and lifestyle-based associations, even when coupled with McJobs, seem likely to be limited to a privileged strata of the most advanced societies. What befalls the rest of society? Certainly, any benefits from 'consumer society' are unlikely to be distributed evenly; likewise the costs of resourcing this new aesthetic. At the same time, there is little doubt that monopoly capitalists (McDonalds, Microsoft, Sony, Westinghouse) are still firmly in control of what commodities are to be produced and consumed, and hence what 'lifestyles' are sanctioned. In this respect, the elements of the Panopticon are extended unambiguously from work into the realm of leisure.

Conclusion

Marx and Engels suggest a remedy for disenchantment with the world that can be found only in revolution and the overthrow of capitalism by the proletariat. Their confidence was based on an understanding of capitalism as a system wracked by contradictions. As the likelihood for revolution fades, sociologists suggest that they ignored subjectivity in the realm of work and class struggle. Similarly, Braverman is criticized for ignoring the potential for the labour process to be perceived and engaged with as a game. In short, workers may (and seemingly do) focus their energies on informal practices that create meaning at work, and so make the (potentially unbearable) passing of time bearable. Yet, disenchantment remains a central element of contemporary society. Cathedrals of consumption dominate public spaces, as do concerns about how to live a meaningful life in a crassly consumerist society (Ritzer, 2001). Bauman proposes that the authenticities of productivism and the certainties of the work ethic are in terminal decline. However, as yet the only replacements for these outmoded norms are partial, fragmented and contradictory. This is the ambit of speculation and futurology. In this respect, two entwined responses may offer a reconfiguration of the control and resistance debate. First, resistance may itself become an object of pleasure. Thus, the recalcitrant worker becomes a subversive agent, stealing pleasure in the form of 'textual poaching' (de Certeau, 1984) from their ironic self-implication in corporate culture. Second, re-enchantment is made possible by the techniques of seduction that are the new basis for control. While at no stage becoming a dupe to corporate culture and consumerism, the new worker-consumer may take full advantage of the illusions and simulations on offer.

Suggestions for further reading

Bauman, Z. (1998) *Work, Consumerism and the New Poor* (Milton Keynes: Open University Press).

Braverman, H. (1974) *Labor and Monopoly Capital: The Degradation of Work in the Twentieth Century* (New York: Month Review Press).

Foucault, M. (1979) *Discipline and Punish: The Birth of the Prison* (New York: Vintage Books).

Haraway, D. (1992) 'A Cyborg Manifesto: Science, Technology, and Socialist-Feminism in the Late Twentieth Century', in *Simians, Cyborgs and Women: The Reinvention of Nature* (New York: Routledge), pp. 149–81.

Ritzer, G. (1996) *The McDonaldization of Society: An Investigation into the Changing Character of Contemporary Social Life* (Thousand Oaks, CA: Pine Forge).

Bibliography

Bauman, Z. (1998) *Work, Consumerism and the New Poor* (Milton Keynes: Open University Press).

Bogard, W. (1996) *The Simulation of Surveillance: Hypercontrol in Telematic Societies* (Cambridge: Cambridge University Press).

Braverman, H. (1974) *Labor and Monopoly Capital: The Degradation of Work in the Twentieth Century* (New York: Month Review Press).

Burawoy, M. (1979) *Manufacturing Consent: Changes in the Labor Process under Monopoly Capitalism* (Chicago, IL: University of Chicago Press).

de Certeau, M. (1984) *The Practice of Everyday Life* (Berkeley, CA: University of California Press).

Du Gay, P. (1996) *Consumption and Identity at Work* (London: Sage).

Edwards, R. (1979) *Contested Terrain: The Transformation of the Workplace in the Twentieth Century* (New York: Basic Books).

Foucault, M. (1979) *Discipline and Punish: The Birth of the Prison* (New York: Vintage Books).

Gabriel, Y. (1999) 'Beyond Happy Families: A Critical Reevaluation of the Control–Resistance–Identity Triangle', *Human Relations* 52(2), pp. 179–203.

Goldthorpe, J. (1969) *The Affluent Worker in the Class Structure* (London: Cambridge University Press).

Haraway, D. (1992) 'A Cyborg Manifesto: Science, Technology, and Socialist-Feminism in the Late Twentieth Century', in *Simians, Cyborgs and Women: The Reinvention of Nature* (New York: Routledge), pp. 149–81.

Hochschild, A. (1983) *The Managed Heart: The Commercialization of Human Feeling* (Berkeley, CA: University of California Press).

Littler, C. (1985) 'Taylorism, Fordism and Job Design,' in D. Knights, H. Willmott and D. Collinson (eds), *Job Redesign: Critical Perspectives on the Labour Process* (Aldershot: Gower), pp. 10–29.

Marx, K. and F. Engels (2004/1848) *The Communist Manifesto* (London: Penguin Books).

Miller, D. (1998) 'Introduction', in D. Miller, *A Theory of Shopping* (Cambridge: Polity Press), pp. 1–13.

Mumford, L. (1973) *Interpretations and Forecasts: 1922–1973* (London: Secker and Warburg).

Ritzer, G. (1996) *The McDonaldization of Society: An Investigation into the Changing Character of Contemporary Social Life* (Thousand Oaks, CA: Pine Forge).

Ritzer, G. (2001) 'Enchanting a Disenchanted World: Revolutionizing the Means of Consumption', in G. Ritzer, *Explorations in the Sociology of Consumption: Fast Food, Credit Cards and Casinos* (London: Sage), pp. 108–44.

Sewell, G. and B. Wilkinson, (1992) ' "Someone to watch over me": Surveillance, Discipline and the J-I-T Labour Process', *Sociology* 26(2), pp. 271–89.

Shields, R. (1992) *Lifestyle Shopping: The Subject of Consumption* (London: Routledge).

Thomas, W. I. and D. Thomas (1928) *The Child in America: Behavior Problems and Programs* (New York: Alfred A. Knopf).

Thompson, P. and S. Ackroyd (1995) 'All Quiet on the Workplace Front: A Critique of Recent Trends in British Industrial Sociology', *Sociology* 29(4), pp. 615–34.

Waring, M. (1996) 'Work', in *Three Masquerade: Essays on Equality, Work and Hu(man) Rights* (Auckland: Auckland University Press).

Weber, M. (1970/1905) *The Protestant Ethic and the Spirit of Capitalism* (London: Unwin University Books).

FEELING: EMOTIONS • BELIEVING: RELIGION • EDUCATING • STRAYING: DEVIANCE • MEDIATING: TECHNOLOGY • INFORMING: MEDIA • RELATING: FAMILY • BELONGING: COMMUNITY • FINISHING

3   85

4 consuming

Steve Matthewman

KEY
POINTS

- Sociology has tended to focus on the symbolic aspects of consumption.

- We should remember the material aspects of consumption: for a significant proportion of the planet and throughout most of human history consumption has primarily related to staying alive.

- There are massive disparities in the ability to consume – vertically (between different social classes within countries) and horizontally (between different countries).

- Sociologists see more than personal preference informing consumption. They look at how individual consumption acts might be shaped by broader issues of ability, age, class, gender, ethnicity and sexuality.

- Consumption is a major source of individual and collective identity. As such it plays a significant part in fostering social cohesion.

- The advertising industry plays a significant role in stimulating consumption. Their trick is to get us to desire things. In so doing, they frequently use celebrities.

- Consumption often figures as 'retail therapy', as a reward for the degradations of work and the banalities of everyday existence.

- The consumer ethic is spreading into all areas of social and public life. For instance, national and international politics are becoming exercises in brand management.

- Increasingly, citizens are acting as consumers, confronting all aspects of public life as shoppers. Considerations are made in terms of individual purchasing power and value.

- Pleasures derived from consumption tend to be short term, hence the need for further consumption.

- Consumption and production are linked. Each presupposes the other.

Introduction

Sociology is founded on the identification of category error. Much of the sociologist's job is devoted to putting people right. 'You think that it is X', says the sociologist, 'but it is *really* Y.' Typically 'Y' will be some form of social function. Irrespective of what they study, then, the real thing always turns out to be something else. Thus when sociologists claim 'to comprehend something they have left aside what the *thingness* of this thing actually is! Either they destroy what they study or ignore what it is' (Latour, 2000, p. 112). The paradigm case for this, as Bruno Latour (2000, p. 109) observed, was religion. Sociologists said that religious rituals, beliefs, even miracles, performed purely social functions. Nothing was happening in Heaven and the hereafter, it was all happening here on Earth right now. Thus they dismissed religious practices as mere fetishes, as false beliefs. What religious belief *really* did was give society its cohesion, and mask its hierarchical structure. Émile Durkheim explained (away) religion as a tool of social cohesion and social control, while Karl Marx (1988, p. 64) famously dismissed it as 'the opium of the people' (see Chapter 13, 'Believing: Religion').

The same can be said of the sociology of consumption. In a tradition stretching from Thorstein Veblen to Pierre Bourdieu and beyond, sociologists insist that consumption is *really* about social distinction. We consume to show status and group identity, and in so doing to mark our difference from outsiders (who are characteristically from a different class). This may be the case, and the insights from such reasoning are considerable. However, this is but one explanation. If we only focus on this we will ignore *what* is being consumed; hence we forget that consumption has material as well as symbolic significance. There is, after all, a thingness to things. Even in the affluent West where eating, drinking and clothing have long since surpassed strictly utilitarian functions, 'direct encounters with the fundamental materiality of goods must surely underpin every individual's experience of consumption, no matter how much attention is paid to the symbolic or "meaningful" features of goods' (Campbell, 1995, p. 117). Besides, which socio-economic strata will get sky blue? How are we to distribute colours amongst the classes, 'or a given engine, or product line, or category of cigarette, or high-top shoe' (Lipovetsky, 1994, p. 153)? Simply put, social distinction is too crude a map to allow us to navigate through the social world. It may delineate land from sea, but how are we to proceed from country to country, city to city, street to street?

Moreover, for much of human history consumption has first and foremost been about staying alive. This is where the standard sociological literature on consumption can let us down. In celebrating the pleasures of consumption it presumes a universal consumer, as if everyone the world over was a Western university lecturer. Thus there are further problems that beset standard sociology: its compact chronology and its restrictive geography. Sometimes it seems as if nothing happened before 1823 or beyond Western Europe. Sociology was so named at this time and in this place. A modern discipline charged with making sense of the modern world, it has tended to extrapolate from this province of privilege ever since (we call this Eurocentrism). We need to remember that abilities to consume are unevenly distributed, and that the gap between rich and poor is growing. Let a few statistics stand for many: Tiger Woods earns more in endorsements from Nike than the entire Indonesian labour force that makes their sporting products (Pilger, 2001). The wealth of the world's richest three *individuals* outstrips the combined Gross Domestic Product of the poorest 48 *nations*. These three people are wealthier than a quarter of the world's countries (Ramonet, 1998). The United Nations believes that US$13 billion would secure adequate sanitation and nutritional requirements for all the world's poor. This is what people in the United States of America and the European Union spend yearly on perfume (Ramonet, 1998). Although constituting only 4 per cent of the planet's population, the citizens of the United States manage to consume a quarter of the world's raw resources (Sattler, 2005). Frightening though it may seem, the fact remains that if you earn over US$47,500 a year you are in the richest one per cent on the planet (see Table 7). In comparison, the poorest 10 per cent of the world's population earn only US$800 a year on average

FEELING: EMOTIONS • BELIEVING: RELIGION • EDUCATING • STRAYING: DEVIANCE •
MEDIATING: TECHNOLOGY • INFORMING: MEDIA • RELATING: FAMILY • BELONGING: COMMUNITY • FINISHING

89

(Global Rich List, 2006). A simple breakdown of share of world income by share of population further underscores massive disparities (ibid.). The richest one per cent of the world's population enjoys 9.5 per cent of its income – that is more than the poorest 50 per cent of the population.

Table 7 **Stratified share of global earnings**

Percentage of world population	Percentage of world income	Yearly individual income (in $)	Daily individual income (in $)
Bottom 10 %	0.8	400	1.10
Bottom 20 %	2.0	500	1.37
Bottom 50 %	8.5	850	2.33
Bottom 75 %	22.3	1,487	4.07
Bottom 85 %	37.1	2,182	5.98
Top 10 %	50.8	25,400	69.59
Top 5 %	33.7	33,700	92.33
Top 1 %	9.5	47,500	130.14

The prospects of the rest of the world enjoying the life of the Western consumer are therefore rather bleak. Zygmunt Bauman's words remind us to check our universalizing tendencies: 'However far and wide it spreads,' he writes,

> the emancipation which modernity brought in its wake (liberation from nature, friability of traditional constraints, infinity of human potential, possibility of an order dictated solely by reason), has been from the start and will remain forever an ultimately local phenomenon, a privilege achieved by some at somebody else's expense; it can only be sustained, for a time, on the condition of *unequal exchange* with other sectors of global society. What we came to call 'economic growth' is the process of *expropriation* of order, not of its global increase. (Bauman, 1993, p. 214)

Here the relationship between West and Rest is laid bare: the former are so rich because the latter are so poor.

Anthony Giddens (1993, pp. 19–20) draws on the work of C. Wright Mills to offer us some useful suggestions for how to think sociologically about consumption. Mills (1971, p. 14) urged us to break free from the 'limited orbits' of our life-world, to locate our individual trajectories within the broader constellations of the social universe in order to truly understand the conditions of our existence. To do so requires a special quality of mind. Mills called it the sociological imagination. When we possess it we are able to see the links between biography and history, to see how the personal relates to the public, and the individual to the structural. Giddens asks that we consider the everyday activity of coffee drinking. As a mundane and habitual practice it tends to escape our notice. However, when we investigate it we learn all manner of things about ourselves and our place in the world. This is the lesson of sociology.

Like most sociologists, Giddens brushes over the 'fundamental materiality' of his subject but he does at least acknowledge that coffee is a drink, and that it involves the intake of fluids. He swiftly moves on to coffee's symbolic elements. The ritual of 'doing coffee' may well be more significant than the act of consuming it. The fact that you are chatting with a cherished friend is probably more important than the fact that you are drinking a long black or she a flat white. Similarly, when mothers meet for a coffee morning, the real point of the occasion is not to drink coffee but to meet. For here are people capable of adult conversation, people one can socialize with, share stories with and seek moral support from. Then again, there are people who privilege the coffee above all else. They are the coffee snobs, who know their arabica from their robusta, and will settle for Jamaican Blue Mountain but would prefer Kopi Luwak if you have it. Coffee taste may serve as a mark of distinction, or an indicator of time or available money. We may be able to tell quite a bit about a person from how they have their coffee. Must it be fine espresso every time, or could it be factory synthesized? Do they insist on Fair Trade, or is it decaffeinated with skimmed milk?

We also need to acknowledge the coffee addicts, people that need their fix. Coffee is a drug, and in countries like America it is *the* drug. Globally it is second only to oil in terms of legally traded commodities. The yearly trade is worth about US$70 billion (S. Brown, 2004). We generally fail to recognize it as a drug, but coffee has caffeine in it, which is an addictive substance. It works on the brain in the same manner as amphetamines. Coffee, like alcohol, is a socially acceptable drug whereas in most Western countries marijuana is not. Sociologists show us that far from being natural, laws are cultural constructs, expressions of social power. They also change across time and place. We mentioned coffee's status as a legally traded substance. This status is by no means universal. Giddens notes that there are countries where marijuana use is perfectly acceptable while coffee and alcohol consumption are not.

Because of our addiction we may have a *physiological* relationship with coffee, and coffee plays a part in our *personal* relationships. But Giddens urges us to look ever broader: 'an individual sipping a cup of coffee is caught up in an extremely complicated set of *social and economic relationships* stretching world-wide' (1993, p. 19). To have consumption we also require production, transportation and distribution. This chain can cross the entire planet. And more than ever before, things like food are transported by air. This results in additional greenhouse gas emissions. It also puts a strain on that limited and highly politicized commodity – oil. In consequence our food supply grows ever more precarious. Nutritional content is also lessened because of the long distances travelled. Three British journalists from the *Guardian* bought a basket of 20 goods from a high street grocery store to see just how far food travels. The beef was local, and that was about it. The wine was from Chile and New Zealand, the broccoli from Spain, the potatoes from Israel, the peas from South Africa, and so on. In all, they calculated that their humble basket of 20 products had clocked up 100,943 miles (Lewis et al., 2003). Returning to our example, we see this pattern confirmed. The world's major coffee producers are not the world's major consumers. Brazil, Colombia, Vietnam, Indonesia and India lead the world in production, whereas the Finns, Swedes, Danes, Norwegians and Austrians are the world's leading consumers (S. Brown, 2004).

In addition to the geographical component of consumption, we also need to be mindful of an historical one. We can only sit and drink a cup of coffee because of a prior series of socioeconomic development. While we take coffee, tea and sugar for granted, they only entered the everyday Western diet in the nineteenth century. Mass consumption of these products is a consequence of Western imperialism. Almost all of our coffee comes from former colonies. A character in Voltaire's *Candide*, bereft in the streets of Surinam, lays the conditions of this production bare: he wears hardly a stitch of clothing, and two of his limbs have been hacked off: 'They give us a pair of linen breeches twice a year, and that is our covering,' he explains. 'When we labour in the sugar-works, and the mill catches a finger, they cut off a hand. When we try to run away, they cut off a leg. I have suffered both of these misfortunes. This is the price at which you eat sugar in Europe' (Voltaire, 1993, p. 55). Although a fictional account, it is based in fact. Sidney Mintz's *Sweetness and Power* (1985) provides the details. European palates were sweetened by slavery. Not that we have left these issues in the dim and distant past. John Pilger's (2001) film *The New Rulers of the World* investigates the sweat shops of Indonesia where a host of brand-name goods like Adidas, Nike, Calvin Klein and The Gap are made under conditions 'bordering on a kind of slave labour'. Then there is actual slave labour. The charitable organization Anti-Slavery notes in its Annual Review (2004) that there are millions of people the world over in bonded labour (where they have been tricked into a loan that may mean generational enslavement), forced labour (where work is done under threat of physical punishment), forced marriage (where women are married against their will into lives of domestic servitude), trafficked from one area to another and compelled into slavery, born into a slave class that society sees fit to use as such, or involved in child labour.

Fashioning modernity: the production and consumption of identity

As a social formation, modernity is unlike anything else, even itself. That is because modernity is primarily about *change*. The classic pronouncement on modernity came from Karl Marx and Friedrich Engels (1848). In *The Communist Manifesto* they wrote that:

> [c]onstant revolutionizing of production, uninterrupted disturbance of all social conditions, everlasting uncertainty and agitation distinguish the bourgeois epoch from all earlier ones. All fixed, fast frozen relations, with their train of ancient and venerable prejudices and opinions, are swept away, all new-formed ones become antiquated before they can ossify. All that is solid melts into air, all that is holy is profaned, and man is at last compelled to face with sober senses his real condition of life and his relations with his kind. (Marx and Engels, in McLellan, 1988, p. 224)

For Marx, identity was determined by class, and classes by their relationship to the means of production. History was driven by the motor of class conflict. All societies, with the exception of the coming communist one, were stratified by class (see Chapter 6, 'Stratifying').There was always a ruling class and a subject class, the former parasitic upon the latter. From Marx we get the idea of production as the source of identity. Man's true nature was to be found in labour, hence the designation *Homo faber* – man the worker. These days it is more common to argue the reverse: that consumption is the prime source of personal identity. Either way, the concern with identity is traced back to modernity. In traditional society identity is fixed at birth. Generation after generation, people are born in the same place, wear the same clothes, work the same jobs, hold the same beliefs. It is only in modern times that society seeks legitimacy in the present, and breaks free from the gravity of custom. New forms of working and living come into being, and the possibility of remaking one's self becomes generally available (see Chapter 11, 'Being: Identity').

Freed from the small world of the village, city life introduced a universe of difference. The city collected people of divergent ethnicities, languages, religions and histories. One was confronted by identity in the plural. This troubled many of the early sociologists. Émile Durkheim's entire intellectual project showed concern for order. How could social solidarity come out of rampant individualism and obvious diversity? As with identity, sociologists are split on the question of stability. Some argue that stability grows out of the production process, others that it comes through shared practices of consumption.

The argument from the production side is that the new industrial labour made cogs of one and all, irrespective of cultural background. It mattered little whether you were previously a smallholder, a farm labourer or an artisan. Whether you were involved in domestic work or handiwork was inconsequential; whatever your tradition, whatever your profession, you were now part of the machine. Writer W. G. Sebald travelled through East Anglia and its history. At one point he reflects on the silk weavers of Norwich. They were the forerunners of the modern factory worker. In the 1700s, before the Industrial Revolution had dawned,

> a great number of people [here, as elsewhere] spent their lives with their wretched bodies strapped to looms made of wooden frames and rails, hung with weights, and reminiscent of instruments of torture or of cages. It was a peculiar symbiosis which, perhaps

> because of its relatively primitive character, makes more apparent than any later form of factory work that we are able to maintain ourselves on this earth only by being harnessed to the machines we have invented. (Sebald, 2002, pp. 282–3)

The Industrial Revolution ushered in rationalized factory work for the masses. Ilya Ehrenburg's non-fiction novel *The Life of the Automobile* records this process for the auto-assembly workers of Saint-Ouen:

> The Citroën works had twenty-five thousand employees. Once, they had spoken different languages. Now they kept silent. A close look revealed that these people came from different places. There were Parisians and Arabs, Russians and Bretons, Provençals and Chinese, Spaniards and Poles, Africans and Annamites. The Pole had once tilled the soil, the Italian had grazed sheep, and the Don Cossack had faithfully served the Tsar. Now they were all at the same conveyor belt. They never spoke to one another. They were gradually forgetting human words, words as warm and rough as sheepskin or clods of freshly plowed earth. They listened to the voices of the machines. Each had its own racket. The giant drop-hammers boomed. The milling machines screamed. The boring-machines squealed. The presses banged. The grinding lathes groaned. The pulleys sighed. And the iron chain hissed venomously.
>
> The roar of the machines deafened the Provençals and the Chinese. Their eyes became glassy and vacant. They forgot everything in the world: the colour of the sky and the name of their native village. They kept on tightening nuts. (Ehrenburg, 1976, pp. 22–3)

From this perspective consumption functions as compensation, as reward. It is retail therapy to remedy the degradations of work.

On the consumption side are those that stress the estrangement from traditional communities. Modernity is rationalization, manifest in industrialization, urbanization, bureaucratization and nationalization. The combined result is a recipe for alienation. No longer tied to customary communities and no longer able to rely on the old ways of assessing character, judgement shifted to 'personality'. And personality tended to be a play at the surface – people got assessed by how they looked and acted, by the clothes they wore and the products they consumed. Without the weight of tradition and the iron rule of religion, social

FEELING: EMOTIONS • BELIEVING: RELIGION • EDUCATING • STRAYING: DEVIANCE •
MEDIATING: TECHNOLOGY • INFORMING: MEDIA • RELATING: FAMILY • BELONGING: COMMUNITY • FINISHING

4   95

bonds became more superficial. People became at once less engaged *and* more tolerant. Identity, like modernity, is made rather than made known, capricious rather than permanent. Fashion, then, may have a much greater significance than we generally credit it. Like the world that we know and the means through which we understand it (sociology), mass fashion emerged in Western Europe in the nineteenth century. It 'stands out as the earliest manifestation of mass consumption: homogenous, standardized, indifferent to frontiers' (Lipovetsky, 1994, p. 59). Fashion is an intriguing mix of mimesis and individualism; it is at once to see and to be seen, to appreciate and to evaluate, to play and to celebrate, to express and to communicate. While this may seem frivolous, Lipovetsky stresses its serious social function.

If tradition equates with custom, then the modern equates with fashion. From this we can conclude that it is the very essence of modernity, one of society's foremost organizing principles. Indeed, asserts Gilles Lipovetsky, 'it has succeeded in shaping society as a whole in its own image' (1994, p. 6). Thus for Lipovestsky (ibid., p. 23) modernity does not give rise to fashion, but precisely the reverse. The historic significance of fashion is that 'it institutes an essentially modern social system, freed from the grip of the present'. Fashion is desire, seduction, diversity and redundancy. Fickle by nature, we put it on and we take it off. It has no permanence. Such 'laws' structure mass production and consumption.

Georg Simmel had already reached similar conclusions. Money abstracts things, personal relations included. Modernity simultaneously increases our interpersonal relations and renders them shallower. We deal with this by cultivating a blasé attitude (see Chapter 12, 'Feeling: Emotions'). We may live in a world of strangers, but this is no bad thing: he 'defended strangerhood as one of the most positive features of the modern world. He thought that strangership made a positive contribution to the social order' (Sznaider, 2000, p. 302). This is also close to Erving Goffman's notion of civil inattention – the subtle ways in which we let others know we know they are there but we wish them no harm. We may both be present but there is no need for us to become involved. 'Indifference is not nothing. It's a very subtle something. It means treating everybody exactly the same. It's not corrosive of morality. It's the basis of modern morality' (Sznaider, 2000, p. 304).

The consumer society

We have already noted that our job as sociologists is to explain the workings of the modern world. According to Jeff Lewis (2002, p. 37), such societies are characterized by ever-increasing diversity, mediatization and consumerism. The twentieth century was marked by forced migration. Mass tourism came into its own; and then there are all those business trips and educational exchanges – the combined effect of which is to take significant numbers of people and ideas to new places. This is underpinned by a global system of communications that similarly works against notions of fixed, bounded and homogenous cultural communities. This media system has given rise to the primacy of the image, and the additional processes of digitization and computer networking are reconfiguring the worlds of work, information and pleasure. These developments are by no means new. In *White Collar*, C. Wright Mills positioned the media as reality brokers: 'We are so submerged in the pictures created by mass media that we no longer really see them, much less the objects they supposedly represent. The truth is, as the media are now organized, they expropriate our vision' (1956, p. 333). It was true then. It is truer now. Since other authors in this collection are dealing with community (Chapter 19), the media (Chapter 17) and (ethnic) diversity (Chapter 8), let us turn to Lewis's final point. Consumerism runs rampant. It is driven by our economic system, capitalism. Capitalism is predicated on the commodification of everything. It is difficult to think of a thing that hasn't been commodified – turned into something that can be bought and sold in the market. Economists regard air as a free good, but you can even buy that in special booths in polluted cities (see Chapter 5, 'Trading').

So, we know that our society is defined by consumerism, but we still have not adequately defined what a consumer society is. John Benson (1994, p. 4) directs us towards a sociocultural definition of consumer societies. For the historian or the sociologist, consumer societies are ones in which: 'choice and credit are readily available, in which social value is defined in terms of purchasing power, and in which there is a desire, above all, for that which is new, modern, exciting and fashionable'. In other words, we cannot have a consumer society without a host of things to consume and the means to do so. The extension of credit means that

FEELING: EMOTIONS • BELIEVING: RELIGION • EDUCATING • STRAYING: DEVIANCE • MEDIATING: TECHNOLOGY • INFORMING: MEDIA • RELATING: FAMILY • BELONGING: COMMUNITY • FINISHING

97

we can 'buy now, pay later'. It doesn't matter that we are poor right now, we can still consume. But with credit comes interest. You can bet you'll be poorer in the future. Even if we have the means to consume and the things to consume, we still require the desire to do so. Capitalism seeks to commodify everything, and to open new markets where they do not already exist. Thus our worthiness as citizens is a judgement of our buying power, our ability to possess. Increasingly this– and not intrinsic qualities like moral conduct and personal character – comes to define our social worth. Where Descartes proclaimed, 'Cogito ergo sum' – 'I think therefore I am' – the modern cogito is: 'I buy therefore I am.' Here manufacturers help us out. They have spread the ethos of fashion from clothes to every other product. This means that we have to have the latest kettle, car and cell phone as well. They have also thought about the resistant consumer, the one not swayed by the fickle winds of fashion. They call their strategy 'built-in obsolescence'. You can keep your old kettle, but it won't work. And to fix it would cost more than getting a new one ... Besides, it's *so* 1999 ... And they have a special on at ... And Brad Pitt swears by the new BoilFast 500 ...

Advertisers are worthy of special mention here. It is they who turn mass-manufactured mundane goods into desirable, near-magical objects of consumer desire. It is said that they sell the sizzle not the sausage, a promise rather than the product. Youth are an ideal market – beyond the dependency of childhood but not yet shackled with the responsibilities of adulthood. What they have they can spend. For the rest of us they sell youthfulness. Like sociologists, advertisers forget the thing and pronounce on something else. When did you ever see an advert for Coca-Cola© that focused on the drink? They never tell you what it is. No Coke© advert announces the 'Real Thing' ™ as a sugar-saturated, caffeine-laced beverage whose ingredients include phosphoric acid. Every Coke© advert shows beautiful young people having a wonderful time. Advertisers are clever. If you have the money you can have the product, but they always infer that something else is involved. That something else is taste. 'You are spending your money on us because you *know*', say the advertisers, 'You are clever'. You might say that advertisers put the con in *con*sumption. That is one strategy. If accentuating the positive does not work, they try the opposite. Thus a favourite strategy is to tell you how terrible you are. Where you might have thought that you were just right, advertisers inform you that you are too wrinkly, too fat, too grey, too smelly, too bald, too impotent. They say nothing sells like sex. That being so, anxiety must come a close second. The subtext of all women's magazines, with their tips on how to dress better, be slimmer, parent with more effectiveness and do your hair the right way, is clear: you are inadequate. This is what concerns George Meyer, the creative consultant on *The Simpsons*. 'I hate [advertising],' he says, 'because it irresponsibly induces discontent in people for one myopic goal, and then it leaves the debris of that process out there in the culture. An advertiser will happily make you feel bad about yourself if that will make you buy, say, a Bic pen' (quoted in Owen, 2000). Sometimes advertisers downplay this power. They claim that they do not shape our consciousness, that advertisements have little effect. If this is so, why does a company like Proctor and Gamble bother spending US$2.9 billion a year on it (Auletta, 2005)?

We often try to build up a resistance to advertisements. But one of the difficulties facing the discerning consumer these days is knowing when advertisements stop and when things like television programmes, films and popular songs – in other words, all of the things that are supposed to happen between the ads – begin. The signal-to-noise ratio is so fuzzy. We used to have advertisements and then television programmes, but now we also have 'infomercials' (which are ads that have appropriated the documentary genre), 'advertorials' within the programmes, programme sponsorship, and any number of shows on home improvement, holidaying or self-improvement which really only tell us how much the things cost, where to get them from, and why we so desperately need them. Then there are product placements in television shows and films. Ford's new Mustang figured prominently in the NBC drama *American Dreams* during 2005, and in a nod towards popular culture and intertextuality it produced ads strongly suggestive of Steve McQueen in his 1968 film *Bullitt*. ABC's *Desperate Housewives* had a character promote a Buick LaCrosse at the shopping mall. Cut to the ads and there's a real Buick ad that looks suspiciously like the fictional one. In a General Motors tie-in, Oprah Winfrey gave each of her audience members a Pontiac. A single 30-second ad slot on *Oprah* would cost around US$70.000. Product-placement specialist Frank Zazza reckons that the publicity value of the 'give-away' would be at least 1,000 times that (Auletta, 2005). Product placement within films and television programmes is common, but in March 2005 McDonald's Corporation brought us a new development. They put out a press release promising to pay top hip hop artists US$5 each time a song mentioning their Big Mac burger gets air play. Burberry, Courvoisier, Gucci and Lexus have been beneficiaries of rappers' bragging. But those events were entirely fortuitous. Rappers mentioned those things because they liked them. McDonald's have moved it a step further and put in an incentive scheme. The polite term for this type of activity is 'referencing'. Jay-Z, 50 Cent and Snoop Dogg have already done it (Anon., 2005). In short, our cultural products and our preferred entertainment forms are often little more than adverts. We might not want to buy. Even so, we are being sold. Radio, television, newspapers, websites and magazines sell us, the audience, to advertisers. What interests advertisers is audience size and demographic profile. We are commodities.

Then there is the celebrity, that strange product of the twentieth century: famous for being famous, whose sole social function seems to be to teach us how to consume. Like advertisements, then, they have an instructive value: what clothes, what perfume, what make-up, what hair style, what diet, what car, whatever. We can get their look – can we get their life? Essentially a media-made product, the blander they are, the better. This seems paradoxical – why would we be interested in someone so fundamentally uninteresting? But the answer makes sense: so that we can project more of our dreams, desires and fantasies onto them. David Beckham is a wonderful example. Granted, he can kick a ball, but so can Thierry Henri. David's pretty, and he dresses well, and his wife's a pop star: 'Posh'n'Becks', a dream (marketing) team. His image is fluid and negotiable. He's open to many readings: a fantasy figure for men and women, a family man, role model, roving lad, significant other to a pop singer, soccer player, rags-to-riches success story, fashionista and franchise. Major soccer clubs are now brands too, selling everything from alcoholic beverages to interior furnishings. That's why Real Madrid paid over US$40 million to sign him up – they want to be the biggest sporting brand of all. (And Adidas were pleased to have him with an Adidas team – former team Manchester United are Nike.) Real don't need a world-class player. They already have a World XI. This was an exercise in 'Beckonomics' (Cashmore and Parker,

2003). This was not about winning on the pitch in Spain; it was about selling soccer shirts in Asia.

All of this is worrying enough, yet the consumer ethic spreads continually, entering ever-greater areas of social life. Politics is a good example. These days it is dominated by the tools of market research. Politicians make extensive use of focus groups, public relations firms, image consultants and media spin merchants. The end product is a brand rather than a policy, and a model of citizenship based on consumer sovereignty (Hobsbawm, 2000, p. 113). Rampant individualism triumphs over older notions like the public sphere, which once provided for collective social action. Indeed, in free-market ideology there is little need for politics. After all, citizens (consumers) 'vote' with their purchases. Small wonder, then, that sociologists talk of the privatization of social life. Seen from this perspective, the people charged with running nation states come to look suspiciously like advertisers. The *Guardian Weekly* once ran an article titled 'America is not a Hamburger'. It emerges that America *is* a hamburger. Lashed by anti-American sentiment upon inaugurating its War on Terror, the White House looked to put things right. The traditional approach would have been to engage in the diplomatic process, have your ambassadors talk to their ambassadors, perhaps offer some aid, or broker a trade deal. The Undersecretary of State for Public Diplomacy and Public Affairs that Bush appointed was of a different kind. Charlotte Beers was one of Madison Avenue's leading lights, a brand manager par excellence. The new politics has nothing to do with building relationships but with building brands (Beers had never previously worked her magic on anti-terrorism or militant Islam, but through J. Walter Thompson and Ogilvy & Mather she had experience with dog food and power drills). 'Now she was being asked to work her magic on the greatest branding challenge of all: to sell the US and its war on terrorism to an increasingly hostile world' (Klein, 2002). The appointment raised eyebrows in some parts, but then Secretary of State Colin Powell's feathers remained unruffled. By way of explanation he said: 'There is nothing wrong with getting somebody who knows how to sell something. We are selling a product. We need someone who can rebrand American foreign policy, rebrand diplomacy. Besides,' he said, 'she got me to buy Uncle Ben's rice.' So we are sold politics and particular policies in the same way that we are sold Big Macs and Eminem CDs. Buyer beware.

FEELING: EMOTIONS • BELIEVING: RELIGION • EDUCATING • STRAYING: DEVIANCE • MEDIATING: TECHNOLOGY • INFORMING: MEDIA • RELATING: FAMILY • BELONGING: COMMUNITY • FINISHING

4   101

Conclusion

When we think about consumption we should never lose sight of the thing being consumed. Recent years have seen the development of what we might call 'Thing Studies' (B. Brown, 2004; Daston, 2004). Although this is welcome, it is not without its flaws. These students of things are all for objects but they largely ignore how they come into the world (clue: they are the products of human labour). It is only after we have acknowledged the thingness of things that we should move on to consider what their consumption may symbolize. When we have regarded consumption as 'something else' it has been in the following ways: consumption as compensation, consumption as social cohesion and consumption as identity. Throughout this discussion we have not lost sight of how such consumption practices impact upon others. Our consumption is someone else's production, and our pleasure may well be someone else's pain. Production and consumption, then, are heavily intertwined: production presumes consumption and vice versa. We have noted distinctions in terms of who can consume and how we consume. Here the gap between the West and the Rest loomed large. Similarly, we should note that there are distinctions in production; we call this the division of labour. Some are bosses, more are managers, most are workers. We have also noted (with alarm) the spread of the consumer ethic into more and more areas of social life.

The sociology of consumption literature supposes that consumption is what binds us together in the modern world; that it gives us something we would otherwise be missing in the absence of custom; that it gives shape and meaning to our existence. Sometimes the argument is pushed even further: consumption entails the re-enchantment of the world. There is talk of the sacralization of consumption: malls are our cathedrals (Ritzer, 2001). Two points need to be made. First, the argument is not new. Walter Benjamin began his attempt to unravel the bourgeois experience of the nineteenth century in 1927. It led him straight into the arcades of Paris. These were the forerunners of the mall. Of the Passage de Panoramas he wrote: 'All at once, they were the hollow mold from which the image of "modernity" was cast. Here, the century mirrored with satisfaction its most recent past' (2004, p. 874). The mall's other prototype was the department store. In *Au bonheur des Dame* (1883) Emile Zola observed that 'the department store tends to replace the church. It marches to the religion of the cash desk, of beauty, of coquetry, and fashion. [Women] go there to pass the hours as they used to go to church: an occupation, a place of enthusiasm where they struggle between their passion for clothes and the thrift of their husbands' (Zola in Miller, 1981, p. 177). Second, we should be sceptical of claims that consumption fills an existential void or provides spiritual sustenance. Its solutions are strictly short-term. This takes us back to capitalism: if one thing satisfied us we would never buy another. The system would soon grind to a halt (see Chapter 5, 'Trading').

In a very real sense, more is less. Take America. The income of someone born in 1940 has risen 116 per cent since the start of their working lives. Between 1950 and 2000 Gross Domestic Product tripled. Goods became more plentiful and cheaper too. We might say that luxuries got democratized. Interestingly, no one has got any happier. Formal surveys began in 1946. Joy has not increased (in fact it has fallen slightly since the 1970s). But what has increased, and spectacularly so, is depression – by a factor of ten since the 1950s (Surowiecki, 2005). None of this would have been news to Sigmund Freud. In *Civilization and Its Discontents* Freud noted how civilization contains its very antithesis. The modern scientific age has many achievements, to be sure. We can now go farther, live longer and control nature to a degree never hitherto imagined. Yet despite all of this people are no happier. Indeed, the things we use to alleviate our misery are frequently their cause. New technologies and products may bring new possibilities, but they are freighted with problems.

> If there were no railway to overcome distances, my child would never have left his home town, and I should not need the telephone in order to hear his voice. If there were no sea travel, my friend would not have embarked on his voyage, and I should not need the telegraph service in order to allay my anxiety about him. (Freud, 2004, p. 32)

We used to consume to live. Now in the privileged West we live to consume. As large tracts of the world suffer because they do not get enough, we suffer from having too much. The popular term for our curious malady is *affluenza*. Let us be truthful about our condition. 'Things' change our lives, but not necessarily for the better.

FEELING: EMOTIONS • BELIEVING: RELIGION • EDUCATING • STRAYING: DEVIANCE • MEDIATING: TECHNOLOGY • INFORMING: MEDIA • RELATING: FAMILY • BELONGING: COMMUNITY • FINISHING

103

Suggestions for further reading

Klein, N. (2001) *No Logo: No Space, No Choice, No Jobs, No Logo* (London: Flamingo).

Mackay, H. (ed.) (1997) *Consumption and Everyday Life* (Thousand Oaks, CA: Sage).

Miller, D. (ed.) (1995) *Acknowledging Consumption: A New Review of Studies* (London: Routledge).

Ritzer, G. (2001) *Explorations in the Sociology of Consumption: Fast Food, Credit Cards and Casinos* (London: Sage).

Scanlon, J. (ed.) (2000) *The Gender and Consumer Culture Reader* (New York: New York University Press).

Bibliography

Anon. (2005) 'Return of the Mac', BBC News. Available: http://news.bbc.co.uk/go/pr/fr/-/2/hi/business/4389751.stm [accessed: 03/29/2005].

Anti-Slavery (2004) *Annual Review*. Available: http://www.antislavery.org/homepage/resources/full%20annual%20report.pdf [accessed: 11/04/2005].

Auletta, K. (2005) 'The New Pitch', *The New Yorker* (28 March 2005). Available: http://www.newyorker.com/fact/content/articles/050328fa_fact [accessed: 29/03/05].

Bauman, Z. (1991) *Thinking Sociologically* (Oxford: Blackwell).

Bauman, Z. (1993) *Postmodern Ethics* (Oxford: Blackwell).

Benjamin, W. (2004) 'The Arcades of Paris', in *The Arcades Project*, trans. H. Eiland and K. McLaughlin (Cambridge, MA and London: The Belknap Press of Harvard University Press), pp. 873–84.

Benson, J. (1994) *The Rise of Consumer Society in Britain, 1880–1980* (London and New York: Longman).

Brown, B. (ed.) (2004) *Things* (Chicago, IL: University of Chicago Press).

Brown, S. (2004) 'Coffee – The Market: The Economics of Coffee', *First Things*. Available: http://www.firstscience.com/SITE/editor/022_ramblings_15082003.asp [accessed: 12/04/2005].

Campbell, C. (1995) in *Acknowledging Consumption: A Review of New Studies*, ed. Daniel Miller (London: Routledge).

Cashmore, E. and A. Parker (2003) 'One David Beckham? Celebrity, Masculinity and the Socceratti', *Sociology of Sport* 20(3), pp. 214–32.

Daston, L. (ed.) (2004) *Things that Talk: Object Lessons from Art and Science* (New York: Zone Books).

Ehrenburg, I. (1976/1929) *The Life of the Automobile* (New York: Urizen Books).

Freud, S. (2004/1930) *Civilization and Its Discontents*, trans. David McLintock (London: Penguin Books).

Giddens, A. (1993) *Sociology*, 2nd edn (Cambridge: Polity Press).

Global Rich List: http://www.globalrichlist.com/how.html

Hobsbawm, E. (2000) *The New Century* (London: Little, Brown and Company).

Klein, N. (2002) 'America is not a Hamburger', *Guardian* (14 March 2000). Available: http://www.guardian.co.uk/Columnists/Column/0,5673,667053,00.html [accessed: 14/04/2005].

Latour, B. (2000) 'When Things Strike Back: A Possible Contribution of "Science Studies" to the Social Sciences', *British Journal of Sociology* 51(1), pp. 107–23.

Lewis, J. (2002) *Cultural Studies: The Basics* (London: Sage).

Lewis, R., F. Lawrence and A. Jones (2003) 'Miles and Miles and Miles', *Guardian* (10 May 2003). Available: http://www.guardian.co.uk/food/focus/story/0,951962,00.html [accessed: 11/04/05].

Lipovetsky, G. (1994) *The Empire of Fashion: Dressing Modern Democracy*, trans. Catherine Porter (Princeton, NJ: Princeton University Press).

Marx, K. (1988/1844) 'Towards a Critique of Hegel's *Philosophy of Right*: Introduction', in D. McLellan (ed.), *Karl Marx: Selected Writings* (Oxford: Oxford University Press), pp. 63–74.

McLellan, D. (ed.) (1988) *Karl Marx: Selected Writings* (Oxford: Oxford University Press).

Miller, M. B. (1981) *The Bon Marché: Bourgeois Culture and the Department Store, 1869–1920* (Princeton, NJ: Princeton University Press).

Mills, C. W. (1956) *White Collar: The American Middle Class* (New York: Oxford University Press).

Mills, C. W. (1971/1959) *The Sociological Imagination* (Harmondsworth: Penguin).

Mintz, S. W. (1985) *Sweetness and Power: The Place of Sugar in Modern World History* (New York: Viking).

Owen, D. (2000) 'Taking Humor Seriously – George Meyer, the Funniest Man Behind the Funniest Show on TV', *The New Yorker* (13 March 2000). Available: The Simpsons Archive: http://www.snpp.com/other/interviews/meyer00.html [accessed: 14/04/2005].

Pilger, J. (2001) *The New Rulers of the World: A Special Report* (Birmingham: Carlton International Media).

Ramonet, I. (1998) 'The Politics of Hunger', trans. Barry Smerin, *Le Monde Diplomatique* (November 1998). Available: http://www.irvl.net/

FEELING: EMOTIONS · BELIEVING: RELIGION · EDUCATING · STRAYING: DEVIANCE · MEDIATING: TECHNOLOGY · INFORMING: MEDIA · RELATING: FAMILY · BELONGING: COMMUNITY · FINISHING

4   105

LE%20MONDE%20DIPLOMATIQUE%20-%20November%201998. htm [accessed: 10/04/2005].

Ritzer, G. (2001) *Explorations in the Sociology of Consumption: Fast Food, Credit Cards and Casinos* (London: Sage).

Sattler, S. (2005) 'A Few Facts That Will Change Your Life', *The Tufts Daily* (23 February 2005). Available: http://www.tuftsdaily.com/vnews/disply. v?TARGET=printable&article_id−421bff6aa7996 [accessed: 01/03/05].

Sebald, W. G. (2002) *The Rings of Saturn* (London: Vintage).

Surowiecki, J. (2005) 'Technology and Happiness', *TechnologyReview. com.* Available: http://www.technologyreview.com/articles/05/01/issue/ surowiecki0105.asp?p=0 [accessed: 01/01/05].

Sznaider, N. (2000) 'Consumerism as a Civilizing Process: Israel and Judaism in the Second Age of Modernity', *International Journal of Politics, Culture and Society* 14(2), pp. 297–314.

Voltaire (1993/1759) *Candide: Or, Optimism* (Ware: Wordsworth Classics).

trading

5

Peter T. Manicas

KEY
POINTS

- Trading has been around for a very long time, even though for most of human history, groups more or less co-operatively produced and shared the basic needs of life.

- The invention of money allowed for extensive impersonal trading, an expanded division of labour, and increasing interdependency, now reaching across the entire globe.

- Markets are always socially constructed and, accordingly, there is enormous variation in the institutional features, conditions, instruments and legal arrangements that make exchange possible.

- There is no such thing as a 'neutral' set of rules governing market exchanges; there is considerable confusion as regards the idea of a 'Free Market'.

- As the unintended product of actors each trying to bring about their goals, markets may create socially disastrous outcomes. Some of these can be addressed only by conscious collective action.

- There is no market mechanism to guarantee work for all who want to work, or which guarantees that all existing jobs will pay a non-poverty wage; still less, that all will get the jobs and wages they 'deserve'.

- Globalization increases uncertainties and inhibits our capacities to solve many problems – environmental, economic and social.

Introduction

Trading has been around for a very long time, although for most of human history groups engaged nature, more or less co-operatively producing what they needed. There was a rudimentary division of labour – almost always rooted in gender – and little in the way of surplus to be exchanged. In such 'subsistence economies' almost everything was consumed by the producers, either as it was produced or later. Peasants made sure, for example, that there would be some rice stored for consumption during the winter.

Adam Smith, one of the first to try to analyze capitalism, offers, in *The Wealth of Nations* (1776), a story of how people left what he called 'the early and rude state of society'. It is an illuminating story, but almost certainly not a true one. He held that the 'early and rude' state of society became 'civilized' because human beings had what he called 'a propensity to truck, barter and exchange one thing for another' (to truck is to carry something). He saw this as a feature of human nature – an assumption that led Karl Marx to say that Smith considered everyone an eighteenth-century English merchant. Smith did not give much thought to his Scottish feudal forebears, still less Native Americans or Maori, who somehow lacked this particular propensity.

But however this may be, he felt that 'trucking and bartering' led to an expansion of the division of labour. Individuals or even groups (so-called hunters and gatherers) could stop trying to do everything to satisfy their needs. Tasks could be divided up and assigned to many different people. They could then exchange with one another for what they needed and wanted.

The invention of money was certainly a critical next step. As John Locke had already argued (in 1690), money was something that could be stored, 'without waste', and could be used to represent the value of things which might then be traded. Smith shared with Locke the idea that the 'value' of something – or more strictly the exchange value of something – was equal to the amount of labour time that went into its production. In a famous example Smith argued that if beavers were to be exchanged for deer, the parties to the trade would trade only if they got their value: if acquiring a deer took twice as long as acquiring a beaver, then the exchange ratio was two to one. Since money could represent these ratios, in this situation, value and price are identical.

Smith held, rightly, that determining values in this way – a version of the labour theory of value – held only in the 'early and rude state of society', before, as he it put it, there was an 'accumulation of stock' and before there were 'landlords' who, he observed, 'love to reap where they have not sowed'. As everyone agrees (including Karl Marx, who also held to a version of this theory), once people own land and the means of production, for example the tools and machines of mass production, it is not so easy to determine prices. Modern micro-economics (or neo-classical price theory – what one gets in the first course in economics) is an effort to do this.

The earliest money had a strictly local reach – the cowry shells of Poly-nesians bought nothing in London or Paris. Still, having something that could represent value permitted non-barter exchange. Instead of trading goods for other goods, if two parties could agree that a given quantity of money did represent a given value, one could use money to buy something – if the other party had it for sale. One cannot overstate the importance of this. As Adam Smith already recognized, not only were the possibilities for a continuously expanding division of labour created but, along with this, conditions for expanding interdependency were created, an interde-pendency which today encompasses the entire globe.

The logic is quite straightforward. When a group could satisfy all its needs using its own resources, individuals and families did not need to trade among the members of the group; they might simply share. But as well, the group and its members did not need to trade with other groups. They were autarchic (self-sufficient). Once trade became widespread and they *needed* to trade to satisfy their needs, they become dependent. Consider, for example, energy needs. Even a nation as large and as powerful as the United States cannot satisfy its energy needs domestically; it must buy oil from oil producers abroad. More generally, as is quite plain, most of us today need the hands of many others if we are to get through the day. Most of these people are quite unknown to us and many of them live in China or Mexico. Indeed, they may live and work anywhere. As individuals we are radically interdependent, even if – a fact of considerable importance – nearly all of these relations are entirely impersonal and anonymous. When we go to a supermarket, the store is filled with commodities, each bearing a price. Although all of these goods were made by human hands, this becomes irrelevant. As Marx neatly put the matter in *Capital*, a social relation between persons becomes an objective relation between things (Marx, 1970, vol. 1: sec. 4).

Impersonal markets

Impersonal markets, the primary mechanisms of exchange, require commodification, the constitution of things as commodities – including the commodification of labour. (A commodity is anything that can have a price attached to it and is available to sell.)

There is a huge amount of folklore associated with the idea of a market. Much of this mythology is promoted by well-established economic theories. Two points need to be mentioned. Markets do function to allocate resources – for example, factors of production – and to distribute– for example, the wages of workers; the obvious alternative is some sort planning or 'command' system. There are distinct advantages to markets, but real markets do not, and never have, satisfied either the too often critically held beliefs about them, or the conditions of modern price theory.

To fix our ideas, consider what may have been the most rudimentary of markets: a place established for vendors who bring products to sell. Perhaps there is a flea market in your town or perhaps you have been to a farmer's market in some city. In this convenient place in physical space, suppliers (people with things to sell) come together with demanders (people who want to buy). Now if everybody knew the (real) value of commodities, buyers would bargain with sellers until each was satisfied that they were getting their money's worth.

But nobody knows the real value of anything and they cannot. The requisite information is not available. Even if each seller does know what it costs her to bring the product to the market, she doesn't know what it costs other sellers to bring their products to the market – and they are not likely to tell her. So she fixes a price on her goods that she thinks she can get. On the other side, buyers do not walk around with a cost/benefit schedule in their heads so that they know what they would be willing to pay for differing amounts of utility to be gleaned from the goods available. What happens is pretty simple. The buyers look at the prices of goods offered and decide whether they are willing to pay what is being asked for the particular good. So perhaps, after some haggling, some things get sold and others don't. You *may* have got a bargain. Nor does help to say that if there is some other seller of the same good, the competition between them will drive the price down to its real worth (technically, the slope of the supply curve: the price at various quantities). On this assumption and assuming that buyers do have cost/benefit schedules in their heads (the slope of the demand curve), the intersection of the two curves will be the price and it will equal the real value. But the buyer has to know that there is another seller of the commodity and that his price is lower. People do shop around, but they do not look everywhere. Indeed, even if in principle they could, the costs of doing so would forbid the effort. This is an example of what are sometimes called transaction costs. Further, the two goods may not be identical. The seller with the commodity with the higher price can argue that it is of better quality. And he may not be lying. The question of what is substitutable cannot be determined in advance. More generally, exchanges need not satisfy constraints of economic rationality.

There are further implications of this. Theory says that in a free market, prices will fall until there are buyers for everything. The vendors all go home with money in their pockets but no commodities: the market clears. But markets do not clear. Buyers go home disappointed (or annoyed); sellers go home with inventories. For nearly all markets, there is no time at which everything evens out, no time when the market is at equilibrium.

Often people speak of a market as being 'free', without considering what this means. It may be assumed that a market is free when government is not interfering. But this is an odd way to think since without the government and its laws and regulations there could be no market. It is the government that establishes the rules of the game. The rules that constitute a market define, for example, the bundle of rights which constitute what we think of as private property. It defines contracts, standards and conditions. Critically, there is no neutral way to do this. In baseball, raising the height of the pitcher's mound is to the advantage of the pitcher, but, accordingly, to the disadvantage of the batter. Labour laws are in the interests of workers, but contrary to the interests of employers.

One cannot assume that there is only one way to do any of these things. Because markets are always socially constructed, as a function of different histories, there is enormous variation in the institutional features, conditions, instruments and legal arrangements that make exchanges possible. The Japanese stock market, for instance, is different in critical ways from the New York Stock Exchange. And given Japanese corporate policy not to fire workers, but to put them in alternative jobs, so too

FEELING: EMOTIONS • BELIEVING: RELIGION • EDUCATING • STRAYING: DEVIANCE • MEDIATING: TECHNOLOGY • INFORMING: MEDIA • RELATING: FAMILY • BELONGING: COMMUNITY • FINISHING

5   111

their labour market is different from the US labour market. Currently, we hear a good deal of talk about marketization in China and the former Soviet Union. This is best understood as the effort to bring into existence the rules and regulations and – even more difficult – the agreed-upon practices which taken together constitute an American-style version of a market. Some writers have referred to the capitalism that is emerging in Russia as 'mafia capitalism' because the key capitalists are able to exploit the current situation with extra-legal means, including intimidation and violence. One recent writer was content to say merely that it was 'weird capitalism', which is just to say that it is not quite like the system which we take so utterly for granted.

There are other problems with the idea of a free market. As conventional theory recognizes, where there is no parity of market power, markets are not free. Giant corporations can (and do) dominate production and sales. They can better control costs, spend millions on advertising, and use other means to restrict competition – for example, by controlling shelf space in a supermarket. Moreover, because of these corporations' size and power, new enterprises are unable to enter the markets that they dominate. Instead of market forces determining organization, organizations determine the nature of markets, or, as Chandler (1993) put the matter, the 'visible hand' replaces the 'invisible hand'. A host of implications follow from this.

Adam Smith (and all those who followed his line of thought) assumed that because producers are self-interested, the invisible hand ensures that goods that are wanted will get produced. As he famously said, 'It is not from the benevolence of the butcher, the brewer, or the baker that we expect our dinner, but from their regard to their own interest' (*Wealth of Nations*, Book 1, Chapter 2).

We may grant that the primary interest of suppliers is profit, but for consumers to be sovereign they need some way to express their wants independently of what is made available to them. This is sometimes true. It is the whole point of market research and ultimately the best argument in favour of entrepreneurs – people who can identify some consumer want and who have the means to respond to it. However, not only are wants shaped and very often created by producers but, as mentioned above, entrepreneurs cannot easily enter the market and become serious competitors.

This is a good place to introduce what economists call elasticity. The demand for a commodity is elastic if it responds to price changes. For example, as the price goes up, people buy less. But since people will pay almost anything for life-saving medications, the demand curve for them is inelastic. In a modern economy demand for many commodities is inelastic because there is little price competition for them. Once a leading corporation determines a price, comparable corporations, on pain of mutual destruction, forego price competition. They shift to non-price competition: built-in obsolescence, brand names, style, extras, service and so on. This also explains the importance of the gigantic effort in marketing in advanced capitalism and of huge consumer debt. The system will break down if needs and wants are not manipulated to ensure that people will buy stuff at the price that has been established. As Schor (1992, p. 117) put the matter, 'consumerism is not an ahistorical trait of human nature, but a specific product of capitalism' (see Chapter 4, 'Consuming').

Nor, for similar reasons, is it the case that a superior product will win out in the marketplace. We now recognize what is called path dependence. This is the fact that small, random events can establish a choice in technology that subsequently becomes nearly impossible to change. Q-W-E-R-T-Y are the first six letters on the upper left of all keyboards that we use. It has been the universal standard since the 1890s. Why? It is clear enough that even if there are much better arrangements, once a relatively small number of people had learned that arrangement, it was effectively locked in. There are more interesting examples: Matsushita's VHS standard over Sony's Betamax; MS-DOS over Macintosh. Indeed, the utter dominance of the gasoline engine cannot be explained by appeal to the idea that only superior products survive in the competitive marketplace. It is also best explained as a case of path dependence. Historians suggest that solutions to the limits of electric cars were on the immediate horizon around 1915, but that a brief price edge was all that was necessary to lock us all into polluting gas-guzzling engines. Some of the same logic is at work regarding the alternative between using cars and mass transportation to commute. The decision to build and sell automobiles led to decisions to build a massive highway system, which, in turn, led to the demise of efficient mass transit. For most people, there is no real choice regarding getting to work: hit the expressway (see Chapter 16, 'Mediating: Technology').

Moreover, there are a host of public goods that private markets have never satisfied. This includes railways, roads, airports, bus systems and national defence. Since these cannot be provided to one person without being available to all others, they will not be provided by private markets (this is a consequence of the so-called free rider problem). Accordingly, government steps in to provide these goods, normally paid for by taxes. But public goods include a narrower set of goods (sometimes called merit goods), which, although they can be privately produced and individually appropriated, generate positive externality effects – that is, the social benefit exceeds the private benefit. Education is an obvious good in this sense. While schools provide benefits to their students, they also inevitably provide benefits to everyone in the community. As well, in the absence of public support for education, private markets would educate only those who could afford their services. The result would be not only increased inequality but a net loss to the community.

The invisible hand also ensured that in the theoretically defined perfectly competitive market production would be accomplished efficiently, where 'efficient' means for the economist that there is no different allocation of resources (inputs) which will improve outputs. But a moment's thought will suggest that an economy could be producing efficiently *and* wastefully or destructively. Destructive but efficient production, for example, destroys the environment – what is often talked about in terms of 'externalities'; wasteful but efficient production generates commodities that fail to serve human needs or wants, or fails to do so as well as it might, like poor-quality housing or Star Wars technology.

There is a further problem with market rationality, often called the isolation paradox. Acting as individuals, each seeks to make the best of his or her position. But because the predicted outcome of the choices that each considers best is affected by the choices of others, the outcome is unintended by all. When each decides to beat the morning traffic jam by leaving for work earlier, the traffic jam occurs earlier. Nothing is gained and everyone loses out on some sleep. When (as Keynes taught us), everyone holds money in order to cope with uncertainty, uncertainty increases. More generally, market outcomes (the range of commodities, their prices, etc.) are the unintended product of the conscious action of different actors each acting to bring about their goals. Since prices provide some guidance in finding and correcting information essential to making economic decisions – a burden not satisfiable in a planned economy (Elson, 1988; Boettke, 1997) – the outcomes may be more efficient than planning could provide. But as is clear enough, micro-rationality may result in macro-irrationality, when, for example, the choices of rational actors produces a serious depression. Globalization increases problems raised by the isolation paradox.

Similarly, problems arise with goods with positional attributes. These include both natural or socially created scarcities and goods subject to crowding problems. Thus beach properties, a BA degree, tourist destinations and automobiles have positional properties. The main idea is caught by noticing that standing on your toes to see better is a good strategy if nobody else follows suit. But when everybody stands on his or her toes, everybody loses. Because education became more widely available, many jobs formerly available to high school graduates now demand college degrees. Again, no one is better off and many are worse off. Automobiles are great on open roads, but they reach their social limits when there are so many that one cannot cross town. The auto confronts natural limits when the pollution becomes unbearable. At this point, the factory that produces automobiles may be efficient, but the result is both wasteful and destructive. In these cases, the rational behaviour of isolated firms and individuals each seeking to satisfy their interests produces outcomes that are neither desired nor even economically rational. Markets themselves cannot solve such problems. Conscious co-ordination of some sort is required.

Markets and work

We have not yet spoken of labour markets. Indeed, these are the distinctive feature of capitalism properly understood. It is confusing (at best) to think that markets *define* capitalism or that capital is merely the means of production. As both Karl Marx and Max Weber insisted, the distinctive feature of capitalism is that workers sell their labour power to people who own the means of production. In this sense, the trading that took place in the ancient European world or in other societies did not make them capitalist. The Greek and Roman political economy was dominated by slavery; in the European Middle Ages, lords commanded serfs who were tied to the land. Lords surely exploited their peasants, but such exploitation took the form of naked coercion. We begin to see capitalism when serfs are 'freed', and are able to sell their labour to employers who produce for exchange, ultimately to generate profit from production. Capitalism is thus a way to produce in the sense that there *must* be labour markets.

It is important to notice that when capitalism was getting started in Europe, the creation of 'free' wage workers involved forcing the peasants off the land. This stimulated an often-bloody resistance (Polanyi, 2001). (The 'enclosure movement' in Europe began when communal peasant land was converted to pasture for sheep in order to satisfy the wool trade. Writing in 1518, Sir Thomas More noted, ironically, that the sheep were eating the people of Europe.) Outside Europe, the process has often been even more disastrous, involving colonial projects that undermined subsistence agriculture and fostered export-led dependent development. A consequence is that today in many post-colonial societies, hundreds of millions are jobless, unable to survive on the land and not absorbed by the modern economy. A recent UN study estimated that globally, in 2001, there were some 921 million living hand-to-mouth existences in slums (Davis, 2004). Indeed, although explaining the emergence of capitalism in Western Europe remains a contested and complicated problem (Pomeranz, 2000; Weber, 2003), the fact that capitalism and modernity did come first to Europe has had enormous consequences regarding the present condition of the nations and peoples of the world.

We can notice here the current myth that capitalism reduced human toil. It is true that in pre-capitalist societies people lacked nearly all of what we now think essential. And if they had enough to eat, it was not *haute cuisine*. But this also meant that once basic food and shelter were provided, people stopped working. Pre-contact Hawai'i has been called 'the first affluent society' because goods were relatively easily provided and there was much time for leisure (Sahlins, 1972). If we look at pre-capitalist Europe, there were but 120 working days in the typical year: some 12-hour days during planting and harvesting, but plenty of holidays and feast days – and the pace of work was slow. A leisure class of nobility did not work.

Capitalism transformed work and the time spent working. First, with the end of feudalism, workers no longer had rights to land or its products;

they became 'proletarian'. If they wanted to eat, they had to sell their labour power to someone. Employers used time to regulate labour and produced a clear division between the work day and leisure time. Second, it was clear enough that capitalists could increase profit by increasing the length of the working day or by making workers more productive – or both. If, in 1300, the typical medieval worker worked 1,440 hours annually, the typical worker in the nineteenth century was working 3,650 hours annually – and always under the watchful eye of the foreman (Schor, 1992, p. 45). In England, beginning in the nineteenth century, labour legislation addressed the question of the length of the working day and, of course, of child labour. A current 40-hour work week, 50 weeks annually, equals 2,000 hours.

Labour markets raise a special problem for the idea of the free market. A plausible sense of 'free' would require that no coercion of any sort be involved in the exchange. But if so, markets would exist only when (paradoxically!) the traders did not *need* to trade: they could refuse to trade if terms were not mutually satisfactory. We may, accordingly, forgo the new car this year or even give up a luxury. But if, as Marx and Weber saw, wage labour is defined by the fact that, as Weber put it (2003, Part IV, Chapter 22), workers are *compelled* to sell their labour power to some employer or another, then obviously coercion is a systematic aspect of labour markets. Persons with only their labour power to sell can refuse any particular offer, but – barring a very strong welfare state – they must accept some offer. It is this fact which most powerfully explains both resistance to 'welfare', *and* low wages. Workers are always in competition for jobs and they will even work at below the minimum wage if they cannot secure a job at a higher wage. They will work part-time without benefits; sometimes at two part-time jobs. But just as it is in the interests of wage workers to get as high a wage as they can, it is in the interests of capitalists to keep their costs as low as possible. Unions were the workers' response to this.

It is a further piece of market mythology that workers get the jobs and wages they deserve. This assumes an appropriate assessment of the skills of the worker and the need for the job. This is perhaps easiest with professional athletes and manual labour, but very difficult for the kinds of skills and competences called for in a modern service economy. Similarly, it is difficult to assess the contribution of the worker, either to the final product or the good of society. To take some obvious examples, one needs to explain why, compared to Japan or Germany, salaries of CEOs (chief executive officers) in the USA are so radically disproportionate to the average salaries of their employees, or why US school teachers with 15 years' experience average $36,219 compared to Switzerland's $62,052 (*New York Times*, 13 June 2001). Moreover, where the product is co-operative product, as is the case in almost all real-world production, it is almost impossible to assess the relative contributions of the co-operators. Indeed, the reality of labour markets is extremely complicated and concretely specific. As Granovetter and Tilly (1988) show, talk of markets collapses a very complicated struggle by a host of parties – capitalists, workers, households, states and organizations, for example trade and labour unions – into a misleading abstraction.

The capitalist has other ways to lower wage costs such as introducing labour-saving technologies. This is a critical part of the dynamic of capitalism since cost reduction (along with product innovation) through technological innovation is built into the system. This is obviously the case where there is price competition, but it occurs even where competition is not over prices. In oligopolistic competition corporate giants do not compete over prices, but, for example, market share. It was widely held that this dynamic was one of the glories of capitalism: it guaranteed progress. But putting aside questions of whether progress can be measured in terms of technological innovation, this belief ignores the consequences for workers and assumes that the self-adjusting mechanisms of the market will produce adjustments in the labour market such that workers who became unemployed would regain desired employment, perhaps doing something else.

Unfortunately, the historical evidence shows that such is not the case. 'Downsized' workers who find jobs generally find ones that pay less and do not require the skills that they had mastered (Uchitelle, 2006). Technological innovation deskills some workers and demands new skills of others. More generally, as theory since the time of Keynes recognizes, there is no mechanism in market capitalism which guarantees either that there will be work for all who want to work or that the available jobs will produce living wages for workers; still less, that everyone will get the jobs they deserve. We call the former structural unemployment.

Today, economists are content to hold that an unemployment rate of 6 per cent or less can be considered full employment. But that means, in the American economy, that as many as nine million workers will be unemployed. Nor does it address the problem of the working poor: that in 2000 some 6.4 million or 41 per cent of America's poor, had jobs that paid *below* the government-defined poverty line (US Bureau of Labor Statistics, March 2002). Similarly, last year in Australia the number of working poor increased by 50 per cent, to some 3 million (*The Australian*, 7 April 2006).

The problem of labour-saving technology was discerned in the early nineteenth century by the so-called Luddites – Nottingham stocking-knitters who smashed the machines then being introduced (17 of them were hanged in York in 1812). And, of course, the problem is hugely exacerbated by the latest generation of technologies. Indeed, Jeremy Rifkin (2004) has recently written a book called *The End of Work*! Rifkin is not predicting a utopia where everywhere enjoys a life of leisure, but a grim world where getting a decent job becomes more and more difficult.

Capitalists have another powerful capacity to cut costs: because capital is mobile they can move it from country to country with ease, and hence they can move production to places where cheaper labour is available. The result is *not* what either Adam Smith or Karl Marx predicted. Both believed that capitalism would encompass the world ('breaking down Chinese walls', as Marx put it in the *Communist Manifesto*) and that, eventually, societies would achieve developmental parity. (It was just this, of course, which led Marx to call for the workers of the world to unite!) But development has continued to be dependent and uneven. When we add to this the alarming growth in the world's population and the destruction of nature that modernizing processes have produced, the result is a new kind of world poverty and a huge acceleration in efforts to immigrate – legally or illegally. Thus the International Labour Organization, a UN body, has estimated that 820 million people – or 30 per cent of the world's labour force – were without a job or underemployed at the end of 1994. Things have worsened since. By one recent estimate, more than two *billion* people – nearly one-third of the total population of earth – live on the equivalent of less than a dollar a day (Reich, 2006). Dividing the globe into north and south, the ILO concludes: 'What we have is a globalization of the labour markets, a new division that is emerging. It means that the south will get more involved in labour intensive production and the north will have to find niches related to high-tech production. *No single country can tackle this on its own anymore*' (*The European*, 24 February–2 March 1995). (See also Chapter 4, 'Working'.)

The present and immediate future

When we think of capitalism we still tend to think in nineteenth-century terms of the factory system which separated household and industry and organized workers with machines into a division of labour on the shop floor, controlled by supervisors and bosses. The smokestacks belching black smoke are gone and so indeed is industrial capitalism as that term is generally used. Of course, there are still factories but even these look little like Henry Ford's automated car-assembly line where workers worked an eight-hour day for a wage which allowed them to buy the cars they were producing.

In *The Condition of Postmodernity* (1989), David Harvey suggests that a new system emerged with Ford and that this system (which he calls 'Fordist–Keynesian') developed, matured and more or less began give way in the 1970s, at the end of the long boom that followed the end of the Second World War. Harvey calls this period of capitalism Fordist–Keynesian because these two names capture two of its key features. From a technological and organizational point of view, Henry Ford's Dearborn, Michigan auto plant was essentially an extension of trends already well in motion. Business organization was already corporate, even if at the end of the century large organizations had been greatly extended through a wave of mergers, trusts and cartels. Similarly, the division of labour and the separation between conception, management, control and execution on the shop floor was by then standard. As Harvey writes: 'What was special about Ford ... was his vision, his explicit recognition that mass production meant mass consumption, a new system of the reproduction of labour power, a new politics of labour control and management, a new aesthetics and psychology, in short, a new kind of rationalized, modernist, and populist democratic society' (1989, p. 126).

Ford would create not only a new type of worker, but a new type of man. He would be hardworking, but he would be a *consumer*, working for his nuclear family, who would also consume in a world where the standard of living would continue to improve: with their new car, they would be mobile, and enjoy both city and country. (Compare Schor, *The Overspent American*, 1998.) The Keynesian part of the term comes from the work of John Maynard Keynes (1936) who wrote the *General Theory of Employment, Interest and Money*. It had long been recognized that, left to its own devices, the capitalist system was subject to recurring booms and busts. This had come to a dramatic head in the Great Depression of 1929. Although this depression had worldwide effects, it had begun in the USA with Black Thursday, the collapse of the New York Stock Exchange. Within months, hundreds of factories closed and unemployment soared. By 1934 over 20 million were unemployed in the USA alone.

A new mode of regulation was invented to remedy this. This emerged in the 1930s, both with the New Deal of Franklin Delano Roosevelt and with the more authoritarian solutions being explored in Japan, Germany and Italy. The Second World War ended the Great Depression exactly because government became involved in the economy, not merely as the safety net of last resort, and regulator of capitalist exchange processes, but – as Keynes had already suggested – as the critical investor in the economy (through massive government spending to build tanks and aircraft).

After the war, under US hegemony, capitalism in the advanced countries realized a long period of strong and sustained growth. Living standards rose and mass democracy was preserved and extended to nations that had no experience of it. Harvey notes that trouble was evident in the 1960s, especially with the full recovery of the West German and Japanese economies, which entered global capitalism as players seeking export markets. The Fordist–Keynesian solution no longer sufficed. Harvey argues that if one word suggests its fundamental flaw, it is 'rigidity'. He writes:

> There were problems with the rigidity of long-term and large-scale fixed capital investments in mass production systems that precluded much flexibility of design and presumed stable growth in invariant consumer markets. There were problems of rigidities in labour markets, labour allocation, and in labour contracts (especially in the so-called 'monopoly sector'). And any attempt to remove

FEELING: EMOTIONS • BELIEVING: RELIGION • EDUCATING • STRAYING: DEVIANCE •
MEDIATING: TECHNOLOGY • INFORMING: MEDIA • RELATING: FAMILY • BELONGING: COMMUNITY • FINISHING

121

> these rigidities ran into the seemingly immovable force of working-class power – hence the strike waves and labour disruptions of the period 1968–72. The rigidities of state commitments also became more serious as entitlement programmes (social security, pension rights, etc.) grew under pressure to keep legitimacy at a time when rigidities in production restricted any expansion in the fiscal basis for state expenditures. (Harvey, 1989, p. 142)

One needs only to look at the daily newspaper to see evidence for current responses to these sorts of 'rigidities'. Thus, we hear constantly about downsizing, subcontracting, the huge increase in part-time benefitless work, especially for females who for the first time exceeded the number of males in the workforce. Similarly, we can recall President Reagan's dramatic attack on PATCO, the air controllers' union; so-called Thatcherism; and, more recently, the Republican 'contract with America' and the adoption of what is termed neo-liberalism, a resuscitation of the laissez-faire policies that were so popular late in the nineteenth century.

Viewed from the point of view of developing capitalism, Harvey calls the new period 'flexible accumulation':

> It rests on flexibility with respect to labour processes, labour markets, products and patterns of consumption. It is characterized by the emergence of entirely new sectors of production, new ways of providing financial services, new markets, and above all, greatly intensified rates of commercial, technological and organizational innovation. (Harvey, 1989, p. 147)

These changes have enormous, if unclear, consequences on a host of other deeply related issues, including the character of contemporary (post-modern?) culture, but especially experience of space and time and, perhaps more critically, our experience of ourselves and of our relations to others and to nature. Thus, to take one example, the annihilation of space through time, which was always part of the capitalist dynamic, has now created the 'Global Village'. As Marshall McLuhan put it:

> After three thousand years of explosion, by means of fragmentary and mechanical technologies, the Western World is imploding. During the mechanical ages we had extended our bodies in space. Today, after more than a century of electronic technology, we have extended our central nervous system itself in a global embrace, abolishing both space and time as far as our planet is concerned. (Quoted in Harvey, 1989, p. 293)

Globalization

Much of the foregoing is often referred to as the consequence of globalization. While it is clear that globalization is a real phenomenon, one can fail to acknowledge its complex and multidimensional character. Depending upon how it is characterized, globalization takes on enormous ideological freight. One popular view, well articulated by Thomas Friedman (1999, p. 7), holds that 'globalization involves the inexorable integration of markets, nation-states and technologies to a degree never witnessed before'. Friedman (2005) has more recently coupled this idea with an idea that 'the earth is flat'. He quotes the co-founder of Netscape: 'Today, the most profound thing to me is the fact that a 14-year-old in Romania or Bangalore or the Soviet Union or Vietnam has all the information, all the tools, all the software easily available to apply knowledge however they want.'

All of this is important, but we must resist the temptation to think of social processes as 'inexorable' – as if there are neither choices nor future surprises. Who would have thought that 'actually existing socialism' in Eastern Europe and the Soviet Union would so precipitously collapse, or that 19 terrorists would destroy the World Trade Center – two events which dramatically altered the world? Similarly, we cannot reduce globalization processes to economics and technology. Technology is socially shaped just as it is socially shaping and, as above, *there are always choices*. Similarly, the governments of the nations of the world have not been passive actors, and their decisions will remain critical factors in outcomes – economic, cultural and educational (Steger, 2005). Here the USA plays a special role. Unfortunately, global poverty and inequality are greatly exacerbated by what is often called 'neo-liberalism', a globalizing myth promoted by the US-dominated International Monetary Fund (IMF), World Bank and World Trade Association (WTO). It insists that for the sake of efficiency the state must withdraw social safety nets and even long-term investment in schools and transportation, and that markets, including international markets, must be free as the neo-classical economist understands this (Stiglitz, 2002).

Thus Americanization is an obvious feature of globalization, because not only is the use of US military power a critical variable, but US corporations are still dominant forces in the global political economy. Moreover, a host of American cultural features, many propelled by new technologies of mass communication, are now global – even if these have a distinctly local look (Ritzer, 2004). But all of these tendencies provoke resistance. Surely, capitalism is the crucial variable in all of this, but given the contingencies of history, it is quite impossible to say what capitalism will look like in the future – even, perhaps, in the relatively near future.

Capitalism's long-term future?

There are those with rose-tinted glasses who now speak of 'virtual capitalism'. Some brief remarks on the implications of digitization conclude this chapter.

It is easy to have a mental image of a virtual university. It is an institution which would grant degrees, would have an administration, students and faculties, but since all the transactions between administrators and students and faculty would take place electronically, it would not exist in *any* place. It would be wherever there are individuals with access to the internet. Indeed, if we think of the learning taking place asynchronically – that is, students and faculty, and students and students interact at their leisure (perhaps within a specified time frame) – then even time loses much of its relevance to the process.

No such image of a virtual capitalism is possible. This is the case because more than electronically transmittable information is essential for any economic system to exist. But the fact that something of what is essential to capitalism is electronically transmittable opens some possibilities. There are a number of visions. One, influenced by Alvin Toffler, the author of *Future Shock*, was articulated by former Speaker of the US House of Representatives, Newton Gingrich. He wrote:

> More and more people are going to operate outside corporate structures and hierarchies in the nooks and crannies that the Information Revolution creates. While the Industrial Revolution herded people into gigantic social institutions – big corporations, big unions, big government – the Information Revolution is breaking up these giants and leading us back to something that is – strangely

enough – much like Tocqueville's 1830s America. (Quoted in Dawson and Foster, 1996, p. 40)

Electronically mediated home work does make possible significant shifts in work activities away from centralized workplaces and this is occurring among both very low waged workers and well-paid telecommunicators; still, it is hardly clear that these tendencies will bring us back to something even remotely like Tocqueville's 1830s America. These are not more or less autarchic yeoman farmers who gather together on the village green to discuss matters of local civic life. Rather, they are much better understood under the heading of flexible accumulation. That is, the information highway is planted on top of the existing structure of highly corporatized global capitalism. This means, at the most elementary level, that home work will be encouraged only if it is cheaper than on-site work and only if it can be readily controlled. Moreover, if there are a host of functions essential to capitalism which can be electronically mediated – direct marketing, data gathering, even forms of decision making – there will remain material production functions which will stay place-based. Indeed, there is a pronounced tendency on the part of many writers to think of capitalism not in terms of production, but in terms of circulation: that is, the whole range of tasks from assembling capital to marketing goods. Bill Gates's (1995) vision of 'friction-free capitalism' is representative of this.

Following the assumptions of standard economic theory, Gates believes that the internet gives us the capacity to have the perfect knowledge that is a condition for a perfectly competitive market. As we noted earlier, on the standard theory, if every buyer knew every seller's price and every seller knew what every buyer was willing to pay for what they wanted to buy, then we would be in a 'new world of low-friction, low-overhead capitalism in which market information will be plentiful and transaction costs will be low'. This is the idealization of consumer sovereignty that we looked at. And, as before, there are a number of problems with this picture. To summarize: buyers are not rational in the sense required. They do not walk around with demand schedules in their heads. Wants and urgencies change. Knowing the price is anything but sufficient information for prospective buyers. Buying from mail order catalogues works, but who has not been disappointed with what came in the mail? In actually existing capitalism, not all sellers are in price-competitive markets and there is no reason to think that electronic communication will change this. Indeed, Gates rightly sees that the big difference will be in marketing. But even here there are serious issues. Gates sees one of them.

For him, the new technologies allow sellers to target buyers more effectively. 'The information highway will be able to sort consumers according to much finer individual distinctions, and to deliver to each a new stream of advertising' (quoted in Dawson and Foster, 1996, p. 51). But, of course, the character and rationale of advertising is not changed by this. After telling us that interactivity will allow buyers to purchase custom-made products, e.g., a pair of jeans, he notes that the menu choice is from predetermined alternatives. This is a superficial sort of consumer sovereignty. As usual, the alternatives are provided for us; our ability to 'choose' is mainly a weapon of mass marketing, producing additional inducements to buy. (Compare here 'choices' on the new car in Schor, 1998.)

Given corporate domination of markets, there is little reason to believe that new technologies will give consumers better information. They may well get less. The *New York Times* ran a piece entitled, 'Why You Can't Tell What Things Cost' (2 March 1997). It concluded:

> Price confusion – the inability to figure out who's offering the best bargain, or even to know the true cost of something after you've bought it – has seldom seemed so universal. The traditional laws of supply and demand once imposed a semblance of order and clarity on prices [it was more price rigidity enforced by oligopoly which did this], but today they are being so haphazardly amended by pell-mell technological changes and new marketing wrinkles that the American marketplace now offers all the certainty of a Mideast bazaar – maybe less.

Airlines, hotels, car rental agencies and so on offer different deals every day: mail order catalogue, corporate discount plans and direct-marketing schemes assault retail markets by offering goods and services 'at reduced or "wholesale" prices whatever that means'. Many of these are simply scams that allow merchandizers 'to change what they want and pocket a substantial profit, with the poor consumer not the wiser'.

Of course, as another recent *New York Times* feature reported, retail stores 'fight back', and evidently one of the more successful ways they are doing this is precisely by doing what electronic marketing cannot do: giving people 'the pleasure of physically being somewhere, of going to a place that was bigger, grander and in every way more exhilarating than anything the customer could experience at home' (*New York Times Magazine*, 6 April 1997). Niketown is an example.

> The first thing you think of when you see Nike's new flagship store on East 57th Street in New York is that this is not a store at all. Niketown's facade is a takeoff on an old New York high-school building. You enter through turnstiles, in the manner of a sport's arena, to find yourself in a sleek, futuristic, five story atrium into which, at 30 minute intervals, a three-story high screen descends and a video softly plugging Nike products is played along with a crescendo of recorded music. There are displays of sports memorabilia and a chance to hit a punching bag. Where are the sneakers?

Retail merchandizing has always sought to enhance the experience of buying and Niketown and the Mall, now under transformation as a Disneyland for shopping, is but the latest step.

Finally, as Gates also sees, information will itself be marketed. Gates notes that there are those who think that the internet will give us unlimited free access to information. He says that while 'a good deal of information, from NASA photos to bulletin board entries donated by users, will continue to be free, I believe that the most attractive information, whether Hollywood movies or encyclopedic databases, will continue to be produced with profit in mind' (quoted in Dawson and Foster, 1996, p. 52).

Mass communication was neatly defined by C. Wright Mills (2000/ 1956). It means that a few people speak to millions and there is little ability to speak back (to raise questions, offer criticisms, point out fallacies, produce evidence that was ignored). By contrast, he defined a public as existing where there were as many speakers as listeners and there was full opportunity to respond. The internet could be a technology which allowed people to bypass the corporate media giants and to communicate globally with one another (McChesney, 1999). In the 1970s most of the world's telecommunications systems were non-profit, state owned (the internet was, of course, a creation of the US Defense Department). Today, most telecommunications systems are owned by a handful of global telecom networks. Indeed, Merrill Lynch is predicting that some 20 per cent of all

FEELING: EMOTIONS • BELIEVING: RELIGION • EDUCATING • STRAYING: DEVIANCE •
MEDIATING: TECHNOLOGY • INFORMING: MEDIA • RELATING: FAMILY • BELONGING: COMMUNITY • FINISHING

127

future investment banking revenues will derive from telecommunications. TCI Chairman John Malone predicted: '[T]wo or three companies will eventually dominate the delivery of telecommunications services over information superhighways worldwide. The big bubbles get bigger and the little bubbles disappear'. Telecommunications giant Rupert Murdock put the matter squarely: 'Monopoly is a terrible thing until you have it' (quoted in Dawson and Foster, 1996, p. 43). Indeed, there is currently a struggle over whether the internet will be a critical feature in the constitution of publics or be reduced to a medium serving the interests of giant corporations (see Chapter 17, 'Informing: Media').

But here, as always, the future will be the product of decisions made by all of us. It is an important goal of this book to give citizens some of the tools needed to be thinking participants in this yet-to-be future.

Suggestions for further reading

Harvey, D. (1989) *The Condition of Postmodernity: An Inquiry into the Origins of Cultural Change* (Oxford: Basil Blackwell).

Manicas, P. T. (2006) *A Realist Philosophy of Social Science* (Cambridge: Cambridge University Press), Chapter 6.

McChesney, R. W. (1999) *Rich Media, Poor Democracy: Communications Politics in Dubious Times* (New York: The New Press).

Polanyi, K. (2001) *The Great Transformation*, 2nd edn (Boston, MA: Beacon Press).

Weber, M. (2003) *General Economic History* (New York: Dover).

Bibliography

Boettke, P. J. (1997) 'Where Did Economics Go Wrong? Modern Economics as Flight from Reality', *Critical Review* 12, pp. 11–74.

Chandler, A. (1993) *The Visible Hand: The Managerial Revolution in American Business* (Cambridge, MA: Belnap Press).

Davis, Mike, (2004) 'Planet of Slums', *New Left Review* 26, pp. 5–34.

Dawson, M. and J. B. Foster (1996) 'Virtual Capitalism: the Political

Economy of the Information Highway', *Monthly Review* (July/August), pp. 40–57.

Elson, D. (1988) 'Market Socialism or Socialism of the Market', *New Left Review* (November/December), pp. 3–44.

Friedman, T. L. (1999) *The Lexus and the Olive Tree: Understanding Globalization* (New York: Farrar, Strauss & Giroux).

Friedman, T. L. (2005) *The World is Flat: A Brief History of the 21th Century* (New York: Farrar, Strauss & Giroux).

Gates, B. (1995) *The Road Ahead* (New York: Viking).

Granovetter, M. and C. Tilly (1988) 'Inequality and Labour Process', in N. Smelzer (ed.), *Handbook of Sociology* (Beverly Hills, CA: Sage), pp. 175–221.

Harvey, D. (1989) *The Condition of Postmodernity: An Inquiry into the Origins of Cultural Change* (Oxford: Basil Blackwell).

Keynes, J. M. (1936) *General Theory of Employment, Interest and Money* (London: Macmillan).

Marx, K. (1970) *Capital*, vol. 1 (London: Lawrence and Wishart).

Marx, K. and F. Engels, (2002) *The Communist Manifesto* (New York: Penguin Classics).

McChesney, R. W. (1999) *Rich Media, Poor Democracy: Communications Politics in Dubious Times* (New York: The New Press).

Mills, C. Wright (2000/1956) *The Power Elite* (New York: Oxford University Press).

More, Sir Thomas (2001) *Utopia* (New Haven, CT: Yale University Press).

Olson, M. (1971) *The Logic of Collective Action* (Cambridge, MA: Harvard University Press).

Polanyi, K. (2001) *The Great Transformation*, 2nd edn (Boston, MA: Beacon Press).

Pomeranz, K. (2000) *The Great Divergence: China, Europe and the Making of the Modern World Economy* (Princeton, NJ: Princeton University Press).

Reich, R. B. (2006) ' "The Poor Get Poorer", review of Joseph Stiglitz and Andrew Charlton, *Fair Trade for All*', *New York Times Book Review* 2 April 2006.

Rifkin, J. (2004) *The End of Work*, updated edn (New York: Tarcher).

Ritzer, G. (2004) *The McDonaldization of Society*, 4th edn (Thousand Oaks, CA: Pine Forge Press).

Sahlins, M. (1972) *Stone Age Economics* (New York: Aldine Transaction).

Schor, J. (1992) *The Overworked American: The Unexpected Decline of Leisure* (New York: Basic Books).

Schor, J. (1998) *The Overspent American: Why We Want What We Don't*

FEELING: EMOTIONS • BELIEVING: RELIGION • EDUCATING • STRAYING: DEVIANCE •
MEDIATING: TECHNOLOGY • INFORMING: MEDIA • RELATING: FAMILY • BELONGING: COMMUNITY • FINISHING

129

Need (New York: Harper Paperbacks).

Smith, A. (2003) *The Wealth of Nations* (New York: Bantam Classics).

Steger, M. (2005) *Globalism: Market Ideology Meets Terrorism* (Lanham, MD: Rowman and Littlefield).

Stiglitz, J. E. (2002) *Globalization and Its Discontents* (New York: W. W. Norton).

Toffler, A. (1971) *Future Shock* (New York: Bantam Books).

Uchitelle, L. (2006) *The Disposable American: Layoffs and Their Consequences* (New York: Alfred A Knopf).

US Bureau of Labor Statistics (2002). http://www.bls.gov/

Weber, M. (2003) *General Economic History* (New York: Dover).

6 stratifying: class

David Bedggood

KEY
POINTS
- The concept 'social class' has been used in sociology, beginning with the classical ideas of Karl Marx and Max Weber, to explain the causes and consequences of social inequality in modern capitalist society.

- Contemporary concepts of class have changed as capitalist society has undergone changes. Concepts such as the middle class, domestic labour, class-consciousness, social movements, indigenous movements are now contested by writers such as Anthony Giddens, Pierre Bourdieu and Erik Olin Wright.

- In Aotearoa/New Zealand class appears to be subordinated to ethnic and gender inequality. In Argentina recent events have suggested that class has given way to social movements of the unemployed. In Iraq the categories of religion and nationality cut across those of class.

- The evidence shows that class relations remain a fundamental feature of modern capitalist society and that other dimensions of social inequality such as race, gender and nationality are rendered more intelligible in their relations to class.

The centrality of social class

The concept of social class is a central one in sociology. Its relevance is to explain the social, as opposed to psychological or biological, causes of persistent and resistant social inequality. Like sociology itself, however, class is open to different interpretations and is a highly contested concept. Sociologists have even been accused of inventing the working class (presumably so they can then pursue careers to escape it). Some sociologists, like Pakulski and Waters, now speak of the 'death of class' as a concept or as a social reality (1996). Hardt and Negri insist that class has been reborn as the 'Multitude' (2000, 2004). Others contest the death notice as premature. For bell hooks (2000), 'Class is the elephant in the room' (a large presence that people politely ignore), and Erik Olin Wright titles one of his books *Class Counts* (1997).

In this chapter I will argue that those who cannot see the 'class elephant' are also like the characters in a dark room who, in yet another elephant story, each feel and describe a different part – tusks smooth and cool, skin rough and wrinkled, trunk like a hose pipe. My purpose is to show that social classes are alive and swinging. As the elephant picks us up and sets off at pace, it becomes obvious that social class is not just an academic curiosity, but a living, moving force that can jump national borders. When widening global gaps between rich and poor cannot be attributed to genetics, non-rational values or mass psychology, then class is left as the single most powerful explanation of its persistent and resistant inequality.

Like the elephant, class has a long memory: it spans several centuries and is as old as sociology itself. We should therefore look first at the two broad historical approaches to class within sociology (Wright, 2005). The first is that of Marxists, who define the nature of modern capitalist society in terms of social class – it is all-important – and their theory stands or falls with class. The second is that of Weberians, who recognize the existence of class inequality in the market without making it a fundamental or necessary feature of modern society (see Chapter 2, 'Modernizing').

This chapter will briefly outline the main elements of each: their basic concepts, the research evidence they draw upon, and their policy outcomes. We can then practically test the explanatory power of both theories by selecting countries where class can be isolated from other important competing causes of inequality. I will conclude that the theory that understands classes as relations of production can account for those 'complex and changing' political and cultural practices of inequality more efficiently and practically than its rivals, allowing the chastened sociologist to at least hang on to the rampaging elephant if not bring it to a halt.

Marx's classes as production relations

Karl Marx defined capitalist society as a relationship between two social classes – wage labour and capital. His interest in class was sparked by the outrage he felt at the treatment of poor peasants denied firewood by wealthy landowners. For him class constituted the essence of capitalism since it involved the systematic exploitation of wage labour and the expropriation of surplus value by capital. Marx distinguished capitalist class society from pre-capitalist society, both classless (primitive communism) and class (slave society, feudalism and the oriental mode of production) and post-capitalist classless communist society (Marx, 1983, pp. 502–6; Miles, 1987, pp. 19–24).

Arising out of this analysis, capitalist society is seen as the most historically advanced mode of production capable of developing the forces of production to the point where a classless socialist society can replace it. However, this process was uneven, and the classes of earlier modes were not always extinguished and sometimes remained 'articulated' to capitalist class relations in what has been called the 'combined and uneven development' of capitalism. This was true of slave or indentured labour, and of tribal, peasant or tributary forms of production, all of which become incorporated as *unfree labour* rather than as free wage labour (Miles, 1987, pp. 313–34). Today, peasant labour, unpaid domestic labour, slave and indentured labour, as well as 'self-employed' and 'temping', remain lucrative sources of unfree labour, alongside wage labour (Cook, 2000) (see Chapter 3, 'Working').

As well as constituting capitalism, the wage workers and capitalist employers are involved in constant struggle over the rate of exploitation. For Marx, class struggle was the 'motor of history', as the demands of workers for better wages and conditions forced capitalists to resort to using the state and law to defend their private property, to pass anti-union legislation and employ 'management' techniques to contain the working class. When this failed, employers would use 'divide and rule' tactics, hiring non-union labour, migrant workers and private armies to break the power of unions. Most importantly, employers were driven to use new technology to increase labour productivity so as to maintain their profits. This had the powerful effect of reducing labour time and the number of workers, creating a pool of unemployed and an industrial reserve army of labour, thus further driving down wages (Marx, 1976, pp. 781–94).

However, the emergence of a working class able to liberate itself from exploitation was not spontaneous or inevitable. The separation of workers from the ownership of the means of production hid from view the actual process of exploitation. Workers did not see that their surplus labour was expropriated to reappear as the value of commodities owned by the employers. Even in the heat of the class war, this productive relation was 'inverted' in the minds of both workers and employers as an ongoing battle over a 'fair' division between wages and profits. Marx called this inversion 'commodity fetishism' because it falsely misrepresented the value of workers' labour as inherent in the 'value' of commodities. This spontaneously generated a 'false consciousness' in which workers saw themselves as being potentially equal with the capitalists (Marx, 1976, pp. 163–77). Class-consciousness would arise only as a result of the intervention of revolutionaries who understood his scientific critique of capitalism and could penetrate the 'appearance of things' to understand their true 'essence' (1981, p. 956).

Weber's classes as market relations

Max Weber's concept of capitalism was that of a market society in which individual actors exchanged commodities. Weber was himself a leading German economic historian and the centre of an influential circle of academics and intellectuals who were generally hostile to Marxism. He viewed economic classes in terms of individuals, such as himself, owning more or less economic 'assets' than others. Individuals also differed according to their access to political power (party) and according to their ability to consume (status). Unlike Marx, however, Weber did not think that individuals were assigned to classes as production relations since they could change their class, status and party positions. Thus, rather than combining together in classes to bring about change in society, Weber saw individuals as having social mobility, acting to change their position in society.

What motivated individuals to try to increase their market share was their rationality – that is, their ability to act as rational actors in the market by buying and selling commodities to improve their asset values. For Weber the capitalist market represented a progressive shift from non-rational society to a rational society where progress was measured by an increasingly efficient division of labour. The economic theory that underpinned this view was the late nineteenth-century marginalist economics that held that the value of commodities was determined by supply and demand (Clarke, 1982, p. 16). The capacity of individuals to act rationally in the market was given by their ability to maximize their assets in the exchange process and determine their share of the distribution of wealth. For this reason, he regarded socialism as a return to the non-market irrationality of 'serfdom' (Gerth and Mills, 1970, p. 49).

For Weber then, economic classes result from individuals' ability to use their knowledge and power in the market to act rationally to determine their relative share of 'assets' or wealth. The capitalists did not combine as a class to exploit wage labour, either in production or in exchange, but rather used their ability to control production and respond to demand in order to increase their market share. Workers, on the other hand, had little power to increase their market share when their only asset was their labour power. Nevertheless capitalists could make bad decisions and go bankrupt, and workers could use their skills and their combined political power to improve their market share. Bargaining over their respective shares of the national wealth then becomes the main economic activity of all actors. Market shares increasingly become determined by relative political power in the formation of 'revenue' classes (i.e., distributional share in the national income).

Neo-Marxism

It did not take long for Marx's prediction of socialist revolution to be falsified by events. Despite the growth of the proletariat during the nineteenth century – in particular the rise of strong trade unions and social democratic and labour parties – workers did not seem to want to turn strikes into revolutions. Where they did revolt, as in Russia in 1917, this did not fit Marx's preconception of a developed industrial society and mass working class. Russian capitalism was in its infancy with a huge

FEELING: EMOTIONS • BELIEVING: RELIGION • EDUCATING • STRAYING: DEVIANCE •
MEDIATING: TECHNOLOGY • INFORMING: MEDIA • RELATING: FAMILY • BELONGING: COMMUNITY • FINISHING

6   135

peasant population. More tellingly, in Germany, where capitalism was well established and a mass working class did exist, workers' revolutionary demands were contained within the Weimar Republic, a 'bloody carnival' of a counter-revolution (Gerth and Mills, 1970, p. 41).

Many Marxists drew the conclusion that economic interests alone were not sufficient to make the working class revolutionary. How can this be explained? Were there political and cultural factors that acted 'independently' of the economy to limit workers' consciousness? Rejecting Marx's theory of commodity fetishism, Antonio Gramsci and the German Frankfurt School highlighted the dominance of capitalist ideology in neutralizing class-consciousness. Some concluded that the proletariat was no longer the 'historic agent' of socialism. The working class appeared to be in decline relative to the 'middle class' and its socialist intellectuals or 'new true socialists' (Meiksins Wood, 1986, pp. 1–11). Over the course of the twentieth century, the apparent weight of such evidence saw the emergence of the contemporary neo-Marxist class theory such as that of Eric Olin Wright and Pierre Bourdieu, who attempted to marry Marx with Weber.

Some went so far as to abandon most of Marx's class analysis altogether and become 'post-Marxist'. For example, Nicos Poulantzas and Ernest Laclau substituted economic with political and ideological 'determinism' in the formation of classes (Meiksins Wood, 1986, p. 34 passim, p. 47 passim). The main message was: 'you're only in a class if you think you are and act like it, in particular voting for your labour or socialist (communist) party'. This redefined Marxist social relations as individual relations compatible with contemporary neo-Weberian 'revenue' classes (Carchedi, 1987, p. 120).

Neo-Weberians

Weber's theory has proven more popular than Marx's among sociologists because it seemed to explain not only the existence of economic classes, and the relative autonomy of economics and politics, but also allowed for individuals to escape particular classes and exercise choice without the inconvenience of overthrowing capitalist society. It therefore seemed to fit better with the actual behaviour of the majority of workers who struggled to improve their living standards without developing a revolutionary class-consciousness.

Not surprisingly, neo-Weberians like Frank Parkin or Anthony Giddens claim that capitalism has outgrown the nineteenth- and early twentieth-century economic scarcity that required classes to compete for zero-sum shares in the national wealth. Today it has become a global, post-scarcity, win–win society in which all can improve their shares of a growing income pool. The persistence of barriers to upward mobility between revenue classes within the urbanized working class can be explained by relative market capacity, i.e. occupations with scarce skills or other 'social capital' (e.g. status and power) that enable them to improve or maintain their income share at the expense of other occupations (Erikson and Goldthorpe, 1992, pp. 366–8, 394–6).

Key to revenue shares are the social status factors that act as gateways to equality. Bourdieu has developed a neo-Weberian theory of revenue classes where the dominant classes can protect their wealth and power by the continuous cultural subordination of the 'lower classes'. He adapts Weber's concept of status in his concept of 'cultural capital', referring to the skills and knowledge necessary to compete for revenue. Access to cultural capital is restricted by the use of 'symbolic capital' such as sexism, which marginalizes women, and nationalism and racism, which stigmatizes migrant workers and blocks class solidarity between nationals and 'aliens' (1998, p. 17) (see Chapter 8, 'Racializing' and Chapter 9, 'Gendering').

Thus for neo-Weberians, the persistence of social, national and cultural barriers to equality is reflected in both the upward movement of individuals into skilled occupations and a downward mobility of individuals into a casualized workforce and a residual marginalized underclass. Far from proving that a Giddens-type post-scarcity society is unobtainable, it reflects the result of the competition of revenue classes over shares of the rising national income. Thus, if individuals act responsibly to minimize risk and maximize opportunity in the marketplace, those with relatively less market capacity can improve their positions and overcome most disadvantages due to class, status or party positions (Giddens, 1998, pp. 110–28).

FEELING: EMOTIONS • BELIEVING: RELIGION • EDUCATING • STRAYING: DEVIANCE • MEDIATING: TECHNOLOGY • INFORMING: MEDIA • RELATING: FAMILY • BELONGING: COMMUNITY • FINISHING

6 137

In the long run, the development of the rationalization of the market in post-capitalist society will eliminate social inequality. On the face of it, this neo-Weberian class theory appears capable of explaining classes in modern or post-modern capitalist society in all their apparent complexity (Lee and Turner, 1996). This accounts for the rise of theories that combine Marx and Weber to arrive at 'hybrid classes'. The next section puts these theories to the test.

Marx–Weber hybrid classes

As we have seen, neo-Marxists have accepted at face value the evidence that the proletariat has declined relative to a 'new middle class' and has ceased to be the universal class agent of revolution. This has caused them to retreat into alliances with neo-Weberians in the hope of explaining the persistence of inequalities. As a result they have made major concessions to neo-Weberian distributional analysis of revenue classes based on occupations, status and political parties. But there are dangers in these concessions. It isn't merely a matter of slotting Weberian concepts into a Marxist theory like diet supplements. There are at least two important objections to such hybrid theories of class formation.

Exploitation vs. 'life chances'
Firstly, for Marx, as we have seen, classes are defined by their relation to the means of production, not by market share of revenue. There is a funda-mental distinction between the two levels of analysis: that of production and that of exchange. For Marxists the preoccupation with 'occupation' reflects a one-sided, technical conception of production. Occupations within a division of labour result from the increasing technological ef-ficiency in harnessing the forces of production in producing use-values, that is, the 'usefulness' of a commodity in satisfying a need. On the whole this is a progressive development, which results from labour becoming more productive. But this ignores the fact that all of these occupations are made up of workers exploited by capital during production and cir-culation, so that the scientist, engineer, machine operator, truck driver

and retail worker are all, despite their occupational and skill differentials, members of the exploited proletariat as the 'global worker' (Marx, 1976, p. 945).

Indeed, Marx anticipated the modern sociology of distributional classes. His only specific reference to 'classes' in this sense was to clearly reject 'classes' categorized by 'revenue sources'. Otherwise 'the same would hold true for the infinite fragmentation of interests and positions into which the division of labour splits not only workers but also capitalists and landowners' (1981, p. 102). Revenue seeking by different occupations (and, as Marx says, employers and landlords) redistributes value that is already produced and expropriated during production. Whatever the share of wages, profits and rents arrived at by means of unequal exchange or redistribution in the market, this has no direct bearing on the rate of exploitation. Marx pointed out the highest paid skilled workers may be the most exploited. That is why he 'averaged' the whole range of skills of different occupations as the 'collective' or 'global' worker (1976, p. 945). Therefore, from his standpoint, any argument that capitalism has become 'post-capitalism' defined by revenue classes is evidence of the 'ideological' obscuring of production relations by exchange relations.

Fetishism of the intellectuals

Thus the second objection to hybrid theories of class is the role played by intellectuals privileging distributional class analysis. The 'fetishized' ideology that makes workers think that they are potentially equal to their employers accounts for their reluctance to overthrow capitalism. For Marx class-consciousness required the intervention of revolutionary intellectuals able to fuse Marxist science with working-class practice. But this is countered by bourgeois intellectuals who reproduce the sanitized, inverted ideology of capitalism as matter of 'fair shares' among revenue classes of workers, employers and landowners.

With the retreat of the neo-Marxists to the neo-Weberian notion of class as an association of individuals competing for revenue shares, the conception of classes rooted in relations of production is lost. If exploitation results from unequal exchange (the unfair distribution of revenue by political and cultural elites – justified on gender, ethnic and national grounds) then the way is opened for the complete abandonment of the concept of class struggle and the substitution of social movements for fair shares.

Social movements

The typical offspring of hybrid theories of class formation that substitute actual groups of individuals in the marketplace (revenue classes) for social relations of production are social movements (Crompton, 1998, pp. 18–19). If the problem of inequality is caused by unequal distribution, or exchange, then the solution must involve a political strategy to equalize distribution or exchange. Such disadvantaged (excluded, marginalized) groups (categorized by class, gender, ethnicity, sexual orientation and indigeneity) are mobilized ideologically and politically to challenge the cultural alibis for inequality.

The political and ideological agenda of social movements are provided by petty bourgeois leaderships that specialize as 'go-betweens' in revenue redistribution. The 'model' social movement is the women's movement. Liberal feminists took over the leadership in the 1960s and 1970s with an agenda to challenge sexist ideology blocking gender equality at the level of distribution. But in the decades that followed, the women's movement failed to equalize access to revenue for most women. A small minority of middle-class women in the OECD (Organization for Economic Co-operation and Development) countries gained access to top jobs and improved their revenue shares. But the vast majority of women in the world continued to be disadvantaged and oppressed in the casualized labour market and/or stigmatized as welfare dependents. Other social movements have made marginal gains in the recognition of rights (gay and lesbian, black, immigrant, indigenous rights etc.) and in equalizing revenue shares (upward mobility). But they all exhibit the same fate as the women's movement – there has been no major advance in the social position of minorities, and even those who have advanced are vulnerable to resistant reactionary backlashes or sexism, racism and patriotism.

What if the problem with social movements is their singularity – each has a 'single issue' focus – which makes them vulnerable to ideological backlashes? A recent attempt to rescue social movements as agents of global change is that of Hardt and Negri (2000, 2004). They define the Multitude as the 'common' element of all the singular social movements capable of challenging the Empire of capitalism. As Empire is the transnational organization of capital, the Multitude must oppose it across national borders. Thus migrants become a critical test of the 'constituent power' of the 'common' insofar as they can liberate themselves from patriotic backlashes. So far, the 'common' has failed the test as migrant workers typically face the hostility of other workers fearful of competition for jobs, housing, as well as alien cultural symbols like headscarves. The migrant movement's demand for jobs is perceived by the existing labour movement as a threat to jobs and welfare, i.e. competition for revenue.

Hardt and Negri's hybrid theory aims to defeat the Empire by 'constituting' the power of the Multitude to overcome 'common' exploitation through the redistribution of revenue. But with no common class interest grounded in the exploitation of wage labour, they fail to show that the singularities or 'differences' that capitalism creates can become non-exploitative without socializing capitalist property. To eliminate the common causes of inequality Hardt and Negri need to become 'anti-capitalist' in the universal sense of abolishing capitalist class relations. Let me try to demonstrate this by taking three examples where the singularities of race, gender, social movements, nationality and religion are widely held to be 'independent' of class relations as the main causes of social inequality. We begin by looking at those social movements that are usually substituted for class – race and gender.

Lands of white settlement: USA, Australia and New Zealand
European settler states allow us to test the explanatory power of race and gender independently of class relations. The claim is that the United States, Australia and New Zealand are relatively open, fluid societies comparatively free of class barriers. The evidence does not support this (Erikson and Goldthorpe, 1992, p. 324). Nevertheless, because race and gender inequality is highly visible, they tend to figure more prominently than class inequality in such societies (hooks, 2000, p. 7).

For example, in the USA the legacy of slavery and the disproportionate numbers of Black and Latino workers allowed employers to use race to divide the working class (Weinberg, 2003, p.168). New Zealand Maori and

Australian Aboriginals tend to be concentrated as blue-collar workers in the industrial reserve army of labour, causing racist divisions that cut across class identity (Poata-Smith, 2004; Armstrong, 1996, p. 67). Similarly, in much of the literature gender is seen as more or less independent of class (James and Saville Smith, 1994, p. 6; Stone, 1996, pp. 79–80; Fraser, 1997, p. 18). This has the effect of relegating class to just another 'single-issue social movement' alongside race and gender. Yet even at this level, multi-factoral studies in these countries show that once gender and race are controlled for, occupational class remains a major determinant of life chances and revenue-seeking capacity (Erikson and Goldthorpe, 1996, p. 378). Thus, if we look for the underlying cause of this 'market capacity', we see it is the polarization of wage labour and capital, the 'global' character of all waged or salaried occupations including the industrial reserve army of labour, that strikes us as the major determinant of class, race and gender revenue shares.

Therefore, explanations of the structural causes of social class have to be located at a deeper level than socio-economic status or occupation. For Marxists, the particularities of race and gender are *effects* of the history of class relations in these White-settler societies. This does not mean, however, that there are no *reciprocal* effects on class. But in none of these societies did race and gender divisions exist before colonization. Gender and racial oppression originated with the impact of the capitalist mode of production on pre-existing lineage, slave and domestic modes of production so that they became 'surrogates' of class relations (Miles, 1987, p. 44).

Perhaps it is no accident that both Martin Luther King and Malcolm X were each assassinated at the point when they broadened their struggle for racial justice and equality into a class struggle across the racial divide (Cohen, 2003, p. 383). The particularity of 'race' or 'people' becomes broken by the widening class divide. Thus the emerging African American and Maori bourgeois have taken most of the increased share of the equal opportunity stakes of the Great Society in the United States and the Treaty Settlement (payment of reparations for acts of the Crown during colonization and afterwards) process in New Zealand at the expense of the bulk of working-class African Americans and Maori who remain concentrated in the working class and industrial reserve army of labour (hooks, 2000, pp. 89–100; Rata, 2003). Such class differentiation of ethnic groups opens up opportunities for cross-ethnic working-class alliances grounded in proletarian class-consciousness (Munck, 2004, pp. 1–14).

In the case of gender, the subordination of the 'patriarchal' or 'domestic' mode of production to capitalism can explain the chronic social position of women as predominantly unpaid domestic workers, as casualized wage workers with dependent children or as stigmatized single mothers on welfare. That is, the social production of women becomes transformed into an unpaid subsidy to capital. That in turn accounts best for the disadvantage of women in the labour market, where discrimination and inequality remain strong. Thus the distributional accounts of gender such as the 'feminization of poverty' are the end result of an historic causal logic that begins with the expropriation of domestic labour as a form of unfree labour subordinated to capitalist production (Bedggood, 2002) (see Chapter 9, 'Gendering').

Thus in these highly developed European settler societies, where social class is seen to be almost dead, the class surrogates of race and gender remain powerful determinates of life chances. The strongest explanation of this reality reveals how the pre-capitalist social relations of tribal, tributary, slave or domestic production survive alongside capitalist social relations, like the dead hand of the past on the free labour of the living. Overcoming this legacy and building a united multi-ethnic and multi-gendered working class is the task facing labour organization today (Luthje and Scherrer, 2001; Bonefeld, 2002). 'Race' and 'gender' equality require the elimination of class relations of production.

The 'multitude' versus the proletariat: Argentina

If the 'social movement' approach is taken to its logical conclusion we arrive at Negri's concept of the Multitude as the 'movement of movements'. Negri revises classic Marxist class analysis and its key concept of the expropriation of labour value with a theory of the immaterial production of bodies 'exploited' (in every sense) by the concentrated wealth and power of global capital (Hardt and Negri, 2000, 2004).

In the case of Argentina, by expanding the definition of 'exploitation' by capital to the 'body' Negri suggests that the working class disappears when factory jobs disappear, leaving the unemployed and self-employed as the 'vanguard' of the Multitude. Yet if capitalism's industrial reserve army of labour functions as part of the labour market, holding down the value of labour power, then this must include all those without other means of subsistence competing to sell their labour power. Therefore, the demands of the unemployed *piquetero* movement in Argentina for jobs and living welfare payments are no different from the campaigns of the oppressed minorities in the reserve army of the developed capitalist economies to defend and improve welfare standards. They are not members of an 'underclass', who voluntarily opt out of the labour market, but members of the International Reserve Army of Labour forced out of the labour market. In Argentina this can be shown by the fact that rather than accept unemployment many thousands of workers have chosen to occupy and to continue producing in hundreds of bankrupt factories in Argentina (Bedggood, 2005).

Elsewhere in Latin America, as well as in Asia and Africa, the rapidly growing population of peasants and unemployed workers living in barrios and slums testifies to the fact that capitalism converts pre-capitalist modes and labour systems into a huge reserve of cheap labour. This is not an argument against, but for, the proletariat as the main class and agent of social change. The peasant movements, landless movements, indigenous peoples' movements are all surrogates for the global proletariat struggling for land, resources, jobs and welfare to provide their means of subsistence in the face of capital siphoning off their economic wealth into the global market.

Arising out of these surrogate working-class movements, it is not the Multitude, or the 'movement of movements' of the World Social Forum, where classes/movements combine in a national patriotic front, that poses the real threat to global capitalism. Rather it is the potential power of the organized proletarian and peasant masses that capital fears. This is why, in an attempt to avoid popular insurrections, the dominant capitalist powers are prepared to allow despotic regimes to be replaced by popular regimes that allow the masses a voice. Their hope is that regimes such as that of Chavez in Venezuela and Lula in Brazil will unite workers with employers behind powerful nationalist or religious ideologies that will pit workers in different countries against one another instead of joining forces across borders to pose a challenge to the rule of international capital (Petras, 2004a).

Iraq: nation and religion against class

Such is the power of ideologies of nation, tribe and religion that today arguably the most persuasive case against class is that nation and religion far outweigh any class-consciousness or mobilization of workers and peasants (see Chapter 8, 'Racializing' and Chapter 13, 'Believing'). Many theorists of post-capitalism or post-modernism assert that productive classes are now dead or dying as social agents of identity, solidarity and change, and that the strongest associations or communities are those of indigeneity, nation and religion. Appeals to nationalism can be progressive or reactionary. Such is the power of nation that the most progressive attempts to unite the 'peoples' in Latin America are inevitably extensions of bourgeois national revolutionary movements. The Bolivarian Movement of Chavez in Venezuela is the most influential today. Reactionary appeals to nationalism are most clearly identified with Islamic states.

Iraq is the obvious test case, where a progressive, secular nationalism combines with a fundamentalist Islamic nationalism to over-ride the class interests of peasants and workers. It is a country in which class seems the most unlikely source of social solidarity and change. Yet if we look at the modern history of Iraq, we find a history of class struggle. We find that the capitalist classes in the West have conspired with the local ruling class to maintain regimes hostile to the mobilization and political power of the working class. The American CIA and the Baath Party conspired in 1963 to overthrow the Qassem regime, which was supported by the Iraqi workers and aligned to the Soviet Union, and then set about systematically eliminating the Communist Party and all organized working-class political activity for 40 years. This policy continued until the USA and Saddam fell out over control of Iraqi oil (Ali, 2004).

Today, after a decade of wars, blockades and occupation, in which the secular labour movement was all but destroyed, it is not surprising to find the working class and the poor peasantry weak and divided by competing nationalist and Islamic factions. It seems that tribalism and religious sectarianism has replaced the Iraqi working-class formation. Yet, out of the most devastating conditions we find that same class re-emerging and reforming itself out of sheer economic necessity. In the oil industry, as well as others, unions have been revived; strikes for basic rights and conditions have been increasing – this in a country that is still occupied by Western powers whose companies are directly exploiting Iraqi resources using Iraqi workers. It seems that in the face of rampant tribal and sectarian rivalry, itself the product of Iraq's neo-colonial legacy, the same old social relations of production are reasserting themselves, and that beneath the forms of a national war of resistance to Western occupation, there is the reality of class war (Petras, 2004b).

Conclusion

Class is a contested category. I have argued that persistent and resistant inequalities of global capitalist society are caused by class relations of production, which underlie and account for the market distribution of revenue classes. Secondary factors such as occupations, status and social movements based on ethnicity, gender, nation or religion are the complicated effects of class relations and are evidence for, rather than against, the historic dynamic of class struggle. This perspective is, however, one of several argued within sociology and the social sciences in general. Each stands or falls on its truth claims as to the causes of persistent and resistant inequality in global capitalist society. As the amateur sociologist V. I. Lenin once said, the test of theory is practice because 'the truth is concrete'.

Suggestions for further reading

Meiksins Wood, E. (1986) *The Retreat from Class* (London: Verso).
Milner, A. (1999) *Class* (London: Sage).

Bibliography

Ali, T. (2004) *Bush in Babylon: The Re-colonisation of Iraq* (London: Verso).
Armstrong, M. (1996) 'Aborigines: Problems of Race and Class', in

R. Kuhn and T. O'Lincoln (eds), *Class and Class Conflict in Australia* (Melbourne: Longman).

Bedggood, D. (2002) 'Abort, Ignore, Retry: On the Domestic Mode of Production', in B. N. Ghosh and P. K. Chopra (eds), *Gender and Development: Theory, History, Policy and Case* (Leeds: Wisdom House).

Bedggood, D. (2005) 'Hardt and Negri's "Empire" and "Multitude" in the Argentinazo of December 2001', *Journal of Iberian and Latin American Studies* 11(1).

Bonefeld, W. (2002) 'European Integration: the Market, the Political and Class', *Capital and Class* 77, pp. 117–42.

Bourdieu, P. (1998) *Acts of Resistance: Against the New Myths of Our Time* (Cambridge: Polity Press).

Carchedi, G. (1987) *Class Analysis and Social Research* (Oxford: Basil Blackwell).

Clarke, S. (1982) *Marx, Marginalism and Modern Sociology* (London: Macmillan).

Cohen, L. (2003) *A Consumers' Republic: The Politics of Mass Consumption in Post-war America* (New York: Alfred A. Knopf).

Cook, C. D. (2000) 'Temps Demand New Deal', *The Nation* (27 March).

Crompton, R. (1998) *Class and Stratification: An Introduction to Current Debates*, 2nd edn (Cambridge: Polity Press).

Erikson R. and J. H. Goldthorpe (1992) *The Constant Flux: A Study of Class Mobility in Industrial Societies* (Oxford: Clarendon Press).

Fraser, N. (1997) *Justice Interruptus: Critical Reflections on the 'Postsocialist' Condition* (New York: Routledge).

Gerth, H. H. and C. W. Mills (1970) *From Max Weber: Essays in Sociology* (London: Routledge).

Giddens, A. (1998) *The Third Way: The Renewal of Social Democracy* (Cambridge: Polity Press).

Hardt, M. and T. Negri (2000) *Empire* (Boston, MA: Harvard University Press).

Hardt, M. and T. Negri (2004) *Multitude: War and Democracy in the Age of Empire* (Harmondsworth: Penguin).

hooks, b. (2000) *Where we Stand: Class Matters* (New York: Routledge).

James, B. and K. Saville-Smith (1994) *Gender, Culture, Power: Challenging New Zealand's Gendered Culture* (Auckland: Oxford University Press).

Lee, D. J. and B. S. Turner (1996) *Conflicts about Class: Debating Inequality in Late Industrialism* (London: Longman).

Luthje, B. and C. Scherrer (2001) 'Race, Multiculturalism, and Labour Organisations in the United States: Lessons for Europe', *Capital and Class* 73, pp. 141–71.

FEELING: EMOTIONS • BELIEVING: RELIGION • EDUCATING • STRAYING: DEVIANCE • MEDIATING: TECHNOLOGY • INFORMING: MEDIA • RELATING: FAMILY • BELONGING: COMMUNITY • FINISHING

6   147

Marx, K. (1976) *Capital*, vol. 1 (Harmondsworth: Penguin).

Marx, K. (1981) *Capital*, vol. 3 (Harmondsworth: Penguin).

Marx, K. (1983) 'Preface to a Contribution to the Critique of Political Economy', in K. Marx and F. Engels, *Selected Works*, vol. 1 (Moscow: Progress Publishers).

Meiksins Wood, E. (1986) *The Retreat from Class* (London: Verso).

Miles, R. (1987) *Capitalism and Unfree Labour* (London: Tavistock).

Munck, R. (2004) 'Introduction: Globalisation and Labour Transnationalism', in R. Munck (ed.), *Labour and Globalisation: Results and Prospects* (Liverpool: Liverpool University Press).

Pakulski, J. and M. Waters (1996) *The Death of Class* (London: Sage).

Petras, J. (2004a) 'Neoliberalism and Class Politics in Latin America', *Counterpunch* (13/14 November) (http://www.counterpunch.org/petras11132004.html) [accessed 9/1/06].

Petras, J. (2004b) 'The Crushing of Fallujah', *Counterpunch* (http://www.counterpunch.org/ petras11192004.html, 2004b) [accessed 19/11/05].

Poata-Smith, E. (2004) 'Ka Tika a Muri, Ka Tika a Mua: Maori Protest Politics and the Treaty of Waitangi Settlement Process', in P. Spoonley, C. Macpherson and D. Pearson (eds), *Tangata, Tangata: The Changing Ethnic Contours of Aotearoa/New Zealand* (New Zealand: Dunmore Press).

Rata, E. (2003) 'Leadership Ideology in Neotribal Capitalism', *Political Power and Social Theory* 16, pp. 46–64.

Stone, J. (1996) 'A Different Voice? Women and Work in Australia', in R. Kuhn and T. O'Lincoln (eds), *Class and Class Conflict in Australia* (Melbourne: Longman).

Weinberg, M. (2003) *A Short History of American Capitalism* (http://newhistory.org).

Wright, E. O. (1997) *Class Counts: Comparative Studies in Class Analysis* (Cambridge: Cambridge University Press).

Wright, E. O. (2006) 'If Class is the Question, What is the Answer?', (http://www.ssc.wisc.edu/~wright, 2005) [accessed 9/1/06].

governing: power

Catherine Lane West-Newman

KEY
POINTS

- Sociologists define the abstract concept of power in various ways and use it in their explanations of many social processes and practices. We see power not as a material object but manifested through its effects.

- Power is frequently understood in terms of quantity, which implies that a finite amount is available and that it is unequally distributed, like money or fame. Possession of power is closely linked to access to resources.

- Sociologists trace the operation of unequal power between racial majorities and minorities, colonial and metropolitan subjects, men and women, different sexual identities and practices, and rich and poor in class relations. In all of these areas, power is at work through socially structured and culturally defined patterns of stratification.

- Power can also be understood as the legitimate right to govern others. Here it is often linked with the democratic state in modern society and associated with a monopoly of sovereign power. Globalization processes challenge the monopoly of sovereign power by the nation state.

- Theories of legitimate democratic power either see it as made up of plural competing interest groups or held by one dominant power elite made up of political, corporate and military interests.

- Foucault's account of capillary power rejects other conventions of theorizing power. He refuses to see power in terms of quantity or as a force operating from above on those below. Power is everywhere, produced in and through all forms of social relations.

- International shadow powers (especially globally linked organized crime) now subvert the power of the nation state and operate on a scale capable of shaping world economies and policies. They are largely invisible to popular and sociological examination and raise questions about the line between legitimate and illegitimate power.

149

Introduction

An online Google search for 'power' will give you more than 310 million potential sources; less dauntingly, an Oxford Dictionary (which brings us also the verb 'to google') still has 18 alternative definitions. Within the workings of the sociological imagination (Mills, 1959), the idea of power is valued for its capacity to explain everything from the nature of democracy to the quality of doctor–patient interaction in a medical consultation. For, as Avery Gordon explains,

> [p]ower can be invisible, it can be fantastic, it can be dull and routine. It can be obvious, it can reach you by the baton of the police, it can speak the language of your thoughts and desires. It can feel like remote control, it can exhilarate like liberation, it can travel through time, and it can drown you in the present. It is dense and superficial, it can cause bodily injury, and it can harm you without seeming ever to touch you. It is systematic and it is particularistic and it is often both at the same time. (1997, p. 3)

So it is hardly surprising that sociologists, too, define power in various ways and use the concept in their explanations of many social processes and practices. What makes all this variation possible is the fact that power is an abstract notion; like electricity (which is also, of course, called electric *power*), we see power not as a material object, but manifested through its effects.

Three dictionary (*New Zealand Oxford Dictionary*, 2004) definitions of power are directly relevant to sociological thought: 'the ability to do or act'; 'political or social ascendancy or control'; and 'authorization, delegated authority'. Each of these aspects of power has a part in the sociological theories of power discussed here. In turn, each theoretical approach offers a way of understanding how power is created, perpetuated and works in the social world, is associated with certain sociologists, and has at some time been strongly influential in sociological thought. This evidence that sociological ideas go in and out of fashion actually raises another important matter you might want to remember when reading about the ideas in social theory: that the particular scholars, books and ideas which dominate in any disciplinary area of thought are not timeless and fixed. They are socially constructed in specific times and places and, like culture itself, reveal a continual process of movement and change. One generation decides what is most important to the material conditions of the world they live in and, on the basis of these, produces ideas and explanations of how society works. Those ideas may then be taken up, even adopted, by a next generation of social theorists, or they may, alternatively, be ignored and disappear almost without trace for many years, only to be rediscovered by a still later generation of thinkers (Connell, 1997) (see Chapter 2, 'Modernizing').

Power here will be explored through three theoretical approaches devised in different times and places; each represents an attempt to understand the social conditions under which their producers lived and wrote. The first treats power as a quantifiable commodity; the second is concerned with legitimate and illegitimate claims of power; and the third (based in the work of Michel Foucault) overturns the assumption that power inevitably works in vertical relationships – directed from above to below. They are all partial and were, for the most part, developed in response to conditions in the West (Europe and the United States). Some overlap with others, and none can be said to explain all aspects of power in societies. But, within these limitations, they still offer a fascinating range of possibilities for understanding both the social world and the place of each of us as individuals whose lives are unavoidably lived out within its constraints and opportunities.

Quantifiable power – how much?

Most of our everyday taken-for-granted assumptions about the nature of power treat it as something that can be measured through ideas of quantity, like money or fame. How much power do I have? How much do other people and institutions have over me, thereby diminishing mine? In this way of seeing, the quantity of power any one of us has is always determined by how much is held by someone or something else. If they have more then I will necessarily have less. The ultimate assumption here is that there is a limited and finite amount of power available within a society (or within the world) and that it will always tend to be unequally distributed. Just as it is with wealth, some individuals, political parties,

FEELING: EMOTIONS • BELIEVING: RELIGION • EDUCATING • STRAYING: DEVIANCE •
MEDIATING: TECHNOLOGY • INFORMING: MEDIA • RELATING: FAMILY • BELONGING: COMMUNITY • FINISHING

7   151

even nations will always have more than others (see Chapter 3, 'Working'; Chapter 5, 'Trading'; Chapter 6, 'Stratifying: Class'). This way of seeing power is often described as a zero-sum game: there are only winners and losers. If you win then I must have lost, and vice versa. In democracies, political parties translate this point of view into the way governments are elected to give dominant power to the winning party (or parties in states where there is an electoral system like Mixed Member Proportional voting in Germany and New Zealand, which tends to prevent single-party dominance in government). This perspective is summed up in a quotation from Max Weber, a German scholar who wrote in the late nineteenth and early twentieth centuries, and whose ideas will also appear in the next section of this chapter. He describes power as 'the chance of a man or a number of men to realise their own will even against the resistance of others' (Weber, 1978, p. 926). This way of seeing power also, of course, suggests by implication that the application of power is a form of coercion. If you and I are determined to achieve different outcomes then only one of us will succeed. So power in these terms means the ability to compel people to do (or refrain from doing) things against their own will.

Since sociology in the 1970s began to rediscover the social significance of racial, cultural, gender, and sexual difference much research has traced the operation of unequal power between racial majorities and minorities, colonial and metropolitan subjects, men and women, and different sexual identities and practices (see Chapter 6, 'Stratifying: Class'; Chapter 8, 'Racializing'; Chapter 9, 'Gendering'; Chapter 10, 'Sexualizing'). In particular, it is recognized that in all of these areas, as well as in class relations, power is at work through socially structured and culturally shaped patterns of stratification. You may have noticed in that quotation in the first paragraph that Weber wrote of a 'man or number of men'. It is true that 'man' was the term then in general use to describe humans (male and female) but in this particular case Weber was also describing the truth of his world. Men had power but women did not; even to use the two words 'women' and 'power' in the same sentence would have seemed strange to him. There are many places in the world where this would still be so, but it is also clear that in many Western nations the gendered distribution of power is less immediately obvious today. Two aspects of social life where power inequalities are still strongly

152 7

DOING RESEARCH • MODERNIZING • WORKING • CONSUMING • TRADING • STRATIFYING: CLASS •
GOVERNING: POWER • RACIALIZING • GENDERING • SEXUALIZING • BEING: IDENTITY •

marked throughout the world are national legal systems and the global distribution of poverty.

The claim to treat everyone equally lies at the heart of law's claim that it has a legitimate right to demand our obedience. In the liberal democracies of the Western world it is known as the 'rule of law' and believed to guarantee justice for all. Critical socio-legal scholars have, however, demonstrated just how unequally legal systems may, in certain areas, treat women, homosexuals, racial and ethnic minorities, people with disabilities, and poor people. There are, of course, very obvious instances of unequal power when whole categories of people are declared legally ineligible to vote, be elected to public office, or enter the medical, legal and other professions. Women, for example, experienced all of these in nineteenth- and early twentieth-century Britain, the United States, Canada, Australia and New Zealand (Sachs and Wilson, 1978). Because, until 1967 in Britain and 1986 in New Zealand, homosexuality was a crime punishable by imprisonment, a whole section of the population in those countries were compelled to conceal their sexual desires, and what many saw as a central part of their identity (see Chapter 10, 'Sexualizing'). The state, then, wielded a huge power over their personal lives that it did not claim over citizens with heterosexual desires and relationships. And the very illegality of their sexual preferences meant that they could only have the power to work politically for changes to the law if they hid under a pretence of heterosexual preference. Or, in other words, the state's power to realize its will over theirs was very strong indeed. And again, under the Jim Crow laws of the southern United States after slavery was abolished, African Americans were systematically stripped of any political and social power that emancipation might have created (Woodward, 1974).

In *Voices of the Poor: Can Anyone Hear Us?*, a book that documents World Bank studies of poverty in 50 countries conducted in the 1990s, poor people reported in their own words common experiences of poverty around the world.

> From Georgia to Brazil, from Nigeria to the Philippines, similar underlying themes emerged: hunger, deprivation, powerlessness, violation of dignity, social isolation, resilience, resourcefulness, solidarity, state corruption, rudeness of service providers, and gender inequity. (Narayan, 2000, p. 3)

FEELING: EMOTIONS • BELIEVING: RELIGION • EDUCATING • STRAYING: DEVIANCE •
MEDIATING: TECHNOLOGY • INFORMING: MEDIA • RELATING: FAMILY • BELONGING: COMMUNITY • FINISHING

7   153

Poor people overwhelmingly report the multidimensional effects of being poor and powerless: hunger, psychological dimensions of dependency, shame and humiliation, and the material deprivations of living without access to roads, transportation, clean water, education and health care. They speak of crumbling family and household structures when, under harsh economic conditions, men cannot earn adequate incomes to support families and women become the main breadwinners. The resulting redistribution of power within households frequently produces 'alcoholism and domestic violence on the part of men' (Narayan, 2000, p. 6). Poverty creates a powerlessness that renders people unable to help themselves, compelled to rely upon largely ineffective state aid and the limited support that NGOs (non-governmental organizations) can provide. The depth and scale of such poverty is, except when television news brings it briefly into our consciousness, invisible and unimaginable to those who enjoy the comforts taken for granted in Western and Westernized capitalist societies.

This brings us to the very important point that power, seen as a resource, has a central place in accounts of how politics, particularly (but not exclusively) in democratic political systems, actually works. Much of the thinking about the distribution of political power has taken place within the debates over the legitimacy of power that will be discussed in the next section.

Legitimate power – who governs?

The power of leadership: Max Weber
When power is defined as 'created through authorization or delegated authority', this captures the idea of something that individuals and groups have and use because they have a generally recognized and accepted right to do so. This conceptualization is generally associated with the sociology of Max Weber, who is now seen as a key thinker on this subject, although this was not so during his own lifetime. His recognition as a central member of a group of grand synthesizing social thinkers who, in the late nineteenth and early twentieth centuries, applied an evolutionary framework to understanding the nature of social institutions and ideas, is

more recent. It began in the English-speaking world only when, during the 1940s, American sociologists (and German sociologists who had sought refuge from Nazi Germany within the United States) translated his ideas and applied their versions of them to contemporary issues in their own society. Because his particular interest in power came out of a desire to understand the nature of political leadership, Weber thought of power as a capacity to be exercised over others. He defined it as 'the probability that one actor within a social relationship will be in a position to carry out his own will despite resistance, regardless of the basis on which this probability rests' (Weber, 1978, p. 53).

Weber sometimes wrote about 'power' under this name but, because he thought the way power was generally understood was not clear enough for good social theory, he more often preferred to use a different word – 'domination'. So, using the term domination, he defined a more sociologically specific form of power: 'the probability that a command with a given specific content will be obeyed by a given group of persons' (Weber, 1978, p. 53). His examples of dominance describe three kinds of legitimate power (which is also leadership): charismatic, traditional and rational-legal (see Table 8). Charismatic leaders hold their position by virtue of some special quality – sacredness, revelation or heroism, for example – that is theirs alone and they are obeyed because their followers believe this leadership can transform their own lives.

> The term 'charisma' will be applied to a certain quality of an individual personality by virtue of which he is set apart from ordinary men and treated as endowed with supernatural, superhuman or at least specifically exceptional powers and qualities. These are such as are not accessible to the ordinary person, but are regarded as of divine origin or as exemplary, and on the basis of them the individual is treated as a leader. (Weber, 1922/1947, pp. 358–9)

Lists of famous charismatic leaders have included Jesus Christ, Mahatma Gandhi, Martin Luther King, Robin Hood, Napoleon Bonaparte, Adolf Hitler and Saddam Hussein. Frank Parkin points out that to hold authority a charismatic leader must be able to 'convince his followers and disciples of his extraordinary powers' by performing 'miracles and heroic deeds' (1982, p. 84). Ian Craib suggests that we might see charisma 'not as a quality of the leader but as a quality projected on to a leader by virtue of situation, opportunity, and events' (1997, p. 134). For example, he says, British Prime Minister Margaret Thatcher seemed to have charisma for a time, especially in the period after victory in the short war against Argentina over possession of the Malvina Islands, but it rapidly vanished when she lost power in 1990.

Traditional leaders are seen as legitimate through 'the 'loyalty and fidelity' felt by subjects toward their master' (Parkin, 1982, p. 81) and their authority rests in their occupation of the designated position: hereditary absolute monarchy and chiefship are both traditional forms of dominance. They claim obedience through the tradition they represent. The exemplary form of traditional domination is often described as the patriarchal power held by a father over his household, where his wife and children are mentally and physically dependent and trained to obedience. This form of family is, of course, increasingly rare in Western societies (see Chapter 18, 'Relating: Families').

In the third form of leadership, present in most contemporary Western societies, a legitimate ruler/leader's claim is grounded in law. The ruler's dominance is based on the fact that they were appointed under impersonal legal rules that specify the proper conditions and processes for appointment of legitimate rulers/leaders. Democratic election is a specific form of such rules and processes and elected presidents and prime ministers claim obedience from their people on the basis of lawful appointment as leader. In effect, 'the actual ruler is necessarily and unavoidably the bureaucracy' (Weber, 1968, p. 1393).

Table 8 **Weber's typology of claims to legitimate power (adapted from Parkin, 1982, p. 77)**

Type of domination	Grounds for claiming obedience
Traditional	Obey me because this is what our people have always done.
Charismatic	Obey me because I can transform your life.
Legal-rational	Obey me because I am your lawfully appointed superior.

J. M. Barbalet has described Weber's overall treatment of power (and of resistance, which is closely connected to power) as 'sketchy, contradictory and poorly grounded in general sociological principles' (1985, p. 535). Nevertheless his ideas about the nature of legitimate rule still influence, if not shape, present-day analyses of political and legal power. Under rational-legal forms of domination the notion of the right to exercise power is intimately connected with the conditions under which a nation state may be governed as a democracy; that is, by the people and for the people. In particular, it is associated with the consent that citizens give when they accept their government's right to control many aspects of their lives, particularly payment of taxes and obedience to laws.

Pluralist power or elite power?

These two theories of power were developed in the United States in the mid-twentieth century and were, quite obviously, the product of local social conditions. Their interest for sociology today lies in the way that these two points of view still shape American political debate and influence the nature and form of that county's intervention in present-day global politics. The central question is whether, within a democratic system of government, power is diffused throughout the society through multiple interest groups who compete for influence, or whether it is monopolized by a dominant elite that shuts out all other citizens from the decision-making process. The former, pluralist theory has been the most widely accepted account of the American system of power and is often associated with the work of Robert Dahl. C. Wright Mills's elite theory was developed at least partly as a challenge to that claim.

In an influential book *Who Governs?* (1961), Dahl described the power structure in the city of New Haven in Connecticut to show how he thought pluralist politics worked. In his account power is represented as a set of forces, all active in political decision making, which compete in power relationships through the mechanisms of consensus and compromise. In this pattern, consumer groups, business, workers, taxpayers and other organized groups all exercise some power but no single interest establishes dominance over the others. This model was thought to be an effective explanation of both local (urban) and national power relationships in politics.

Pluralist theory offers an optimistic vision of power in politics. The role of class is minimized and the significance of diversity and differentiation in modern industrial societies emphasized. Trade unions, consumer groups, occupational groups, ethnic and religious groups are all thought to share a common interest in maintaining a democratic framework within which they can compete (on an equal footing) for satisfaction of their sectional interests. But movements that signal real social divisions – black power, student or anti-war radicals, striking workers – are characterized as a damaging threat to the power consensus essential to democratic pluralism. The role of the state in this competition of organized interest groups is to maintain a balance of competition, favouring no particular group and ensuring policy is formed not through the operation of monopoly power but within a complex and constantly shifting power structure. This might be likened to the ideal school, overseen by a benevolent headmaster, where the playing fields are all level, the teachers treat all students with scrupulous fairness, there is no bullying, no hierarchy of merit, and, most important of all, economic resources are unlimited and therefore irrelevant.

The question of consent also underlies questions about the way power (in the quantifiable sense discussed in the previous section) appears now in nations such as the United States to be concentrated in the hands of a (relatively) small number of very rich people. It was already preoccupying C. Wright Mills in the 1940s and 1950s when (in a still influential book and articles), he identified the existence of a power elite created through the convergence of political, military and economic power in the United States and argued that this had important negative implications for the democratic rights of ordinary Americans. Mills, whose conception of the sociological imagination features in our opening chapter, demonstrates in his work on power just how that imagination may create a convincing explanation of society in a particular moment that may also shed light on later events (see the Introduction, 'On Being Sociological').

In opposition to what he saw as fictions of democratic pluralism, Mills argued that power in the United States was concentrated in the hands of a single power elite. He did not deny that forms of pluralist power did exist in some contexts, but he thought that Dahl's 'moving balance of many competing interests' was true only of 'the middle levels of power'. At the highest levels the power elite decided the shape of the nation's economy, and its involvement in war or peace. Only at the middle level were there the 'competing interests which make up the clang and clash of American politics' and these were only 'concerned with their slice of the existing pie' (Mills, 1958, pp. 35–6).

> The power to make decisions of national and international consequence is now so clearly seated in political, military, and economic institutions that other areas of society seem off to the side and, on occasion, readily subordinated to these. The scattered institutions of religion, education and family are increasingly shaped by the big three, in which history-making decisions now regularly occur. Behind this fact there is all the push and drive of a fabulous technology; for these three institutional orders have incorporated this technology and now guide it, even as it shapes and paces their development. (1958, p. 32)

It has generally been true in history, he says, that explicit decisions by individuals have had less social effect than 'the innumerable actions of innumerable men' whose actions gradually modify the social structure of their world, as, for example, 'innumerable entrepreneurs and innumerable consumers by ten-thousand decisions per minute may shape and re-shape the free-market economy'. But he detected in the middle of the twentieth century a quite different power dynamic at work in the United States and Soviet Union, where

> a few men may be so placed within the structure that by their decisions they modify the milieux of many other men, and in fact nowadays the structural conditions under which most men live. Such elites of power also make history under circumstances not chosen altogether by themselves, yet compared with other men, and compared with other periods of world history, these circumstances do indeed seem less limiting. (1958, p. 30)

Mills's work on power, as Todd Gitlin points out, can be seen as specific to its time – the Cold War era – when, in controlling national strategies for nuclear war, the elite also 'controlled weapons of mass destruction and were in a position not only to contemplate their use but to launch them' (Gitlin, nd, p. 4). This concept of power, central to Mills's social thought, is directly linked with the state: where Marxist explanations would rely on the labour process, and Weberian accounts on the economic function of the market, Mills assumes that elites are institutionally constituted (Aronowitz, 2003, p. 12). The corporate, political and military, although institutionally and spatially independent, are combined in an elite composed of individuals at the top levels of each of these three orders. Their relative strength is historically variable; during and after wars

FEELING: EMOTIONS • BELIEVING: RELIGION • EDUCATING • STRAYING: DEVIANCE •
MEDIATING: TECHNOLOGY • INFORMING: MEDIA • RELATING: FAMILY • BELONGING: COMMUNITY • FINISHING

7   159

the military is likely to attain particular dominance. During the 1950s superpower confrontation between the United States and the Soviet Union, the military and corporate defence industry held a combined position of strength.

In Mills's *The Power Elite* (1956), interlocking networks of association embracing all these social spheres are empirically traced and described. And, when he pointed out the ways in which celebrities, the products of mass society and its entertainment industry, were recruited to attract popular support to political parties and interests, Mills also identified another aspect of the elite power constellation that is familiar to us today. He depicted how, as individuals move between all of these spheres, the lines are further blurred:

> corporate executives regularly mingle with celebrities in Hollywood and New York at exclusive clubs and parties; and 'warlords' – high military officers, corporate officials, their scientists and technologists engaged in perfecting more lethal weapons of mass destruction, the politicians responsible for executive and congressional approval of military budgets – congregate in many of the same social and cultural spaces as well as in the business suites of warfare. (Aronowitz, 2003, p. 13)

Dying of a heart attack when he was 46, Mills did not live to see Ronald Reagan in the White House or Arnold Schwarzenegger as Governor of California, but he did describe the social processes through which, decades later, they came to be in those places.

Legitimacy and globalized power

Both the elite and the pluralist accounts of legitimate power assume that it will inevitably be held by the sovereign state alone and by nothing else. But processes of globalization, which, it is widely recognized, characterize the late twentieth and early twenty-first centuries, raise doubts about the capacity of this formulation to encompass all there is to be said about power and legitimacy. Although the precise meaning and implications of the term are widely contested, there is wide sociological and popular understanding that information and capital now flow so freely and widely within an international sphere that there has been a significant change in the degree of autonomy and power enjoyed by individual nation states.

Manual Castells describes new social phenomena – network society and the network state. These are born out of the conflicting trends of globalization and assertions of identity through which

> [t]he instrumental capacity of the nation-state is decisively undermined by the globalization of core economic activities, ... of media and electronic communication, ... of crime, ... of social protest, and ... of insurgency in the form of transborder terrorism. (Castells, 2004, p. 304)

Under these conditions, 'global flows of capital, goods, services, technology, communication, and information' undermine state control while state-defined national identity and tradition are 'challenged' by autonomously defined plural identities based in, for example, ethnicity, indigeneity and religion (see Chapter 8, 'Racializing' and Chapter 13, 'Believing: Religion'). State attempts to recuperate, through membership of supranational institutions (for example the World Trade Organization, or the European Community), their lost control over the definition of historical tradition and national identity only further undermine national sovereignty.

Castells (2004, p. 321) argues that the power of the nation state is also subverted through globally linked organized crime, which generates a criminal economy of a 'scale and dynamism' that conditions economic and political international relations and deeply penetrates to eventually destabilize national states. Recent research describes what Carolyn Nordstrom (2000, p. 36) has called 'international shadow powers' that now operate on a scale 'capable of shaping world economies and policies' and yet remain largely invisible to popular knowledge and sociological analysis. By this she means the shadow networks of goods and services that operate outside formal state and legal channels in war zones and international non-state trade in legal and illegal commodities. These relationships of power and exchange are non-formal but not insubstantial. Such transnational networks are worth more than a trillion dollars annually and employ millions of people. These shadow networks

> fashion economic possibilities, they broker political power and, importantly, they constitute cultures, for these networks of power and exchange are governed by rules of exchange, codes of conduct, hierarchies of deference and power – in short, they are governed by social principles, not merely the jungle law of tooth and claw. (Nordstrom, 2000, p. 37)

The scale of this can be glimpsed through statistics: up to 20 per cent of the world's financial deposits are in unregulated banks and offshore locations (Lopez and Cortwright, 1998, cited in Nordstrom, 2000); illicit drugs earnings (UNRISD, 1995) and weapons sales (Castells, 1998) are each estimated at US$500 billion a year. In 1994 the United Nations Conference on the Global Criminal Economy estimated that about US$750 billion each year from illegal sources is laundered in the global financial system (Castells, 2004, p. 321).

As such a substantial proportion of the world's economy, these networks are also a significant part of its power grids. In pursuit of an extended notion of power that includes 'informal', non-state sources and locations of power and recognizes organized international crime as an economically significant part of global power, Nordstrom describes the situation in Angola. After a war of independence against Portugal, Angola now has civil war between Unita rebels and the MPLA (Movimento Popular da Libertação de Angola) government. In this society, where one side controls the main centres of population, roads, airports and oil production and the other the rural, food-producing areas, legal and illegal trade merge in the movement of precious gems, armaments, food and general supplies – all traded through complex informal networks of people as well as international smugglers. Covert financial channels are used by organized criminal groups, terrorist and revolutionary groups, and ordinary people who may be trading quite legally. Illicit transactions and development are closely linked with political power as people gain the wealth from the former to move into legal enterprises, gather economic power and social status, and be elected to political positions. They may also hold appointments with the United Nations or in international non-governmental organizations. Nordstrom points out that if the diamonds/armaments trade in all the gem-producing areas of the world is considered, then

> The number of people involved can rival populations of states. The revenues generated can far surpass the GNP of smaller nations. The power the leaders in these extra-state empires wield can rival that of state leaders. These vast networks shape the course of international affairs to as great a degree as the formal state apparatuses of some countries. When we expand out from

> gems and armaments to add in all extra-state industries, we are discussing a series of power grids that shape the fundamental economic–political dynamics of the world today. (Nordstrom, 2000, p. 44)

The lines between legitimate and illegitimate power, legal and illegal transactions, public and private power are now, it seems, irretrievably blurred. This raises interesting questions about the relationship between these shadow global networks that operate on the boundaries of criminality and the ability of nation states to maintain legitimacy and sovereign status. There is more to learn about how shadow networks operate their behavioural rules and codes of conduct; how and when authority (dominance) is exercised within them; and the relationships between shadows and states. Castells concludes that

> while nation states continue to exist, and they will continue to do so in the foreseeable future, they are, and will increasingly be, *nodes of a broader network of power*. They will often be confronted by other flows of power in the network, which directly contradict the exercise of their authority, as happens nowadays to central banks whenever they have the illusion of countering global markets' runs against a given currency. Or, for that matter, when nation states, alone or together, decide to eradicate drug production, traffic, or consumption, a battle repeatedly lost over the past two decades everywhere – except in Singapore. (2004, p. 257)

Control of the nation state is now just one competing means to assert power. In seeking to understand how the diminishing effect of state sovereign power may be understood, it is useful to look to a third, quite different, version of power.

Power everywhere – capillary power

So far, the explanations of power we have considered suggest that it is created and exercised within specific institutions, circumstances, groups and individuals, and is imposed by those in high positions on to those below them. This next form, though, is very different. It comes from a

French scholar whose work is associated with several different disciplines – philosophy, history and sociology. The following quotation from Foucault's book *Discipline and Punish*, when carefully read, gives a clear description (or at least as clear as Foucault's descriptions ever are) of what he calls a 'micro-physics of power', which

> presupposes that the power exercised on the body is conceived not as a property, but as a strategy, that its effects of domination attributed not to 'appropriation', but to dispositions, manoeuvres, tactics, techniques, functionings; that one should decipher in it a network of relations, constantly in tension, in activity, rather than a privilege that one might possess; that one should take as its model a perpetual battle rather than a contract regulating a transaction or the conquest of a territory ... Furthermore, this power is not exercised simply as an obligation or a prohibition on those who 'do not have it'; it invests them, is transmitted by them and through them, just as they themselves, in their struggle against it resist the grip it has on them ... Lastly, they are not univocal; they define innumerable points of confrontation, focuses of instability, each of which has its own risks of conflict, or struggles, and of an at least temporary inversion of the power relations. (Foucault, 1977, pp. 26–7)

Because power, then, is productive we must give up describing it in negative forms as 'excluding', 'repressing', 'censoring', 'masking', 'concealing', and recognize instead that 'it produces reality; it produces domains of objects and rituals of truth. The individual and the knowledge that may be gained of him belong to this production' (Foucault, 1977, p. 194).

Foucault's account rests on an intricate and inseparable connection between power and knowledge within the social order that he developed and explicated throughout much of his work. He is concerned with 'the role of knowledge in the reproduction of relations of dominance', especially in the political struggles around 'identities' (Haugaard, 2003, p. 88). This leads him to conceive of power neither as a quantifiable resource nor existing through the legitimacy of its claims, but as a network of relations. In this formulation power connects with knowledge, including self-knowledge, to form part of the historical production of truth. His purpose is:

> to expose the political and strategic nature of those ensembles of knowledge previously thought to be either relatively independent of power (the 'human science'); or (as in the case of criminology or sexuality) linked only in a vague or inadequate way to political institutions. (McHoul and Grace, 1993, p. 60)

These micro-explanations of power connect the knowledge claims of, for example, the medical profession, with associated power claims; similarly, authoritative knowledge as practised in institutions such as asylums and hospitals has direct power. Pronounced sick, or mad, by the experts, the individual is then under the direct control of those who so define her.

Foucault's account of power is intentionally shaped to reject the conventions of theorizing power described earlier in this chapter. In refusing to see power in terms of quantity and as a force operating from above on those below, exercised by the 'powerful' over the 'powerless', Foucault, as he so often does, deliberately seeks to undermine and overturn conventional sociological assumptions. As a thinker whose work refuses positioning in a single discipline as he traverses the territories of philosophy, history and sociology, he uses the freedoms of transdisciplinary positioning to give us new ways of thinking about old questions. And for this reason his insights have been adopted and adapted for many sociological purposes. In fact the way Foucault goes about explaining social phenomena effectively demonstrates the kind of thinking C. Wright Mills had in mind when he described the starting point for this book – the sociological imagination.

This radically new explanation of power serves several purposes for Foucault. First, it allows him to move away from what he sees as the Marxist tradition's tendency to see all power as repression and thus inevitably bad. Second, he rejects the idea that power is a possession that some have and others do not. Third, by claiming that power is present in all forms of social relations he can also argue that where there is power there must also be resistances to that power. These resistances 'are formed right at the point where relations of power are exercised' (Foucault, 1980, p. 142) and though they will necessarily be marginalized and silenced by the power effect, can be actively listened for. Most importantly, it opens the way to replace the earlier focus on power as legitimate domination. Together with the refusal to couple power and repression, this leads Foucault to reject concepts of sovereign power wielded through right as the principal

FEELING: EMOTIONS • BELIEVING: RELIGION • EDUCATING • STRAYING: DEVIANCE •
MEDIATING: TECHNOLOGY • INFORMING: MEDIA • RELATING: FAMILY • BELONGING: COMMUNITY • FINISHING

7   165

twentieth-century mechanism of dominance, together with notions of legitimate and illegitimate power. Instead, the distinguishing feature of the twentieth century is the ascendancy of what he calls 'disciplinary power', which, in the shape of small and dispersed 'capillary power', is networked throughout all levels of society.

Disciplinary powers are made up of a range of techniques of power that do not rely on coercion or force; they can be seen from the eighteenth century onward. New ways of controlling and training people, which Foucault describes as 'technologies of the body', produced 'docile' human bodies – as, for example, in the training of soldiers through endless minutely choreographed marching drills into regimented bodily obedience. Also associated with disciplinary power are the practices of observation, measuring and recording that comprise the techniques of surveillance. Hierarchical observation is conducted through the collection of census data, issuing of birth, marriage and death certificates, and much more recently the employment practice of requiring annual performance reports and reviews for every worker. Hunt and Wickham (1994) point out that modern forms of imprisonment whose purpose, using systems of permanent observation, is to produce bodies now disciplined into docility and usefulness might well be thought 'more cruel than the old physical cruelties of torture' because, even more invasively, 'disciplines impinge on the soul, will or personality of the prisoner' (1994, p. 13). Normalizing judgements define the attributes of properly conducted citizens – good soldiers, feminine women, well-behaved children, co-operative patients. Disciplinary power exists to train individuals through small, repeated, everyday physical mechanisms and the discipline operates not so much through punishment as by a careful mix of carrots and sticks (rewards and micro-penalties) in the form of prizes and privileges or humiliations and fines.

In the late twentieth century considerable effort was devoted to tracing the effects of these disciplinary powers at work. Feminist scholars explored the many ways in which women practised self-surveillance as they monitored their docile female bodies to achieve appropriate forms of feminine beauty. Eating disorders, plastic surgery and body sculpting through exercise were all examined as writers traced the effect of micro-technologies of power over women's lives (Bordo, 1990; Tate, 1999).

166 7

DOING RESEARCH • MODERNIZING • WORKING • CONSUMING • TRADING • STRATIFYING: CLASS •
GOVERNING: POWER • RACIALIZING • GENDERING • SEXUALIZING • BEING: IDENTITY •

Others studied their effects in medicine, criminology, psychology and psychiatry. At the same time, many looked for instances of the resistance that Foucault believed to be always associated with power. In the process they discovered that although it was relatively straightforward to identify the presence of power, it was altogether less simple to decide what actually constituted domination or subordination. When the pop singer Madonna in the 1980s made herself the ultimate male fantasy of a female sex object, she claimed to be subverting male dominance. Others, though, thought that she had simply succumbed to a comforting self-delusion while actually reinforcing stereotypes of female oppression (Kellner, 1995).

Power is abstract, everywhere and endlessly interesting. Through the lens of the sociological imagination its myriad traces and effects can be found, explored and even (if we believe Foucault) perhaps resisted.

Suggestions for further reading

Castells, M. (2003) *The Power of Identity* (Malden, MA: Blackwell).
Egan, D. and L. Chorbajian (eds) (2005) *Power: A Critical Reader* (Upper Saddle River, NJ: Pearson Prentice Hall).
Foucault, M. (1980) *Power/Knowledge: Selected Interviews and Other Writings, 1972–1977*, ed. Colin Gordon (New York: Pantheon Books).
Hindess, B. (1995) *Discourses of Power: From Hobbes to Foucault* (Oxford: Blackwell).
Mills, C. W. (1956) *The Power Elite* (New York: Oxford University Press).

Bibliography

Aronowitz, Stanley (2003) 'A Mills Revival?' *Logos* 2(3) (Summer 2003) http://www.logosjournal.com/aronowitz.htm [accessed 30/1/2005].
Barbalet, J. M. (1985) 'Power and Resistance', *The British Journal of Sociology* 36, pp. 531–48.
Bordo, S. (1990) 'Reading the Slender Body', in M. Jacobus, E. Fox Keller and S. Shuttleworth (eds), *Body/Politics: Women and the Discourses of Science* (New York: Routledge).

FEELING: EMOTIONS • BELIEVING: RELIGION • EDUCATING • STRAYING: DEVIANCE • MEDIATING: TECHNOLOGY • INFORMING: MEDIA • RELATING: FAMILY • BELONGING: COMMUNITY • FINISHING

7   167

Castells, M. (1998) *End of Millennium* (Malden, MA: Blackwell Publishers).

Castells, M. (2004) *The Power of Identity*, 2nd edn (Malden, MA: Blackwell Publishing).

Connell, R. W. (1997) 'Why is Classical Theory Classical?', *American Journal of Sociology* 102, pp. 1511–57.

Craib, I. (1997) *Classical Social Theory* (New York: Oxford University Press).

Dahl, R. (1961) *Who Governs? Democracy and Power in an American City* (New Haven, CT: Yale University Press).

Foucault, M. (1977) *Discipline and Punish: The Birth of the Prison*, trans. A. Sheridan (Harmondsworth: Penguin).

Foucault, M. (1980) *Power/Knowledge: Selected Interviews and Other Writings, 1972–1977*, ed. Colin Gordon (New York: Pantheon Books).

Gitlin, T. (nd) 'C. Wright Mills, Free Radical'. http://www.uni-muenster. de/PeaCon/dgs-mills/mills-texte/GitlinMills.htm [accessed 30/1/2005].

Gordon, A. (1997) *Ghostly Matters: Haunting and the Sociological Imagination* (Minneapolis and London: University of Minnesota Press).

Haugaard, M. (2003) 'Reflections on Seven Ways of Creating Power', *European Journal of Social Theory* 6(1), pp. 87–113.

Hunt, A. and G. Wickham (1994) *Foucault and Law: Toward a Sociology of Law as Governance* (London: Pluto Press).

Kellner, D. (1995) *Media Culture* (London: Routledge).

McHoul, A. and W. Grace (1993) *A Foucault Primer: Discourse, Power and the Subject* (Melbourne: Melbourne University Press).

Mills, C. W. (1956) *The Power Elite* (New York: Oxford University Press).

Mills, C. W. (1958) 'The Structure of Power in American Society', *The British Journal of Sociology* 9(1), pp. 29–41.

Mills, C. W. (1959) *The Sociological Imagination* (New York: Oxford University Press).

Narayan, D. (2000) *Voices of the Poor: Can Anyone Hear Us?* (New York: Oxford University Press).

Nordstrom, C. (2000) 'Shadows and Sovereigns', *Theory, Culture & Society* 17(4), pp. 35–54.

The New Zealand Oxford Dictionary (2004) (Melbourne: Oxford University Press).

Parkin, F. (1982) *Max Weber* (Chichester and London: Ellis Horwood and Tavistock Publications).

Sachs, A. and J. Hoff Wilson (1978) *Sexism and the Law: A Study of Male Beliefs and Legal Bias in Britain and the United States* (Oxford: Martin Robertson).

Tate, S. (1999) 'Making your Body your Signature: Weight-Training and Transgressive Femininities', in S. Roseneil and J. Seymour (eds), *Practising Identities: Power and Resistance* (Basingstoke: Macmillan).

UNRISD (United Nations Research Institute) (1995) *States of Disarray: The Social Effects of Globalization* (London: UNRISD).

Weber, M. (1922/1947) *The Theory of Social and Economic Organisation* (New York: Oxford University Press).

Weber, M. (1968) *Economy and Society*, ed. Guenther Roth and Claus Wittich (New York: Bedminster Press).

Weber, M. (1978) *Economy and Society. An Outline of Interpretive Sociology* (Berkeley, CA: University of California Press).

Woodward, C. V. (1974) *The Strange Career of Jim Crow*, 3rd rev. edn (New York: Oxford University Press).

FEELING: EMOTIONS • BELIEVING: RELIGION • EDUCATING • STRAYING: DEVIANCE •
MEDIATING: TECHNOLOGY • INFORMING: MEDIA • RELATING: FAMILY • BELONGING: COMMUNITY • FINISHING

7   169

8 racializing

Ivanica Vodanovich

KEY
POINTS

- Definitions of race, and its associated concepts ethnicity and nationality, are situationally determined and used.

- Race, ethnicity and nationalism are social/cultural constructions. Their use and the meaning attached to them is negotiated and contested in social interaction. We need to be reflexively aware of the discourse of race, ethnicity and nationality in our culture, the way in which it varies historically and contextually, and the way in which we and others use it.

- As cultural concepts they structure our perception and interpretation of a situation, guide behaviour and provide a system of moral evaluation.

- These concepts can function as ideologies serving economic and political interests, though they do not always do so. As ideologies they maintain structures of power and domination and can serve to determine control over and access to resources.

- In the post-modern global world we can choose from a range of identities. Individuals are more mobile and personal identity is more fluid and fragmented. Race, ethnicity and nationality, whether chosen or ascribed by the 'other', have re-emerged in this context as significant for the ordering of collective and individual identities. They can serve as mechanisms for centring identity and bridging the local and global. The interesting question in studying race, ethnicity and nationalism is to identify the situations (economic, political, demographic) in which an issue is defined in racial/ethnic terms and those in which they are seen as irrelevant.

- The focus on 'racializing' draws attention to the ideological process by which ideas of racial/ethnic/national origins are used to classify individuals into groups and order social relations. It requires us to consider the specific historical context in which this occurs, the groups subjected to this process and, of equal importance, those which are excluded.

Introduction

Early sociologists were largely unconcerned with the concept of race and its consequent social effects. Their desire to explore and understand the evolving industrial capitalist society they lived in led them to analyse the changing forms of social relations, and the emerging class structure and political institutions they perceived. But despite the fact that the nineteenth and early twentieth century was the period of imperialist expansion that laid the foundation for the development of many of today's racial issues, race was not explicitly addressed in their work.

Today the 'problem of race' and issues of racialization are quite central to sociology. In a globalizing world, conflicts and patterns of violence and disorder are increasingly defined in racial terms. This upsurge in socio-logical interest illustrates two important characteristics of the sociological enterprise. Firstly, sociologists are part of the social reality they inhabit. Their work reflects the issues and problems of that world. Even when it is not explicitly acknowledged, history, as lived individual experience and as learnt culture, is always part of it. Secondly, because the ideas and concepts we use in sociology are social constructs, the meaning they are given varies historically and situationally.

Race is, in a sense, a phantom concept. Nineteenth-century 'scientific theories' and claims about the biological foundations of 'race' have long been discredited in scientific thought (Barzun, 1937/1965). But the many ways in which the idea of 'race' permeates our social world clearly exemplify W. I. Thomas's famous dictum that 'if men define situations as real, they are real in their consequences' (Thomas and Thomas, 1928, p. 572). Widespread ideas about race provide a powerful system of symbolic representations that influence behaviour. The continued use of this concept to describe or explain patterns of order and disorder, conflict and inequality, encapsulates the paradox and the problem of race for sociologists today. The difficulty is, as Osborne and Sandford observe, that 'race is a concept with a disreputable past and an uncertain future yet it continues to trouble the present both politically and intellectually' (2002, p. 1). The vocabulary of race is an element of everyday language, part of the stock of cultural capital we draw on to organize our world, ascribe or claim identity, and guide our interaction with others. As a cultural concept it influences our perception and actions and is part of our system of moral evaluation. Race always refers to membership of a group or collective. It is used to organize sets of social relationships and access to resources both within and between states. As such it is an element in the power structure of states and communities.

In the past 20 years many sociologists have moved from a static representation of 'race' and racism as part of something called 'race relations' to the more process-oriented concept of racializing. This has been, at least in part, a response to a concern that the former emphasis on race or race relations might give credibility and legitimacy to claims for the objective existence of race. In contrast, 'racialization' emphasized the constructed nature of the concept as a social and cultural process. It drew attention to the contexts in which it – rather than, for example, concepts of class, age, gender or religion – was used to explain social phenomena. Racialization was defined as an 'historically specific ideological process ... that results in certain social collectivities being thought of as constituting naturally (often biologically) distinct groups, each possessing certain ineradicable features' (Miles and Small, 1999, p. 141) and the accompanying structures – political, economic, legal and cultural – that reinforce and maintain these beliefs. The resulting institutionalization of these beliefs so they are seen as 'natural' ensures that racialized patterns of social action become routinized. In a continuing process of mediation and negotiation, symbolic representations of racial/ethnic groups within the culture construct and maintain racialized social processes. Through this, the past is brought into the present and the defined social groups are placed within a social, and frequently geographical, space.

The roots of contemporary racism, and its pervasiveness, lie in the structures and processes of globalization (see Chapter 5, 'Trading', and Chapter 7, 'Governing: Power'). Racialization serves to define and maintain the boundaries of the contemporary state within the global system. The cohesion of contemporary states, most of them multi-ethnic, is based on an assumed commitment by the population to a common 'national' identity. Within the state race/ethnicity is one of the categories used to organize and structure relationships between constituent groups. Citizenship provides legitimacy for full membership of this political community and full access to social and civil rights. The study of race must therefore

FEELING: EMOTIONS • BELIEVING: RELIGION • EDUCATING • STRAYING: DEVIANCE • MEDIATING: TECHNOLOGY • INFORMING: MEDIA • RELATING: FAMILY • BELONGING: COMMUNITY • FINISHING

8 173

also consider the related issues of ethnicity, nationality and citizenship. Together, these ideas make up a set of overlapping ambiguous concepts, used inconsistently or interchangeably.

Globalization processes

The dimensions of the globalization process relevant to contemporary forms of racism lie in the disjunctions between the working of the global economic system (which creates economic interdependence through multiple systems of exchange in production, trade and finance) and the political autonomy of the nation states that make up the system (see Chapter 4, 'Consuming'; Chapter 5, 'Trading'; Chapter 7, 'Governing: Power'). This is allied with increased cultural interaction through the accelerated growth of modern technology, especially communication systems (see Chapter 17, 'Informing: Media'). Castells (1997) argues that this gives rise to the 'network society' and collapses time and space to allow a culture of virtual reality. It ensures immediate awareness of events in other societies and facilitates the creation of international communities of interest, a basis for collective movements including those based on race or ethnicity (see Chapter 11, 'Being: Identity'). Increased personal mobility is one outcome of this global pattern.

Globalization is not a uniform process. It operates on a system of differentiation of production and inequality of power that creates an uneven system of accumulation and control skewed towards the core states (Wallerstein, 1974; Hirst and Thompson, 1996). Increased mobility brings previously separate populations into close contact in their everyday life and work and increases competition for resources. Transnational migration in all its forms, including illegal migration and the growth of refugees and internally displaced persons, is part of this process. In 2002 185 million people lived outside their country of origin, compared with 80 million in the early 1970s (GCIR, 2005). The growth of distinct ethnic minorities within modern democracies is a result, as is the re-emergence of claims for local identity in both core and peripheral states. The continuing reassertion of Basque, Welsh and Scottish nationality, the dissolution of the Federal Republic of Yugoslavia and the separation of the Czech and Slovak states are just a few examples of this trend. It is a result of the contradictions created between the disjunctions of the world system, on the one hand, and the pressures for homogenization, on the other. These localized movements emerge where discrete populations exist that can claim common ethnic and historical roots.

These simultaneous processes of economic and cultural integration on the global level, within a structure grounded on the independence of the constituent states, threaten the autonomy of the state. At the same time the parallel growth of multinational and international organizations, which set international standards, usurp some of its authority over its culture (cf. Hall, 1991a) by establishing a degree of political integration based on transnational norms. Taken-for-granted national identity can become problematical in this situation because it confronts challenges from within and without the state. Together, these processes provide the context in which new forms of racism emerge, often hidden under the guise of cultural incompatibility.

The United Nations, through the establishment of an international system of universal standards, contributes to the process of political integration. This system provides a degree of homogeneity in norms and standards and a framework for the way in which states address issues of racial discrimination while at the same time implicitly limiting their autonomy. The Universal Declaration of Human Rights, adopted by the General Assembly of the United Nations in 1948, was the starting point. It asserted the universality of rights for all individuals equally without distinction of 'race, colour, language, religion, political or other opinion, national or social origin, property, birth or other status'. This Declaration was complemented by the work of a variety of international and regional organizations such as UNESCO (United Nations Educational, Scientific, and Cultural Organization), ILO (International Labour Organisation), the Council of Europe, NAFTA (North American Free Trade Agreement), the International Court of Justice and, more recently, the World Court. The Council of Europe, a broader grouping of European states than found within the European Union, drew up the European Convention on Human Rights in 1950 and established the European Court of Justice. The Universal Declaration was supplemented by further Covenants including one on the Elimination of all Forms of Racial Discrimination. This

Covenant, adopted by the General Assembly in 1965, was influenced by the then South African system of apartheid. It reinforced the principles of racial equality and added ethnic origin to the list. However, it specifically maintained the rights of states to distinguish between citizens and non-citizens and their right to determine processes of naturalization, provided they did not discriminate against a particular nationality.

States and regional groupings have taken a variety of steps to implement these Covenants but there is considerable variation in the way in which they accept, interpret and implement them. Within the European Union the Amsterdam Treaty (1999), building on the work of the Council of Europe, directly addressed issues of discrimination and required member states of the European Union to take appropriate action to combat discrimination based on sex, racial or ethnic origin etc. (Stepanek, 2002). Member states vary in the rights accorded non-citizens, refugees or migrants as opposed to citizens of member states. Bhabha (2003) cites differences in acceptance of refugee claims as illustration. In 1991, while about 5 per cent of refugee claims were successful in Germany, Italy, Belgium, the UK and the Netherlands, about 20 per cent were recognized in France (Bhabha, 2003, p. 105).

This international system of human rights is a based on recognition of individual rights. However, the right to practise one's own religious, ethnic or racial culture provides the basis for the organization of collectives and collective action. This poses a dilemma for contemporary pluralistic states as they seek means to recognize and allow for diversity within their borders, often for discrete groups with historical allegiances outside its frontiers, and at the same time ensure the cohesiveness and stability of the state through the commitment of the population to a common identity. In everyday discourse this is referred to as 'national identity' even among multi-ethnic/national states. Not only is racialization at work in defining and maintaining the boundaries of the contemporary state but it is also used to organize and structure relationships between its constituent groups, often defined in terms of ethnicity rather than race or nationality.

Practical instances of racialized ethnic diversity are now found in many places. For example, Ghassan Hage, in his studies of Australian society, effectively dissects white responses to life in an increasingly multicultural society. He describes multiple instances of ethnic stereotyping and group allegiances, sometimes enacted through violence, that form a counterpoint to official rhetoric of inclusion. Even where the language of tolerance is in place a sub-text may also be found, as in this commentary from an elderly man from Marrickville:

> I say hello to the neighbours and they say hello back to me and ... I just do my thing and they do their thing. The lady next door, she's Italian: I might go into the bathroom there and she's singing opera next door. ... And the people next door, ah, they're Vietnamese school teachers, you know, they all got young kids ... like they're all nice people. There's a couple of Greeks, in the street, they're all nice people ... you get the Greeks up there near the post office with their beads, you know, in the hand you know, sittin' there and, you get some Aborigines up there near the other end of the post office drinking their plonk or whatever, you know, they never cause no trouble ... The only problem are those new Vietnamese up the road. They are like ... they don't want to know ... they only talk among themselves as if they're plotting or something. (Hage, 1998, p. 98)

Race, ethnicity and nationalism

These three ideas, together with the concept of citizenship, share a common reference point. They are used to order collective identities and structure relations between them within a political community. However, the way we use them and the distinctions we make between them is inconsistent and varies between societies and within societies over time. We often slip from one usage to another. As Fenton (2003) observes, they are overlapping concepts that share a common core, occupy the same social territory, but differ at the margins. He argues that instead of trying to separate them it is more useful to identify the contexts in which one or other of these ideas becomes a basis for social action.

The process of constructing and ordering social groups entails recognition of similarity with those accepted as belonging to the same ethnic/race-based group, and differentiation from other groups. It involves the drawing of boundaries, of varying degrees of permeability; thus it is simultaneously an inclusive and exclusive process. Within a given territory or state the groups are usually organized hierarchically. Membership is ascribed on the basis of a variety of assumed shared characteristics that identify their common core and differentiate them from other groups. The most important characteristic that the three terms – race, ethnicity and nationality – share is the assumption that members of the group share biological descent (historical or mythical) – a common ancestry or genealogy at some point in time. As well as a putative common descent they assume a common history, culture (way of life) and language. Religion may also be a central element. These are used to distinguish them from other groups sharing the same or an adjoining social space. Given this core of similarities, the most useful way of distinguishing between the three concepts is to examine the way in which they are used today in specific contexts and how their use has varied over time.

Nationalism and nationality

Nationalism and nationality are today associated with the 'nation state'. However, no totally homogeneous nation states exist. Human mobility and miscegenation ensure that 'nation' states always contain pockets of distinct 'ethnic' minorities to a greater or lesser degree. Also, national/ethnic groups are not totally closed. Nationality is always constructed. The development of the centralized modern 'nation' state in Europe is the story of the welding and melding together, over a long and bloody history, of people whose original identities derived from myriad sources: ethnic group, locality, feudal estate, principalities, province, tribe or clan. The twentieth-century ideal of the 'nation' state emerged with the break-up of the multi-ethnic Austro-Hungarian and Ottoman empires in 1918 and the establishment of new states in Eastern Europe. The principle of nationality, linked to the ideal of self-determination, was used to reorganize Eastern Europe into new states (Hobsbawm, 1990). The model of nationalism/nation state was also taken as the blueprint for the formation of the newly independent states in Africa and Asia, following the dissolution of the European imperial system in Asia, Africa and the Middle East after the Second World War. We can currently see it at work in the reorganization of Eastern Europe and Central Asia following the break-up of the Soviet Union. However, the principle of self-determination had a more limited application. Not all 'nationalities' have been successful in achieving an independent state. The Kurds are one such example and the Basques are another. The people of Chechnya and of Tibet, though residing within a distinct territory, have not been able to maintain political autonomy within a geographical space.

Nationalism provides a simple method of creating solidarity, cohesion and commitment for governments with few other resources (Nairn, 1975). As such, it is an inclusive concept as opposed to race, which is more usually used to exclude. In newly emerging states, following the demise of colonial powers after the Second World War, it could also usually draw on the support of the liberation movements that had led the fight for independence from the imperial powers.

Contemporary states are all multi-ethnic, albeit usually with one dominant culture. Despite this, both governments and people still employ the discourse of nationality and the idea of the 'nation' state as a basis for solidarity and patriotism, drawing on ideas of a shared history, culture and experience rather than common biological descent. At the same time, 'national identity' – either defining it, establishing its essence, questioning it or regretting its absence – appears to be a central problem of contemporary consciousness at the level of both the individual and the collective. In Anderson's definition, a nation 'is an imagined political community – and imagined as both inherently limited and sovereign' (1991, p. 6). This identifies the distinctive characteristics of nationality (as opposed to ethnicity and race) when it is allied to the term 'state'. Nation states control political power and the legitimate means of force within a defined territory. National movements generally aim for some form of political independence. National identity is the identity acquired by membership of the political community. It is the basis for the acquisition of citizenship that allows full participation in society.

The increasing cultural/ethnic diversity of the contemporary state, reinforced by processes of mobility and migration, poses particular problems for the construction of national identity. The assumed uniformity of cultural beliefs has lost its taken-for-granted quality. This is reinforced by the almost universal recognition of the United Nations Conventions on Human Rights, which include cultural as well as political rights. The problem today, then, is the creation of unity through recognition and incorporation of diversity in culture, language and religion. Different societies have adopted different approaches in addressing this issue.

FEELING: EMOTIONS • BELIEVING: RELIGION • EDUCATING • STRAYING: DEVIANCE • MEDIATING: TECHNOLOGY • INFORMING: MEDIA • RELATING: FAMILY • BELONGING: COMMUNITY • FINISHING

8 179

Stepanek (2002) claims that, within the European Union, France has adopted a policy of assimilation relegating distinct cultural/ethnic practices to the private sphere; the British system of 'hierarchical cultural pluralism' maintains the notion of the superiority of British culture while recognizing and supporting minority cultures; Germany uses a system of 'temporary incorporation', which makes it extremely difficult for migrant groups – for example, the large Turkish minority – to obtain citizenship, thus marginalizing them. In the United States of America ideas of assimilation prevalent in the 1960s and encapsulated in the idea of the 'melting pot' gave way to acceptance of biculturalism or multiculturalism. These different approaches demonstrate that there is a continuing historical dialectic at work. Accommodations may settle particular situations but they do not necessarily resolve the problem.

States control the right to citizenship. Withholding citizenship marginalizes individuals or populations. As noted, international covenants recognize states' authority in this area. However, the conflation of culture with 'national identity' can provide the opportunity for discrimination on the basis of perceived racial or ethnic differences. Bhabha (2003, p. 118) cites the example of three children, with French nationality but of Algerian origin, who were refused entry at a Belgian airport in 1996 while in transit to France. Their parents were waiting for them but were not given the chance to explain their status. This action, which Bhabha identifies as an example of the 'racialized understanding of what constitutes a European identity', was explained as being sent back rather than expulsion. It illustrates the ambiguities and contradictions in the mélange of national identity, citizenship, racial/origins and culture. European identity, as a member of the European Union, was not traditionally a 'racial category' although it appears, from this example, to be an emergent one. This could pose problems of definition because not all European states are members of the Union. The rise of anti-immigration political parties and their relative success in the polls, in France and Holland, is a reaction to the increased numbers of migrants from Islamic countries and the perceived threat they are believed to pose to 'European culture', thus adding religion and culture to the mix of race, nationality and ethnicity.

The Federal People's Republic of Yugoslavia addressed the problem of recognizing distinct 'ethnic' identities within one political territory by distinguishing between citizenship and nationality. The linguistic terms made the different sources of the concepts clear. The term for nationality was '*narod*', from '*rod*' meaning family or parentage. In contrast, the word for citizenship was *drzavljanstvo*, from the word *drustvo* meaning society. This linguistic distinction between the word for nationality, rooted in notions of common blood, and the term for citizen, which draws on notions of civil status, is found in many languages. In the Federal Republic, citizenship was Yugoslav, but national identity was defined in 'ethnic terms', membership of which was embedded in the constituent republics that made up the Federal Republic – Croatia, Serbia, Slovenia etc. But, as the subsequent break-up of the Federal Republic demonstrated, this did not resolve the problem of ethnic diversity within a pluralistic state.

'Race' and 'ethnicity'

The definitions and everyday use of the terms 'race' and 'ethnicity' are more problematic. Fenton (2003) argues that there is no clear consistent meaning given to these terms or to the distinction between them. Both concepts are rooted in the belief of common biological origins. Race was frequently used to refer to a larger grouping such as European, Asian or American. It is also often used even more widely in everyday discourse to refer to larger groupings such as the 'white race' or the 'black race'. The term has an ascriptive quality and appears to be used to describe a population rather than a social group. The use of colour in identifying race/ethnicity in everyday discourse points to an important element in the process of constructing racial and ethnic collectivities. We look for and use visible markers – language, dress, names and colour. Of these the most obvious is colour and the term 'race' in everyday discourse often appears to be based on colour differentiation.

Fenton (2003) points out that the term 'ethnic' emerged in the discourse in the 1960s, popularized in the work of Glazer and Moynihan. It was used to distinguish between white populations within a multi-ethnic state, in terms of their countries of origin. In the United States the term 'race' was applied to the Negro population. Ethnicity was used for European migrant groups. Now it is used more generally. A hierarchy always exists within ethnic groups. In the United States, WASPS (white Anglo-Saxon Protestants) were at the top of the European groups, as opposed to the lower-ranked Irish Catholics. In Britain during the late 1960s and early 1970s, Pakistanis had the lower status within the coloured migrant population and 'Paki' bashing occurred. The fact that Pakistani is a national identity rather than a racial category again demonstrates the inconsistencies and ambiguities in the ways these categories are used. 'Pakistani' refers to membership of the state of Pakistan. The name Pakistan is an acronym of the constituent provinces that make up the state. There is no such historical racial or ethnic grouping.

In contemporary multi-ethnic states, a sense of common origin can provide a basis for identification and mobilization for social, communal or political action. Discrete 'ethnic' groups can thus be perceived as a potential threat. Equally, their marginalization means a greater reliance on the communal support of their cultural ethnic community. This is a two-way process of interaction that draws on forms of symbolic representation to interpret the lived-in experience of the collective and renegotiate social space and identity. The process is not always purely one of exclusion by the dominant group. It can include the embracing of the ethnic/racial identity by the ethnic minority and subjective identification with the group. The 'Black is Beautiful' movement, which, in various forms, spread from the United States to many other places, is one such example (see Chapter 11, 'Being: Identity').

Fenton (2003) notes the demise of the term 'race', pointing out that the term 'ethnic' is more commonly used today. So while the Holocaust, and its rationale in the supposed purification of the 'Aryan' race, is referred to as a 'racial cleansing', conflicts in more recent times – for example, in Bosnia and Rwanda – have been called 'ethnic cleansing'. The term 'race' is vanishing from the discourse; however, although it is now rarely used to describe a social group, it is still used for a population. The adjective 'racist' persists, to describe unacceptable behaviour towards a group that would usually be described as an 'ethnic' group. Similarly, 'racism' is used to describe such behaviour. In everyday discourse a trend emerged which equated ethnicity with a distinctive culture and saw it as positive, but viewed 'race' as discriminatory.

This is an interesting and, for sociologists, paradoxical development. In the sociological perspective race (and nationality) have always been seen as cultural/social constructs or at least accorded a cultural dimension.

In the evolving contemporary discourse culture is increasingly separated from ethnicity and race and used for assessing acceptability. This framing of problems of differentiation in terms of culture allows charges of racial discrimination to be sidestepped. Miles (1993) discusses this 'new racism' in which biological determinism is replaced by culture as a basis for discrimination. Culture becomes a synonym for racial/ethnic differentiation. This can be seen in political or policy statements justifying or legitimating exclusion on the grounds of cultural incompatibility. The discourse is ideological, as it conceals the racial underpinning. The statement of Christian Democrat leader Angela Merkel (who subsequently became Chancellor of Germany) that 'immigrants must adapt to Germany's majority Christian influenced culture because efforts to create a multicultural society are doomed to failure' (*New Zealand Herald*, 8 December 2004), is an example. It is debatable whether this is actually a 'new racism' or simply the persistence of old forms of discrimination in a different guise. Reassertions of the primacy of a more homogeneous national culture in Holland and France are similar markers, although these reactions are amplified by the global security situation.

Anderson's definition of the nation as an 'imagined community', in which individuals do not ever know all members of the community but nevertheless feel an identity with them, is to a degree common to all three concepts – race, ethnicity and nationality. The communities created on these grounds, whether imposed or embraced, are all, in a sense, 'imagined communities'. Nation states differ from ethnic or race-based communities in some important respects. They always include control over a given political territory, including the monopoly of the legitimate use of force and authority to grant or withhold citizenship. Processes of racialization – discrimination on the basis of supposed biological distinctiveness and the institutionalization of economic, legal and political arrangements based on these assumptions – draw on and employ all three concepts.

Sociological analysis of race

It will by now be evident that race, ethnicity and nationality make up a set of contested concepts. There is no unitary phenomenon of race. Therefore

FEELING: EMOTIONS • BELIEVING: RELIGION • EDUCATING • STRAYING: DEVIANCE •
MEDIATING: TECHNOLOGY • INFORMING: MEDIA • RELATING: FAMILY • BELONGING: COMMUNITY • FINISHING

8   183

there is no distinct field of study (Miles, 1993). Race can be both the problem and the explanation, used to describe patterns of disorder or social problems or, in a circular loop, to explain them. A variety of theoretical approaches can be identified. Depending on the issue, whether for example the study is examining a question of race and gender, race and class, race and identity, or race and religion, authors draw on the relevant body of theory. We are dealing with a variety of political and social discourses and the resulting social action, in a range of areas of social life.

The emergence of a concern with 'race' reflects the way in which these ideas are rooted in the particular historical context and the interaction between sociology and its subject matter. Its development in Britain in the 1960s emerged as a response to the increasing presence of migrant ethnic groups from the colonies and recognition of changes taking place within the society. As would be expected, American sociologists had an earlier concern with these issues; they initially examined issues of segregation, immigration and perceptions and awareness of race. By the 1960s they had moved to a focus on the dynamics of ethnic groups.

Despite the lack of an explicit concern with race in the work of the founding fathers, many of their more general insights provide the starting point for sociological work in this area. The theorists of particular significance are Marx, Weber and Gramsci. Studies exploring race, inequality and the racialization of social relations have their staring point in theories of the work of Marx and theories of the capitalist mode of production. In this approach, nationalism and race, as part of the superstructure and culture, reflected the material conditions rather than acting as causal factors. Marx's argument that material conditions determine consciousness is a starting point for the study of race as ideology and for considering the way in which ideas of race are embedded in the social, historical and economic context and vary over time. The work of Robert Miles draws on the Marxist tradition.

Weber (1968) addresses the issue of race, albeit indirectly. His debate with 'the ghost of Marx' emphasized the role of ideas in social action and argued that culture had a degree of autonomy. It was not purely reflective of economic conditions. This approach, which recognizes the interaction between cultural ideas and economic conditions in patterns of social action, has proved useful in analysing the global re-emergence of racial/ethnic conflicts. For example, the conflicts that led to the break-up of the Federal Republic of Yugoslavia had an economic and political underpinning although they were presented as ethnic conflicts and acted upon in those terms. Remington (1997) presents a Weberian analysis of these events. In a detailed examination of the processes leading to the implosion of the Federal Republic, he shows the complexity and multi-layered nature of conflict and argues that the different historical contexts in which Serbian and Croatian nationalism developed provide the framework within which conflicts presented. The federal structure of the Republic validated ethnic nationalism (although not all ethnicities were fully recognized – for example, the large Albanian population in Kosovo) and hampered the development of effective central political institutions. The death of charismatic leader Tito exposed the weaknesses of the political structure and provided the situation for the reassertion of ethnic nationalism throughout the Republic. This drew on the long-standing resentment of the northern republics of Slovenia and Croatia about the economic support they were obliged to provide to the less-developed southern regions of the country, allied to their concern at the action of the predominantly Serbian army. External support from Germany reinforced the stand of Croatia. Thus the different historical experiences of the north and south, allied to the different cultural, linguistic and religious patterns, encapsulated in ethnic differences, meant that the conflicts developed along the fault lines of the old historical ethnic divisions. Underpinning these events were the forms of political and economic institutions and the influence of external forces. In a more recent study, Sekulic (2004) argues that in Croatia a civic identity is now becoming more prominent in certain parts of the Republic, in particular in the larger metropolitan regions and the more geographically marginal areas such as Istria. This is compared with the focus on a narrower ethnic identity functional in the period leading to the dissolution of the Federal Republic.

Weber's second contribution derives from his work on status groups. He viewed ethnic groups as akin to status groups; bounded groups, defined by life style and consumption patterns, as opposed to classes, were defined by their position in the capitalist mode of production. He identified the potential for ethnic groups to mobilize for social political action. The work of John Rex and Michael Banton (who first used the term 'racialization' in 1977) can be located within this tradition. Their work focused on race relations, race conflicts and a concern with policy development.

Robert Miles was one of the leading critics of this earlier approach. He argued that races are purely ideological constructs that hide the underlying economic reality. If there are no races, there can be no race relations. Focusing on them reifies them and gives them legitimacy. There is not a 'race problem' but a problem of 'racism'. For this reason he criticized the institutional and legal systems put in place in national states and regional organizations such as the European Union to combat racism, arguing that they reinforce the idea of race. He proposed instead to focus on racialization and, in later work, on racism. Racialization is the process through which ideas and beliefs about race, together with class and gender, shape social relationships: in other words, the social construction of race. Racism applies to the set of ideas involved in this process. He argues that it serves as one more mechanism to effect and legitimate the allocation of scarce resources (Miles, 1993). Racialization is located within the capitalist world mode of production. Miles is particularly interested in the effect of the global capital economy on migrant workers and saw relations between groups of workers from different ethnic communities as manifestations of class conflict and the powerlessness of migrant workers.

Gramsci's theory of hegemony, a system of domination through consent, influenced the work of Stuart Hall and the Birmingham Centre for Contemporary Cultural Studies and identifies an important body of work which approaches the problem through cultural studies. The engineering of consent is through a process of negotiation rather than coercion. A particular hegemonic configuration is the outcome of a historically specific struggle between competing classes and groups. In this process power is mediated so that the outcome embodies ideas from both the dominant and the subordinate groups. This is a continuing process that expresses a shifting pattern of negotiated interests between the state, institutional structures and groups in civil society. Hall's framework focuses in particular on racism as ideology. For Hall, racism is always historically and culturally specific. His work on this subject links with his focus on culture and the media and offers insights for the study of identity. Rejecting the notion of an 'essential black subject' requiring representation by 'black artists and black cultural workers themselves', he asserted 'the extraordinary diversity of subject positions, social experiences and cultural identities which compose the category "black"' and pointed out that neither the effectivity of any cultural practice nor its aesthetic value will be guaranteed or determined through 'some composite notion of race around the term black' (1996, pp. 442, 443).

This selective brief overview of some of the significant British theorists of race and racialization illustrates the complexity of the field and the continuing evolution and transformation of our construction of the 'problem'. Solomos and Back (1996, p. 229) think that 'no one theoretical perspective is dominant at the present time'. However, the idea of race provides a powerful system of symbolic representations through which groups of individuals locate themselves and others, and interpret their own experience as racialized others. In doing so, they also racialize 'the other'. Racialized categories can emerge in all areas of social life – cultural, economic, political and social. No one theory is likely to be able to explain the myriad of 'races' this gives rise to. Rather, we need to draw on a range of theoretical perspectives – feminist, cultural, political, philosophical, economic or sociological – chosen in terms of relevance for the historically specific issue we are analysing.

However, there is no doubt that the concept of racialization has become akin to a core concept in this field of study. Murji and Solomos (2005) argue that the use of this concept in social sciences to address such a wide variety of social issues and analyse institutional structures has led to a conflation of the concept, and the lack of clarity has led to inconsistent use. Still, the concept has value because it draws attention to the constructed nature of race as a social process and to the institutional and social contexts – political, economic and cultural – in which it occurs. Rattansi (2005) argues that it is an indispensable concept because it allows us to explore the multidimensional and complex character of the phenomenon.

Racialization and identity

Identity, and the location of this identity in the construction of social space, are two significant features of contemporary multi-ethnic societies usefully examined through the lens of racialization. Modernity has always provided a challenge to identity (Hall, 1991b). Contemporary identity is decentred and fragmented. We can choose between a range of identities in different contexts. Bauman (1992) argues that the relativity inherent in post-modernity accentuates the dilemma for the individual. It gives them responsibility for moral choice but deprives them of universal norms to guide conduct. Individuals must rely on their own subjectivity and take responsibility for their own choice.

National identity did provide a mechanism for ordering and integrating this multiplicity. However, the growth of large migrant communities provides a particular problem for the negotiation and construction of national identity, and for marginalized migrant communities it does not provide a viable option. Assimilation may be impossible or resisted by the migrants. In a mass society where 'strangers' are brought into close proximity, presumed common origins become a source of instant recognition and identification and provide the migrant with a mechanism to overcome the existential dilemma posed by Bauman. Hall (1991a, p. 33) argues that a return to the local is 'often a response to globalisation'. The local re-emerges in the global society as a source of identity by linking past and present. In migrant communities this process, by the positioning of identity, links social space in the host community and homeland. Again, numerous examples from many places now exist. Macpherson has, over more than 30 years, studied and reported on the experiences of Samoan migrants to New Zealand, and on the next generation of locally born children growing to adulthood but still deeply touched by traditional Samoan cultural beliefs and practices (Pitt and Macpherson, 1974). The negotiation of identity between places is brought to life in Carrington's (1999, p. 17) study of the Caribbean Cricket Club in Chapeltown, Leeds. Nicholas, born in England, sees himself as English and West Indian. In cricket tests he supports the West Indies:

> Because they're all black and, well ... also they're all better than the English team anyway and I don't agree, you know, when people say like 'If you're born in England you have to support England', I don't agree with that, because it's like, your choice you can support whoever you like ... The only way I'll support England is if they're playing Australia 'cause I don't really like Australians much.

Race and ethnicity provide the starting point for the narrative construction of identity through negotiation with others. This is not a linear or unproblematic process and local ethnicities can threaten national identity. The rejection of modernity, which lends itself to the rediscovery of an identity grounded in a form of fundamentalism, is one example (Hall, 1991a). (See Chapter 13, 'Believing: Religion'.)

Identities are never completed; they are always in the process of becoming through negotiation and interaction with the other (Hall, 1991b). This narrative process draws on systems of symbolic representation derived from the culture of origin but mediated through interaction in a dialectical process. The explosion of forms of cultural expression from migrant cultures in art, literature, film, mass media and theatre, which explore the lived experience of migrants in interaction with the culture of the others, is part of this dialectic. It may be (though is not necessarily) ideological and it brings into the debate on racism a focus on cultural production and the politics of identity and gives powerful expression to the experience of being 'other'.

Conclusion

Race, ethnicity and nationality are social (and cultural) constructs that provide the basis for the systems of symbolic representations we draw on in constructing the social groups we inhabit and in ordering relationships with other groups. The force of these ideas lies in the way they serve as referents for presumed common origins and provide a powerful emotional mechanism which links individuals with their past. They function to structure perceptions, action and evaluations. As Nairn (1995) argued in relation to nationalism, they persist as potential fault lines, which, in times of crisis or conflict, can serve to channel behaviour, action and reaction – and our reading of it – irrespective of the actual causes of the problem.

There is therefore no unitary phenomenon we can define as race and no single theory to address it. It may function as ideology; it may be a basis for discrimination, and thereby serve to maintain dominant economic and political interests that legitimate exploitation. Alternatively, it may provide a basis for resistance and political mobilization and a source for the construction of identity in a multi-ethnic society.

FEELING: EMOTIONS • BELIEVING: RELIGION • EDUCATING • STRAYING: DEVIANCE • MEDIATING: TECHNOLOGY • INFORMING: MEDIA • RELATING: FAMILY • BELONGING: COMMUNITY • FINISHING

8   189

In the global world of today we confront multiple racisms. The forms in which they manifest themselves vary over time and in different situations. Despite scientific rejection of the validity of racial categories, sociology cannot ignore the study of this phenomenon. It has real objective consequences in our social world.

Suggestions for further reading

Anthias, F. and G. Lazaridis (eds) (2000) *Gender and Migration in Southern Europe* (Oxford: Berg).

Anthias, F. and C. Lloyd (eds) (2002) *Rethinking Anti-racisms: From Theory to Practice* (London: Routledge).

Bulmer, M. and J. Solomos (eds) (1999) *Racism* (Oxford: Oxford University Press).

Hughey, M. W. (ed.) (1998) *New Tribalisms: The Resurgence of Race and Ethnicity* (Basingstoke: Macmillan).

Knowles, C. (2003) *Race and Social Analysis* (London: Sage).

Rowe, M. (1998) *The Racialisation of Disorder in Twentieth-Century Britain* (Aldershot: Ashgate Publishing).

Said, E. W. (1995) *Orientalism* (London: Penguin).

Stone, J. and R. Denis (eds) (2003) *Race and Ethnicity: Comparative and Theoretical Approaches* (Oxford: Blackwell).

Bibliography

Anderson, B. (1991) *Imagined Communities* (London: Verso).

Banton, M. (1967) *Race Relations* (New York: Basic Books).

Barzun, J. (1937/1965) *Race: A Study in Modern Superstition* (New York: Harper & Row).

Bauman, Z. (1992) *Intimations of PostModernity* (London: Routledge).

Bhabha, J. (2003) 'Enforcing the Human Rights of Citizens and Non-Citizens in the Era of Maastricht: Some Reflections on the Importance of States', in B. Meyer and P. Geschiere (eds), *Globalization and Identity: Dialectics of Flow and Closure* (Oxford: Blackwell), pp. 97–124.

Carrington, B. (1999) 'Cricket, Culture and Identity: and Ethnographic Analysis of the Significance of Sport within Black Communities', in S. Roseneil and J. Seymour (eds), *Practising Identities* (Basingstoke: Macmillan), pp. 11–32.

Castells, M. (1997) *The Power of Identity* (Oxford: Blackwell).

Fenton, S. (2003) *Ethnicity* (Cambridge: Polity Press).

GCIR, InternationalMigrationStatistics.http://www.gcir.org/about_immigration/world_map_intro.htm [accessed 7/8/2005].

Gramsci, A. (1991) *Prison Notebooks* (New York: Columbia University Press).

Hage, G. (1998) *White Nation* (Annandale, NSW: Pluto Press).

Hall, S. (1991a) 'The Local and the Global: Globalization and Ethnicity', in A. D. King (ed.), *Culture, Globalization and the World System* (New York: Macmillan), pp. 19–40.

Hall, S. (1991b) 'Old and New Identities', in A. D. King (ed.), *Culture, Globalization and the World System* (New York: Macmillan), pp. 41–68.

Hall, S. (1996) 'New Ethnicities', in D. Morley and Kuan-Hsing Chen (eds), *Stuart Hall: Critical Dialogues in Cultural Studies* (London: Routledge), pp. 441–9.

Hirst, P. and G. Thompson (1996) *Globalization in Question* (Cambridge: Polity Press).

Hobsbawm, E. J. (1990) *Nations and Nationalism since 1780* (Cambridge: Canto).

Macpherson, C., P. Spoonley and M. Anae (eds) (2000) *Tangata o te moana nui: The Evolving Identities of Pacific Peoples in Aotearoa /New Zealand* (Palmerston North: Dunmore Press).

Miles, R. (1993) *Racism after 'Race Relations'* (London: Routledge).

Miles, R. and S. Small (1999) 'Racism and Ethnicity', in S. Taylor (ed.), *Sociology: Issues and Debates* (Basingstoke: Palgrave), pp. 136–57.

Murji, K. and J. Solomos (2005) 'Racialisation in Theory and Practice', in K. Murji and J. Solomos (eds), *Racialisation: Studies in Theory and Practice* (Oxford: Oxford University Press), pp. 1–28.

Nairn, T. (1995) 'The Modern Janus', *New Left Review* 94, pp. 3–29.

Osborne, P. and S. Sandford (eds) (2002) *Philosophies of Race and Ethnicity* (London: Continuum).

Pitt, D. and C. Macpherson (1974) *Emerging Pluralism: The Samoan Community in New Zealand* (Auckland: Longman Paul).

Rattansi, A. (2005) 'The Uses of Racialization: the Time–Spaces and Subject–Objects of the Raced Body', in K. Murji and J. Solomos (eds), *Racialization: Studies in Theory and Practice* (Oxford: Oxford University Press), pp. 271–301.

FEELING: EMOTIONS • BELIEVING: RELIGION • EDUCATING • STRAYING: DEVIANCE • MEDIATING: TECHNOLOGY • INFORMING: MEDIA • RELATING: FAMILY • BELONGING: COMMUNITY • FINISHING

8 191

Remington, R. A. (1997) 'Ethnonationalism and the Disintegration of Yugoslavia', in W. A. Van Horne (ed.), *Global Convulsions. Race, Ethnicity and Nationalism at the End of the Twentieth Century* (Albany, NY: State University of New York), pp. 261–80.

Sekulic, D. (2004) 'Civic and Ethnic Identity: the Case of Croatia', *Ethnic and Racial Studies* 27, pp. 455–83.

Solomos, J. and J. Back (1996) 'Race and Racism in Social Theory', in R. Barot (ed.), *The Racism Problematic: Contemporary Sociological Debates on Race and Ethnicity* (New York: Edwin Mellen Press), pp. 212–30.

Stepanek, L. (2002) *Minorities in Europe: The Divergence of Law and Policy.* http://www.eumap.org/journal/features/2002/jan02/minorities [accessed 21/9/2005].

Taylor, B. K. (ed.) (1996) *Race, Nation, Ethos and Class* (Brighton: Pennington Beech).

Thomas, W. I. and D. S. Thomas (1928) *The Child in America: Behavior Problems and Programs* (New York: Alfred A. Knopf).

Wallerstein, I. (1974) *The Modern World System 1* (New York: Academic Press).

Weber, M. (1968) *Economy and Society: An Outline of Interpretive Sociology*, ed. G. Roth and C. Wittich (New York: Bedminster Press).

gendering

Chris Brickell

<table>
<tr>
<td>KEY
POINTS</td>
<td>

▪ Our gender is central to our identities as individuals, and is lived and embodied by each one of us every day of our lives.

▪ Gender is socially constructed and operates in hierarchies of power.

▪ The theorizing of gender has a rich history within sociology.

▪ Men's as well as women's lives are deeply affected by gender; we do femininity and masculinity as an everyday part of who we are.

▪ Contemporary sociology suggests that we might think of gender as important in our lives without assuming that current gender arrangements are inevitable.

▪ Sociological studies of gendering can focus on gender as difference, gender as division, and gender as something we 'do'.

</td>
</tr>
</table>

Introduction: the importance of gender in sociology

Whether we are men or women, girls or boys, our gender influences many aspects of our lives. Our clothing and leisure activities reflect pervasive ideas about what is appropriate for male or female persons, while gender profoundly affects our experiences of education, employment and the family. Our gender is central to our identities as individuals, and is lived and embodied by each one of us every day of our lives (see Chapter 11, 'Being: Identity'). While our gender does not represent the sum total of our experience, it is always with us, as Don West and Candace Zimmerman have suggested:

> Individuals have many social identities that may be donned or shed, muted, or made more salient, depending on the situation. One may be a friend, professional, citizen, and many other things to many different people or to the same person at different times. But we are always women or men. (1991, p. 26)

The individual, however, is but one focus in the sociology of gender. Who we are as individuals does not fill out the whole story, because gender is not only an individual matter. It is also an integral dynamic of social arrangements and social order. Our sense of ourselves as boys and girls, men and women, develops as we interact with other members of our society. We become who we are, reflect upon our lives, and change over the years, all in the context of our relationships with significant and not-so-significant others and the culture in which we are immersed. In other words, gender involves social processes as well as individual identities.

Culture is expressed through a number of social institutions – large-scale forms of social organization that influence what we do and how we think about our place in society. These include governments and their laws, the family in all its permutations, medicine, religion, literature, the news media, the paid and unpaid work we engage in, the education system in which we learn to think about the world, and the forms of popular culture we enjoy or react against (see, for instance, Chapter 13, 'Believing: Religion'; Chapter 14, 'Educating'; Chapter 17, 'Informing: Media'). As the wider culture and the social circles in which we move change over time, so too do our expectations about society and our relationship to it. Social change is a key concern for sociologists of gender, as it is for sociologists in general. We are interested in how and why gendered activities and expectations have changed in recent decades, for example. Sociologists take a critical stance towards these questions, challenging taken-for-granted assumptions, asking why things are the way they are and how they might change under particular circumstances.

By now it will be obvious that there are many interrelated factors involved in a sociological analysis of gender. We are concerned not only with individuals, but also the different institutions and processes through which gender might be reproduced (the family, the media and so on). Gender implicates individuals, groups and larger patterns of social interaction and behaviour. In order to explore these in more detail, we might break down our analysis of gender into three interrelated approaches: gender as a *difference*, gender as a *division*, and gender as something we *do*.

First, what does it mean to think of boys and girls, men and women as 'different'? A number of ways of conceptualizing difference have been influential in sociology, including the notion of gender 'roles' and the distinction between 'sex' and 'gender'. Second, gender gains its social importance in part because men and women are distinguished from each other in ways that involve relations of power. These include hierarchical divisions between men and women ('patriarchy'), and between men ('hegemonic masculinity'). Third, although gendered relationships reflect the larger structures and processes of society, as individuals we also 'do' 'femininity' or 'masculinity' (or both) in our everyday lives. The following discussion takes each of these three aspects of gender and explores it in greater detail, while the conclusion briefly considers how we might bring these three approaches together in a multi-faceted sociology of gender.

Gender as a difference

'Men and women are different.' This idea has long held sway within popular understandings of gender and its place in society. But what does it mean, exactly? It would be easy to assume its obviousness if we presume that 'being a man' or 'being a woman' is a stable state determined directly by 'natural' processes. However, sociologists have long struggled with the notion that men and women are members of unchanging and unchangeable 'natural' categories.

During the Second World War women took up traditionally male jobs, such as factory work, farming and non-combatant military roles, while large numbers of men were engaged in armed combat on the battlefields. In the shadow of these wartime disruptions to the gender order, Czechoslovakian-born author Viola Klein challenged the idea that masculinity and femininity were immutable states of being. Instead, she wrote in her 1946 book *The Feminine Character: History of an Ideology* that they involved *roles*: expectations about which behaviours, aptitudes and spheres of action were suitable for men and women. Klein argued that gender roles are shaped within human societies:

> As people generally tend to live up to what is expected of them, it seems important to expose the particular set of views held in our culture with regard to woman's social role, characteristic traits and psychological attributes. These views [are] transmitted by custom, social attitudes, public opinion … But this cultural pattern itself is far from static. In our own civilization it has been subjected to radical changes, particularly during the last century. (1946, p. 1)

Thus, the work, emotions, leisure, talk and so on associated with boys and girls, men and women, express the gender roles transmitted through society and acted out by the individuals within it. These mirror broader social changes, and shift over time. Klein quoted various anthropological studies in order to argue that roles and expectations differ cross-culturally, too. She argued that while members of some tribal societies expect that men will be domineering hunters, women take a leading role in some other cultures, and in others both sexes play a significant, co-operative role in tasks such as child raising (Klein, 1946, p. 131).

Together with Alva Myrdal, Klein went on to explore changing social expectations about married women's social roles in the post-war years: ought they to remain in the home, or might they enter the paid workforce? Myrdal and Klein (1956) argued the latter, suggesting that an increase in the numbers of married women in paid employment would result in an improved range of options for women and a more productive economy overall.

In the post-war decades men's roles were investigated less than women's, but the lives of men were not totally immune from scrutiny. Helen Hacker (1957) and Ruth Hartley (1959) suggested that social changes led to 'role strain' for men. Women were entering the paid workforce in increasing numbers, and some men took this as a challenge to the male 'breadwinner' ideal (see Chapter 18, 'Relating: Family'). At the same time as the man's erstwhile status as the sole economic provider was coming under challenge, in the home he was now expected to be more emotive and democratic. Hacker wrote that he had 'lost the security of the old *paterfamilias*, who was the autocrat of the breakfast table, and experiences difficulties in establishing a satisfying new role' (Hacker, 1957, p. 230). Moreover, his status as a mediator between the community affairs of the outside world and the inner sanctum of the family was eroded by the advent of radio, television and women's social and political organizations. Men's roles, it was suggested, were becoming increasingly uncertain in the face of social change in general and 'women's emancipation' in particular.

Women, it was argued, were also having difficulty adjusting to the 'feminine role' laid out for them, and Betty Friedan explored this problem in the context of suburban life in the United States of American during the 1950s. She suggested that many women felt 'trapped' at home, and experienced feelings of emptiness and a lack of self while tirelessly devoting their time to the care of others. The 'feminine role', Friedan argued, offered too few options for women, and was defined almost exclusively in terms of household matters: 'wife, mistress, mother, nurse, consumer, cook, chauffeur; expert on interior decoration, child care, appliance repair, furniture refinishing, nutrition, and education' (Friedan, 1965, p. 28). During the following decades, sociologists remained critical of the narrowness of the gender roles on offer. Like Friedan, Klein, Hacker and Hartley before them, Fenwick, Novitz and Waghorne (1977, p. 116) argued for the loosening of rigid expectations about women's and men's respective places in society. They noted that those who deviated from traditional sex roles were often seen as unusual at best, or pathologically disordered at worst.

As we can see, some social commentators questioned the rigidity of gender roles by suggesting that society might offer a much wider range of roles to both women and men. Others proposed a separation between 'sex' and 'gender' (Oakley, 1972). In this model, 'sex' referred to those biological characteristics, such as chromosomes (XX or XY), genitalia, breast and beard development, that make us female or male. 'Gender' denoted the roles and appearances we enact in our lives that mark us out as feminine or masculine, girls or boys, women or men. Although we are born with either a male or female sex, it was argued, we have to be 'socialized', trained into either a 'feminine' or 'masculine' gender, as we grow up. Therefore, while our maleness or femaleness were assumed to be biologically fixed, new ways of being men and women remained possible because masculinity and femininity might be reinterpreted and modified.

Ironically, although this distinction between sex and gender has gradually become influential outside of sociology, it has lost its appeal within the discipline (Delphy, 1993). Why is this? There are three main reasons. First, the biological distinctions denoted by the term 'sex' are not always as clear-cut as we might think. Chromosomal patterns are sometimes more complex than a simple XY or XX; some people have genitalia that look ambiguous and do not allow an easy classification into either a male or a female category. It has been argued that such 'intersexed' individuals demonstrate how the process of assigning a sex to a body is actually a social rather than a biological one (Kessler, 1998). If it is not always clear whether an individual can be classified as 'male' or 'female', then how enduring is such a distinction? The social character of this attribution process becomes clear when such classifications are not obvious and decisions need to be made.

Second, our bodies are always experienced in social contexts, and so their biological properties can be constrained and modified through social norms surrounding food, comportment and exercise (Guillaumin, 1993). Therefore, bodies are fundamentally affected by the societies in which they are maintained and transformed. For example, through athletics training women's and men's bodies can become capable of feats of strength, agility and endurance that could not be achieved without that training. What training is available to whom is, in turn, a product of expectations about what is socially acceptable for which bodies: often men rather than women have been seen as the 'proper' recipients of heavy training regimes. As Alison Jaggar (1992, p. 84) suggests, the rate 'at which women's athletic records are being broken and the speed at which women's bodies have changed even over the last decade shows that in the past, social norms have limited the way in which women fulfilled their genetic potential, so that we have no idea of the extent of that potential'. The distinction between biological 'sex' and social 'gender' starts to lose its grip once we recognize the very real impact of social and technological forces upon basic biological capabilities.

Third, the ways we understand biology – and therefore 'maleness' and 'femaleness' themselves – are deeply affected by social presumptions (see Chapter 10, 'Sexualizing'). Scientific knowledge is itself gendered, and powerful ideas from our culture are smuggled consciously or unconsciously into investigations of the biological body (Bleier, 1984). For example, the way many biologists describe the process of conception owes much to gendered assumptions that maleness is active and conquering, but that femaleness is languid and passive. In many medical textbooks, for instance,

> The egg is seen as large and passive. It 'is swept' or 'drifts' along the fallopian tube ... [the sperm in contrast are] 'streamlined' and invariably active ... they have a 'velocity' that is often remarked upon ... they need 'energy' and 'fuel' so that with a 'whiplash movement and strong lurches', they can 'burrow through the egg coat' and 'penetrate' it. [Some writers] liken the egg's role to that of Sleeping Beauty: 'a dormant bride awaiting her mate's magic kiss, which instills the spirit that brings her to life'. (Martin, 1991, pp. 489, 490)

In this discussion of such representations of human conception, Emily Martin makes the point that although bodies and bodily processes are undoubtedly 'real' in one way, they come to make sense to us only when we interpret them. In doing so, she argues, we take up what we think we already know about masculinity and femininity. This, in turn, affects how we think about bodily processes.

In summary, decisions about what biology 'is', and where it stops and 'society' starts, are themselves affected by social beliefs and norms. Where we draw the line between the two depends on the frameworks of knowledge that guide us in our attempt, because what we 'see' is conditioned by what we expect to see. This is important for a discussion of sex and gender, because it means that judgements about which attributes 'belong' with (biological) sex and which 'belong' with (social) gender depend upon the ways knowledge is socially constructed. Therefore, it is difficult to separate biology from society. In this sense, the sex/gender distinction over-simplifies complex social – and hence political – processes. So, how else might we think of gender 'difference'?

Gender as a division

To summarize so far, most sociologists agree that 'differences' between men and women are not 'natural', and that the precise character of these varies across time and between cultures and contexts. This is not to say that we must dispense entirely with the notion of difference. Instead, we can understand it as a sociological reality in the sense that social inequalities divide men from women and men from each other, and constitute them as 'different' in the process. Although there is nothing immutable or eternal about these divisions, in their current form they play a significant part in the lives of actual women and men. Difference, then, is not a matter of inherent distinctions between people. Instead, 'men' and 'women' owe their very existence to the social hierarchies in which they are located.

One key term used in feminist sociology to describe gender inequality is 'patriarchy'. Traditionally used to refer to the rule of older male heads of households over women and younger men, in recent decades the term has been employed within sociology to describe how men of any age establish and maintain dominance over women. Some have suggested that the term implies a lack of historical change in gender relations and leads to an over-simplified analysis of social inequality (for example, Pollert, 1996). However, Walby (1990) has reworked the concept of patriarchy by suggesting that it can be divided into six related 'structures': paid employment, household production, culture, sexuality, violence and the state. This is a useful approach, because it allows us to examine gender inequality systematically and manageably.

In terms of paid employment, Walby (1986) argues that women, particularly those who are married, have historically been excluded from paid work on the grounds that men should be their household's breadwinner. In recent decades, the situation has become more complex. In general, men tend to be clustered in the jobs which are highest paying and those that offer the best prospects for autonomy and promotion (Tomaskovic-Devey, 1993). Even in those areas of the labour force where women predominate, such as in service work, men earn the highest wages and occupy the most senior positions.

Pay differentials may exist even where men and women carry out exactly the same tasks. In her study of British telephonists, Janet Siltanen (1994) found that the members of the predominantly male night shift were paid at a higher rate than women who answered the phones during the daytime. She suggests that men have not infrequently sought to maintain gendered wage differentials, supporting equal pay only if it looks as though large numbers of women might enter the workplace and threaten to replace the more highly paid male workers. Within many multinational corporations in newly developing countries, labour forces tend to be highly segregated by gender. Women are seen as a source of low-cost labour, particularly in the garment industry, as Juanita Elias (2004) demonstrates in her study of clothing workers in Malaysia who make items for the British market.

Sociologists of work argue that inequality is demonstrated not only by wage levels, but also by how work is valued more generally. For example, caring and customer service work tends to be carried out mostly by women and is generally afforded negligible social status and lower wages than those sectors of the labour force that employ predominantly male workers. It has also been argued that because status is gendered, in industries where large numbers of women workers displace male workers, the status of the jobs starts to decline (Tomaskovic-Devey, 1993, p. 10). As we can see, questions of inequality in the workplace are a matter of complex social processes, rather than the result of particular individuals' traditional attitudes to men's and women's social roles.

Women also carry out more unpaid labour than men, especially in the household. Even where all adult members of a household work for pay outside the home, women do most of the housework as well. This situation is known as the 'double burden' (see Chapter 18, 'Relating: Family').The fact that many women spend a lot of time outside the paid labour force dramatically affects their total income across the time span. Brian Roper (2005) has suggested that some of these inequalities are closely related to the way capitalism works: if women carry out child care and household labour for free, wages paid to male employees can be lower than they would be if all domestic labour had to be purchased on the open market. So, the capitalist economic system has a vested interest in devaluing – or not valuing – women's unpaid work (Waring, 1988).

Walby suggests that men are privileged over women in respect of other social structures. Our culture encodes a diverse set of patriarchal practices: men's contributions to literature and art are often valued over women's, and men occupy dominant positions within religion and the news media. A further example involves the sexualization of women in advertising and computer animation, where they frequently appear in submissive poses that men very rarely adopt. Within the realm of sexual relations, a 'sexual double standard' allows men more sexual activity than women

FEELING: EMOTIONS • BELIEVING: RELIGION • EDUCATING • STRAYING: DEVIANCE • MEDIATING: TECHNOLOGY • INFORMING: MEDIA • RELATING: FAMILY • BELONGING: COMMUNITY • FINISHING

9   201

without being subject to the kinds of social judgements made of their female counterparts. In popular writings on sex – such as John Gray's 'Mars and Venus' series – men are frequently portrayed as active desirers and orchestrators, while women appear as passive and awaiting direction (Potts, 2002). This type of division between actively desiring men and sexually passive women is also frequently encoded in new cultural forms such as cyber-pornography (Streitmatter, 2004, p. 218). Such beliefs about female sexual passivity can, as a set of British studies on young people's sexuality concluded (Holland et al., 1992), sometimes make it difficult for women to negotiate safe and pleasurable sex in relationships with men.

Walby's two remaining structures of patriarchy are violence and the state. Violence may take the form of domestic beatings, rape, sexual harassment or sexual assault. Feminist sociologists regard male violence as a systemic social problem, not merely something carried out by a few psychologically maladjusted men. They argue that violence requires a certain social legitimacy in order to take hold (Hamner and Maynard, 1987). Even when not directly exercised, the threat of violence may cause women to practise self-surveillance and alter their conduct and patterns of movement. Most sociologists argue that the state holds a monopoly over legitimate coercion. It is gendered in its structure: for the most part men hold positions of authority, and women in powerful government positions are exceptions rather than the rule. In addition, the state's actions have effects that are differentiated by gender. For instance, cutbacks to social welfare programmes disproportionately disadvantage women, who do most of the unpaid caring for others and must pick up the burden, even when their own incomes are reduced (Else, 1996).

Although men are generally advantaged in relation to women, they too must negotiate prevailing forms of masculinity and the social expectations that accompany these. R. W. Connell (1987) coined the term 'hegemonic masculinity' to describe the form of masculinity that occupies a dominant position in society, and affects the lives of individual men and women. The term 'hegemony' is Antonio Gramsci's, and refers to the process by which people are ruled by consent rather than brute force. Therefore, Connell suggests that hegemonic masculinity relies on a broad social consensus about which forms of masculinity are the most socially desirable.

What is hegemonic, however, changes over time. Connell has

suggested that traditional masculinities based on a hard day's labour and physical confrontations with others have largely been replaced by newly hegemonic forms. The growth of capitalist enterprise and the legal and regulatory apparatuses that accompany them have created new masculinities, such as the competitive businessman and the bureaucrat. Connell argues that today's hegemonic masculinity is more technocratic than confrontationist, and is defined by rationality and expertise rather than physical force (Connell, 1993). This often involves a formality of both attire and human relationships, and the close control of one's emotions and actions (Whitehead, 1999). The emphasis on physicality has not entirely disappeared, as the kudos still granted to rough and risky male sports attests.

As this discussion demonstrates, hegemonic masculinity is not a static or unchanging phenomenon. Instead, it is a variable 'state of play' that might be contested or challenged by other forms of masculinity (Connell, 1987, p. 184). For instance, family-centred masculinities may sometimes dilute the competitive, technocratic forms, especially when men make conscious decisions to prioritize domestic responsibilities over career advancement (Whitehead, 1999). To give a second example, gay masculinities offer to rework male identity by challenging the prevailing assumption that a man's masculinity depends upon his involvement in sexual relationships with women (Nardi, 2000). Differences of class, ethnicity and ability also mean that men's experiences vary. A number of authors have explored the complex ways in which black masculinities relate to white masculinities as well as to white and black femininities. Allen (1999) argues that in education, for instance, black men in the USA tend to be marginalized within the education system and elsewhere relative to white men. Respondents to his study on higher education reported 'unfavourable campus racial climates characterized by serious racial conflict, racial separation, and low sensitivity to Blacks' concerns' (Allen, 1999, p. 206). This said, black and white women have differently gendered experiences, and Carbado (1999) adds that black women's disadvantage tends to attract less critical attention than black men's.

Ironically, hegemonic masculine ideals (the sporting hero or the corporate raider, for instance) do not necessarily reflect the lives of the majority of men, even many of those who aspire to them. For instance,

FEELING: EMOTIONS • BELIEVING: RELIGION • EDUCATING • STRAYING: DEVIANCE • MEDIATING: TECHNOLOGY • INFORMING: MEDIA • RELATING: FAMILY • BELONGING: COMMUNITY • FINISHING

203

not every man can represent his country on the international sporting stage. Also, although a certain stoicism remains an ideal masculine trait, it sometimes masks feelings of fear, insecurity and uncertainty. Clearly, the relationship between wider social processes and individual men's – as well as women's – lives are relatively complex.

Gender as 'doing'

When we analyse gender as a social division we work on a large scale, examining social processes and power relations in the widest sense. However, our discussion of hegemonic masculinity indicates that what is going on at the individual level is also important. Therefore, some sociologists focus upon exploring how we produce and express gender in everyday life. Two related schools of thought have been influential here: ethno-methodology, the study of the methods people use to carry out their everyday lives; and symbolic interactionism, the examination of the ways social relationships influence the meanings we make of the world around us. Both of these approaches suggest that our sense of who we 'are' is primarily the result of what we 'do' within our social settings.

Two well-known North American authors developed such ideas in relation to gender: Erving Goffman and Harold Garfinkel. Goffman argued that our sense of ourselves as men or women is heavily influenced by the ways we manage impressions of ourselves to those around us (Goffman, 1969, p. 26). He suggested that we all want to present or perform gender in ways that gain a favourable reception from others. The term 'perform' is quite deliberate, because Goffman used the theatre as a metaphor to explain how we present ourselves to others. Our gender 'performances' involve 'frontstage' and 'backstage' zones, just like in a theatre. Each of us performs publicly, up 'front' and under the scrutiny of others, after we have prepared ourselves and practised our technique out 'back', away from prying eyes. So, while we might 'appear' as an acceptably gendered man or woman out in the street, the pub or the lecture theatre, we first prepare our appearance, emotions and deportment in our own living room and in front of the bathroom mirror (see Chapter 11, 'Being: Identity').

In adopting such an analysis, sociologists manage a delicate balance between constraint and freedom. On the one hand, we see that the specific ways in which we perform our genders are not fully constrained by societal ideals and directives, so it is possible for us to resist the expectations placed upon us in particular times and places to some extent. On the other hand, this is not a matter of complete freedom. For example, in his work on gender and advertising, Goffman suggested that our gender performances are limited somewhat by the 'schedules' society makes available to guide our 'portrayals of gender' (Goffman, 1979, p. 8). Put simply, ways of being 'feminine' or 'masculine' are made available to us by our cultures, and these are adopted, modified or resisted by each of us as we 'do' our gender.

Garfinkel elaborated upon this idea. He suggested that we are expected to adhere to the codes of appearance, activities, talk, dress, attitudes and emotions considered appropriate for our gender (Garfinkel, 1967, pp. 123–5). For example, some occupations are coded feminine (nurse, florist) and others masculine (firefighter, construction worker); rules govern what men and women can wear in particular situations; and women are often assumed to be more empathetic and men to be stoic and competitive.

None of this is to say that we all 'do' our gender in the same way, nor that we wholeheartedly embrace the social expectations to which we are subjected. Shirley Tate's (1999) study of female weightlifters, for instance, explores how such 'body projects' provide women with ways of reworking conventional notions of femininity. Tate suggests that while weightlifting women are to some degree constrained by the category of 'feminine woman', they can do feminine embodiment in new ways that provide a pleasurable and empowering sense of strength and control over their bodies and their lives. Although these women have to carefully tread a line between a socially acceptable muscularity and less accepted notions of 'butchness', Tate argues, weight training does provide some possibilities for transgressing prevailing modes of doing gender.

Goffman and Garfinkel both suggest that 'maleness' and 'femaleness' are social accomplishments. By this they mean that people usually strive to present themselves to others as coherently and 'properly' gendered. Over time this becomes a matter of routine, and we 'do' our masculinity or femininity without consciously thinking about the processes involved (Garfinkel, 1967, p. 181). As a consequence, the deliberate accomplishment of gender disappears from view, and we adopt what Garfinkel calls the 'natural attitude'. Because most in society assume a certain inevitability towards the way the majority of men and women 'do' their gender, those with an idiosyncratic gender presentation are not considered 'real' men or women. They might be thought improper or 'unnatural', and subject to negative comment or even ostracism.

Such widespread assumptions about gendered 'nature' indicate that there is a moral aspect to the way gender is created and presented (Garfinkel, 1967, p. 124). Both Goffman and Garfinkel challenged taken-for-granted ideas about 'naturalness', and developed a sophisticated critique of the very idea that particular ways of doing gender are 'natural'. First, Goffman never adopted a distinction between sex and gender, rejecting the idea that we could easily distinguish between 'biological' and 'social' aspects of maleness and femaleness. Instead, he argued that the division of each individual body into one of two sexes is itself the result of social practices such as naming and talk (one example would be the phrase 'It's a girl!' uttered at birth) (see Chapter 10, 'Sexualizing').

Second, Goffman argued that such naming practices do not reflect any pre-existing 'natural' difference, but produce the very notion that gender differences are somehow biological rather than social in the first place (Goffman, 1977, pp. 319, 324). 'Nature', then, is an idea rather than an absolute. Goffman's writing is interesting in its reversal of the way 'naturalness' and gender are usually thought about. He wanted to consider *how* we come to believe that particular ideas about gender are natural, rather than ask *what* 'is' or 'is not' natural about men and women as we currently know them.

More recently, other authors have expanded Goffman's and Garfinkel's ideas about the ways we 'do' gender. In their article titled 'Doing Gender', Don West and Candace Zimmerman (1991) agree that gender can be seen as a routine, methodical and recurring accomplishment, guided by social expectations and notions that particular ways of doing gender are the most 'natural'. They add that though we 'do gender' in the actual presence of others, we are likely to continue with many of the same behaviours even when nobody else is present. This is partly because our modes of talking, walking and acting 'like a woman' or 'like a man' become ingrained, as Garfinkel pointed out, but also because we are always regulating our own behaviour to make sure we are doing our gender correctly. We exercise surveillance over ourselves in private as well as in public, in order to ensure the consistency of our presentation. After all, when each of us goes out into the world, we must ensure our competence by appearing as a 'culturally correct' boy or girl, man or woman. Why is this so? To do gender is to risk being assessed by others of doing it incorrectly, and being called to account. In turn, our adherence to overarching cultural standards of gender competence reinforces the idea that particular modes of gender expression (emotiveness, attentiveness, stoicism, competitiveness, aggression) are somehow 'natural' for men or for women.

Ways of 'doing gender' have changed over time. Women can now wear trousers and work on construction sites; more men teach in primary schools and push prams along the street than they did 20 or even 10 years ago. Meanwhile, 'metrosexual' men look neater and smell sweeter than their predecessors, and women's rugby or extreme sports are no longer unheard of. Gendered patterns of alcohol consumption are changing as notions of femininity and masculinity change, and members of both genders can adopt a gay, lesbian or polysexual identity more openly than at any time in the past. This is not to say, of course, that there are no longer clear patterns in gendered expectations, or that inequalities have disappeared.

Conclusion

We always live our lives with a sense of ourselves and others as gendered beings, because expressions of gender occupy every corner of our society. They may circulate at the most mundane level of the everyday: how we walk down the street, who drives the car and in what manner, who cooks our dinner, and who cleans up afterwards. Similarly, gendered practices are embedded in less common situations: weddings, televised election campaigns, street marches, music festivals, high school dances, sporting events. Everybody in these places appears to have a gender, and most often behaves in ways that accord with social expectations of that gender.

Our focus on what happens in these situations depends on our particular sociological viewpoint. Some of us focus on the roles that are assumed to characterize men's and women's lives; others examine the inequalities that persist within paid and unpaid work, culture, the state and so on; while others are particularly interested in how we 'do' gender in ways that mark us out as credible, competent men and women. Very few of us assume that how we imagine gender now is the same as how it was imagined in the past or will be in the future. For sociologists, gendered performances and relationships vary over time as a response to social contestation and broad economic and cultural changes.

The complexities of gender, as we experience them in our own society at the start of the twenty-first century, demonstrate the usefulness of examining the different aspects of gender together. Men and women are faced with different expectations about gender roles, although we ought not to neglect the relationships between roles and questions of power. In this way, discussions of patriarchy and hegemonic masculinity can add useful insights to a gender role analysis. Similarly, as we enact roles we perform our genders in particular ways: gender roles might be seen as things we 'do' rather than as an expression of what we 'are'. In turn, some of these performances accord with dominant relations of power, while other performances resist or contest widespread social expectations. As we consider the complex interrelationships between different aspects of gender, we can also bear in mind gender's intersection with class, sexuality, ethnicity, age, geographical location and so on.

Without a doubt, gender is complex. Notions that 'men and women are different', that 'gender differences are natural', or even that 'everybody knows' what a man or a woman 'is', belie these complexities. Complexity need not be a problem: as sociologists, we can explore the nuances, contradictions and changes in the social organization of gender by breaking it down into its many components. In this way, we can start to think more systematically and critically, and a whole new world opens up to us. The sociological study of gender is as fascinating as it is multi-layered.

Suggestions for further reading

Connell, R. W. (2002) *Gender* (Cambridge: Polity Press).
Delamont, S. (2003) *Feminist Sociology* (London: Sage).
Jackson, S. and S. Scott (2002) *Gender: A Sociological Reader* (London: Routledge).
Kimmel, M. (2004) *The Gendered Society* (New York: Oxford University Press).

Bibliography

Allen, W. (1999) 'Missing in Action: Race, Gender, and Black Students' Educational Opportunities', in D. Carbado (ed.), *Black Men on Race, Gender, and Sexuality* (New York: New York University Press).
Bleier, R. (1984) *Science and Gender: A Critique of Biology and Its Theories on Women* (New York: Pergamon).
Carbado, D. (1999) 'Introduction: Where and When Black Men Enter', in D. Carbado (ed.), *Black Men on Race, Gender, and Sexuality* (New York: New York University Press).
Connell, R. W. (1987) *Gender and Power* (Cambridge: Polity Press).
Connell, R. W. (1993) 'The Big Picture: Masculinities in Recent World History', *Theory and Society* 22, pp. 597–623.
Delphy, C. (1993) 'Rethinking Sex and Gender', *Women's Studies International Forum* 16(1), pp. 1–9.
Elias, J. (2004) *Fashioning Inequality: The Multinational Company and Gendered Employment in a Globalizing World* (Aldershot: Ashgate).
Else, A. (1996) *False Economy: New Zealanders Face the Conflict between Paid and Unpaid Work* (Auckland: Tandem).
Fenwick, P., R. Novitz and M. Waghorne (1977) 'Symposium on Sex Roles and Sexuality: Introduction', *Australian and New Zealand Journal of Sociology* 13, pp. 116–18.
Friedan, B. (1965) *The Feminine Mystique* (New York: Penguin).
Garfinkel, H. (1967) *Studies in Ethnomethodology* (Englewood Cliffs, NJ: Prentice Hall).
Goffman, E. (1969) *The Presentation of Self in Everyday Life* (London: Penguin).
Goffman, E. (1977) 'The Arrangement between the Sexes', *Theory and Society* 4(3), pp. 301–31.
Goffman, E. (1979) *Gender Advertisements* (London: Macmillan).
Guillaumin, C. (1993) 'The Constructed Body', in C. Burroughs and J.

FEELING: EMOTIONS • BELIEVING: RELIGION • EDUCATING • STRAYING: DEVIANCE •
MEDIATING: TECHNOLOGY • INFORMING: MEDIA • RELATING: FAMILY • BELONGING: COMMUNITY • FINISHING

9   209

Ehrenreich (eds), *Reading the Social Body* (Iowa: University of Iowa Press).

Hacker, H. (1957) 'The New Burdens of Masculinity', *Marriage and Family Living* 19, pp. 227–33.

Hamner, J. and M. Maynard (eds) (1987) *Women, Violence and Social Control* (London: Macmillan).

Hartley, R. (1959) 'Sex-role Pressures and the Socialization of the Male Child', *Psychological Reports* 5, pp. 457–68.

Holland, J., C. Ramazanoglu, S. Sharpe and R. Thomson (1992) 'Pleasure, Pressure and Power: Some Contradictions of Gendered Sexuality', *Sociological Review* 40, pp. 645–74.

Jaggar, A. (1992) 'Human Biology in Feminist Theory: Sexual Inequality Reconsidered', in S. Himmelweit (ed.), *Knowing Women: Feminism and Knowledge* (Cambridge: Polity Press).

Kessler, S. (1998) *Lessons from the Intersexed* (New Brunswick, NJ: Rutgers University Press).

Klein, V. (1946) *The Feminine Character: History of an Ideology* (London: Kegan Paul).

Martin, E. (1991) 'The Egg and the Sperm', *Signs* 16, pp. 485–501.

Myrdal, A. and V. Klein (1956) *Women's Two Roles: Home and Work* (London: Routledge and Kegan Paul).

Nardi, P. (2000) 'Anything for a Sis, Mary: an Introduction to Gay Masculinities', in P. Nardi (ed.), *Gay Masculinities* (Thousand Oaks, CA: Sage).

Oakley, A. (1972) *Sex, Gender and Society* (New York: Harper Colophon).

Pollert, A. (1996) 'Gender and Class Revisited: or, the Poverty of "Patriarchy"', *Sociology* 30, pp. 639–59.

Potts, A. (2002) *The Science/Fiction of Sex: Feminist Deconstruction and the Vocabularies of Heterosex* (London: Routledge).

Roper, B. (2005) *Towards Prosperity or Poverty? The Keynesian Era, Neoliberal Restructuring and the Third Way in New Zealand* (Palmerston North, NZ: Dunmore).

Siltanen, J. (1994) *Locating Gender: Occupational Segregation, Wages and Domestic Responsibilities* (London: UCL Press).

Streitmatter, R. (2004) *Sex Sells! The Media's Journey from Repression to Obsession* (Boulder, CO: Westview).

Tate, S. (1999) 'Making Your Body Your Signature: Weight-training and Transgressive Femininities', in S. Roseneil and J. Seymour (eds), *Practising Identities: Power and Resistance* (Basingstoke: Macmillan).

Tomaskovic-Devey, D. (1993) *Gender and Racial Inequality at Work* (New York: ILR Press).

Walby, S. (1986) *Patriarchy at Work* (Cambridge: Polity Press).

DOING RESEARCH • MODERNIZING • WORKING • CONSUMING • TRADING • STRATIFYING: CLASS • COVERNING: POWER • RACIALIZING • **GENDERING** • SEXUALIZING • BEING: IDENTITY •

Walby, S. (1990) *Theorizing Patriarchy* (Oxford: Blackwell).

Waring, M. (1988) *If Women Counted: A New Feminist Economics* (San Francisco, CA: Harper & Row).

West, D. and C. Zimmerman (1991) 'Doing Gender', in J. Lorber and S. Farrell (eds), *The Social Construction of Gender* (Thousand Oaks, CA: Sage).

Whitehead, S. (1999) 'Contingent Masculinities: Disruptions to 'Man'agerialist Identity', in S. Roseneil and J. Seymour (eds), *Practising Identities: Power and Resistance* (Basingstoke: Macmillan).

FEELING: EMOTIONS • BELIEVING: RELIGION • EDUCATING • STRAYING: DEVIANCE •
MEDIATING: TECHNOLOGY • INFORMING: MEDIA • RELATING: FAMILY • BELONGING: COMMUNITY • FINISHING

9   211

10 sexualizing

Michael Stevens

KEY
POINTS

- Human sexual behaviour is a complex and nuanced field. The social patterning of it over time has shown great variety, rather than following one particular 'natural' paradigm.

- Sociology examines how modern society benefits from particular forms of sexual patterning and privileges them over others.

- The dominant heteronormative model privileges the monogamous heterosexual couple as the family unit and as a key social element in providing capitalism with a stable unit capable of producing more workers and consumers.

- Societies based on the three Abrahamic religions (Judaism, Christianity and Islam) tend to show a much more restrictive attitude to sexuality than others.

- The sociology of sexuality has tended to focus on those groups that fall outside the norms and seeks to explain why modern societies regulate sexuality in particular ways.

- The study of homosexuality in particular has provided fertile ground for examining sexuality in a sociological manner as a whole.

- Sexuality has become one of the key flashpoints in contemporary society as some groups seek to claim full moral and legal equality that others do not wish them to have.

- The original push for gay liberation grew out of the same historical and social impetus that drove the civil rights and feminist movements in the developed world.

- Today many now base the call for equality of homosexuals around a neo-liberal version of the self that locates the person first and foremost as a tax-paying consumer rather than as a member of a socially oppressed minority.

- Some academic theorists have worked to place sexuality as a social marker equivalent to the more traditional sociological categories of class, race, gender and age.

- They have developed the idea of 'queer', encompassing all non-heteronormative forms of sexuality, as a new way of seeing human sexuality.

Introduction

Sex is for many one of the greater pleasures of being alive. Sex with a loved partner is valued and extolled in most societies today – and has been through time and history – as one of the great and fulfilling experiences of human existence (see Chapter 12, 'Feeling: Emotions'). The sexual act between a man and a woman has, until the advent of new technologies, been absolutely necessary to ensure the continuation of the species. Sexual desire and love is a strong motivator for individual action and how this motivation is expressed and patterned is reflected in social organization. The collective history of humanity is layered with stories based around happy – or more often unhappy – tales of how these forces can come into play and the consequences they carry in their wake. The story of Helen of Troy has been famous in Western culture for millennia (Homer, 1960), as has the love of Leyla and Mejnun in Turkic culture (Fuzuli, 1970) or Zhang Junrui and Cui Yingying in classical Chinese culture (Xu, 1992). The example of the lovers Harmodius and Aristogeiton in classical Athens, who were revered for overthrowing the Peisistratid tyranny in 514 bce, shows us these stories were not only based around the love of men for women (Crompton, 2003, pp. 25–8).

What is central to these stories is how they reflect the societal mores of their time. They tell us about the sexual patterns and behaviours that were accepted, praised, idealized, tolerated, winked at, condemned or rejected. A close examination of them reveals a wealth of variety and numerous points of convergence and divergence between cultures and societies.

How human sexuality is expressed and patterned has been the subject of regulation in societies over centuries. This regulation has typically been based in religious understandings of the world and society and the proper and divinely sanctioned roles of men and women (see Chapter 13,

'Believing: Religion', and Chapter 9, 'Gendering'). However, it should be borne in mind that what is officially sanctioned by approved societal teachings and what is practised by the population at large have often been at variance. We can see here evidence of a private culture versus a public one. Although we are all aware of the rules that exist, we recognize that there are times when we and those around us do not follow them. If sexual behaviour in societies followed all the societal rules laid out for it, then how much less complex, yet also how much poorer, our societies, cultures and individual lives would be.

In this quest to regulate and control and also to celebrate what is acceptable sexual behaviour – and to limit and punish what is not – we gain an insight into understandings of religion, science and health, of property rights, of gender relations, of age and class, and of how the entire world of the social is conceived. Sexuality is a fundamental force in how our societies are structured and in how we live in them. For example, Jenkins mentions the fact that in many societies in Papua New Guinea adultery is considered a more serious crime than murder (Jenkins, 1997, p. 372). Any glance through the news media will also show us how often sexual acts that fall outside socially accepted norms are the cause for extreme reaction in modernized societies as well.

What interests us as sociologists is how these patterns of human sexual behaviour have been shaped and reformed by the modern world, the world shaped by the Industrial Revolution and its great motor, the capitalist economy. Sociology's arena is the modern world and a core part of sociology is the way that modernity has shaped and shifted social patterns as a result of the changes brought about by the economic, political, social and technological advances of the last 200 years. Social patterns and, with them, the accepted sexual patterns of Western society have been dramatically reshaped and reformulated in this period – the intense urban environments that have become one of the most obvious identifying forces of the modern developed world. Industrialization demanded a new concentration of urban population and concomitant shifts in labour relations and this had a marked effect on all our social relations including our sexual life (see Chapter 2, 'Modernizing').

Sexuality has become a central area of social theory and debate over the last century. The term 'sexuality' itself is scarcely more than a century old. Although a wide variety of sexual practices have been recognized in all human societies across time, the study of sexuality as an academic area is very much a product of the modern Western world (Herdt, 1984, 1997; Foucault, 1990; Hinsch, 1990; Weeks, 1991; Treat, 1999; Crompton, 2003). A cursory study of the literature available on the topic today shows how vast the field has become in a short time. What was once an area surrounded by taboos and not fit for speech or print has become a major site of production in both academic and general contexts. To understand the context and appreciate the vast changes that have occurred in modernized societies, we need to consider the historical background and place of sexuality in the pre-modern world.

In Western societies, strongly influenced by Christian teaching and thought for the last two millennia, the social aspect of the sexual has been, until very recently, dictated largely by the thoughts and teachings of the Church, whether explicitly stated or not. The Christian Church, strongly shaped by the writings of the Apostle Paul, and later St Augustine of Hippo, has had a largely negative attitude to the body and to sexuality throughout its history. The body is the site of sin and corruption, and it is the soul and the afterlife that matters. The female body is especially dangerous because it was Eve who lured Adam into temptation and is responsible for humanity's fall from grace into the state of sin. This religious centring of the sexual act as the definitive rupturing event for humanity from the divine continues to echo down the years in the social attitudes expressed in these cultures. It is woman who is made to bear the blame – characterized at once as lascivious, lustful, potent, devious, dangerous and destructive yet at the same time weak, passive, ignorant and dependent upon the man, from whose rib she was made. The body, and especially the female body, led humanity away from the divine and redemption from this earthly life that ends in death. Thus in Western culture we can see sex and death as almost inextricably intertwined (Bauman, 1992).

The sexual act could only be justified if it was in the context of procreation within the bounds of marriage. This is still the official teaching of the Roman Catholic Church, hence its ban on contraception, including condom use to prevent the transmission of the HIV virus. All other sexual acts are sinful. This includes a husband and wife having sex as a means of celebrating their love for each other without the desire for children to come from this act at the time. In these terms, all sex outside marriage is of course sinful, as is masturbation, and especially homosexuality. The origins of this way of thinking can be found in St Thomas Aquinas' theology, with his attempts to make theology 'rational' by the lights of his era. He argued that the only natural and therefore legitimate and sinless form of sexual expression was for procreation; thus, all sexual acts that did not have procreation as their intention were sinful. This idea has had immense impact over the years in forming official and popular discourses on sexual behaviour and society.

As the realm of authority moved away from the Church – as Western societies modernized and secularized and the state emerged as the unifying force with the power to punish – so the categories of sexual acts were reclassified. What had been the province of religion and priests – sin, with the prospect of eternal damnation – moved instead into the realm of doctors, illness, medicine and law, and lawyers and questions of sanity and perversion (Freud, 1962; Foucault, 1990). Human sexual behaviour became subject to the great cataloguing, rationalizing project of modernity, with attempts to fit all sorts of aspects of human life and its varieties into neat organizational categories. Instead of appealing to theological categories of sin, with the threat of damnation, we can see evidence of Weber's 'iron cage' of rationality enclosing humanity. Sexual acts and the persons performing them could be classified and categorized into 'value free' varieties and schemes. Again with reference to the supposedly immutable biological rules of males and females being needed to mate, anything outside this pattern was viewed as abnormal. What is remarkable is how, as Western Europe modernized, the sexual acts that were condemned stayed the same, but the means used to justify their social exclusion and opprobrium were moved from the religious to the scientific. Heterosexual marriage was still enshrined as the ideal state. Sex outside marriage was officially frowned on, though in popular discourse winked at as fun and to be expected. Masturbation was now a sign of moral degeneracy and a site of moral panic (Friedman, 2001, pp. 86–102), and homosexuality, instead of sodomy, demanded incarceration in prison and, in some more enlightened societies, treatment to 'cure' it.

Thus were terms such as 'sadist', 'masochist' and 'transvestite' born, and the terms 'homosexual' and later still 'heterosexual'. What had once been categories of behaviour defined as sinful or not and endangering the soul now become part of individual identities that could be defined instead as natural or perverted, legal or illegal (MacCulloch, 2003, p. 622). If they were perverted or unnatural then it was only right to look for a cure for them and to seek a way to impose 'normalcy' on the deviant. The origin for such deviancy was sought in either physical or psychological illness, and correspondingly cures were also claimed. Most influential in the late Victorian era was Richard von Krafft-Ebing's classical work *Psychopathia Sexualis* (Krafft-Ebing, 1935). Monogamous heterosexuality was seen as the norm and variations from this were seen as deviant and in need of correction. Where the 'patient' (for they were suffering a sickness) could not be cured then incarceration was seen as normal. In this era women were treated for 'hysteria' – the condition of a wandering womb – and men were treated for 'spermatorrhea' and masturbation amongst other problems (Friedman, 2001). Such medical-sexual conditions have now disappeared and tell us more about the attitudes of the society that invented them than they do about the human body, desires and sexual behaviour.

While the early editions of Krafft-Ebing's work saw deviations from the heterosexual norm as curable medical abnormalities of some sort, later editions shifted to the idea that they were innate and incurable. Throughout much of the nineteenth and early twentieth centuries academic discussion around sexuality tended to focus on homosexuality as an obvious example of deviation from the norms of heterosexual behaviour. This discourse, typically framed by discussions of what it was to be a 'normal' male or female, made assumptions about masculinity and femininity that reflected standard social mores of the time. These social mores were still based in pre-modern understandings of human life.

Following on from Krafft-Ebing's work, the British sexologist Havelock Ellis (1859–1939) took a view of sexual behaviour that we would see as more recognizable today. It understood sexuality as a normal part of being human and not reducible to the simplistic categories of 'natural' and 'unnatural'. Ellis is notable as one of the first academics to consider seriously the notion that what others viewed as sexual deviations from an essential fixed biological norm were in fact social constructions. One of the ongoing points of debate in the field of sexuality has been just what deserves to be counted as 'normal' sexual behaviour and what should be excluded. The categories for establishing the grounds for this have been and continue to be contested. However, in seeking to establish taxonomies and classifications of sexual behaviour, these early sexologists at least opened the door for discussion on what had been in most societies a social taboo.

Possibly the most influential sexologist was Alfred Kinsey. He and his interviewers carried out thousands of two-hour interviews with men and women to try to gain an understanding into just what made up their sexual lives (Kinsey et al., 1948; Kinsey and Institute for Sex Research, 1965). People were asked deep questions about their sexual experiences, fantasies and desires, and the results provided some startling and important information about the sexual life of typical American men and women. His findings showed far greater variety from the accepted social norm of sexual behaviour was common, and this in turn raised questions about the validity of attempting to impose these social norms on people, and to punish those who broke them. He is perhaps most famous for his 'seven-point' scale, which rates just how attracted people are to either men or women, with someone who is a '0' rating as exclusively heterosexual, a '3' as someone who is equally homosexual and heterosexual and a '6' as someone who is exclusively homosexual (Kinsey et al., 1948, pp. 638–41). Treating sex in this explicitly scientific and positivistic manner had enormous social repercussions. If, as his results showed, many people had sexual lives that did not conform to heteronormative monogamy, then it could be argued that this social model (and the laws supporting it) was in fact deeply flawed. His research was often cited by many seeking more liberal laws around sexuality, and condemned by those who wished to preserve the status quo. Although his work has been criticized by many for both its methodology and its underlying assumptions (Irvine, 2002), its influence has been enormous.

Gender and sexuality: who do we desire and why?

In Plato's *The Symposium* Aristophanes tries to explain human sexual desire by way of a myth. In his telling, there were originally three types of human. There were males, females and hermaphrodites (those made up of an equal measure of male and female). Each human was round like a ball, with four arms and four legs, and two faces on one head, four ears and two sets of genitals. The gods feared them and so Zeus split each one down the middle, not killing them but leaving instead humans, as we know them today. Zeus' actions left each half desperately yearning for the other. Thus those that had been exclusively male desired men, those who had been female desired other females, and those who had been hermaphrodite desired the opposite sex (Plato, 1935, pp. 189–91). While this myth may strike us as an odd way of conceptualizing things, it demonstrates some attempt to understand just how and why some humans desire certain other types of humans. Generally speaking, our sexuality is driven by a desire for another person of a particular type based on our attraction to them. The gender of the other that we desire is commonly used to identify our sexuality. This other person – this object to our subject – that we desire continues to define the understanding of sexuality and sexual orientation in most areas of discourse.

If a woman desires a man, or a man a woman, we use the word 'heterosexual' as a descriptor; if a man desires other men, or a woman other women, then we employ the term 'homosexual', and if they claim to desire both, we label them 'bisexual'. While this scheme has an attractive simplicity and neatness to it, it fails to capture the complexity of actual human behaviour. Although some theorists query the validity of these terms, they continue to hold popular sway and are resorted to even by those who critique them and wish to do away with them. They are powerful and widely understood descriptors of basic human sexual behaviour. They exist as social categories and are applied by individuals and groups to describe themselves, their identities and behaviours. They are not unproblematic terms, but they do relate to just who we perceive as a desirable and attractive sexual object, and their currency is still very strong. These terms themselves are in fact of very recent origin, with the term 'homosexual' pre-dating 'heterosexual'. The first recorded use of it was in German in 1868 by Karol Maria Kertbeny (1824–82), who invented and employed it as a more dignified and scientific term than existing terms such as 'sodomite'. He is also credited with inventing the term 'heterosexual' 11 years later (Norton, 1997, p. 67).

Gender as a concept intersects with sexuality in a fundamental manner. Typically, sexual attraction and desire is seen as based on gender. The heteronormative world in which we live sees the attraction and sexual expression between a man and a woman as the normal mode of sexual behaviour. In this model there are only two genders – male and female (see Chapter 9, 'Gendering'). This simple binary model of humanity appears to be a common understanding in human cultures across time, as we can witness from the Book of Genesis (1: 27): 'male and female he created them'. While this may seem blindingly obvious to many, in fact a number of cultures have recognized more than one possible gender. For example many pre-Conquest Native American cultures had room for third and fourth gendered people – men who did not fit the traditional role of the male but occupied an accepted space and role that we would construe as feminine, and likewise some also allowed a role for those we would perceive to be biologically female but who lived and identified themselves in a way that we would label masculine. Many Polynesian societies continue to give room to men and women who do not fit imposed Western colonial and Christian notions of gender.

Hocaoglu (2002, pp. 147–9) gives examples in contemporary Turkish society of men who see the men they sleep with as gay because they allow themselves to be penetrated, but do not in any way regard themselves as being gay or less than real men so long as they are performing the penetrative act. Here we can see an interesting and not uncommon intersection of ideas of gender roles (real men do not get penetrated, but retain their masculine status as long as they penetrate) and ideas about what constitutes sexual identity. In my own experience, living in Turkey for eight years, I found this to be a typical understanding of many men. These ideas about the 'active' man not losing any status by performing these roles while the 'passive' one does are also well documented by writers on Latin American sexuality (Murray, 1995; Girman, 2004). What is striking in these examples is how the masculine 'active' partner's status is not socially diminished, while the man who takes the 'passive' role loses.

This wider shift can be seen as signalling the impact of modernity itself on social organization. When measured in human terms, it may have seemed a slow progression taking more than a hundred years, but in historical terms these changes are quite sudden and mark a point of disruption in the previously slower pace of social change. Accepted social norms and institutions reformed into new modes of social organization and life, including dramatic changes in marriage, especially in the role and legal status of women. (See Chapter 9, 'Gendering', and Chapter 18, 'Relating: Family'.)

Essentialism and constructionism

Academic and popular discourse on sexuality has tended to alternate between the positions that can be identified as *essentialist* and, in opposition to this, as *social constructionist*. While it may be argued that taking a position at either pole of this continuum is unproductive and unsupported by evidence, these extremities are where much of the debate has coalesced and been fought. Essentialist and constructivist interpretations are applied not only to sexuality, but also to debates on gender, ethnicity and even emotions (see Chapter 8, 'Racializing'; Chapter 9, 'Gendering'; and Chapter 12, 'Feeling'). In its crudest, most 'commonsense' form, the essentialist argument claims that humans are all possessed of a 'hard-wired' form of sexuality, and that this is most often heterosexual. An essentialist viewpoint can also be used to explain the existence of homosexuality and bisexuality as a pre-set genetic disposition. The social constructionist views sexuality as much more fluid and malleable in make-up – a result of how certain societies privilege and shape the sex drives of its members – and seeks to explain it as something we 'learn'.

Essentialist thinking in its most basic form holds to the notion that sexuality is a fixed biological part of human nature, hence it is seen as consisting of, or as part of, one's essence. The essentialist view works on the basis that we are born with some fixed and unalterable basic sexual orientation. We are, in this view, born attracted either to our own gender or to the opposite one, with a small group of people attracted equally to both genders. In this view there are only three possible sexual orientations – heterosexual, homosexual and bisexual. There might be some variations of this desire and its manifestations but desire itself is seen as a biological and innate quality within each human being. Heterosexuals, homosexuals and bisexuals are human kinds in the way that redheads or people born with blue eyes are. This is a commonly held view and is often seen as simply common sense. Much of the work that has been done to support this view searches for the genetic basis of sexual attraction and operates on the assumption that a force as important as the reproduction of the species must have some sort of innate genetic basis. Typical of this sort of work is the biological work often dubbed the search for the 'gay gene' (Hamer, 1994).

The social constructionist position understands sexual orientation and gender as social artefacts that arise from specific sets of social and historical forces at play within a society. Perhaps most famously, in terms of gender, the French philosopher and feminist Simone de Beauvoir (1952) claimed: 'One is not born a woman, one becomes one.'

These two opposing poles signal a very important and as yet ongoing debate about more than just human sexuality or gender. This debate points to a much deeper question about basic ontological positions: how much of our life is under our own control, and how much is created by our cultures, societies and perceptions of reality, and how much lies beyond our control? This is important as it highlights the role of human agency – how much lies in our hands and how much is determined by the evolutionary history of our species? Arguments about the morality or otherwise of, for example, homosexuality, fall away if it is held to be a natural and unchangeable aspect of a person's life. If instead, sexuality is seen as something one has control over and is a 'choice' then the argument can be made that it does not have to be chosen and that there are certain moral choices involved in making one choice over another. Thus, the state should have an active role to play in legislating for good choices.

The role of evolutionary psychology, or socio-biology, in this debate is also of note. Why, given the basic evolutionary idea of the best genes being passed on to ensure the survival of a species, would evolution favour the emergence of exclusive homosexuality in individuals? On the other hand, if it is not an innate and natural trait, why do so many men and women insist that they were born this way, that it is a deep and real part of their selves and that they have known they were 'different' from a very early age?

The study of sexuality as a subject in itself signals a marked change in thought and life. While talk on the subject of sex has never been in short supply in society, its official rise as a subject worthy of academic discussion and investigation tells us something has changed. Along with this development of the subject as a field of academic inquiry we can match a rise in the open discussion of sexual matters in Western literature. Works at the start of the twentieth century by writers such as James Joyce or D. H. Lawrence that seem to us today to be tame or even boring were in their time treated as scandalous and outrageous in their frank treatment and discussion of the subject. Thus we can see a wider cultural shift taking place in the public discourse on human sexual behaviour in general.

There remain questions still inadequately answered by both camps. If constructionists are correct and sexuality is a socially constructed pattern of human sexuality, why do so many people swear that they cannot change their sexuality? Why have so many gay men been put through various programmes that have claimed to alter or 'cure' their gayness and come out the other end still physically attracted to other men? Why do so many gay men and lesbians swear that this is the way they were born and have always been? Can they all be wrong and the social theorists correct? And if the essentialists are correct, what evolutionary advantage is there in gay-ness? Why would there be some gene or set of genes that is inherited for gayness when gayness presupposes that most gay men and women will not reproduce? What evolutionary advantage can there be for homosexuality? And if it is an essential and inherited human trait like left-handedness, then why is there such turmoil around the concept in so many cultures?

Queer theory

Queer theory lies in what is often termed 'the postmodern turn' (Jagose, 1996; Sanderon, 2001). Broadly speaking, post-modernism challenges the modernist assumptions of rationality, and over-arching narratives that can be used to explain any phenomenon. This challenge has been both popular and controversial in the academic world. Where modernity and structuralism offer certainty and claim an objective field of knowledge, post-modernity and post-structuralism see the world and our knowledge of it in a much more relativistic fashion, one that is dependent more on the observer's own social and cultural understandings than on any notion of objective truth.

Queer theorists all place the origins of their work in the thought of the French philosopher Michel Foucault and especially his *History of Sexuality*

(Foucault, 1980). Broadly speaking, the stance taken by queer theory is a constructionist one: that sexuality, gender and identity are constructs of society. This stance rejects the essentialist idea of an innate identity, regarding things such as gender and sexuality as social constructions that vary over time, cultures and societies rather than having any innate presence as part of a 'natural' human condition (Butler, 1990; Halperin, 1990; Stein and Plummer, 1994). Foucault's biographer, Didier Eribon, points out that much of what Foucault says in the *History of Sexuality* was in fact hypothetical and abandoned by Foucault himself soon after (Eribon, 2004, pp. xiii–xiv), a point rarely noted by the queer theorists themselves.

Kirsch claims that the term 'queer theory' was first used by Theresa de Lauretis at a conference in 1989 (Kirsch, 2000, p. 33). The socio-political background needs noting here. It was at this time that AIDS was wreaking its havoc and seemed unstoppable. The existing gay political world, based on the ideas of gay liberation and its descendents, was seen (rightly or wrongly) as ineffective in dealing with the crisis, distant from its radical roots and largely white, male, middle-class and assimilationist. This provided fertile ground for the more radical approach that queer promised. Kirsch, citing Edgar and Sedgwick, describes queer theory:

> What demarcates Queer theory from its postmodernist and poststructuralist foundations is its referral to a range of work 'that seeks to place the question of sexuality as the centre of concern, and as the key category through which other social, political and cultural phenomena are to be understood'. (Kirsch, 2000, p. 33)

These writers here are calling it the *key* category above or at least equal to issues of race, class and gender. Queer theorists in their most radical form seek to reshape accepted sociological and political norms in identity politics and to at least 'trouble', and at best rid, them of heterosexist assumptions. They differ from the ideas that inhere in the Gay Liberation movement that grew out of the 1960s civil rights movement, which focused on reinforcing and strengthening group identities derived from class, ethnicity or gender.

These movements, such as Black Power and Women's Liberation and Gay Liberation, sought to claim legitimate social and cultural space and power by affirming their difference as real and identifiable groups within society that deserved equal rights and opportunities. Queer theorists do not see this reinforcing of identity through difference as liberating because it is still, in their view, based in heterosexist assumptions that cannot be anything but oppressive to the very group trying to emancipate themselves. Taking their lead from Foucauldian theory, which sees identity formation as being at least in part regulatory and disciplinary in nature, queer theorists such as Seidman (1997) see the self as limited and constrained by the application of identity labels such as gay or straight that restrict the possible spectrum of imagining the self. Dillon, citing the work of Stein and Plummer (Stein and Plummer, 1994) encapsulates the project of queer theorists:

> Queer theorists call for a radical 'queering' of all aspects of sociology and not just the study of sexuality. Emphasizing the contextual intersectionality of biographical, sexual, gender, racial, and class identities, they call for new analytical approaches that inject sexuality into 'mainstream' sociological analyses of, for example, stratification, education, and gerontology, asking what happens when a (nonheterosexist) sexual lens is used in our apprehension of the social world. (Dillon, 2005, p. 225)

How successful this radical approach to sociological thought has been remains to be seen. While extremely popular throughout much of the 1990s on university campuses, the radical theoretical notions attached to queer theory seem to have gained little traction. Their strength lies, in this writer's opinion, in challenging preconceived notions of gender and sexual identity. Their weakness, however, seems to lie in putting too much weight onto the area of sexuality alone. It is hard to see how this one aspect of human life can be made to carry such ideological weight successfully. Many people outside the heterosexist norms of contemporary society do not define themselves purely on the basis of their sexuality. For some it is central, for others a concern, for yet others merely a peripheral concern, and for some it is of no issue whatsoever. Hurley makes the point that gay men are certainly 'doing gay' in a very different way today than before – different from before the time of Gay Liberation and its subsequent development of identity politics, different from the time of AIDS's initial dreadful impact (Hurley, 2003), and this also seems to apply to others who fall outside the heterosexist norms that are still predominant.

Perhaps the necessary accommodation with simply living along with the generally more benign (though certainly not perfect) social environment for gay men and lesbians that has resulted in the developed world over the last 40 years has made many of the concerns of queer theorists seem trivial outside the academy. Indeed, Stein and Plummer locate the origins of queer theory 'in the most elite American universities in the late 1980s' (Sanderon, 2001, p. 55).

Perhaps expecting such a disparate group of people, united only through some sense of being 'different' in terms of their sexual practices and desires, was building upon foundations too weak to sustain much. 'Queer' currently seems to simply occupy a space as an umbrella term to mean those who fall outside the heterosexist norm – an easier way of being inclusive without having to run through the familiar list of 'Gay Lesbian Bisexual Transgender' (GLBT). This seems a long way removed from the original radical plans for the notion, but perhaps is where it will remain.

Conclusion

Louis Crompton points out that there seems to be a broad and obvious distinction between those societies that have their origins in the Abrahamic religions of Judaism, Christianity and Islam, and the rest when it comes to matters of sexuality and homosexuality in particular (Friedman, 2001; Crompton, 2003). All societies seek to impose some sort of regulation upon sexual behaviour, whether it is in the form of an age of consent or legislating which people of which gender may legally have sex with others. However, the three Abrahamic religions show a particularly strong aversion to any form of sexuality outside married heterosexuality.

The reduction of sexuality to simply the mechanical actions of sex and its pleasures does us a disservice as humans – we are emotional beings as well and now, more than ever, perhaps, we desire from our sexuality not just a sense of identity but also that the object of our desire, our loved one and our partner, occupy some space that transcends the everyday for us. Bauman points out the way we now live in an age where we place a gigantic expectation on our partner in love: we expect our relationship with them, our 'universe of two', to use his words, to provide us with a vicarious immortality (Bauman, 1992, p. 28). Bauman points out the contradictory role our society in this period has given itself, placing such a high value on the functional importance of love while its carrying capacity appears to have been reduced so drastically. Love, and the technical display of sexual prowess, have come to take on a new social meaning in his analysis, similar to that of the record-breaking sportspeople: it is a way to escape the limitations of the body, to deny the inherent finitude and mortality of our selves (Bauman, 1992, p. 30). Sexuality and its expression and regulation can be viewed as a lens through which society seeks to understand and hold at bay mortality. If we view it in this light it is no wonder that it is such a contested area of our social world.

Different societies have shown different levels of tolerance and intolerance to different forms of sexual expression over time. We can see that most strikingly in recent times in the legalization of 'gay marriage' by the Spanish government. As the world has modernized and as the concept of moral and political rights has widened in its scope as a direct result of this modernizing force, so old certainties have been challenged. The debate is by no means settled as yet, and debates around sexuality – what is and is not appropriate, moral, socially acceptable or otherwise – continue to arouse great passion. In many ways the semiotic/symbolic space occupied by sexuality within a culture seems to point to something deeper, some greater fundamental sense of anxiety about itself. Eribon (2004) points to how the dominant paradigm of heteronormative societies maintain their position by the use of the insult. Perhaps the current debates signal a slow lessening of the power of the force of this insult in modern and post-modern societies, perhaps not.

To examine sexuality is to examine both one of the central delights of human existence and one of its central points of tension and control. Sexuality, like much else that modernization has touched, has changed and exerts a level of change on its surrounding society. Society still sees a need to control and regulate sexual expression, as a way of controlling and regulating itself.

Suggestions for further reading

Crompton, L. (2003) *Homosexuality and Civilisation* (Cambridge, MA: Belknap Press of Harvard University).

D'Emilio, J. (2002) *The World Turned: Essays on Gay History, Politics and Culture* (Durham, NC: Duke University Press).

Foucault, M. (1978) *The History of Sexuality*, trans. R. Hurley (New York: Pantheon).

Kirsch, M. (2000) *Queer Theory and Social Change* (New York: Routledge).

Weeks, J., J. Holland and M. Waites (eds) (2003) *Sexualities and Society: A Reader* (Malden, MA: Polity Press).

Bibliography

Bauman, Z. (1992) *Mortality, Immortality and Other Life Strategies* (Cambridge: Polity Press).

de Beauvoir, S. (1952) *The Second Sex* (New York: Alfred A. Knopf).

Butler, J. (1990) *Gender Trouble: Feminism and the Subversion of Identity* (New York: Routledge).

Crompton, L. (2003) *Homosexuality & Civilization* (Cambridge, MA: Belknap Press of Harvard University Press).

Dillon, M. (2005) 'Sexuality and Religion: Negotiating Identity Differences', in M. Jacobs and N. Hanrahan-Weiss (eds), *The Blackwell Companion to the Sociology of Culture* (Oxford: Blackwell), pp. 220–33.

Eribon, D. (2004) *Insult and the Making of the Gay Self* (Durham, NC: Duke University Press).

Foucault, M. (1980) *The History of Sexuality*, trans. R. Hurley (New York: Viking).

Foucault, M. (1990) *The History of Sexuality* (London: Penguin Books).

Freud, S. (1962) *Three Essays on the Theory of Sexuality* (New York: Basic Books).

Friedman, D. M. (2001) *A Mind of its Own: A Cultural History of the Penis* (New York: Free Press).

Fuzuli, M. (1970) *Leyla and Mejnun*, trans. Sofi Huri, with a history of the poem, notes and bibliography by Alessio Bombaci (London: Allen and Unwin).

Girman, C. (2004) *Mucho Macho: Seduction, Desire, and the Homoerotic Lives of Latin Men* (New York: Harrington Park Press).

Halperin, D. (1990) 'Homosexuality: a Cultural Construct – an Exchange with Richard Schneider', *One Hundred Years of Homosexuality and Other Essays on Greek Love* (New York: Routledge), pp. 41–53.

Hamer, D. H. (1994) *The Science of Desire: The Search for the Gay Gene and the Biology of Behaviour* (New York: Simon and Schuster).

Herdt, G. H. (1984) *Ritualized Homosexuality in Melanesia* (Berkeley, CA: University of California Press).

Herdt, G. H. (1997) *Same Sex, Different Cultures: Gays and Lesbians across Cultures* (Boulder, CO: Westview Press).

Hinsch, B. (1990) *Passions of the Cut Sleeve: The Male Homosexual Tradition in China* (Berkeley, CA: University of California Press).

Hocaoglu, M. (2002) *Escinsel Erkekler: Yirmi Bes Taniklik [Homosexual Men: Twenty-five Interviews]* (Istanbul: Metis Yayinlari).

Homer (1960) *The Anger of Achilles: Homer's Illiad* (London: Cassell).

Hurley, M. (2003) *Then and Now: Gay Men and HIV* (*Melbourne*: The Australian Research Centre in Sex, Health and Society, La Trobe University, Monograph Series Number 46).

Irvine, J. M. (2002) 'Toward a "Value Free" Science of Sex: the Kinsey Reports', in K. M. Phillips and B. Reay (eds), *Sexualities in History: A Reader* (New York: Routledge).

Jagose, A. (1996) *Queer Theory* (Dunedin: University of Otago Press).

Jenkins, C. (1997) *Qualitative Methods in Sex Research in Papua New Guinea. Researching Sexual Behavior* (Bloomington, IN: Indiana University Press).

Kinsey, A. C. and Institute for Sex Research (1965) *Sexual Behavior in the Human Female* (New York: Pocket Books).

Kinsey, A. C., W. B. Pomeroy et al. (1948) *Sexual Behaviour in the Human Male* (Bloomington, IN: Indiana University Press).

Kirsch, M. H. (2000) *Queer Theory and Social Change* (London: Routledge).

Krafft-Ebing, R. v. (1935) *Psychopathia Sexualis, with Especial Reference to the Antipathic Sexual Instinct: A Medico-Forensic Study* (New York: Physicians and Surgeons Book Co.).

MacCulloch, D. (2003) *Reformation: Europe's House Divided* (London: Penguin).

Murray, S. O. (1995) *Latin American Male Homosexualities* (Albuquerque, NM: University of New Mexico Press).

Norton, R. (1997) *The Myth of the Modern Homosexual* (London: Cassell).

Plato (1935) *The Symposium* (New York: E. P. Dutton).

Sanderon, S. K. (2001) *The Evolution of Human Sociality: A Darwinian Conflict Perspective* (Lanham, MD: Rowman and Littlefield).

Seidman, S. (1997) *Difference Troubles: Queering Social Theory and Sexual Politics* (New York: Cambridge University Press).

Stein, A. and K. Plummer (1994) 'I Can't Even Think Straight: "Queer Theory" and the Missing Sexual Revolution in Sociology', *Sociological Theory* 12, pp. 178–87.

Treat, J. W. (1999) *Great Mirrors Shattered: Homosexuality, Orientalism, and Japan* (New York: Oxford University Press).

Weeks, J. (1991) *Against Nature: Essays on History, Sexuality, and Identity* (London and Concord, MA: Rivers Oram Press).

Xu, Y. (1992) *On Chinese Verse in English Rhyme: From The Book of Poetry to the Romance of the Western Bower* (Beijing).

FEELING: EMOTIONS • BELIEVING: RELIGION • EDUCATING • STRAYING: DEVIANCE • MEDIATING: TECHNOLOGY • INFORMING: MEDIA • RELATING: FAMILY • BELONGING: COMMUNITY • FINISHING

231

11 being: identity

Martin Sullivan and Catherine Lane West-Newman

KEY
POINTS

▪ The idea of possessing an individual identity is socially and historically specific.

▪ Language is an essential precondition for a sense of self, and we learn that language through the processes of socialization acquired through our connection with families, communities and formal education systems.

▪ Cooley and Mead describe a self that emerges in social interaction and may be seen as social structure incorporated in an individual.

▪ Goffman developed the idea of roles to describe the reflexive process through which identity is constituted for individuals through exchanges with others, and managed, accepted or rejected by a conscious self.

▪ The concept of stigma refers to the notion of undesirable and spoiled identity and the associated strategies for role management.

▪ Identity politics developed in the new social movements of the 1960s that exposed and contested social inequalities of gender, race, sexuality and disability. They sought to change the objective conditions of oppression and to change the consciousness of insiders and outsiders by transforming discredited and undervalued identities into sources of pride and positive self-image.

▪ In contrast to the more or less unitary 'modern self', the 'postmodern self' is seen as fractured and fragmented, subject always to external influence and likely to change without notice. For individuals, construction of the self has become a more self-conscious and problematic project.

Introduction

> [Y]our essence, your character, your consistent and self-revealing patterns of behaviour are not something you were born with. You acquired them as you grew up, acted, behaved, and sometimes as you made choices of what to do, occasionally when you decided what to be, who to be. (Hacking, 2004, p. 282)

When Ruth Reichl became restaurant critic for the *New York Times* she learned that she could do her job better when she avoided recognition and the special treatment that inevitably followed. As adviser to the thousands who looked for her guidance in choosing where to eat, she needed to know what eating out was like for ordinary people. So, with the help of excellent wigs and appropriately matching clothes, she ate out under several different identities, devising appropriate biographies for each to help her behave in character. She even became her mother. At some of the most famous restaurants she rapidly discovered what it is to be the 'wrong' kind of customer, the one whose style is not right for the place. At the same time she also found, to her surprise, that looking different, and having people respond in various ways to that look, came to shape and colour her behaviour in ways far beyond what she had intended. She felt like the different characters – her voice became softer or louder, her approach to others more or less aggressive. The multiple identities, or rather the people she became, seemed at times to be taking over her life. Some of them her family found to be not only quite unpleasant but even frightening (Reichl, 2005). This story introduces the idea that we all locate ourselves in the world through a sense of personal identity and that this 'self' each of us experiences as uniquely our own is also a social construct. It also signals that in the present-day world under conditions of post-modernism it is possible to conceive of human individuals as fabricators and bearers of multiple selves, often self-consciously (reflexively) constructed in and through various social situations, experiences and relationships in which we find ourselves.

Concern with the nature and consequences of selfhood has been central in the social sciences since the early 1980s. This revitalization of interest has been attributed both to theoretical developments in cultural studies, post-structuralism and feminism and to a world where, '[a]s the globalization processes of late capitalism continue to destabilize traditional practices and cultural assumptions, the self is exposed in various ways' (Callero, 2003, p. 115). Concepts of self and identity used by sociologists for the previous 80 or so years developed out of social psychology and were based in a theoretical and methodological position known as symbolic interactionism. This approach to understanding how society works focuses on the creation of meaning in human social interaction. Because humans have complex nervous systems and the capacity for language, they are able to remember large numbers of symbolic meanings and to express them in actions and words. We learn these meanings through social interaction with others (Bullock and Trombley, 1999, p. 851). Recent sociological understandings of the self, however, have taken into account the significant connections between power and the self, which are identified and examined in the work of Michel Foucault (for example, 1980). They have also explored the notion of the multiple and shifting selves that make up what Kenneth Gergen (1991, p. 150) has called pastiche personality – 'a social chameleon, constantly borrowing bits and pieces of identity from whatever sources are available and constructing them as useful or desirable in a given situation'.

Discussions of self and identity are quite commonly illustrated with examples of gendering, racializing and sexualizing social practices and the discriminatory differentiation that so often underlies such categorizations (see Chapter 8, 'Racializing'; Chapter 9, 'Gendering'; and Chapter 10, 'Sexualizing'). In this discussion, although some examples will be drawn from these, the principal focus will be on the relationship between identity and disability. In this way, we hope to refresh some old discussions while also showing how the sociological imagination can envisage still more ways of being in the social world and thereby critique existing explanations of the social self.

The self under Modernism – Cooley and Mead

How we conceptualize the notion of the 'self' and understand what it might mean to have or be that self is produced as an epistemological effect. In other words, the very idea of what shall count as knowledge of individual identity is socially and historically specific. The modernist self is a unitary – but nevertheless social – self, for as Charles Taylor (1989, p. 35) observes: 'One is a self only among other selves. A self can never be described without reference to those who surround it.' This means that language is an essential precondition for a sense of self, and we learn that language through the processes of socialization acquired through our connection with families, communities and formal education systems. Through this same process we also develop the vocabulary for a sense of self. 'The concept of identity offers an answer to the question of who I am through a definition of where I am speaking from and to whom … [through] reference to a defining community' (Taylor, 1989, p. 36). As we will see later, the post-modern 'self', on the other hand, is both more fragile and more diverse.

The concept of the unitary self as it has been used in modernist sociology is developed and explained in the work of three foundational thinkers – Charles Horton Cooley, George Herbert Mead and Erving Goffman. The first of these was a pioneering social psychologist who, in *Human Nature and the Social Order*, first published in 1902, considered how we conceive of ourselves within the world of others. In many cases, he thought, this took the form of a 'reflected or looking-glass self' perceived through the eyes of someone else:

> As we see our face, figure, and dress in the glass, and are interested in them because they are ours, and pleased or otherwise with them according as they do or do not answer to what we should like them to be; so in imagination we perceive in another's mind some thought of our appearance, manners, aims, deeds, character, friends, and so on, and are variously affected by it. (Cooley, 1902, p. 184)

The imagination, then, plays an important part. We believe that those who see us also make judgements about all aspects of our existence – and in response to what we imagine they are thinking (and they may of course give us clues about this by their own behaviour towards us), we value or devalue our 'self'. Most people, Cooley suggests, are not strongly conscious of this 'social self-feeling' unless or until 'failure or disgrace arrives' (1902, p. 208). But then they will 'perceive from the shock, the fear, the sense of being outcast and helpless' their 'existence in the minds of others', all unknowing. Although there are always other participants in the interactions Cooley describes, his focus remains on the issues of self-perception; for him, 'all social interactions depend upon the imaginations of the individuals involved ... society really has no existence except in the individual's mind' (Mead, 1934, p. 224). The author who here describes Cooley's psychologically focused assumptions is George Herbert Mead, the next important figure in this developing sequence of ideas.

Mead places this production of self through the socially interactive consequences of the mirror experience squarely within an external and objectively defined social context. The existence of language, he says, makes it possible for humans to envisage themselves as objects. This means that we can name ourselves as both subject and object simultaneously and therefore identify two distinct aspects of the self – an 'I' and a 'me'. In this scheme the 'I' is a spontaneous and creative element of the self, which responds to others' reactions towards the ('me') self as an object. The 'me' is an explicitly social product – 'a bounded and structured object' (Callero, 2003, p. 121), which incorporates the perceptions of others' attitudes to that self and responds appropriately. The 'me', then, is a whole repertoire of the social behaviours and performances that make up the organized expectations of others incorporated into the self. It is the product of each individual's birth into a social structure and an institutional order already in existence and the constraints and limitations of established languages, codes, customs and laws. It is what others see. But although the 'me' knows what is socially expected, even required, the 'I' – 'the response of the organism to the attitudes of the others' (Mead, 1934, p. 175) – 'is never entirely calculable ... it is always something different from what the situation itself calls for' (p. 178). When Aboriginal resistance to Australian settler society takes the form of deliberate drunkenness in public spaces, the 'I' might be said to be insisting on its own response to norms that are both known and consciously rejected (Russell, 2005).

What Cooley and Mead share is their view of the self as something that is neither entirely individual nor entirely social. For them, the self emerges in social interaction; it is a social product, a social structure incorporated in an individual. Erving Goffman, the next important contributor to the symbolic interactionist theories of self, is squarely located within sociology. The psychological dimensions of (individual) selfhood still underpin his

FEELING: EMOTIONS • BELIEVING: RELIGION • EDUCATING • STRAYING: DEVIANCE • MEDIATING: TECHNOLOGY • INFORMING: MEDIA • RELATING: FAMILY • BELONGING: COMMUNITY • FINISHING

237

understanding but the focus is now on the conscious management of self and identity as each individual represents him- or herself *within the social world*.

Roles and identities – Erving Goffman

Goffman's first research was as a participant observer in a tourist hotel in the Shetland Islands. There he discovered that staff and guests played different roles, according to where and with whom they were interacting. Previously he had, while a student, worked for the National Film Board of Canada on documentaries that won international prizes for their depiction of detailed interactions between people involved in their everyday lives in various and diverse Canadian villages and towns. It is this experience, a biographer suggests, that shaped his attention to the significance of 'social exchanges between individuals, not only the words but also the tone, the accent, the body language, the gestures, the withdrawals, the silences' (Hacking, 2004, p. 278). Throughout all his work Goffman's particular sociological imagination envisages and reports the lives of individual 'selves' constructed always and necessarily in the context, and through the lives, of others. His purpose is to create an account of the reflexive process through which identity is constituted for individuals through exchanges with others, and managed, accepted or rejected by a conscious self.

The concept of role, embedded in a wider metaphor of theatre and performance and summarized as a dramaturgical approach, is central to both his empirical observations and theoretical framework. It is first developed in *The Presentation of Self in Everyday Life* (1959). Roles are defined as context specific, multiple, and to be played according to scripts and scenarios that are socially determined and known to the performer. The roles are part of the person – some brief and relatively insignificant and others lifelong and deeply significant. For example, people who divorce and remarry – perhaps many times – may play the husband or wife or partner role for a large part of their lives but with different people playing opposite them. This could be likened to having Brad Pitt, Tom Cruise and Russell Crowe playing opposite at different times; indeed some movie stars seem to do marriages as if they were temporary film roles.

Some roles we may freely choose and enjoy, but others are imposed and may be deeply resented, to the point where they must be managed, avoided, denied, rejected. The term 'role' describes, then, the socially ascribed content of an inevitable aspect of social life through which we produce and present a range of 'selves' to the world and thereby offer ourselves to the judgement of others. Not everyone is pleased to find their social existence represented in such terms: Kenneth Gergen suggests that in offering a sense of self as 'strategic manipulator', Goffman 'most poignantly capture[s] the nagging sense of guilt pervading the daily life of ... beings struggling toward efficacy in a socially complex world' (1991, p. 149). There is, in fact, some disagreement about the extent to which Goffman recognizes the strategic component of this process. Tseelon (1992, p. 116) argues that while Goffman's dramaturgical metaphor simply depicts 'people's presentational behaviour as a process of negotiation' through which 'people offer definitions of themselves in various interaction contexts which the audience either accepts or challenges', the related impression management literature (developed for and by the 'management professions') extends this to interpret self-presentations as strategic moves undertaken to acquire benefits. In other words, for Goffman it is a game of representation rather than, as management professionals would have it, one of misrepresentation. We will return to this point later when considering the idea of 'post-modern' selves.

Goffman, disability and identity

In *Stigma: Notes on the Management of Spoiled Identity* (1963), Goffman expands his earlier ideas on impression management and directly relates them to the notion of identity as an individual and collective experience. His approach inevitably reflects the assumptions and attitudes of 40 years ago towards disability and stigma in ways that one of us, as a disabled person reading it today, finds quite offensive in places and embarrassing and laughable in others. Nevertheless, it also offers some deep insights into the creation of meaning around stigma and the consequent construction of personal and social identities.

In his account of the social location and effects of stigma Goffman distinguishes three forms of identity: social, based on relationships with other people; personal, derived from individual personal biography;

and ego, the subjective sense of self that emerges out of experience. The processes of stigmatization occur within the social identity but at the same time personal identity provides the space for information control – decisions about concealment and disclosure, where these might be possible. The notion of social identity is extended to distinguish two dimensions – *virtual* and *actual*. In the former we internalize the 'attributes felt to be ordinary and natural' (1963, p. 11) for established categories of persons. We regard these as deserved indications of the kind of person we are and how we would like others to see us. The actual social identity, on the other hand, rests on the category and personal attributes that one can actively demonstrate. This means that if evidence can be produced to show that individual to have 'an attribute that makes him different ... less desirable' than others in that category of persons then the person is reduced in the observer's mind from a 'whole and usual person to a tainted, discounted one' (1963, p. 12). If the discrepancy between virtual and actual identity is 'deeply discrediting', it is what Goffman terms a stigma, which will, in his terms, 'spoil' that individual's social identity (1963, p. 31).

Goffman (1963, p. 15) identifies three types of stigma: physical abnormalities, character blemishes (e.g. weak will, unnatural passions, dishonesty) and tribal stigma of race, nation or religion. Through the creation of these named categories of undesirable difference, a category of the desirable is simultaneously constituted in the unmarked remainder who are 'normals'. For those so defined, the stigmatized are not quite human and it is this assumption that opens the way for those discriminatory practices that reduce their life chances. By way of justification, normals also construct a 'stigma theory' to provide an explanation of the inferiority and danger that those with stigma represent. How deep this non-acceptability reaches, Goffman says, can be seen in the ways in which terms such as 'cripple, bastard, moron' are used as metaphors in everyday discourse (1963, p. 5). Given these circumstances, Goffman suggests that a stigmatized person may feel quite alienated in the company of normals and, despite what they say, will not feel readily accepted as an equal when with them. Indeed, a pivotal fact of mixed interaction is that the stigmatized individual tends to share the same beliefs about identity and normality as the normals they meet. It follows that, when in the company of normals, those who have been stigmatized may, even momentarily, find themselves becoming intensely aware of the extent to which they fall short of what they ought to be. Thus, finding him/herself a discredited person in an unaccepting world, the stigmatized person may then seek out the company of sympathetic others who will accept them as human and 'essentially' normal in spite of their own self-doubts. This category of people is made up of two kinds of people – 'the Own', who share the stigma, and 'the Wise', who are normal persons 'whose special situation has made them intimately privy to the secret life of the stigmatized individual and sympathetic to it' (1963, p. 41).

Personal identity is related to personal biography and in this instance it is about managing information about one's stigma. For Goffman there are two sides to personal identity. First, there is the visible or freely available information such as personal appearance, those parts of one's biography one makes known, and information on public record. Second, there is the information about you that is known only to a small group of friends and family. In the first instance the person has a *discredited* identity because everyone knows of the stigma or it is self-evident (for example, amputee or gay activist); in the second, s/he has a *discreditable* identity because the stigma is neither known nor obvious (e.g. someone with a colostomy or gambling addiction) (see Chapter 15, 'Straying'). For someone with a discredited identity the problem is one of managing the tension produced by the fact that others are aware of that which discredits one's identity. For a person with a discreditable identity it is a problem of concealment and disclosure. Strategies of concealment include 'passing' (for example, the closeted homosexual living an ostensibly straight life, the ex-mental patient living in the community without revealing his past) and 'covering' – a way of passing in the community by acting in an expected way (for example, someone who is hard of hearing relying on their spouse to give hints about what is being discussed at a dinner party) (1963, p. 127).

This description of Goffman's work reveals both the many strengths of his perception (which lie in an amazing capacity to operate at the margins of individual and social experience) and an absence – the lack of a broader social context than the local and specific sites of encounter and interaction. It is precisely this absence that is remedied in later work on social selves and identities that has developed, under the influence of processes of globalization and conditions of post-modernity, as experience and in new theoretical insights. The recent resurgence of interest in identity noted earlier has been fuelled by the conjunction of interest by sociologists, social psychologists, and cross-disciplinary interest in the characteristics of global culture under the influence of new technologies. It has been noted that in general the structural features of that society which shapes personal and social identity is largely (and intentionally) invisible in Goffman's work. Consequently, the absence of power in his analysis raises questions that can be seen subsequently to have been addressed by Foucault in ways that also bear upon ideas about self and identity (Hacking, 2004). But at this point the self in question is one constructed under very different terms and conditions.

Collective identity: the new social movements and identity politics

Identity politics is the name given to the orientation of a series of challenges mounted in response to 'the declining ability of democratic nation-states to represent adequately the interests of large segments of their constituencies' (Bullock and Trombley, 1999, p. 413). The identities in question have been asserted through social movements emerging in response to perceived social conditions. They are contentious and oppositional manifestations of popular feeling that offer a collective challenge to the way things are. Their goal is social (and political) change and they seek to achieve this 'through collective action outside the sphere of established institutions [such as class]' (Giddens, 1997, p. 511). Indeed, in *Farewell to the Working Class*, Andre Gorz (1982) argued that class was dead and that identity now rested more on culture and consumption than on work. From the 1960s, issues such as civil rights, women's rights, gay and lesbian rights, the environment, nuclear disarmament and disability rights began to emerge as points of greater importance than class in identity formation and around which to mobilize for social and political change. (For an alternative view on this see Chapter 6, 'Stratifying: Class'.)

What are generally known as the new social movements of the mid-twentieth century began with the United States Civil Rights Movement, where the leadership of Martin Luther King Jr ultimately brought him to the iconic recognition of a national holiday in his name. In mass public gatherings, peaceful protest marches and sit-ins, African Americans and their supporters campaigned to bring their profoundly unequal experience of life in American society under public scrutiny. Their goal was the dismantling of systemic discrimination under the Jim Crow laws of the South and legislation to support their demand for equal rights. Their protests ultimately brought about the Civil Rights Act 1964 and the Civil Rights Voting Act 1965. Inspired by the effectiveness of the black campaign (while noting also the virtual absence of women from significant leadership roles and power in that movement), the women's liberation movement (now more generally known as the women's movement), with feminism providing the analysis, demanded an end to all forms of discrimination against women and the right to legal abortion as a valid social choice. Gay liberation campaigned to abolish laws that outlawed consensual, homosexual sex and an end to the pervasive discrimination which lesbians and gay men experienced in their everyday lives. Indigenous peoples in settler nations, generating and drawing on post-colonial theory and analysis, asserted claims for self-determination (and sometimes sovereignty) within the settler states.

These new social movements were not just about changing the objective conditions of oppression; they were also about conscientization – that is, about changing the consciousness of both insiders and outsiders alike by transforming discredited and undervalued identities into sources of pride and positive self-image and by promoting this image to wider audiences. Because the basis of their claims lay precisely in identities that were ascribed to them (on the basis of gender, race/ethnicity, physical and mental characteristics and qualities, historical contingency) rather than freely chosen, their activism acquired the name of 'identity politics'. Under this description activists asserted interest-based demands for social change and intellectuals developed critical analyses that supported these claims.

The disability rights movement

The following account of the history, positioning and debates within the disability rights movement (DRM), though simplifying the differences between the countries described, effectively illustrates the processes of identity politics in action. In the United States the movement adopted a minority group model, which focused on the denial on the basis of disability of individuals' constitutional rights. In contrast, the British movement adopted a structural analysis of disability and focused on changing social structures as a means to the elimination of disability and discrimination. Pivotal to this was the redefinition of disability generated by disabled people (UPIAS, 1976) which, by asserting a distinction between *impairment* (the deficit of body or mind an individual has) and *disability* (able-bodied society's negative reaction to impairment), reframed it from an individual problem to a social one. This social model differed considerably from the hegemonic individual model (which incorporates medicalization, welfarism and charity), where to have an impairment is to be disabled; where disability is an individual problem, located within individuals who properly seek medical intervention for cure, amelioration or care. This account is underpinned by a personal tragedy theory (Oliver, 1990), which casts disabled people as the victims of some tragic happening or circumstance. Unsurprisingly, the individual medical model had come to dominate mainstream perceptions of disability and disabled people, and, as such, created entirely negative social and personal identities for 'the disabled'.

According to Shakespeare and Watson (2001), the social model was hugely important for the British disability rights movement (and for the whole Western disability movement generally) in two ways. First, it provided a political agenda of barrier removal. If barriers were what created disability then we must organize for their removal and the creation of a non-disabling society in which disabled people could participate as fully as they wished and on their terms. Second, it changed the consciousness of disabled people. Disability no longer resided in our bodies or minds but out there in society; it was now a problem of social oppression and we were an oppressed minority. We were no longer at fault – society was; we didn't need to change – society needed to change; we didn't have to be sorry for ourselves and apologize for our existence – we could be angry! Once conscientized, disabled people were empowered to mobilize for equal citizenship; to demand their rights to be economically and socially productive rather than existing in a state of forced dependency on welfare, charity and goodwill (Shakespeare and Watson, 2001). This then became the identity politics of the disability rights movement.

But with an identity politics based on oppression there was a danger of sliding into fatalism and a passive acceptance of the dominant discourse through 'internalized oppression'. To counter this, energy was devoted to uncovering, creating and promoting images that undermined negative stereotypes of disability. This began with a politics of naming, in which the dehumanizing category 'the disabled' was assigned to the dustbin and some became 'people with disabilities', to indicate that we were people first before the disability. The more politically attuned became 'disabled people', asserting that disability is not something we have but something which is done to us (Sullivan, 2000). Concomitantly, the 'able-bodied' became the inverted 'non-disabled', and disability pride ('We're OK, but what happens to us is not') emerged to underpin positive personal identities for disabled people. Membership of the DRM soon became dependent upon individuals consciously choosing to identify as a disabled person, and the war cry of the movement became: 'nothing about us without us' (Charlton, 2000).

This, however, is not the complete story on identity politics in the disability rights movement. The epistemological basis of Disability Studies, especially within the United Kingdom, has been overwhelmingly one of materialism and the social model. Under these conditions, a 'disability correctness' (Shakespeare, 1998) emerged in which the social model was sacrosanct and any talk of the body or impairment was regarded with much suspicion by leading activists and academics. With the notable exception of Jenny Morris (1991), academic writing until relatively recently steered clear of the role of the body in disability identity (see Crow, 1996; Sullivan, 1996; Hughes and Paterson, 1997; French, 1999). There is now, however, a growing literature on the body and disability identity with the embodied experience of impairment increasingly accepted as a valid part of identity formation.

In some quarters the social model was routinely criticized for not offering a complete theory of disability (which it had never claimed to do) and for its inability to explain the experience of disability for all people because of its failure to include other forms of oppression. For example, should disableism be prioritized as the main form of oppression for disabled people who are also subject to sexism and/or racism and/or heterosexism and/or ageism and/or classism? Vernon (1998) asks if a disabled woman is properly considered to be doubly oppressed or if she experiences two forms of oppression simultaneously or if it is something different like disableism plus? Does she only experience disableism when with her non-disabled women friends and sexism within the disability community or is she always other in multiple ways? This questioning can usefully be seen as the assertion of identity politics within identity politics. It alerts us to the fact that the new social movements consist of people who may be similar in one key respect but who also have many different, and sometimes competing, interests and identities. It also contains a warning against reverting to a kind of essentialism where one identity has hegemonic salience and is seen as representing the core, authentic person or, as in this case, one overarching identity for a whole movement of people.

Through this account of the identity politics of disability a characteristic common to all such politics can be clearly seen – the identities in question are social constructions and, as such, explanations of their foundations are always contestable and under debate. There can be, then, no general agreement on whether they are best understood as strategic 'statements of resistance to the status quo' or, more deterministically, as 'expressions of essential characteristics possessed by subaltern groups' (Bullock and Trombley, 1999, p. 413).

Post-modern selves

It is apt to conclude this chapter with a consideration of identity and post-modernism that returns to the starting point of the sociological concern with identity: the self. The depiction of the modern self developed by Cooley, Mead and Goffman, and upon which modern notions of identity are predicated, is, however, a quite different proposition from what is now called 'the post-modern self'. Notions of identity have been secured in a variety of long-standing relationships with friends and communities, in established social structures (for example, family, church, the state) and in recurring situations. Identity under these conditions could be envisaged as genuine, real, reflexive, self-conscious and autonomous (Vryan et al., 2003). But in the latter part of the twentieth century Jacques Derrida, Jacques Lacan, Michel Foucault and Jean-François Lyotard have all questioned whether this modern self ever existed as such a coherent entity. They further argued that the conditions under which the self was constituted had changed and moved beyond the modern to a social climate and milieu some theorists describe as post-modern (see Introduction, 'On Being Sociological'). Under these conditions, individuals now have to rely on their own authority to make judgements and decisions about how to construct and live their selves and identities. Moreover, with the growth of information technology there is a proliferation of fragmented and incoherent images in the media to draw upon, as well as virtual worlds in which one can construct virtual identities free of the constraints and frameworks of modern social structures like the family and community (see Chapter 17, 'Informing: Media', and Chapter 19, 'Belonging: Community').

The term 'identity' traditionally described 'the relatively stable and enduring sense' that individuals have of themselves (Bullock and Trombley, 1999, p. 413) and carried an implication that this sense endured over time. The modernist self was envisaged in the form of a central 'I' around which multiple aspects or identities were generated during interaction with others. Somewhere in the background, assumed rather than described, lurks the notion of 'a real self', the person who can, like the actor, relinquish a role and leave that stage. In contrast, descriptions of the self and identity under post-modern conditions emphasize the multiplicity and fluidity of selves constructed and experienced in the context of today. Under post-modern conditions – particularly through the bombardment of media effects – Gergen (1991, p. 147) describes a saturated self that has no essence, just multiple representations.

> As the self as a serious reality is laid to rest and the self is constructed and reconstructed in multiple contexts, one enters finally the stage of the relational self. One's sense of individual autonomy gives way to a reality of immersed interdependence, in which it is relationship that constructs the self.
>
> Characteristics of the postmodern condition that produced this change include not only the growth in information technologies and culture industries but also a commodification of images, diversification of social worlds, rise of consumption-oriented society and the crumbling of previously dominant modernist values of rationality, autonomy, and authenticity. (Sandstrom and Fine, 2003, p. 1050)

FEELING: EMOTIONS • BELIEVING: RELIGION • EDUCATING • STRAYING: DEVIANCE • MEDIATING: TECHNOLOGY • INFORMING: MEDIA • RELATING: FAMILY • BELONGING: COMMUNITY • FINISHING

247

The self, then, is a fractured and fragmented thing, subject always to external influence and likely to change without notice:

> The world of friendship and social efficacy is constantly expanding, and the geographical world is simultaneously contracting. Life becomes a candy store for one's developing appetites. (Gergen, 1991, p. 149)

But alongside this 'optimistic sense of enormous possibility' there is also an uneasy recognition of the instability of the mutable self. If others are simply a source of self-gratification for each individual then that is all we can be to each other. If there is no self outside external social construction then we must rely on public presentation of that self through clothing, style, body shaping and presentation to construct an acceptable self. Television reality games about mating, surviving on desert islands and fighting fear are all about this kind of impression management. In effect, they are constructed to create situations where the possibility of management is stripped away in tense interpersonal and physically dangerous situations. The audience sees character traits revealed in public humiliations that participants may not even recognize until they see the resulting programme (see Chapter 12, 'Feeling: Emotions').

Recent sociological studies have inquired into the effect, especially on young people, of constructing the self under such conditions. British sociologists, for example, interviewed 140 young males to discover how they experienced themselves as embodied identities and found support for 'the idea that the surface of the body has come to constitute a "project" and key source of identity for young men' (Gill et al., 2005, p. 41). They also discovered this to be a fraught and difficult kind of self-construction that demanded work on body discipline through exercise (gym and sport) and decoration (tattoo and piercing) and simultaneous disavowal of any inappropriate vanity or even interest in personal appearance (see Chapter 9, 'Gendering').

We've looked here at sociological understandings of identity as an individual experience and project, and as a collective socio-political phenomenon. The role of identity politics in transforming discredited identities has been described and we have looked forward to a future of floating and multiple selves. Identity remains the source of the capacity to describe and locate our selves and others socially in mutually agreed-upon ways. It makes behaviour predictable and understandable. It is the basis of social life. This is why, as the twenty-first century progresses, identity is likely to remain a key field of sociological inquiry, tracking new and transformed identities as they emerge from changing social realities.

Suggestions for further reading

Charlton, J. (2000) *Nothing about Us without Us: Disability Oppression and Empowerment* (Berkeley, CA: University of California Press).

Goffman, E. (1959) *The Presentation of Self in Everyday Life* (London: Pelican Book).

Roseneil, S. and J. Seymour (eds) (1999) *Practising Identities: Power and Resistance* (Basingstoke: Macmillan).

Sarup, M. (1996) *Identity, Culture, and the Postmodern World* (Edinburgh: Edinburgh University Press).

Taylor, G. and S. Spencer (eds) (2004) *Social Identities: Multidisciplinary Approaches* (London and New York: Routledge).

Bibliography

Bullock, A. and S. Trombley (eds) (1999) *The Fontana Dictionary of Modern Social Thought*, 3rd edn (London: HarperCollins).

Callero, P. L. (2003) 'The Sociology of the Self', *Annual Review of Sociology* 29, pp. 115–33.

Charlton, J. (2000) *Nothing about Us without Us: Disability Oppression and Empowerment* (Berkeley, CA: University of California Press).

Cooley, C. H. (1902) *Human Nature and the Social Order* (New York: Charles Scribner's).

Crow, L. (1996) 'Including All of Our Lives: Renewing the Social Model of Disability', in C. Barnes and G. Mercer (eds), *Exploring the Divide: Illness and Disability* (Leeds: The Disability Press).

Foucault, M. (1980) *Power/Knowledge: Selected Interviews and Other Writings, 1972–1977*, trans. and ed. C. Gordon (Brighton, Sussex: Harvester Press).

French, S. (1999) 'The Wind Gets in My Way', in M. Corker and S. French (eds), *Disability Discourse* (Buckingham: Open University Press).

FEELING: EMOTIONS • BELIEVING: RELIGION • EDUCATING • STRAYING: DEVIANCE • MEDIATING: TECHNOLOGY • INFORMING: MEDIA • RELATING: FAMILY • BELONGING: COMMUNITY • FINISHING

249

Gergen, K. (1991) *The Saturated Self: Dilemmas of Identity in Contemporary Life* (New York: Basic Books).

Giddens, A. (1997) *Sociology*, 3rd edn (Cambridge: Polity Press).

Gill, R., K. Henwood and C. McLean (2005) 'Body Projects and the Regulation of Normative Masculinity', *Body & Society* 11(1), pp. 37–62.

Goffman, E. (1959) *The Presentation of Self in Everyday Life* (London: Pelican Books).

Goffman, E. (1963) *Stigma. Notes on the Management of Spoiled Identity* (London: Penguin Books).

Gorz, A. (1982) *Farewell to the Working Class: An Essay on Post-industrial Socialism* (London: Pluto Press).

Hacking, I. (2004) 'Between Michel Foucault and Erving Goffman: between Discourse in the Abstract and Face-to-face Interaction', *Economy and Society* 33, pp. 277–302.

Hughes, W. and K. Paterson (1997) 'The Social Model of Disability and the Disappearing Body: Towards a Sociology of Impairment', *Disability & Society* 12, pp. 325–40.

Mead, G. H. (1934) *Mind, Self and Society from the Standpoint of a Social Behaviorist* (Chicago, IL: University of Chicago Press).

Morris, J. (1991) *Pride Against Prejudice* (London: Women's Press).

Oliver, M. (1990) *The Politics of Disablement* (London: Macmillan).

Reichl, R. (2005) *Garlic and Sapphires: The Secret Life of a Critic in Disguise* (London: Penguin Press).

Russell, P. H. (2005) *Recognizing Aboriginal Title: The Mabo Case and Indigenous Resistance to English-Settler Colonialism* (Toronto: University of Toronto Press).

Sandstrom, K. and G. Fine (2003) 'Triumphs, Emerging Voices, and the Future', in L. T. Reynolds and N. J. Herman-Kinney (eds), *Handbook of Symbolic Interactionism* (Walnut Creek, CA: AltaMira Press).

Shakespeare, T. (ed.) (1998) *The Disability Reader: Social Science Perspectives* (London and New York: Cassell).

Shakespeare, T. and N. Watson (2001) 'The Social Model of Disability: an Outdated Ideology?', in S. Barnartt and B. Altman (eds), *Exploring Theories and Expanding Methodologies: Where Are We and Where Do We Need to Go?* (Oxford: JAI).

Sullivan, M. (1996) 'Paraplegic Bodies: Self and Society', Ph.D. thesis, Department of Sociology, University of Auckland.

Sullivan, M. (2000) 'Does It Say What We Mean, Do We Mean What It Says, Do We Know What It Says? Problematising the Way Disability is Written and Spoken About', *New Zealand Journal of Disability Studies* 8, pp. 36–46.

Taylor, C. (1989) *Sources of the Self: The Making of Modern Identity* (Cambridge, MA: Harvard University Press).

Tseelon, E. (1992) 'Is the Postmodern Self Sincere? Goffman, Impression Management and the Postmodern Self', *Theory, Culture, and Society* 9, pp. 115–28.

UPIAS (1976) *Fundamental Principles of Disability* (London: Union of the Physically Impaired Against Segregation).

Vernon, A. (1998) 'Multiple Oppression and the Disabled People's Movement', in T. Shakespeare (ed.), *The Disability Reader: Social Science Perspectives* (London and New York: Cassell).

Vryan, K., P. A. Adler and P. Adler (2003) 'Identity', in L. T. Reynolds and N. J. Herman-Kinney (eds), *Handbook of Symbolic Interactionism* (Walnut Creek, CA: AltaMira Press).

FEELING: EMOTIONS • BELIEVING: RELIGION • EDUCATING • STRAYING: DEVIANCE •
MEDIATING: TECHNOLOGY • INFORMING: MEDIA • RELATING: FAMILY • BELONGING: COMMUNITY • FINISHING

251

12

feeling: emotions

Catherine Lane West-Newman

KEY
POINTS

- Western thought has, since ancient times, made a conceptual divide between reason and emotion, seeing them as fundamentally opposed. Many societies, though, have not done this and it is now increasingly recognized that feeling and thinking are part of the same processes in the human brain and it is a mistake to see them as entirely separate.

- Present-day sociologists agree that neither biology nor society is entirely responsible for emotions. Certain foundational emotions – for example, fear, anger, depression and satisfaction/happiness – seem to be common to all humans and therefore part of our biological make-up. We share these emotions as humans who are social actors and whose existence is mediated through the experiences of body as well as of mind.

- There are also named emotions which seem to be particular to specific cultures or to be understood and valued differently in different societies. In a world where we increasingly live in multicultural societies these differences can have very important consequences in the way they share social life.

- Because sociologists are interested in the ways emotions shape and are shaped by social processes, institutions and power relations, they often explore the connections between emotional states and individuals' social location in gender, class and ethnic groupings.

Introduction

As self-conscious individuals we absolutely know that feelings matter. Some of our best (and worst) experiences involve love or grief or joy or shame or anger or even some quite confusing mixture of these. Alphonso

Lingis, in a book called *Dangerous Emotions*, writes about these deep emotions and our capacity to feel them in a way that is quite astonishing. Consider this:

> We take emotions to be distinctively human phenomena. Outside the crystal ball of the human psyche, there are only grass that does not wince when we tread on it, trees that are impassive as the chain-saw slashes them, water that does not shiver with pleasure when we stroke it, atoms drifting through the void without anxiety and colliding without pleasure or pain. (Lingis, 2000, p. 15)

The passage is interesting because it can be seen to work on two levels at once, speaking to the head *and* to the heart. In a curious and not easily explained way we comprehend, through reason, that these are ideas that the author wants to communicate and at the same time he also evokes in us at least some fragments of the actual feelings he describes. So, in creating this dual experience in our minds and bodies Alphonso Lingis achieves an experience more often created in fiction – novels, plays and movies – than in the social sciences. This is because, although many societies and cultures make no conscious division between thought and feeling, Western thought since ancient times has usually done so. Through this separation into two distinct and opposing worlds of feeling and reasoning our experience of and in everyday life has been conceptualized as two quite different modes of being which, by their very existence, work to undermine each other. Social science has long been given over to the world of reason alone.

In this division reason was always the more valued way of knowing both ourselves and our world, and with the Enlightenment it was honoured as the ground of scientific thought, the source of justice, the triumphant crown of human cultural and social achievement. In contrast, emotion was tied to an inferior, less admired, association with nature, bodies and the failure of reason. The qualities of each realm were also strongly linked with a gendered division of capacities in which men epitomized reason and all its virtues and women represented the unruly (and often messy) qualities of nature, embodiment and feeling.

All of this goes a long way towards explaining why sociology, from its invention in the early nineteenth century until very recently, has managed almost to ignore the social origins, effects and importance of feelings. There are, however, some interesting exceptions to this general rule. Although German sociologist Georg Simmel (1858–1918) is now less well known than the famous three founding sociologists – Karl Marx, Max Weber and Émile Durkheim – his work is currently seen as helpful in understanding some of the questions that most interest present-day sociologists. The writing of phenomenologist Max Scheler (1874–1928) now seems to be closer to philosophy than to research-based sociology, but it too offers ideas about what we now call the 'emotional self'.

Georg Simmel and Max Scheler

Simmel's famous essay 'The Metropolis and Mental Life' describes the relationship between the nature of city life and the way individual personalities adapt to existence within that environment. He explains that although feelings shape individual and collective behaviours, when people live in large cities they are likely to develop a self-preserving attitude that blanks out the extremes of emotional experience in everyday life. His picture of urban life, written over a hundred years ago, seems even more relevant to the vastly accelerated experience of big city life today. As individuals, he says, each of us needs to feel that although we are part of overwhelming social forces, historical heritage, culture, and 'the technique of life' we need to see ourselves as also and above all independent and meaningful beings (Simmel, 1950, p. 409). We need to preserve a sense of personal identity and significance. So, in response to the *intensification of nervous stimulation* that cities create, we develop a particular kind of personality that is able to adjust to the external forces that surround us. Cities create an environment with 'rapid crowding of changing images, the sharp discontinuity in the grasp of a single glance, and the unexpectedness of onrushing impressions' (ibid., p. 410). These psychological conditions demand our attention and ultimately exhaust our capacity to receive and respond to all the things around us. Our senses are bombarded by such rich and varied impressions that we eventually, in self-defence, make a perceptual wall between us and them. This wall comes, Simmel says, through suppressing our feeling responses – reacting not with the heart but with the head, a part of the body less sensitive and 'quite remote from the depth of the personality' (p. 411). Reason replaces emotion.

There is another reason, too, why emotions have been seen as less relevant to the modern world. Big cities are the heart of a money economy that is understood as intrinsically connected to the dominance of reason and the mind.

> Money is concerned only with what is common to all: it asks for the exchange value, it reduces all quality and individuality to the question: How much? All intimate emotional relations between persons are founded in their individuality, whereas in rational relations man is reckoned with like a number ... (Simmel, 1950, p. 411)

Emotion is not only irrelevant to capitalism but, because our feelings in personal relations distract us from the intellectual calculations of commerce, actually undermines it. In contrast, the blasé attitude preserves us from inappropriate distractions because when everything appears 'in an evenly flat and gray tone' then 'no one object deserves preference over any other' (Simmel, 1950, p. 414). The blasé attitude fits us not only for the instrumental relations of business but also to be docile consumers of the goods that capitalist economies must produce (see Chapter 2, 'Modernizing' and Chapter 4, 'Consuming').

However, if all that were not depressing enough, the blasé attitude is also at work in our interpersonal relations. Because we live and work alongside thousands, even millions, of other people, self-preservation in the big city requires us to shut out others – to adopt a reserved indifference, even 'a slight aversion, a mutual strangeness and repulsion' which 'will break into hatred and fight at the moment of a closer contact' (Simmel, 1950, pp. 415–16). In compensation, though, we obtain greater personal freedom to do as we wish, shedding obligations to family and friends but free also to be lonely and lost in the crowd. The more intense metropolitan life becomes, the harder we have to try to be noticed; to attract others we may have to adopt dramatic forms of being different because only then will we stand out from the crowd (ibid., p. 421) (see Chapter 11, 'Being: Identity').

This connection between the social conditions of modernity and the social and sociological recognition of public emotions returns in some present-day sociological studies of public and private grief and of revenge inside and outside the law. We will return to this, and to associated questions about the authenticity of twenty-first-century emotional life, later in the chapter.

Max Scheler, who, like Simmel, was as much a philosopher as a social theorist, is almost more famous for his public failure to manage his emotions in either his personal or professional lives than he is for the classic studies of resentment and of sympathy which formed part of his development of a phenomenology of emotions (Bershady, 1992). His love life created public scandals and his relationships with the universities that employed him were disruptive and usually brief. Nevertheless his perceptions about how we actually feel in particular situations and the effect those feelings have on our social environment are still at the heart of our thinking about such matters. In any case, understanding how emotions work in individuals and in societies is not, of course, any guarantee that we will actually be able to control our own emotions (or lives).

Sociologists are particularly concerned to understand how collective sentiments – the feelings that we share and experience intersubjectively – come into being and how they operate in particular societies. Scheler's account of this is 'valuable in developing an understanding of "we-feeling"' (Turner, 1993, p. 506). For example, people recognize the idea of human rights because there is a collective awareness that we are dependent upon each other for survival. This finds expression in the belief that helping others is a proper recognition of our shared human frailty. Present-day sociologist Bryan Turner argues that 'rights, as a system of mutual protection gain their emotive force' (1993, p. 507) from precisely these recognitions. Disaster can happen to any of us and so those whose lives are shattered by war, terrorism or natural disasters deserve our help. International response to the Indian Ocean tsunami at the end of 2004 – the giving of billions of dollars in aid by Western nations and the individual donations of private citizens – is a good illustration of these feelings in action.

Scheler defined four forms and levels of emotional connection between people. The first is immediate community of feeling, where the same event provokes emotion felt in common, for example the grief of two parents at the death of their child. The second involves a shared feeling about something; rejoicing in another's joy, commiserating with their sorrow. The third Scheler calls 'mere emotional infection', where our emotion free-rides on that of the other; and the fourth is 'true emotional identification' or empathy that takes another's emotions as one's own (van Hooft, 1994,

FEELING: EMOTIONS · BELIEVING: RELIGION · EDUCATING · STRAYING: DEVIANCE · MEDIATING: TECHNOLOGY · INFORMING: MEDIA · RELATING: FAMILY · BELONGING: COMMUNITY · FINISHING

12   257

p. 18). These rather fine-grained distinctions identified by van Hooft alert us to some interesting distinctions which have become highly relevant to present-day debates about public and private as well as authentic and inauthentic emotions under contemporary social conditions. Ultimately, though, Scheler understood emotions as psychological inner states and was less interested in how they were related to interpersonal experiences. Therefore his contribution is probably most important as a reminder of the ultimately personal and individualistic nature of even those feelings whose social effect is most widely acknowledged.

Explaining emotions

Modern sociologists are generally agreed that neither biology nor society is entirely responsible for emotions. Certain foundational emotions – fear, anger, depression and satisfaction/happiness are the ones identified by Theodore Kemper (1978) – seem to be common to all humans and therefore part of our biological make-up. These we share as what Simon Williams (1998) describes as 'embodied agents', that is, humans who are social actors and whose existence is mediated through the experiences of body as well as of mind. But over and above these are a complex of emotional beliefs, experiences, practices, norms and values, all of which are socially formed, and historically and culturally variable. Kemper identifies 'secondary' emotions such as guilt, shame, pride, gratitude, love and nostalgia as socialized adaptations of the (physiologically grounded) primary ones. They are part of the power relations of different groups: they shape and are shaped by politics, are experienced and performed as gendered practices, and their effect on human action and reaction is still greatly underestimated by social scientists and in everyday life (Kemper, 2002).

Probably the clearest example of biological explanations is found in Charles Darwin's treatment of emotions as direct biological imperatives common to humans and animals. They were, he thought, a form of physiological arousal based in instinctual drives. In *The Expression of the Emotions in Man and Animals* (1872/1965) anger is described simply as a process of physical arousal where

> the action of the heart is a little increased, the color heightened, and the eyes become bright. The respiration is likewise a little hurried; and as all the muscles serving for this function act in association, the wings of the nostrils are somewhat raised to allow for a free indraught of air ... The mouth is commonly compressed, and there is almost always a frown on the brow. (Darwin, 1965, p. 244)

His theoretical approach is that emotion can be explained by observing outward signs of expression on the face and body. Human interaction and social context are irrelevant – emotions function physiologically (and involuntarily) within the individual who experiences them. Present-day biological explanations have also been developed by neurophysiologists who, with access to brain chemistry not earlier available, have identified specific parts of the brain (hypothalamus, limbic system and, particularly, amygdala) that are directly associated with emotions (Damasio, 1996; Le Doux, 1996). But in demonstrating the physiological processes of emotional response these researchers do not claim that social and cultural context is irrelevant; rather, they see themselves as addressing just one aspect of the much more complex shape of human emotional experience.

In direct contrast, almost all sociologists tend to favour social constructionist explanations that locate the origins of emotions in the social and cultural world. This explanation suggests that individuals are taught through the processes of socialization how they should act and feel emotionally in the correct and appropriate ways for their culture. They learn when it is proper to feel sad, happy, angry and ashamed, and also under what circumstances these feelings should be hidden or revealed. In this account emotions are 'manufactured aspects of social reality' (Finkelstein, 1980, p. 119) and their place is explicitly in the moral and social order of things. Social theorists of emotions tend to be divided on the extent to which they acknowledge a place for biological antecedents of emotions alongside the strictly social influences. The most extreme view is held by those who claim that emotions have no biological source but are entirely learnt and contextual. Rom Harré's social constructionism says that there is no such thing as 'an emotion'; there are only ways of acting and feeling emotionally. The task of the sociologist then is to describe the emotional vocabulary of a society, the conditions under which they are used, the moral order that gives them their meanings, and

FEELING: EMOTIONS · BELIEVING: RELIGION · EDUCATING · STRAYING: DEVIANCE · MEDIATING: TECHNOLOGY · INFORMING: MEDIA · RELATING: FAMILY · BELONGING: COMMUNITY · FINISHING

12   259

the social functions they perform (Harré, 1991, pp. 142–3). But Harré is a philosopher and psychologist and most sociologists today accept that neither explanation is exclusively and wholly correct and that emotions have both physiological and social dimensions.

Cultural differences in emotions

Do people in different cultures experience similar emotions or are the emotions of people in different cultures actually different? For many years it was assumed in European thought that humans shared a common, biologically determined repertoire of emotions and had (or should have) the same norms about their expression and meaning. But now we have many illustrations from anthropologists and psychologists of the range and variation in ways that members of different ethnic groups (and therefore different cultures) will experience emotions, name them, and develop social norms about their significance and appropriate context of expression. In a world where we increasingly live in multicultural societies, these differences can have very important consequences for the shape of social life.

If we ask the questions: 'What is shameful?', 'What causes grief?', 'When and where should love be felt (and expressed)?', 'What are the proper occasions of anger?', will people from different cultures give the same answers? It seems that the answer is yes – and no. There are certainly some cross-cultural emotional similarities. In a study of the causes of jealousy (Buunk and Hupka, 1987), male and female students from Hungary, Ireland, Mexico, The Netherlands, the Soviet Union, the United States and Yugoslavia all said that sexual relationships with a third party would make them jealous. And, although the intensity of that feeling differed among the nationalities, they all thought that flirtation caused jealousy.

But there are also significant differences. The Utku Inuit are apparently made happy by enjoyable experiences like 'chasing lemmings or stoning ptarmigans' and 'traveling under good conditions' (Briggs, 1970, pp. 327–8) but these are unlikely sources of happiness for those who live in tropical countries. A comparison of Israeli and European emotional responses to particular circumstances found that Israelis associated joy with achievement, sadness with death and bad news, fear with interaction with strangers, and anger with injustice and interaction with strangers. Europeans, on the other hand, found joy in relationships, sadness in death and relationships, fear in traffic, and anger in relationships. These differences seem quite obviously to be connected with the differing social conditions under which these Israelis and Europeans live (Scherer et al., 1986).

When names for emotions are compared across different languages it becomes evident that there are some feelings that have no direct equivalences across cultures. Rosaldo, an anthropologist who studied the lives of Ilongot people in the Philippines, thought at first that their word '*liget*' described the feeling of anger. Later, when she had come to understand its deep connection with the practice of headhunting, which is central in Ilongot culture, she realized that it was far more complex than that. The emotion of *liget* involved notions of passion, energy and anger simultaneously (Rosaldo, 1980). When one or more Ilongot men had heavy feelings of *liget*, they went out with a group of others to kill and then, after the beheading, returned home feeling purged of violence. *Liget* which was acted out in this way was seen as socially useful; but when *liget* was not focused on headhunting then it caused chaos and disturbed social life. In a complex, and very un-Western, way of thinking, the colour red that appears in the sky at sunset is seen as a kind of *liget* which can make people sick. Such ways of experiencing feelings in the world are not universal – they are particular to a specific culture.

Sometimes emotions may initially look quite similar but be experienced through very different social dynamics (West-Newman, 2005). In the English-speaking world, the notion of shame is strongly linked with individualism. It is felt as a lonely, exposed, personal failure but it does not contaminate others who are associated with the person shamed (Schweder, 2003). But in New Zealand, Maori have a concept which, although it can be likened to shame and embarrassment, is embedded in a quite different pattern of social meanings and consequences. *Whakama* works on individuals because they feel it when they transgress the values of their community. The actions of an individual can bring about collective *whakama* that affects *whanau* (family), *hapu* (sub-tribe) and *iwi* (tribe) and, according to the nature of the action or event, can be intense. Its result may be violence, withdrawal, or even, in traditional times, suicide (New Zealand Ministry of Justice, 2001, p. 313). In Chinese, Japanese and Korean cultures, the associated concept of 'face' is also related to shame and embarrassment but, again, it is experienced and managed within a complex set of quite different social beliefs and practices (Ha, 1995; Liem, 1997).

Studying particular emotions

Because sociologists are interested in the ways emotions shape and are shaped by social processes, institutions and power relations, they often explore the connections between emotional states and individuals' social location in gender, class and ethnic groupings. Some, for example, use a Marxist perspective to point out the resentment, boredom and misery of the proletariat living under the oppressions of capitalist society (see Chapter 6, 'Stratifying: Class'). Marx and Engels' *Manifesto of the Communist Party* declares:

> Not only are they slaves of the bourgeois class, and of the bourgeois State; they are daily and hourly enslaved by the machine, by the overlooker, and above all, by the individual bourgeois manufacturer himself. The more openly this despotism proclaims gain to be its end and aim, the more petty, the more hateful and the more embittering it is. (1848/1977, p. 43)

Present-day studies in the sociology of emotions concern themselves with such a wide range of social phenomena that we can look, here, at only a small tasting of them. Nor is it possible to go far into an empirical exploration of the social conditions and effects of emotion without moving quite rapidly to deal with emotions not as a generic category but as specific named feelings. Grief, fear, love, resentment, anger and revenge, for example, all have distinctly different social characteristics. Here, we will look briefly at revenge, love and grief.

Revenge
Sociologists who are concerned particularly with the effect of emotions in the social structure inevitably find themselves studying, also, aspects of

power in society. Revenge is an interesting example of an emotion involving the experience of unequal power, which, while formally treated as socially unacceptable, in fact operates within the legal system and often forms the subject of movie and television plots. At the core of revenge is a concern to set things right after a (perceived) injury. It has been described as an emotion that works to correct imbalanced or disjointed power relationships. It is concerned with reasserting human dignity or worth and restoring social actors to their rightful place in relationships. So it is both an appeal against a denial of rights and an assertion of an individual's right to their position and their entitlement to punish those who try to take away their rightful place (Barbalet, 1998).

Revenge may operate in one-to-one relations as private retaliation for wrongful treatment. Researchers have found many forms of sabotage practised by workers against employers they thought had wronged them (see Chapter 3, 'Working'). Computer data have been destroyed and altered, products on supermarket shelves contaminated with metal, glass and noxious substances, and even aircraft dangerously sabotaged during production. Other vengeful strategies have included bomb threats, setting fires, death threats toward supervisors, spreading rumours, and placing sleeping pills in a supervisor's coffee. A fired bakery worker broke into the bakery after closing to replace the inscriptions on pre-ordered decorated cakes with insulting messages. At the Encyclopaedia Britannica Company a fired editor substituted Allah for Jesus Christ and changed the names of other historical figures to those of current Britannica executives in computer files for the encyclopaedia (Crino, 1994). In each case the point is to cause enough trouble to feel that proper retribution has been delivered. Nevertheless, in Western societies revenge is not generally seen as a publicly admissible motive for individual action and so an even richer fantasy life of revenge is offered in popular culture fictions.

Revenge may also be collective, perhaps involving an extended family, ethnic group or even a whole nation. At this level vengeance works through legal systems, traditions of feud or payback, and even through acts of terrorism and warfare. Although it is not always acknowledged, there is a particularly strong connection between revenge and law. Indeed, European legal history reflects a development from physical (blood) revenge, to compensation payment by one kin group to another that

FEELING: EMOTIONS · BELIEVING: RELIGION · EDUCATING · STRAYING: DEVIANCE · MEDIATING: TECHNOLOGY · INFORMING: MEDIA · RELATING: FAMILY · BELONGING: COMMUNITY · FINISHING

12   263

has been wronged, to present-day systems of compensation made under a state-administered legal system. Through civil law people can obtain compensation for personal injuries; in criminal law the state acts on behalf of all citizens to prosecute crimes and punish convicted offenders. But we seldom call this revenge. Instead it is described as state retribution in which punishment is carefully calculated in proportion to the seriousness of the crime (Leiser, 2001). In modern Western society revenge is portrayed as 'crazed, uncontrolled, subjective, individual', an unreasoned taking of the law into one's own hands' (Miller, 2000, p. 162).

But although this is the official version, it is clear that revenge is an important part of how people think about crime and punishment. William Ian Miller (2000) has argued that there is a public appetite for movies with a vengeance theme, whether they are about getting even with cheating lovers, triumphing over mean employers, or substituting for inadequate policing. This reflects, he says, a widespread popular belief in revenge as an understandable, and even acceptable, motive for action. The implications of this point of view are often disquieting for those who believe that self-help is social as well as legal anarchy and that only the state should exact retribution for wrongs.

Love and romance

Francisco Alberoni, in *Falling in Love* (cited in Lindholm, 1998), argues that there is no adequate ordinary language for talking about romantic love. 'Poetry renders love ineffable, obscenity reduces it to the comic, so that any study of romantic love appears either to be missing the point altogether, or else to be engaging in voyeurism under the guise of research' (Lindholm, 1998, p. 247). Love, you might suppose, has to be more positive than revenge; but that is not necessarily so. Sociological interest in love is directed not to the euphoria of romantic love but rather towards understanding the social functions it can be made to fulfil. Indeed, by the time sociologists have finished with it, romantic love looks more like an ideologically constructed trap than the rapturous meeting of minds and bodies celebrated in movies, books, plays and music (see Chapter 18, 'Relating: Family').

Social constructions of love, as sociologists see it, differ from class to class, gender to gender. It may exist differently, or not at all, within different cultures. 'The idea of love in heterosexual relations has always been extremely unstable and as likely to change as any other social ideology' (Evans, 1998, p. 273). The idea that love is a necessary condition for marriage is a peculiarity of modern Western societies and explained as a consequence of a supposed absence in those societies of extended kin relations with their networks of support and obligations. Many theorists link this to the rise of capitalist individual freedoms so that 'the economic market finds a correspondence in the market of free emotions' (Bertilsson, 1986, p. 28). In the modern world love is a vehicle of symbolic exchange, an integrative force which alleviates the social distance that typifies this world.

Among Simmel's recently rediscovered ideas are some useful thoughts on love that fit well with current perceptions of its nature as a very domestic, personal, individualistic kind of emotion. They are a good starting point for understanding how modern sociologists treat love as an emotion, felt between individuals but always socially constructed and experienced. Erotic love, he says, only occurs in humans, the most evolved species on the evolutionary scale, whose high level of individualization sees love and flirtation involved in our 'mechanisms of procreation' (Bertilsson, 1986, p. 23). Thus, love among humans has two aspects: it ensures the future of the species and it has meaning for individual subjectivity. However, there is an antagonism between these two elements which is the source of what might be described as the tragedy of love. It is the second aspect – the subjective one – that causes humans so much trouble. Other animals mate. We, alone (as far as we know) reflect on what it *is* we are doing when we love. That is, we are self-conscious about our mating, and about our relating to each other, and we construct it in a process of examining what is happening, how we feel, and what it all means.

> For Simmel, to love means to be connected with another person in such a way that, while still maintaining their own individualities, the loving person and the loved one permeate one another. It means to apprehend the other directly and entirely. It means that no social or cultural object lies between the lover and the beloved, that no element of the intellect plays any part in the experience of loving. (Arditi, 1996, p. 96)

If he is right, then it is hardly surprising that being in love is more inclined to make people miserable than happy. 'The procreation of life cares little for the highly individuated demands of ... absolute love' (Bertilsson, 1986, p. 24). Misunderstanding, loss, separation (or just divorce) – the great love stories are tragedies.

Stevi Jackson, in an article charmingly titled 'Even Sociologists Fall in Love' (1993), says the pervasiveness of love as a representational theme in high and popular culture is related to its institutionalization in marriage and family life. Love is important in family ideology because romantic love is functional for modern society. It helps to maintain the structures of heterosexual monogamy and patriarchal marriage. These institutions are valued because they are seen as providing a place for communication and self-realization in a complex, impersonal and anonymous world. Much of the saga of the Prince Charles–Princess Diana 'fairytale' wedding and failed marriage, Mary Evans (1998) argues, is a clear demonstration that '[f]ar from liberating women from patriarchal control or the pressures of arranged marriages, romantic love actually traps women in false expectations and psychologically crippling demands' (1998, p. 269). Indeed, it is true that almost all sociological consideration of love sees it as somehow disadvantageous for women.

Current debates about love and the nuclear family often focus on the extent to which love has become a shifting experience of intimacy; a temporary and promiscuous experience undertaken for instrumental reasons. Zygmunt Bauman (2003) frames the matter as a choice between commitment and 'liquid love' and takes a negative view of its social effects. But Ulrich Beck, the author of theories about how present-day life is preoccupied with the management of risk, and Elisabeth Beck-Gernsheim (1995) claim that although present-day conditions in modern individualized society complicate the development of close relations, they also offer a platform for experimenting with new ways of feeling and doing love.

Grief
Sociologists studying grief in the late twentieth century have focused on social norms in Western societies that define how and when sorrow should be concealed and revealed and what kind of events might give rise to public demonstrations of emotion. Although we may feel grief for many different kinds of losses – of youth, of love, of physical functions,

of nation, of place, and of other things that we value deeply – the main emphasis of grief studies is on the kinds of grieving connected with death. There has been considerable historical and cultural variation in norms of grieving that surround death. Nineteenth-century Britain celebrated it with intense emotionality and a romantic cult of the dead. The United States for most of the twentieth century was a death-denying society. Erika Doss (2002) has observed that the 1927 bombing of a Missouri school that killed 46 students and the 1958 arson of a Catholic school with 95 people dead were not recognized with memorials. But events over the past ten years – from the Columbine High School massacre to the Oklahoma Bombing to September 11 – together with AIDS, euthanasia and international terrorism, have dramatically altered that.

Among these changes the norms of appropriateness in keeping grief private or making it a public display have also been transformed. Biddle and Walter (1998) point out that the English norm was, for most of the last century, self-control and a 'brave face' in public but that an underlying desperate unhappiness in private, signalled just enough to reveal that one was not actually heartless, were also expected. Recently, though, celebrity deaths and mass public death – especially as the result of terrorist actions – have produced particular manifestations of expressive grief. Biddle and Walter point out that in England, 'In the week following Princess Diana's death, the press generated an impression of an entire nation indulging in expressive grief, bringing flowers by the million to local and national ad hoc shrines, baring its soul in books of condolence and on cards attached to the flowers, and regularly breaking down in public' (Biddle and Walter, 1998, p. 97). The British royal family, though, were criticized both for failing to perform expressive grief in public and for showing not even the accepted signals of private grief bravely endured. There was even talk of a constitutional crisis because the monarchy was so (emotionally) out of touch with its subjects.

After the Oklahoma City bombing in 1995, the media showed to the world the many objects placed in memorial on the wire fence surrounding the building; public grief and ritual enacted by local residents and tourists was accompanied by interviews where victims and visitors showed their loss and suffering on camera (Doss, 2002) (see Chapter 17, 'Informing: Media'). The site of the 1999 Columbine High School killings was similarly decorated and memorialized for the world. And, after the murder of Italian designer Gianni Versace, a website offered the world a space for an 'electronic mourning' (Harris, 1998). Hundreds of fans posted messages in which they competitively asserted the intensity of their loss and grief.

One way of understanding this phenomenon of mass public grief is through Émile Durkheim's concept of 'collective effervescence'. It is, he said, through such collective rituals of emotional experience that we experience sociality; events such as public grieving are a mechanism of social integration which bind together members of the society who share them. In this process of collectively effervescing (literally, fizzing up together) our emotions are shaped through rites that symbolize group identity and enable us, as individuals, to experience ourselves, collectively, as moral communities who share beliefs, values and behaviours (Durkheim, 1912/1961).

Emotions and authenticity

Recently, some sociologists and social commentators have become increasingly involved with distinguishing between 'genuine' and 'false' emotional expressions. The interest may, in many cases, be traced to the work of Arlie Hochschild, who, in the early 1980s, developed the concept of emotional labour as a means of describing the developing employer practice of training workers to express feelings appropriate to their job. In *The Managed Heart: The Commercialization of Human Feeling* she argued that in an age where everything becomes a commodity – available for sale – employers in search of greater profits were trying to control even their workers' feelings. The experiences of cabin crew working for Delta Airlines who were required to smile and be charming in the face of abusive language, sexual advances, and sometimes physical injuries like the deliberate pouring of hot coffee over them, led Hochschild to argue that emotional labour exerted serious 'human costs' from these workers, who talked of 'burnout', feeling 'phony', 'cynicism', 'emotional deadness', guilt and self 'blame' (Hochschild, 1983).

Managing one's emotions is now recognized as an important part of many different jobs (see Chapter 3, 'Working'). A convincing performance may entail both simulating the required feelings and suppressing the undesired ones. Repetition may render this virtually automatic, performed without effort, or it may exert a conscious strain. Such performances may involve speech, body language and facial expression and may involve disliked and humiliating behaviour. Studies of workers on American supermarket checkouts (Tolich, 1993) and in New Zealand fashion stores (Williams, 2005) have found that some workers, at least, develop their own ways of managing such situations so that they find some personal satisfaction in performing this emotional labour. And whether the performance is virtually automatic or a conscious strain, it seems that workers are generally unwilling to see their behaviour as inauthentic. Barbara's claim: 'I might do it unconsciously. I may, but I don't consciously. ... when someone walks through the door I am happy and I think great, how can I help you?', is a typical response (Williams, 2005).

This distaste for inauthenticity also pervades Stjepan Meštrović's (1997) notion of 'postemotionalism' in the late twentieth century. Post-emotional societies are, he says, characterized by the disappearance of genuine feelings, even in the face of wars, famines and genocide. Instead, under the barrage of media representations of suffering, people in the Western world indulge themselves in emotional conditions which, he argues, characterize the turn of the twenty-first century. We have become, he says, 'post-other-directed' types who are able to deal only in pre-packaged emotions that we have learned from those second-hand feelings delivered to us in the media. As a result, we have largely lost our capacity for spontaneous (and authentic) emotional response, preferring private realms of fantasy to real life and feeling only 'eviscerated compassion' and sentimental pseudo-grief for famous strangers such as Gianni Versace and Princess Diana. Looking back to Simmel's life in the metropolis, here is the blasé attitude in its most extreme form, where television brings us mass death and endless objects of consumption in rapid sequence.

It is tempting to suggest that this is where the blasé attitude described by Simmel ultimately leads. Over-stimulated by consumption and drained by compassion fatigue, we dwell in a twilight world of fake feeling. Or do we? Simon Williams argues that the 'nature of human embodiment' as well as our unruly minds ensure that 'from the loss of self in eroticism to the aggression vented in gang warfare, and from the "unruly" behaviour

FEELING: EMOTIONS · BELIEVING: RELIGION · EDUCATING · STRAYING: DEVIANCE · MEDIATING: TECHNOLOGY · INFORMING: MEDIA · RELATING: FAMILY · BELONGING: COMMUNITY · FINISHING

12 269

of a child to New Age movements, communal festivities, sporting and musical events, spontaneous emotions are "hard at work" in apparent defiance of social conventions, for better or worse, richer or poorer' (1998, p. 764). Consider, also, the way in which, at the end of 2004, the overwhelming mass death toll of the Indian Ocean tsunami aroused a media response focused less on signs of visible overwhelming public grief than on the enormity of death. We saw bodies heaped up mechanically into mass graves, and endless rows of burning funeral pyres. In the countries of devastation people appeared too emotionally numbed by disaster to engage in media-directed performance of grief rituals. In the West, the focus was not on individual emotional performance but on practical aid. In New Zealand the formal silence on the official day of mourning went unobserved on beaches and in shopping malls, but the donations from a population of four million continued to climb for many months afterwards. Feelings continue to exercise their considerable effect in all aspects of our individual lives and to shape collective social interaction.

Suggestions for further reading

Franzen, J. (2002) 'My Father's Brain', in *How to Be Alone* (London: Fourth Estate).
Lupton, D. (1998) *The Emotional Self* (London: Sage).
Williams, S. (2001) *Emotion and Social Theory* (London: Sage).

Bibliography

Arditi, J. (1996) 'Simmel's Theory of Alienation and the Decline of the Nonrational', *Sociological Theory* 14(2), pp. 93–108.
Barbalet, J. M. (1998) *Emotion, Social Theory, and Social Structure: A Macrosociological Approach* (Cambridge: Cambridge University Press).
Bauman, Z. (2003) *Liquid Love: On the Frailty of Human Bonds* (Cambridge: Polity Press).

DOING RESEARCH • MODERNIZING • WORKING • CONSUMING • TRADING • STRATIFYING: CLASS • GOVERNING: POWER • RACIALIZING • GENDERING • SEXUALIZING • BEING: IDENTITY •

Beck, U. and E. Beck-Gernsheim (1995) *The Normal Chaos of Love* (Cambridge: Polity Press).

Bershady, Harold (ed.) (1992) *Max Scheler on Feeling, Knowing, and Valuing* (Chicago, IL: Chicago University Press).

Bertilsson, M. (1986) 'Love's Labour Lost? A Sociologial View', *Theory, Culture & Society* 3(2), pp. 19–35.

Biddle, L. and T. Walter (1998) 'The Emotional English and Their Queen of Hearts', *Folklore* 109, pp. 96–111.

Briggs, J. L. (1970) *Never in Anger: Portrait of an Eskimo Family* (Cambridge, MA: Harvard University Press).

Buunk, B. and R. B. Hupka (1987) 'Cross-cultural Differences in the Elicitation of Sexual Jealousy', *Journal of Sex Research* 23, pp. 12–22.

Crino, M. (1994) 'Employee Sabotage: a Random or Preventable Phenomenon?' *Journal of Management Issues* 6, pp. 311–30.

Damasio, A. (1996) *Descartes' Error: Emotion, Reason, and the Human Brain* (London: Picador).

Darwin, C. (1965) *The Expression of the Emotions in Man and Animals* (Chicago, IL: University of Chicago Press).

Doss, E. (2002) 'Death, Art and Memory in the Public Sphere: the Visual and Material Culture of Grief in Contemporary America', *Mortality* 7(1), pp. 63–82.

Durkheim, É. (1912/1961) *The Elementary Forms of the Religious Life* (London: Allen and Unwin).

Evans, M. (1998) '"Falling in Love with Love is Falling for Make Believe": Ideologies of Romance in Post-Enlightenment Culture', *Theory, Culture & Society* 15(3–4), pp. 265–75.

Finkelstein, J. (1980) 'Considerations for a Sociology of the Emotions', *Studies in Symbolic Interaction* 3, pp. 111–21.

Ha, F. (1995) 'Shame in Asian and Western Cultures', *American Behavioral Scientist* 38, pp. 1114–31.

Harré, R. (1991) *Physical Being: A Theory for a Corporeal Psychology* (Oxford: Blackwell).

Harris, D. (1998) 'The Electronic Funeral: Mourning Versace', *The Antioch Review* 56(2), pp. 154–63.

Ho, D. Y. (1976) 'On the Concept of Face', *American Journal of Sociology* 81, pp. 867–84.

Hochschild, A. (1983) *The Managed Heart: The Commercialization of Human Feeling* (Berkeley, CA: University of California Press).

van Hooft, S. (1994) 'Scheler on Sharing Emotions', *Philosophy Today* 38(1), pp. 18–28.

Jackson, S. (1993) 'Even Sociologists Fall in Love: an Exploration in the Sociology of Emotions', *Sociology* 27(2), pp. 201–20.

FEELING: EMOTIONS · BELIEVING: RELIGION · EDUCATING · STRAYING: DEVIANCE · MEDIATING: TECHNOLOGY · INFORMING: MEDIA · RELATING: FAMILY · BELONGING: COMMUNITY · FINISHING

12 271

Kemper, T. (1978) *A Social Interactional Theory of Emotions* (New York: John Wiley).

Kemper, T. (2002) 'Predicting Emotions in Groups: Some Lessons from September 11', in J. M. Barbalet (ed.), *Emotions and Sociology* (Oxford: Blackwell/The Sociological Review), pp. 53–67.

Kim, U., Y-S. Park and D. K. Park (2000) 'The Challenge of Cross-cultural Psychology: the Role of the Indigenous Psychologies', *Journal of Cross-Cultural Psychology* 31(1), pp. 63–75.

Le Doux, J. (1996) *The Emotional Brain: The Mysterious Underpinnings of Emotional Life* (New York: Simon and Schuster).

Leiser, B. (2001) 'Capital Punishment and Retributive Justice', *Free Inquiry* 21(3), p. 40.

Liem, R. (1997) 'Shame and Guilt among First- and Second-generation Asian Americans and European Americans', *Journal of Cross-Cultural Psychology* 28(4), pp. 365–92.

Lindholm, C. (1998) 'Love and Structure', *Theory, Culture & Society* 15(3–4), pp. 243–63.

Lingis, A. (2000) *Dangerous Emotions* (Berkeley, CA: University of California Press).

Marx, K. and F. Engels (1848/1977) *Manifesto of the Communist* Party (Moscow: Progress Publishers).

Meštrovíc, S. (1997) *Postemotional Society* (Sage: London).

Miller, W. I. (2000) 'Clint Eastwood and Equity: Popular Culture's Theory of Revenge', in A. Sarat and T. Kearns (eds), *Law in the Domains of Culture* (Ann Arbor, MI: University of Michigan Press), pp. 161–202.

New Zealand Ministry of Justice (2001) *He Hinatore ki te Ao Maori – A Glimpse into the Maori World: Maori Perspectives on Justice* (Wellington: Ministry of Justice).

Rosaldo, M. (1980) *Knowledge and Passion: Ilongot Notions of Self and Social Life* (Cambridge: Cambridge University Press).

Scherer, K. R., H. G. Wallbott and A. B. Summerfield (eds) (1986) *Experiencing Emotion: A Cross-cultural Study* (Cambridge: Cambridge University Press).

Simmel, G. (1950) 'The Metropolis and Mental Life', in *The Sociology of Georg Simmel*, trans. and ed. Kurt H. Wolff (New York: The Free Press), pp. 409–24.

Simmel, G. (1921–2/1984) *On Women, Sexuality and Love*, trans. and ed. G. Oakes (New Haven, CT: Yale University Press).

Shweder, R. (2003) 'Toward a Deep Cultural Psychology of Shame', *Social Research* 70, pp. 1109–30.

Tolich, M. (1993) 'Alienating and Liberating Emotions at Work; Super-market Clerks' Performance of Customer Service', *Journal of Contemporary Ethnography* 22(3), pp. 361–81.

Turner, B. (1993) 'Outline of the Theory of Human Rights', *Sociology* 27, pp. 489–512.

West-Newman, C. L. (2005) 'Feeling for Justice? Rights, Laws and Cultural Contexts', *Law & Social Inquiry* 30, pp. 305–35.

Williams, L. (2005) 'Counter Emotions: Emotional Labour in Retail', MA thesis, Department of Sociology, University of Auckland.

Williams, S. (1998) 'Modernity and the Emotions: Corporeal Reflections on the (Ir)rational', *Sociology* 32, pp. 747–69.

FEELING: EMOTIONS · BELIEVING: RELIGION · EDUCATING · STRAYING: DEVIANCE ·
MEDIATING: TECHNOLOGY · INFORMING: MEDIA · RELATING: FAMILY · BELONGING: COMMUNITY · FINISHING

12 273

13 believing: religion

Tracey McIntosh

KEY
POINTS
- ▪ Religion is a basic element of human experience.

- ▪ Sociologists see religion as a social phenomenon and religious belief as a quest for meaning.

- ▪ Early sociologists believed that reason and science would triumph over faith and religion. Their confidently asserted prediction of the end of religion has not been borne out, though the way that religion is articulated and responded to has changed considerably.

- ▪ Both early and later sociologists tend to see religion as a tool of social control and of social cohesion.

- ▪ Secularization is used to describe the belief that religion is losing its significance in modern societies. While it is evident that certain aspects of religious life show a marked decline in Western societies, we do not see a disappearance of religion altogether but an ongoing process of meaning attribution and sacralization. The existence of a plurality of belief systems simultaneously creates a great diversity in 'believing'.

- ▪ Religious beliefs inform social structures, even in modern secular societies. Legal codes are a good example of this.

- ▪ Understanding religion helps us understand both collective action and individual action.

In the beginning ...

Karen Armstrong (1994) argues that *Homo sapiens* is also *Homo religiosus*. From our earliest times, some form of believing has been intrinsic to all human endeavours. This chapter looks at the persistence of faith and the resurgence of religion in contemporary society. Peter Berger (1967, pp. 36–7) defines religion as the 'audacious attempt to conceive of the universe as being humanly significant'. Religion has been, amongst other things, an important tool to make sense of human experience and consciousness. Early sociologists prophesied that the deliverance of humanity from a world-view imbued with religious symbols and fanciful imagery to a world-view formed by the rational and scientific would be one of modernity's major accomplishments. If we accept that the position of religion has changed in modern society, what effect does this have on how we derive meaning in our world? What is it to believe? In the modern age, does religion matter?

I will argue that not only does religion matter but that it matters whether one is a believer or not. It is impossible to have a deep understanding of the world and its complexities at a cultural, social, political and even economic level without having some understanding of the way that religious beliefs inform and influence societal structures. There was a time in our recent past where many social commentators assumed that religion, outside of purely personal considerations, had ceased to be of much import, yet present global conditions underscore its continuing relevance in our day-to-day lives. Religion and faith may have been pushed to the periphery, from the public to the private sphere in some societies, but religion still matters. This is clearly shown by the ways in which faith and belief can be seen to be embedded in codes of law. If a country has been historically Muslim or Christian, for example, then the law will reflect this, even when religious practice is no longer central in terms of governance. Similarly, social norms and values tend to be based on religious ethical codes and individual attitudes are often informed by religious tenets. Another, more jarring, example is the role that religion plays in conflict at the national and international levels (see Chapter 8, 'Racializing').

The problems of definition, a perennial sociological quandary, prove particularly challenging when applied to questions of religion and faith. Religion is yet another of those concepts that we sense we immediately understand yet, when pushed, we find it difficult to come up with an inclusive definition that captures its many qualities. We could say that religion is connected with those socially shared ways of thinking, feeling and acting that have as their central focus some transcendent otherness. This attempt at a definition in a few words goes from the concrete (thinking, feeling and acting) to the abstract (transcendent otherness). So, while being an inadequate definition, it does manage to capture the elusive nature of pinning a label on religion. Steve Bruce acknowledges that no one definition will totally suffice but he does give us a working description. Religion can be defined as:

> Beliefs, actions and institutions predicated on the existence of entities with powers of agency (that is, god or gods) or impersonal powers or processes possessed of moral purpose (the Hindu notion of karma, for example), which can set the conditions of, or intervene in, human affairs. (2002, p. 2)

Defining faith presents its own problems. While a faith is a religion or a recognized community of religious believers, it is also an acceptance of beliefs and ideals that may not be amenable to verification through experimentation and reason. Faith, by its very nature, is beyond reason. Religion, faith and belief are many things and are understood very differently from the perspectives of belief or non-belief. However, whether we are theist or atheist – or somewhere else in this continuum – we can be assured that whatever else religion is, it is decidedly a social phenomenon. As James Beckford explains:

> Regardless of whether religious beliefs and experiences actually relate to the supernatural, superempirical or noumenal realities, religion is expressed by means of human ideas, symbols, feelings and practices and organizations. These expressions are the products of social interactions, structures and processes and, in turn, they influence social life and cultural meaning to varying degrees. The social scientific study of religion ... aims to interpret and explain these processes. (2003, p. 2)

Throughout history – and further back into pre-history – religion has been a vital and pervasive feature of human existence. To understand human history, and human life and experience more generally, it is necessary to understand the way that religious thought and action – particularly the actions of individuals or communities of believers – have influenced and informed personal, regional, national and global narratives. In the contemporary world it becomes increasingly more urgent to understand other groups' systems of belief in order to grasp perspectives often very different from our own. Ninian Smart (1984) argues that understanding religions is important in three ways. First, they are a fundamental element in the varied story of humanity's various experiments in living. Second, in order to grasp the meaning and values of the plural cultures in the contemporary world we need to know something of the world-views that underlie them. For example, to better understand the 'Palestine question' you need to know something about Islam, Judaism and Christianity as they were experienced in the Middle East. Third, having an understanding of religion allows us to attempt to form a coherent picture of reality (Smart, 1993, p. 9). There is also an intrinsic satisfaction in studying the significant ideas and practices of many cultures and civilizations.

Classical sociology of religion

Sociology and religion have historically had very close ties. James Beckford (2003, p. 1) argues that religion was at the very centre of the first generation of sociological and anthropological theorists' thinking. It is significant that the 'classic' theorists of sociology – Auguste Comte, Émile Durkheim, Max Weber, Karl Marx and Georg Simmel – were all exponents of the sociology of religion (Cipriani, 2000, p. 1) and that Marx, Durkheim and Weber made particularly important contributions to this field.

Karl Marx (1818–83)
Marx was an important social theorist for sociology as well as other disciplines. He was born into a German family of Jewish origin that later converted to Lutheranism for social rather than religious reasons. His famous dictum that 'religion is the opium of the people' is often quoted but rarely fully contextualized. Marx was a 'social atheist' but he was not an anti-theist; that is, his work is 'concerned with the *social function* of religion, not with the philosophical disputes about the existence or non-existence of God' (Johnson et al., 1990, p. 143). He was not interested in entering into theological disputes on the existence or non-existence of God but rather was a critic of what he saw as religion's reactionary social role.

Marx, drawing on Ludwig Feuerbach's work, held that 'man makes religion, religion does not make man' (Marx and Engels, 1964, p. 41). He believed religious consciousness arose out of actual human conditions. For the masses, religion was a solution to and consequence of their material poverty (Cipriani, 2000, p. 23). Capitalist society, he argued, is a two-class system where the ruling class exploits the oppressed working class (see Chapter 6, 'Stratifying: Class'). Moreover, because the worker is treated merely as a cog in the production process he is effectively alienated from his own humanity: 'what he produces is alienated from him, since it is not the fulfilment of his own creativity, nor for his personal use nor is he in any way involved in the decisions governing production; he is only a producer of commodities made for the purpose of capitalistic profit' (Johnson et al., 1990, p. 157). Religion was the result of social alienation. This then is the context for understanding Marx's full statement that,

> Religious distress is at the same time the *expression* of real distress and the *protest* against real distress. Religion is the sigh of the oppressed creature, the heart of a heartless world, just as it is the spirit of a spiritless situation. It is the *opium* of the people. (Marx and Engels, 1964, p. 42)

Marx's critique of religion begins from the premise that the exploitation and class conflict of capitalist society produce human alienation. Religion is a projection reflecting this alienation. This projection represents a protest of the exploited proletariat suffering under oppressive conditions. It is, therefore, a narcotic protest, which provides relief and comfort at the price of addicting the proletariat to the status quo that exploits them. The compensatory fantasy world of religion is an immobilizing drug that rationalizes and legitimates the oppressive capitalist system. It teaches and maintains the servile virtues of submission, suffering, weakness, humility, patience and forgiveness of enemies, thereby repressing revolutionary energies. The capitalist class with its vested interests in the status quo is the true profiteer from religious sublimation and compensation. Only the revolutionary overthrow of the class structure of capitalist society will abolish the reactionary social role of religion and remove the conditions on which it thrives (Johnson et al., 1990, pp. 157–61). In later work Marx did not fully develop many of the ideas sketched here, but his critique remains a forceful one and is still engaged with in sociological debate.

FEELING: EMOTIONS · **BELIEVING: RELIGION** · EDUCATING · STRAYING: DEVIANCE · MEDIATING: TECHNOLOGY · INFORMING: MEDIA · RELATING: FAMILY · BELONGING: COMMUNITY · FINISHING

13   279

Émile Durkheim (1858–1917)

Durkheim was a French sociologist who strongly influenced the discipline of sociology. Because he believed that religion served a key function in creating social cohesion and was an important agent of social control, he saw it as critically important in all societies. The study of early religious forms would, he thought, enable a greater understanding of the religious disposition, which he saw as a permanent and essential aspect of humanity (Cipriani, 2000, p. 66). For Durkheim, religion was a product of society:

> Religion is an eminently social thing. Religious representations are collective representations that express collective realities; rites are ways of acting that are born only in the midst of assembled groups and whose purpose is to evoke, maintain, or recreate certain mental states of those groups. But if the categories are of religious origin, then they must participate in what is common to all religion: they, too must be social things, products of collective thought. (Durkheim, 1912/1995, p. 9)

His classic study *The Elementary Forms of the Religious Life* (1912) used one in-depth case study, the Australian Aborigines, and focused on the role of the totem in their culture. Durkheim chose this group because he felt they represented the most basic, elementary forms of religion within a culture. He believed that religion is centred in beliefs and practices that are related to sacred as opposed to profane things and argued that all societies divide human experience into these two categories. The profane, as the realm of the everyday, involves those aspects of social reality that are routine and secular. The sacred is extraordinary and awe-inspiring, beyond the profane realm; it evokes an attitude of reverence. It is important to note that nothing is inherently sacred or profane but rather it becomes such after being defined and labelled by individuals and groups. So religion, for Durkheim, was not divinely but rather humanly inspired. He saw it as having a vital role in ensuring social cohesion, social order and in creating the norms and values of any given society. His analysis suggested that there was no society that 'does not experience the need at regular intervals to maintain and strengthen the collective feelings and ideas that provide its coherence and distinct individuality' (Durkheim, 1912/1995, p. 429) (see Chapter 19, 'Belonging: Community').

Max Weber (1864–1920)

Weber, another German social theorist, is often associated with Marx because much of his work has been seen as a debate with Marx's ghost. Although he admired Marx, Weber nevertheless believed that economic determinants were over-emphasized in his studies of human society. Weber acknowledged that economic factors were important but was also concerned that other factors – for example, religious ideas and values – should not be under-estimated.

Weber was convinced that ideas developed within religious traditions could influence behaviour; that belief could (and did) influence action. Whereas Marx saw religion as largely a reactionary force, Weber thought that it could, in certain social conditions, be revolutionary. In *The Protestant Ethic and the Spirit of Capitalism*, Weber argued that Calvinism (an ascetic form of Protestantism) offered an ideological basis for capitalistic development (Cipriani, 2000, p. 75). He found that Calvinism had developed a set of beliefs around the concept of predestination. John Calvin (1509–64), one of the most influential Protestant theologians of his time (whose teachings are still influential), was born in France a generation later than Martin Luther. He claimed that God has already divided all the people into categories of the 'saved' and 'unsaved', that is, the 'chosen and the rejected' (Bruce, 2002, p. 7). This was the doctrine of predestination. Under this belief, one could not change one's status by faith, good works or repentance – one's fate had been divinely determined. You were either one of the elect or you were not. This, Weber believed, created anxieties for the believer. However, since wealth was taken as a sign of election, this provided an incentive for its acquisition. Steve Bruce argues that 'John Calvin and his followers inadvertently created a climate in which the Puritans could see worldly success, provided it was achieved honestly and diligently by pious people, as a proof of divine favour. These elements combined to produce a new 'ethic' (Bruce, 2002, p. 7).

Weber's main point here was that his analysis showed 'the influence of certain religious ideas on the development of an economic spirit, or the *ethos* of an economic system. In this case we are dealing with the connection of the spirit of modern economic life with the rational ethics of ascetic Protestantism' (1976, p. 27). The Protestant ethic, then, can be seen as

FEELING: EMOTIONS · **BELIEVING: RELIGION** · EDUCATING · STRAYING: DEVIANCE · MEDIATING: TECHNOLOGY · INFORMING: MEDIA · RELATING: FAMILY · BELONGING: COMMUNITY · FINISHING

13   281

providing the religious sanction that fostered a spirit of rigorous discipline (spiritually, socially and economically) that encouraged individuals to work towards rationally acquiring wealth (the spirit of capitalism). Weber claimed that:

> The religious valuation of restless, continuous, systematic work in a worldly calling, as the highest means of asceticism, and at the same time the surest and most evident proof of rebirth and genuine faith, must have been the most powerful conceivable lever for the expansion of ... the spirit of capitalism. (1946]/1958, p. 172)

He was not arguing that this factor alone could account for the rise of modern industrial capitalism but he was able to illustrate effectively how ideas, in this case religious ones, can inform and influence actions.

Weber's study of religion was extensive, much of it of a historical and comparative nature. His work was an attempt to document the move from traditional to modern society and from traditional to legal/rational authority. It focused on a growth of rationalization in all aspects of modern society. Raymond Lee and Susan Ackerman suggest that Max Weber provided, in the early part of the twentieth century, 'the most explicit statement on the transformation of Enlightenment science into an institution of world mastery' (2002, p. 2). A world that relied less on religious explanation and increasingly explained itself using the tools of science and reason was a world that becomes 'disenchanted'. Weber saw, and in many ways foresaw, that modern science and governmental rationalities drain the world of intrinsic meaning and therefore we must proceed bureaucratically. This bureaucratic social order he likened to an 'iron cage'. Weber's work speaks to many issues that are still salient today, in discussions both of religion and of modern society in general (see Chapter 2, 'Modernizing').

The sociology of religion today

Religion continues to be an important dimension in all societies and, whether at the margins or at the centre, continues to play an influential role in many aspects of contemporary life. The sociology of religion seeks to understand religion in its varied manifestations as a social institution, as a cultural practice, and as a pattern of beliefs and activities that are shaped by societal conditions and that, in turn, shape these conditions. These studies focus on such current topics as religious movements, religious organizations, and the relationship of religion to gender, culture, politics, globalization and social change. Sociologists of religion are characterized by a wide range of religious beliefs, as well as non-belief, and embrace a variety of theoretical and methodological orientations. One of the most sustained areas of interest, commented on by Marx, Durkheim and Weber and still significant today, is the secularization thesis. The rest of the chapter will focus on this thesis and on the related issues of the decline and resurgence of religion.

The secularization thesis is as old as the discipline of sociology itself. As Rodney Stark notes,

> For nearly three centuries, social scientists and assorted western intellectuals have been promising the end of religion. Each generation has been confident that within another few decades, or possibly a bit longer, humans will 'outgrow' belief in the supernatural. (1999, p. 249)

'Secularization', like other sociological terms, is one that has been adapted from its original usage. James Beckford recounts how the term can be traced back to Roman civilization and later to the medieval Catholic Church. He notes that whereas the term previously referred to the process of releasing priests from their vows, within the sociological lexicon it came to refer to 'relations between religious institutions and the spheres of politics and commerce, which were gaining independence at the time' (Beckford, 2003, p. 33). Bryan Wilson provides us with a detailed and rather lengthy explanation when he writes,

> Its application covers such things as the sequestration by political powers of the property and facilities of religious agencies; the shift from religious to secular control of various erstwhile activities and functions of religion; the decline in proportion of their time, energy and resources which men devote to supra-empirical concerns; the decay of religious institutions; the supplanting, in matters of behaviour, of religious precepts by demands that accord with strictly technical criteria; and the gradual replacement of a specifically

FEELING: EMOTIONS · **BELIEVING: RELIGION** · EDUCATING · STRAYING: DEVIANCE ·
MEDIATING: TECHNOLOGY · INFORMING: MEDIA · RELATING: FAMILY · BELONGING: COMMUNITY · FINISHING

13   283

> religious consciousness (which might range from dependence on charms, rites, spell or prayers, to a broadly spiritually-inspired ethical concern) by an empirical, rational, instrumental orientation; the abandonment of mythical, poetic and artistic interpretations of nature and society in favour of matter-of-fact description and with it, the rigorous separation of evaluative and emotive dispositions from cognitive and positivistic orientations. (Quoted in Bruce, 2002, p. 3)

In talk of our supposedly irreligious present there is a tendency to compare ourselves with a past where individuals and collectives were religiously observant and pious. Rodney Stark is scathingly critical of this presentation and goes to great length, often very humorously, to rid us of this notion. He argues that there is a myth of past piety to match the myth of religious decline. In example after example from medieval records he is able to paint a picture that illustrates that not only were the general population not overly enthusiastic about carrying out their religious obligations but the clergy were often totally ignorant of even the most basic doctrines (1999, pp. 253–4).

He also says the official records show that even when people did attend church, their behaviour was often poor. The historian Keith Thomas noted from ecclesiastical court records that in late medieval times there were occasions when 'members of the population jostled for pews, nudged their neighbours, hawked and spat, knitted, made coarse remarks, told jokes, fell asleep, and even let off guns' (quoted in Stark, 1999, p. 258). A church record from Cambridgeshire in 1598 reports a man charged for misbehaviour in church after his 'most loathsome farting, striking and scoffing speeches' had resulted in 'the great offence of the good and the great rejoicing of the bad' (in Stark, 1999, p. 258). Doubtless the religious piety of the past has been over-stated, but this in itself is not sufficient to deny that religion played a *greater* part in our past than it does today. Steve Bruce (2002, p. 17) convincingly demonstrates that the life cycles of individuals and of the community were celebrated in church. Births, baptisms, marriages, deaths, harvest festivals, the passage of agricultural seasons, and every important contract and promise were sworn before God. Religious expression and explanation permeated all aspects of lived experience. Religious officials and institutions may have been objects of jest but religion was embedded deep in the social polity.

God is dead? Belief in modernity

The secularization thesis involves an assumption, simply put, that religion is losing its significance in modern societies. For a considerable period this assumption was taken as an absolute given. Auguste Comte enthusiastically and somewhat optimistically suggested that 'as a result of modernization, human society was outgrowing its "theological stage" of social evolution and a new age was dawning in which the science of sociology would replace religion as the basis for moral judgments' (quoted in Stark, 1999, p. 250). Certainly in intellectual circles since the Enlightenment period some had toyed with the idea that the end of God's dominion was nigh. Friedrich Nietzsche (1844–1900) was not the first to suggest that God was dead but his presentation of the idea was unusually powerful and compelling.

Nietzsche, whose parable of the madman who announces the murder of God first appeared in his 1892 book *The Gay Science*, saw the modern world in a state of cultural decline – in what he called a condition of nihilism. He saw himself 'between two worlds, one dead the other powerless to be born' (Livingston, 1971, p. 195). The 'madman' is ridiculed by a group of people watching him; they taunt and mock him, asking if God is lost, or hiding, on a voyage, or emigrated. Incensed, he jumps into their midst and answers:

> Wither is God? He cried 'I shall tell you. *We have killed him* – you and I. All of us are his murderers. But how have we done this? How were we able to drink up the sea? Who gave us the sponge to wipe away the entire horizon? What did we do when we unchained this earth from its sun? ... God is dead. God remains dead. And we have killed him. How shall we, the murderers of all murderers, comfort ourselves?' (Quoted in Kaufmann, 1968, pp. 95–6)

The claim that Nietzsche is making is not a theological one; it is a social one. For him, the 'death of God' is not the result of a philosophical or spiritual investigation but a social fact, the consequence of which, he argued, had not yet been fully revealed to Western consciousness. He is making the point that whether or not individuals hold a personal belief in God is unimportant. God is dead, he suggests, for *all intents and purposes* because whether some personally believe in his existence or not, the world we live in *acts* as if he were dead. The powerful use of this parable caught the mood of the time and it still has resonance today. Nietzsche was not claiming that religion was a false or childish illusion – he was proclaiming that it was no more. He argued that the belief or presence of Christian belief no longer had any significant social consequences for life in modern society. He was, in fact, reflecting on a world where religious explanations no longer dominate. He avowed that the death of God meant the loss of commitment to absolute values as well as the loss of purpose and meaning. Like Weber, he realized that science and rationality would never plug up the metaphysical gap, what Jean-Paul Sartre called the 'God-shaped hole in the human consciousness, where God had always been' (quoted in Armstrong, 1994, p. 378).

Removed from a time when religion formed the main weave of many of our societies, it may seem that the persistence of faith and the resurgence of religion in contemporary society is some form of anomaly. Surely the modern project's accomplishment can be seen in humankind's deliverance from a world-view that was imbued with religious symbols and fanciful imagery into a world-view informed by the rational and the scientific. No longer forced to live within the constraints of a society dominated by religious institutions, instead we are free to make sense of the world around us with the tools of science and logic. Yet this very disruption and emancipation from earlier mind-sets seems to have brought forth problems both of meaning and of legitimation. What then has been the cost of this relegation (if indeed this is what it was) of religion to the periphery of society?

Jonathan Sacks (1990) argues that modernity left religion with a restricted territory within which to operate: 'no longer the vehicle by which all meaning was formulated and expressed', it was now seen as a 'mode of experience, a voice of conscience, a spring to social action or a mystical way of knowing'. Religion, it seemed, was increasingly a *private* rather than a *public* affair. Within the modern world it was now science that investigated nature and history; that examined the past, the ways of business, the new technologies, governments and the mediation of conflicts. All of these had passed 'outside the canopy of faith' (Sacks, 1990). Secularization and its processes took up the position once held by religion.

If secularization can be seen as the liberation of humankind 'from religious and metaphysical tutelage' (Cox, 1990, p. 15) and the focusing of attention away from other worlds and towards this one, what can religion now be seen as? If the position of religion is changed, what effect does this have on how we derive meaning for our world? Seidman sees the transformation of European society in the rise of modernity as bringing forth problems of meaning. By this he means the existence within the modern life of a pervading uncertainty about ultimate beliefs and values; confusion in regard to images of self, society and nature, and a never-ending conflict over the way personal and collective life is organized and legitimated (Seidman, 1983, p. 46). Modernity signals a break from the established cultural structures that had until then framed social life into some form of acceptable and meaningful pattern. Modernity effectively moves that which was previously seen as a rational arrangement of knowledge and set of beliefs into the realm of the fundamentally irrational (Whimster and Lash, 1987, p. 265). Just as magic had become subordinate to religion, so now did religion become subordinate to science.

Max Weber acknowledged that once a previously religiously understood world was perceived through a scientific perspective, then religious belief would lose its centrality in the way the world was seen. This shift in perception also corresponded with a similar shift in expectation of what else science was able to accomplish. Science was called upon to attempt to answer that which had previously been within the domain of the religious world. However, Weber states that in matters concerning ethics and belief the individual and the community must make its own decisions independent of any 'scientific crutches' (Whimster and Lash, 1987, p. 260). Seidman argues that it was the claim of science to construct a world-view that Weber set out to destroy. He named Marxism, Comtean positivism and social evolutionism as examples where science projected itself 'as a secular ideological replacement for religion' (Seidman, 1983, p. 271). Weber understood that all religions demanded that the way of the world be somehow meaningful. Even if religion had been placed on the margins of society, the need for meaning persists in the modern world and this need was unable to be met by a scientific response. Seidman contends that although Weber held that neither religion nor science can generate systems of meaning that could hold as a structure of social unity, he did not succumb to cultural pessimism or to the metaphysical pathos of an absurd existence (Seidman, 1983, p. 272).

Technology is now a facet of all parts of our lives. If technology is seen as an attempt 'to provide the most efficient means for certain ends', and we have accepted its introduction even in the social sphere of our lives, we must become more committed to a highly rationalistic organization of our everyday life. Where once there was a reliance on a strong moral code put into place as a form of social control, electronic surveillance and data retrieval systems have largely superseded the reliance of social virtues such as honesty, goodwill and responsibility (see Chapter 16, 'Mediating: Technology').

Technology demands more rational ways of thinking. At a red light we must obey traffic signals and not what we might see as a personal courtesy to another individual. Stopping at a green light so that an elderly driver may pass would not be seen as a courtesy but as an irrational act. Bryan Wilson (1982, p. 43), in one of his earlier works, noted that it was reflections such as these that made us aware that our sense of control over our everyday lives can seem both artificial and superficial. Moreover, it seems evident that an increasing number of people are distressed by the anonymity of modern bureaucracy, by the loss of personal relationships and a sense of ennui in the face of working within a rational technical system (Wilson, 1982, p. 46). So, although we may have been released from moral controls, we are further restrained by the new technological order.

While the contemporary ethos stresses equality, democracy and individualism, it does not adequately address questions of doubt and the position of trust. Modernity has forced one to face the problems of meaning yet has been unable to console us with sure and comforting words: where once we sought to analyse, now we are hesitant to even conceptualize. The whole notion of certainty often seems redundant. Though questioning has increased, the expectation of resolution becomes more remote. Questions long thought asked and answered are now thrown open to a shifting and retreating and shifting foundation of knowledge. The mere notion of knowledge, let alone secure knowledge, is increasingly problematic. One is left with a feeling of ambiguity, contingency and ambivalence (Bauman, 1991).

Personal and impersonal relationships are further weakened by a loss of trust in both the individual and collective worlds. Society may not signify security or identity but instead be found to be abrasive and soul-destroying. So though we cannot doubt the enormous progress of science and the resulting evident decline in religion and religious commitment, most Western nations have also witnessed the continual appearance of new religious movements. Marc Galanter (1999) and George Chryssides (1999) note that new religious movements emerge as, among other factors, a response to the industrialization and rationalization of contemporary, technologically advanced society (see Chapter 12, 'Feeling: Emotions').

Religion's resurgence

While the religious revival has affected a wide and pluralistic range of religious movements, it is hard not to be aware of the resurgence of many groups that we term 'fundamentalist'. Where they stand out from mainstream political and religious groups is that, unlike the secularists or the religious liberals, they know exactly what they believe in. In times of rapid change and movement their beliefs are rigid and static. Sacks (1990), quoting Robert Bellah, says that they speak with the 'rarest of modern accents – authority'.

Although their content is more often than not traditional, religious conservatives and evangelicals enthusiastically utilize mass media, including the internet. The use of modern mass communicative forms has made Christian and Islamic fundamentalist groups a significant political force. Whereas the 1960s and 1970s may have belonged to the radical and the liberal, it seems that the following decades have been the years of the conservative.

Heller and Feher conceptualize fundamentalism as, 'the voice of the bad conscience of the post-modern condition flagellating itself for its excessive indulgence in relativism' (1988, p. 7). These new religious fundamentalist movements are not an attempt to rediscover the grand narratives of earlier times but usually focus instead on one aspect of the dogma, 'one "text of foundation" to which they declare all attempts at hermeneutics politically subversive' (Heller and Feher, 1988, p. 7).

In the last decades, and particularly after the events of September 11, there has been a substantial increase in sociological works that attempt to make sense of the resurgence of religion, especially as it pertains to fundamentalist orientations and to the possibilities of it engendering religious violence (Bruce, 2000; Juergensmeyer, 2001; Ruthven, 2004). The Fundamentalist Project was launched in the early 1990s and has amassed a vast amount of data presented in substantial volumes. In Volume Five (1995) fundamentalist groups are classified into categories of orientation: 'World Conqueror', 'World Transformer' and 'World Renouncer'.

World Conqueror movements are hegemonic and tend to seek to export the revolution, to renew the faith and orthodoxy of the tepid believer and convert the unbeliever. Ideologies often exhibit strong nationalistic or theocratic elements. Examples include: Revolutionary Shi'ism in Iran, the Sunni Radical Movement in Eygpt, Hamas in the Middle East, US fundamentalist Protestants, Sikh Militants in India and Gush Emunim in Israel. Movements in the World Transformer mode occupy a niche in society but are constrained from hegemonic activity and forced to negotiate their circumstances and transform their environment over time. Leadership may be diffuse, shared by a number of authoritative leaders, mobilizing followers on various issues; the teachings or fate of any one leader is less important than in the World Conqueror pattern. Examples include: Pentecostalism in Guatemala, Habad and Christianity in South India. World Renouncer movements often emerge from an existing, long-standing tradition that is abruptly modernized. The leadership is charismatic, authoritarian, renegade and prophetic – often defining the movement in contrast to tepid, compromising, liberalizing religious leadership that is seen as jeopardizing the integrity of the religious tradition. Examples include: French Catholic Lefebvists and Haredi Jews (Marty and Appleby, 1995, pp. 447–79). Looked at in this way, we can see that fundamentalism is a religious phenomenon, a political movement and a state of mind.

Like all other concepts, fundamentalism is not easily amenable to definition. However, there are certain 'ideal type' characteristics that are present. It is generally characterized by the affirmation of religious authority as holistic and absolute, admitting of neither criticism nor reduction. It is expressed through the collective demand that specific creedal and ethical dictates derived from scripture be publicly recognized and sometimes even legally enforced. The following are characteristics of fundamentalist groups. They see themselves as a righteous remnant. Even when they are numerically a majority, they perceive themselves as a minority. They are oppositional and confrontational towards both secularists and 'wayward' religious followers. Often, they are led by charismatic males. Fundamentalists generate their own lexicon. This language may not always be readily understood by those outside of it. Such a form of religious idealism is seen as a basis for personal and communal identity. This may involve seeing themselves as part of a cosmic struggle. Historical events may then be interpreted in light of this struggle. Opponents may be demonized or vilified. Fundamentalists are distrustful of modernist cultural hegemony (Almond et al., 2003, pp. 116–30).

Religious revival is not only a reaction to the modern but also a form of opposition. Sacks (1990) argues that many religious believers experience the modern condition not as a process to be endured but as an assault to be resisted. Islamic fundamentalism can be seen as both a movement of renewal and purification but also as a rejection of Western notions of progress. Some commentators see the resurgence of religion and the renewal of religious symbolism as an attempt to restore the social bond. Secularization may be seen to be failing the individual and the community by its inability to give meaning, even when it has been remarkably successful in becoming the dominant ethos. For others, the higher profile afforded religion is an attempt to recreate a return to the sacred. Resacralization may be a response from diverse sectors of society who may reject some of the basic premises of secular culture. Religion remains present in society. Though it may be articulated in a number of ways, it still exists to – among other things – give form and meaning to lives. The structure of religion is not static and its images are not uniform or consistent, but it never went away. We may simply have failed to sense its ongoing presence.

Suggestions for further reading

Armstrong, K. (2000) *The Battle for God* (New York: Alfred A. Knopf).

Fenn, R. (ed.) (2001) *The Blackwell Companion to the Sociology of Religion* (Oxford: Blackwell).

Hamilton, M. B. (1995) *The Sociology of Religion: Theoretical and Comparative Perspectives* (London: Routledge).

FEELING: EMOTIONS • **BELIEVING: RELIGION** • EDUCATING • STRAYING: DEVIANCE •
MEDIATING: TECHNOLOGY • INFORMING: MEDIA • RELATING: FAMILY • BELONGING: COMMUNITY • FINISHING

13   291

Haynes, J. (1998) *Religion in Global Politics* (London: Longman).
Watson, J. and M. Watson (eds) (2000) *Religion and Global World Order* (Cardiff: University of Wales Press).

Bibliography

Almond, G., R. Appleby and E. Sivan (2003) *Strong Religion: The Rise of Fundamentalism around the World* (Chicago, IL: University of Chicago Press).

Armstrong, K. (1994) *A History of God* (New York: Ballantine Books).

Bauman, Z. (1991) *Modernity and Ambivalence* (Cambridge: Polity Press).

Beckford, J. A. (2003) *Social Theory and Religion* (Cambridge: Cambridge University Press).

Berger, P. (1967) *The Social Reality of Religion* (Harmondsworth: Penguin Books).

Bowen, J. R. (ed.) (1998) *Religion in Culture and Society* (Boston, MA: Allyn and Bacon).

Bruce, S. (2000) *Fundamentalism* (Cambridge: Polity Press).

Bruce, S. (2002) *God is Dead: Secularization in the West* (Oxford: Blackwell Publishing).

Chryssides, G. (1999) *Exploring New Religions* (London: Cassell).

Cipriani, R. (2000) *Sociology of Religion: An Historical Introduction* (New York: Aldine de Gruyter).

Cox, H. (1990) *The Secular City: Secularization and Urbanization in Theological Perspective* (New York: Collier Books).

Durkheim, E. (1912/1995) *The Elementary Forms of the Religious Life: The Totemic System in Australia*, trans. K. E. Fields (New York: Free Press).

Galanter, M. (1999) *Cults, Faith Healing and Coercion* (New York: Oxford University Press).

Haynes, J. (1998) *Religion in Global Politics* (London: Longman).

Heller, A. and F. Feher (1988) *The Postmodern Political Condition* (Cambridge: Polity Press).

Johnson, R. et al. (1990) *Critical Issues in Modern Religion* (Englewood Cliffs, NJ: Prentice-Hall).

Johnston, D. and C. Sampson (1995) *Religion: The Missing Dimension of Statecraft* (New York: Oxford University Press).

Juergensmeyer, M. (2001) *Terror in the Mind of God: The Global Rise of Religious Violence* (Berkeley, CA: University of California Press).

Kaufmann, W. (1968) *Nietzsche: Philosopher, Psychologist, Antichrist* (Princeton, NJ: Princeton University Press).

Lee, R. and S. Ackerman (2002) *The Challenge of Religion After Modernity: Beyond Disenchantment* (Hants: Ashgate Publishing).

Livingston, J. C. (1971) *Modern Christian Thought* (New York: Macmillan).

Marty, M. E. and R. S. Appleby (eds) (1995) *Fundamentalisms Comprehended* (Chicago, IL: Chicago University Press).

Marx, K. and F. Engels (1964) *On Religion*, introduction by Reinhold Niebuhr (New York: Schocken Books).

Ruthven, M. (2004) *Fundamentalism: The Search for Meaning* (Oxford: Oxford University Press).

Sacks, J. (1990) 'The Persistence of Faith', *The Reith Lectures*. Available: http://www.bbc.co.uk/radio4/reith/historic_audio/reith_historic.shtml.

Seidman, S. (1983) 'Modernity, Meaning and Cultural Pessimism in Max Weber', *Sociological Analysis* 44, pp. 267–78.

Smart, N. (1984) *The Religious Experience of Mankind* (New York: Charles Scribner).

Smart, N. (1993) *The World's Religions* (Cambridge: Cambridge University Press).

Stark, R. (1999) 'Secularization, R.I.P.', *Sociology of Religion* 60, pp. 249–73.

Weber, M. (1946/1958) *From Max Weber*, trans. and ed. H. H. Gerth and C. Wright Mills (New York: Galaxy).

Weber, M. (1976) *The Protestant Ethic and the Spirit of Capitalism* (London: Allen and Unwin).

Whimster, S. (1987) 'The Secular Ethic and the Culture of Modernism', in *Max Weber: Rationality and Modernity*, ed. S. Whimster and S. Lash (London: Allen and Unwin).

Whimster, S. and S. Lash (1987) *Max Weber: Rationality and Modernity* (London: Allen and Unwin).

Wilson, A. N. (1999) *God's Funeral* (London: Abacus).

Wilson, B. (1982) *Religion in Sociological Perspective* (Oxford: Clarendon Press).

Woolacott, M. (1995) 'Keeping our Faith in Belief', *Guardian*, 23 December 1995.

FEELING: EMOTIONS • **BELIEVING: RELIGION** • EDUCATING • STRAYING: DEVIANCE • MEDIATING: TECHNOLOGY • INFORMING: MEDIA • RELATING: FAMILY • BELONGING: COMMUNITY • FINISHING

13 293

14 educating

Roger Dale

KEY POINTS

▪ National education systems are the major means by which societies seek to define, replicate, celebrate and ensure their national distinctiveness; to strengthen their national economies; to address their social problems, and to influence the distribution of individual life chances.

▪ At the same time, 'education' as an institutional means of delivering knowledge is the most significant example of intervention by nation states in the lives of their subjects.

▪ Sociologists of education have approached the complexities of education through a triple framework: their project – the goals they sought to achieve through it; their location – the conditions under which they worked; and the context – the political frameworks within which they worked.

▪ Education has offered the possibility of simultaneously improving economic development, social efficiency and social justice through social mobility. However, there are major tensions between these objectives.

▪ Sociologists – such as Pierre Bourdieu and Basil Bernstein – explore the ways in which education operates to secure social reproduction and the continuity of existing social arrangements.

▪ In large part because of the global impact of neo-liberalism, education is undergoing deep changes that call for the application of a new sociological imagination.

▪ This new imagination must address new 'Education Questions' relating to educational practice, education policy, the politics of education and the outcomes of education.

Introduction

Education may be seen to represent the quintessence of the central claim of modernity – that humanity was capable of understanding the social world in the same ways as it did the physical world; and, moreover, was as capable of controlling and changing it on the basis of that knowledge as physical science had shown itself to be in respect of the natural world. We can see this in a number of ways. For instance, the formal and systematic provision of 'education' is the key means through which such pre-modern features of social life as the allocation of privilege on the basis of one's father's place in the social order – what is known as *ascription* – could be replaced by a system of allocation of status on the basis of individual *achievement* (see Chapter 6, 'Stratifying: Class'). People's fate would no longer be determined at birth. Education offered the means of breaking the tight link between social origins and social destinations. At the same time, it promised to liberate each individual's full potential, and to make available to all the knowledge of most worth.

Another major feature of modernity is its emphasis on the importance and capacities of 'science', whether in the mastery (and potential exploitation) of nature, or in the rationalization, 'scientization' and professionalization of an ever-increasing range of social issues and problems. In the latter case this includes sexual mores and practices, for instance, and improving citizenship, which either cease to be subject to, or have come to be seen as beyond the capacities of, 'local' interpretations and remedies (Drori, 2003). In both these instances, there is frequent and close to universal resort to 'education' as the institution that is most appropriately held responsible for delivering these various kinds of valued knowledge, extending its scope into the labour market and national culture, the household and the individual 'soul'. However, at the same time, 'education' is the institutional means of delivering all these promises; it represents the most powerful and extensive example of the nation state – another key institution of modernity – intervening in the lives of its subjects (see Chapter 2, 'Modernizing'). It is the only institution through which it is compulsory for everyone to pass, or (where it is not compulsory) the institution to which states expose more of their subjects than any other.

Already, it is clear that what we call education is both an enormous field of human endeavour and an exceptionally complex one. The term can apply to purposes, processes, organizations and institutions that are closely related to the lives of individuals and of collectivities. It thus presents a uniquely formidable challenge to sociologists, the more so since, as I shall suggest below, those very features of modernity from which it has drawn its promises, processes and character are themselves undergoing changes that are likely to shape the nature of 'education' and its sociological analysis. Since taking on that challenge is clearly beyond the scope of a single chapter, individual or lifetime, I have chosen to divide this chapter into two halves. In the first half I will try to indicate very briefly how that challenge has been interpreted by sociologists of education, and in the second half I will try to suggest how the sociological imagination might be applied in an attempt to understand more effectively the changes to which I have just referred.

Sociological approaches to education

Though their precise focus and purposes have varied, sociologists of education from Durkheim onward have taken the promises of modernity seriously and these remain close to the heart of their endeavours. Their work has been normatively as well as analytically shaped; one of the defining texts of the sociology of education declares that 'sociology has been influenced more by its social context than by any "inner logic" of the development of the discipline' (Karabel and Halsey, 1977, p. 28).

I have attempted elsewhere (Dale, 2001) to trace some of the ways in which the agendas of the sociology of education were shaped (rather than moulded or determined) over the second half of the last century. Briefly, I argued that the subject had been shaped by three main sets of issues: its project – what its practitioners sought to achieve through it; its location – the conditions under which it was practised; and its context – the political frameworks within which it operated. In terms of the first, I suggested that its practitioners had been attracted to the sociology of education precisely because of its promise that the class-bound nature of education systems could be overturned and that the sociology of education had the tools to do it, if only governments would listen. I referred to this as a 'redemptive' project.

FEELING: EMOTIONS • BELIEVING: RELIGION • **EDUCATING** • STRAYING: DEVIANCE • MEDIATING: TECHNOLOGY • INFORMING: MEDIA • RELATING: FAMILY • BELONGING: COMMUNITY • FINISHING

14   297

The main institutional base from which the sociology of education has operated has been in teacher training rather than sociology departments of universities. This had a number of implications – in particular the relatively low academic status it has enjoyed – and a somewhat uncomfortable relationship with the teaching profession, in that it created difficulties in analysing the work of teachers and encouraged a reluctance to do so.

'Context' refers to the external conditions under which states were operating and their internal responses to these conditions. Over the 50 years following the Second World War, both external conditions and states' responses created an increasingly less propitious climate for the sociology of education, as all the countries that had subscribed to it in the 1950s and 1960s abandoned the redemptive political project. It has, though, continued to be a crucial basis of sociological approaches to education.

This framework led to preoccupations with education's relationship with its purposes and what inhibited their achievement, on the one hand, and school practices, on the other. One significant consequence of this agenda shaping has been that:

> The main lines of thought in the sociology of education ... rise as sociological *commentary* on the institutionalized science of education. They ... tend to accept the assumptions and explanations built into the system itself and then to question whether they are *real* in actual social life ... Sociological commentary on these issues is almost all *pro-education*, that is, in support of the official theory if this theory could be made to work ... Most critics dream of the improvement, not the elimination, of education. (Meyer, 1986, pp. 341–3, emphases in original)

In the remainder of this section of the chapter I will focus briefly on work done on what has been the dominant issue for sociology of education, the relationship between education and social reproduction, in the course of which I will refer to the work of the two leading sociologists of education, Basil Bernstein and Pierre Bourdieu.

Education and social reproduction

As may be inferred from the list of responsibilities imputed to them, and from their centrality in and to modern societies, education systems have been deeply implicated in the reproduction both of major structural and institutional elements of societies and of individuals, their identities and opportunities. Education has offered the possibility of simultaneously improving economic development, social efficiency and social justice through social mobility. Partly in recognition of and response to this promise, the dominant redemptive project of sociological studies of education has driven them in the direction of enquiring into the extent to which education's promise to bring about greater social equality and social justice through severing the links between social origins and destinations has been delivered, and thus the relationship between the structures, processes and practices of education, and its outcomes.

The answer provided by sociologists of education to the question 'How far have these aspirations been achieved?' has been a very clear one – 'Hardly at all'. Numerous national and international studies have come to the same conclusion, summed up in the title of perhaps the most authoritative of such accounts, *Persistent Inequality* (Shavit and Blossfeld, 1993). Shavit and Blossfeld studied the relationship between educational achievement and father's occupation in 13 countries (including Taiwan, Israel and Eastern European countries as well as Western ones), and found that despite strenuous policy efforts in many of them, the relationship between father's occupation and educational achievement had not weakened.

More recently, there has been evidence of greater social *mobility*, with increasing numbers of people from working-class origins taking up non-manual occupations. However, it appears (a) that this is a consequence of changes in the structure of the labour market, as the basis of economic activity shifts away from productive to service industries, and (b) that it has not reduced social *inequality* (see, for example, Ianelli and Paterson, 2005) and thus does not represent a weakening of the link between origins and destinations. It should be noted here that these relationships rest on correlations within populations and that consequently nothing may be inferred about the prospects of any given individual.

These relationships are explained in different ways by major schools of sociological theory. Neo-Marxists explain them as demonstrating a 'correspondence' between the structures of education systems (for

FEELING: EMOTIONS • BELIEVING: RELIGION • **EDUCATING** • STRAYING: DEVIANCE • MEDIATING: TECHNOLOGY • INFORMING: MEDIA • RELATING: FAMILY • BELONGING: COMMUNITY • FINISHING

14 299

example, selection) and the needs of capitalism for a stratified, docile and variously skilled workforce (see Chapter 3, 'Working'). Further, by giving the impression that education offers equal opportunities to all, it legitimates the capitalist system by placing responsibility for the lack of social mobility on individuals (Bowles and Gintis, 1976). The Gramscian version of neo-Marxism points to education as part of a hegemonic system, whereby systems of thought and conceptions of common sense that enable the continuing domination of the capitalist class suffuse the contents and practices of education (Apple, 1995, 1996).

Weberian scholars have seen the forms taken by education systems as arising from struggles between different social groups, such as religious groups, different regional groups and so on (Archer, 1979). Randall Collins's arguments about social mobility in the twentieth century being the result of changes in the demand for credentialed labour and consequently not reducing inequality (see Collins, 1984) illustrate another version of this approach. However, the strongest version may be found in theories of social closure, which see particular social groups seeking to establish and maintain control over entry to desired social assets, such as are provided by education (see Murphy, 1988).

For functionalist theorists, these relationships are explained on the basis that schooling enables the provision of differentiated technical skills, where economic rewards are based on the level of technical skill attained. Because these different levels of reward are based on different levels of educational achievement, education provides the possibility of fairer distribution of social and economic rewards, which in turn produce greater social cohesion because the process is supported by a value consensus on the relationship between ability, effort and success. The most prominent example of this is found in Talcott Parsons's classic article 'The School Class as a Social System' (Parsons, 1959), in which he links the processes of differentiation and selection within schools to the wider social process of the allocation of socially desired assets, and suggests that this also provides the basis of the social acceptance of the differences thus created.

There are three significant limitations to these major explanations. The first is the blurring of the two-stage nature of the relationship between class origin and occupational designation, where the first stage is the relationship between social origins and educational achievement, and the next the relationship between educational achievement and occupational destination. The second is that they tend to downplay the role of agency, reducing individual actors – students and their families – to 'cultural dupes', limited to playing out scripts, determined elsewhere, over which they have no control. And the third is an associated tendency to reduce the workings of the system to a black box, where classed, gendered and raced subjects are inserted at one end and come out further differentiated at the other.

In terms of the first of these, there is significant evidence that educational achievements are not only related to social class of origin, but, once achieved, are differently valued and 'cashed in' according to the recipient's social class, gender and ethnicity. This is especially evident in the case of gender, where girls have produced increasingly stronger educational achievements than boys, but have not seen these reflected in labour market rewards (see Arnot, 2002).

Classic accounts of the role of agency in the distribution and outcomes of educational processes have been provided by Connell et al. (1982) and Willis (1979). These demonstrate that the social classes discussed by sociologists (typically based on the categorization of father's occupation), useful though they are in assembling descriptive statistics and providing broad pictures, are not homogeneous categories, and that in no sense does class location determine *individuals'* occupational and social destinations. Connell et al. focused not just on the life histories of teachers and pupils and pupils' reflections on their school experiences, but their home and family lives, too. They studied not just how schools produced different results for pupils from both working-class and upper-class backgrounds (in itself unusual), but they studied families and their strategies, with a view to understanding the relationship between class inequalities in education as arising from the intersections between family practices, personal trajectories and the institutional arrangements of education systems.

Willis studied a small group of working-class boys in an English secondary school, who rejected both the achievement ideology that promised better rewards for better academic results, and what they saw as the school's bargain with them to exchange co-operation for lack of harassment. Central to their attitudes and practices was the importance to

FEELING: EMOTIONS · BELIEVING: RELIGION · **EDUCATING** · STRAYING: DEVIANCE ·
MEDIATING: TECHNOLOGY · INFORMING: MEDIA · RELATING: FAMILY · BELONGING: COMMUNITY · FINISHING

14   301

their identity of their masculinity, itself associated with their class position, which they saw as contradicted and denied by the school. They were thus seen as not merely complicit in their social immobility, but actively involved in it; not passive victims of social forces, but active constructors of a future they chose and valued.

More broadly, these studies demonstrate the limitations of the assumption built into most theories of the relationship between social origins, educational achievement and social destinations: that everyone sees the links in the same way, and wishes for the same thing – upward social mobility – through the same process of educational achievement. It is not difficult, for instance, to think of identities other than gender that might be held more important than economic and social success – ethnic or religious identities, for example.

Three main bodies of work have sought to explain, rather than rest on correlational evidence of, the meagre contribution of education to social mobility and social equality. One major set of studies has concentrated on the influence of the home, another on the processes of schooling, and a third on the structure of the education system; for comparison of these approaches see Flude (1974) and Dale (2000a). There have been numerous studies of a range of aspects of this issue, from studies of classroom practices, to studies of the allocation of educational opportunities, which have recently become heavily centred around the possibilities of parental choice of schools.

However, in this section I will focus on the work of the two leading theorists of the sociology of education, Basil Bernstein and Pierre Bourdieu, who both died recently, but whose work is widely accepted as representing the most significant current contributions to the sociology of education. What distinguishes their work is that, first, they both focus on education as a topic of study in itself, rather than on its correlates or proxies, and that, second, they both, though in rather different ways, see education and educational practices as key mediators of wider social forces.

For Bourdieu, education is a social field where actors struggle over resources and status. For Bernstein, education is the key institution and medium for the investigation of modes of symbolic control. As he famously put it:

> How a society selects, classifies, distributes, transmits and evaluates the educational knowledge it considers to be public, reflects both the distribution of power and the principles of social control ... (Bernstein, 1971, p. 41)

Bernstein's early work focused on social class differences in the communication codes of working-class and middle-class children (Bernstein, 1971, 1995, 2003). He distinguished between a 'restricted' code and an 'elaborated' code. Restricted codes are context dependent and particularistic, whereas elaborated codes are context independent and universalistic. He associated these codes with the working class and the middle class respectively, suggesting that while working-class children were perfectly capable of using an elaborated code, the social relations of working-class families were more likely to assume a common context and hence not need to elaborate. However, the communication code of schooling and education is an elaborated code, and this immediately puts working-class children at a major disadvantage.

Bernstein also focused on wider relations of power and schooling, seeking to show how both curriculum and pedagogy reflected and reinforced existing relations of power though education, and the consequences of this for different social groups. More specifically, Bernstein compared what he called visible and invisible pedagogies as a means of linking micro-educational processes to the macro-sociological levels of social structure and class and power relations. The two pedagogies are based on different social class assumptions. Visible pedagogies are based on explicit sets of rules that are made clear to all. Invisible pedagogies are largely implicit and rest on assumptions of shared but tacit understandings of what is required of students. This clearly parallels the linguistic code thesis, with the invisible pedagogy inaccessible to working-class children who are not aware of its tacit rules, but clear, if implicit, for middle-class children, whose own 'rules' it is based on.

For Bourdieu, too, it was crucial to move beyond commonsense views that regard academic success and failure as an effect of natural aptitudes. He elaborates his argument as follows:

> By giving individuals educational aspirations strictly tailored to their position in the social hierarchy, and by operating a selection procedure which, although apparently formally equitable, endorses

FEELING: EMOTIONS • BELIEVING: RELIGION • **EDUCATING** • STRAYING: DEVIANCE •
MEDIATING: TECHNOLOGY • INFORMING: MEDIA • RELATING: FAMILY • BELONGING: COMMUNITY • FINISHING

14   303

real inequalities, schools help both to perpetuate and legitimize inequalities. By awarding allegedly impartial qualifications (which are largely accepted as such) for socially conditioned attributes which it treats as unequal 'gifts', it transforms *de facto* inequalities into *de jure* ones and *economic and social* differences into *distinctions of quality*, and legitimates the transmission of cultural heritage. In doing so, it is performing a confidence trick. Apart from enabling the elite to justify being what it is, the *ideology of giftedness*, the cornerstone of the whole educational and social system, helps to enclose the underprivileged classes in the roles which society has given them by making them see as natural inability things which are only a result of their inferior social status, and by persuading them that they owe their social fate (which is increasingly tied to their educational fate as society becomes more rationalized) to their individual nature and their lack of gifts. The exceptional success of those few individuals who escape the collective fate of their class apparently justify educational selection and give credence to the myth of the school as a liberating force among those who have been eliminated, by giving the impression that success is exclusively a matter of gifts. (Bourdieu, 1974, p. 39)

This difference he attributes to the distribution of cultural capital between classes. Cultural capital has three components – dispositions of body and mind, cultural goods and educational credentials. The last of these is particularly important not only because it operates in itself but also because it can act to 'confer entirely original properties on the cultural capital (they) are presumed to guarantee' (Bourdieu, 1997, p. 48).

Questioning education

I suggested in the introduction to this chapter that education in all its forms and meanings is currently undergoing profound changes that call for the application of a new sociological imagination. In this final section I will not even attempt such a hubristic account, but I will try to carry out some humble preparation of the ground it might occupy. I will do this by (a) seeking to identify the causes and consequences of the major changes that are taking place; (b) indicating how we might locate a means of coming to terms with those changes through the device of a set of

'Education Questions'; (c) suggesting very briefly what kinds of inquiry are suggested by those questions and how they might be addressed.

Neo-liberal globalization and education

Here, I want to consider the changes brought about for education by neo-liberal globalization and the associated decline and erosion of institutions of modernity such as education. This will clearly not be an overnight process, and may take decades to emerge, but the existing traces are sufficiently established to make it more than mere speculation.

There have been qualitative shifts in the expectations of education and of how it is – and should be – governed since the fall of the Berlin Wall in 1990, which we might take as the emblematic moment of globalization. The end to the division of the world into two hostile camps, based on different principles for organizing the economy, allowed the successful form – capitalism – to advance rapidly. The idea that the whole world was now for the first time part of a single system created the space for major initiatives in the scope and governance of capital worldwide. In particular, the relationship between capital and states changed, as the boundaries of the free world no longer needed protecting in the same way, and as old boundaries eroded. This gave an enormous boost to the free movement of capital, labour and production, which made borders of all kinds, including those of states, into impediments to such free movement. The key issues are beautifully caught in this quotation from Santos: 'The state ceased to be the controlling agency over the articulations among the three pillars of modern regulation (State, market and community) to become the servant of the market and redesign the community to become the same' (Santos quoted by Dale and Robertson, 2004, p. 154). Put very simply, neo-liberalism swept away some of the key bases of modernity with which it had lived for so long, but which it now found to be an obstacle.

The key elements of that change over the final quarter of the last century have been very usefully spelled out by Bob Jessop (1990):

1   The relationship between the state and the economy has shifted from state planning and intervention to minimal state involvement in the economy (though, as neo-liberalism advances, this changes to a relationship where the state becomes an active enabler of free

trade rather than merely not being an obstacle to it). For education, this erodes the national economic basis on which the resourcing of education was premised.

2 A shift from state to individual responsibility for security and risk, especially in the area of employment, means, for education, a shift in the relationship between its social and economic functions – from one where the latter supported the former, to its opposite.

3 A shift from a national to a post-national focus reflects the decreasing level of 'national' ownership of the economy and the declining influence of borders, as well as the growth of international organizations that carry out many of what were formerly regarded as national prerogatives and responsibilities. For education, this means that the state is no longer necessarily the only party involved in the governance of education. It also requires a rethinking of the methodological nationalist assumption that nation states and their boundaries are the 'natural' containers of societies and hence the appropriate unit of analysis for sociology (Dale 2005).

4 Changes in the nature and sources of governance, especially of the public sector, involve a shift from 'state does it all' to a variety of forms and agents of governing activities, and from the assumption that the state is the source and means of all governing activity. For education, this means that the national is no longer the only level at which education systems are to be found, and their activities governed.

All these changes add to the already extensive range and dense complexity of the meanings of education. In particular, they mean that existing and established meanings and assumptions may need to be revisited, since their relationship to, and contribution to, the purposes, organizations, structures and processes of education may have altered significantly. In terms of the approach suggested here, this increases the need for and the importance of a means of constructing a research agenda for the sociology of education that is based on mutual and reciprocal intelligibility between the competing assumptions around, and aspirations for, education. So, while 'education' is subject to numerous and different interpretations and definitions, it is possible to identify a core set of *questions* that are entailed by and contained in those different definitions and assumptions. Further, it is necessary to recognize that issues and definitions of education are frequently addressing different aspects or levels of education; for instance, it is rarely thought necessary to make clear whether what is being referred to is education as a (set of) outcome(s), a set of practices, a set of policies or a set of relations between states, families and economies (Dale, 2000b).

These 'Education Questions' lie at the heart of sociological approaches to education, and form the basis of a critique (in the sense of not taking for granted) of education systems, practices and outcomes. They cover four different levels of education: educational practice, education policy, the politics of education and the outcomes of education. They are all intimately and necessarily related to each other. It is not possible to address any one of them without recognizing that it is related to all others. That said, there is a difference between 'the outcomes of education' aspect and the three levels of activity. While the latter necessarily, if frequently implicitly, make up mutually dependent and co-constitutive congeries, the outcomes may be seen as permanent – if frequently implicit – 'transversals', the aims, ends or purposes for which the activities are carried out, and against whose achievement they are judged. For instance (to take one central issue of sociology of education), the distribution of educational opportunities, questions and discussions about the activities at all three levels and positions within those discussions always take place in the shadow of an assumed most desirable, or least bad, outcome, be it in the long, medium or short term – or indeed, all three.

Education questions

The key Education Questions are:

1 *Level of Educational Practice*: Who is taught what, how, by whom, where, when: for what stated purposes and with what justifications; under what (school/classroom) circumstances and what conditions, and with what results?
2 *Level of Education Politics*: How, by whom, and at what scale are these things problematized, determined, funded, provided, regulated, governed, administered and managed?
3 *Level of Politics of Education*: What is the scope of 'Education' and

what are its relations with other sectors of the state, other scalar units and national society?

4 *Outcomes of Education*: Is Education seen as an end in itself or as a means to other (economic, social, political, community, personal) ends? What are the individual, private, public, collective and community outcomes of 'Education'?

I will conclude this chapter by suggesting two complementary ways that the Education Questions may be used. The first involves starting from the level outcomes of education, because it is there that the massive range (covering personal identity and national economic development, social mobility and road safety, personal fulfilment and collective survival, the pursuit of any of which has implications for the pursuit of all the others) of expectations of what education is, could and should be are located. This involves us in considering how education is implicated in defining and delivering these objectives, and that makes up the core of the second way of using the questions.

Outcomes of education

The form of the questions about outcomes of education suggests a range of variation of kinds of outcomes but specifies only one major dimension of difference between them: whether they are of instrumental or intrinsic value. However, in order to address the question effectively, a number of other distinctions are useful.

We might first make the distinction between outputs, the 'products' of education, and outcomes proper, the ends that they deliver or enable. Here, we may recognize different outputs, such as Knowledge (what we have learned), Understanding (what we make of what we have learned) and Credentials (how what we have learned may be recognized and valorized). Each of these may be public (goods that cannot be produced for a profit but are essential to the continuity of societies), private (goods whose value may be restricted to particular individuals or organizations) or positional goods (goods whose value is determined by their scarcity).

Outcomes may be intended or unintended. Among commonly intended outcomes of education we might expect to find 'educated individuals', 'a knowledge society', 'good citizens' and 'social justice' – all worthy but possibly not easily made mutually complementary. Among unintended outcomes we may find a sense of personal failure, teaching to the test, trade-offs between quality and accessibility and limited conceptions of human possibilities. Outcomes may also be more or less fully achieved. Just as in the relationship between social class of origin and occupational destination, there are two steps involved here: the relationship between the outputs of education systems and the outcomes with which they may be associated; and the relationship between the outputs and the extent to which they are achieved through the education system, which has been the central concern of sociologists who have looked at education, and to which we now turn.

How education is implicated in defining and delivering objectives

The final argument of this chapter is that education as a set of practices, processes and structures is usefully conceived of as a particular and always-changing architecture. This architecture might be conceived as made up of four components, which are fundamentally grounded in education's links with modernity, on the one hand, and capitalism, on the other. They are: modernity, the core problems of capitalism, the 'grammar of schooling', and education's relationship with national societies. These four elements combine, in different and changing ways, to provide the architecture through which educating takes place in contemporary societies. This architecture constitutes the means of defining education and its purposes, and the means through which it will be delivered. It has been spread from and by advanced countries to the point where it constitutes a 'world model' for education systems. Despite this, it is held in place by national states, and consequently permits of enormous variation. I will now briefly discuss each element in a little more detail.

The link between modernity and education has been the focus of a group of theorists who advance the argument for a standardized world model of education, based on the principles of the Enlightenment, that applies equally to all nation states. Since the fundamental basis of modernity has been spelled out in Chapter 2 ('Modernizing'), we will consider the elements that bear most directly on the study of education, where education is seen as comprehensively framed by those principles and ideas. First, as John Meyer (who may be seen as the intellectual inspiration of this group) puts it, 'the two main goals of the proper modern national state – individual equality and collective progress – come together in an extraordinary worldwide wave of astonishingly homogeneous educational expansion' (2001, p. 6). Meyer and his colleagues have supplied compelling evidence of this homogeneous expansion, which has come to include effectively all the countries of the world, certainly at a formal level (Meyer et al., 1992a; Meyer et al., 1992b). However, the spread of the model is not as 'spontaneous' as may sometimes be implied, and indeed this relationship between the model and its current sponsors/diffusers (foremost among which is the World Bank) points us very clearly to the need not to consider modernity in isolation from the nature of its links with capitalism.

The key to understanding education systems lies in recognizing their relationship to the core problems of capitalism, that capitalism cannot solve and that need an institution like the state to facilitate (Dale, 1989). These core problems are ensuring an infrastructure for continuing accumulation and economic development – such as the provision of a diversely skilled labour force, ensuring a level of social order and social cohesion, and legitimating the inherent inequalities of the system.

The solutions to these problems are as likely to be mutually contradictory as mutually complementary. The practice of streaming is a good example here, for although it is claimed to enhance the identification and development of academic strength, thus serving the accumulation purpose, it is at the same time widely regarded as unfair, thus threatening the legitimation purpose. Attempts to resolve these contradictions lie at the heart of education policy. Essentially, these problems set the limits of the possible for education systems, not in the sense that they *require* particular curricula (for instance, capitalism has shown itself capable of living quite comfortably with a range of different social preferences and movements, such as feminism, and has successfully lived with a wide range of different education systems and curricula) but in the sense that they *exclude* what is not in the interests of capital. Such limits are difficult to predict, and may only be recognized when they are breached, but their reality is reinforced by the increasing mobility of capital, which permits rapid shifts from educational regimes deemed to be insufficiently supportive.

The 'grammar of schooling' is a term (see Tyack and Tobin, 1994) used to refer to the set of organizational assumptions and practices that have grown up around the development of mass schooling and have come to define what education is – to become, in effect, education as practised. They take their fundamental form from the set of assumptions that has characterized organized education since mediaeval times – that its clients are male and of high social standing. This grammar is represented in numerous ways. It is present temporally through the timetable – the division of the day into lessons and playtime – and the 'school year', which has become deeply embedded into the fabric, rhythms and even the calendar of contemporary societies, with its effects on such unconnected items as the cost of holidays. It is also present spatially through specialist buildings with a characteristic architecture and classroom layouts. It is present in an age- and subject-based school system; systems of discipline and examinations; universalism (all may attend and be treated on a common basis). And it is also present in professionalism – education is typically seen as a job for professional experts, with a dedicated teaching force, and this in itself has major consequences for the provision and experiences of education (see Robertson, 1999); and a particular, educator–educandum relationship between the school and the society. A clear indication of the pervasiveness of these assumptions can be found in Robin Alexander's fine comparative study of pedagogic practices in France, India, Russia, the USA and the UK, where he found comparable sets of practices and processes common to all five systems (Alexander, 2001).

Finally, national education systems are the major means by which societies seek to define, replicate, celebrate and ensure their national distinctiveness, to strengthen their national economies, to address their social problems, and to influence the distribution of individual life chances. It is this image of 'Education' that most people have in mind when they think about the issue. It provides the grist for national education politics. These national traditions and issues grow from nationally specific path dependencies, that is, policies and practices that take their form from what has gone before; Archer (1979) offers a highly detailed comparative analysis of these processes.

The precise forms taken by these four elements, and the relationships between them, vary, but they lay down the parameters of what is to count as education. These elements are all historically associated with the West, and their relevance to the rest of the world depends on the West using its economic and political power to impose them as the global definition of education, what may be expected of it, and how it should be done. Each of the elements separately, and their mutual relationships, permit broad interpretation within the limits they set. Alongside the wider changes discussed above, there have been changes in each of the components of the architecture of education and in the relationships between them that together alter it, and hence the activities it shapes, in significant ways. In essence, the architecture of education was dependent upon and held together by the state. However, the changes to the nature of the state discussed above inevitably have repercussions upon the architecture of education. This is a crucially important point. It does not claim that the state has disappeared from education, or even that it has a necessarily diminished role in funding, providing and regulating it. It would be foolish to suggest that the state is not still the single most important institution involved in these activities. Nevertheless, neither the role nor the scope of the state's activity in education is the same as it was 15 years ago, nor is it the same 'state' as it was then. It is especially difficult to grasp the nature and importance of these changes when the same term is used to apply to what is apparently the same institution, but we need to follow Jessop's analysis to see both that it is and is not the same institution.

At the same time, and through the same processes of neo-liberalism, accumulation became clearly the dominant core problem, to the point where it might be seen to be its own legitimation, if effectively pursued, through the operation of the 'trickle down' effect. The grammar of schooling, too, is subject to a range of pressures. Among these are assaults on elements of the grammar that are taken to be inhibitions to the development of a neo-liberal Knowledge Economy. For instance: universalism could be addressed by increased differentiation, personalization, and 'just for me'; limited temporal and spatial scope by education 'any time and anywhere'; and state monopoly by 'any provider'. In addition, there are clear changes in the relationship between schools and parents. The direction of responsibility has changed to put a heavy onus on schools to respond to parents' preferences; parents now compete to gain admission for their children to successful schools.

Conclusion

My concern in this chapter has been to show the importance and variety of the area covered by 'education' within societies, and to give some flavour of sociology's potential for making sense of that territory. I have tried to provide a sense of the key problems that have concerned sociology in its approaches to education, and of how sociologists interpreted and addressed them. In the second half of the chapter I have tried to do the same in describing how the nature of those problems is now changing, and how we may usefully revisit the sociological imagination to find a means to understand them.

Suggestions for further reading

Bernstein, B. (1995) *Pedagogy, Symbolic Control and Identity: Theory, Research and Critique* (London: Taylor & Francis).

Bourdieu, P. (1997) 'The Forms of Capital', in A. H. Halsey et al. (eds), *Education: Culture, Economy, Society* (Oxford: Oxford University Press).

Bowles, S. and H. Gintis (1976) *Schooling in Capitalist America: Educational Reform and the Contradictions of Economic Life* (London: Routledge & Kegan Paul).

Dale, R. (2000) 'Globalisation and Education: Demonstrating "A Common World Educational Culture" or Locating "A Globally Structured Educational Agenda?"', *Educational Theory* 50(4), pp. 427–49.

Halsey, A. H., H. Lauder, P. Brown and A. S. Wells (eds) (1997) *Education: Culture, Economy, Society* (Oxford: Oxford University Press).

Lauder, H., P. Brown, J. Dillabough and A. H. Halsey (2006) *Education, Globalisation and Social Change* (Oxford: Oxford University Press).

Bibliography

Alexander, R. J. (2001) *Culture and Pedagogy: International Comparisons in Primary Education* (Oxford and Boston, MA: Blackwell).

Apple, M. W. (1995) *Education and Power* (New York: Routledge).

Apple, M. W. (1996) *Cultural Politics and Education* (New York: Teachers College Press).

Archer, M. (1979) *Social Origins of Education Systems* (London: Sage).

Arnot, M. (2002) *Reproducing Gender? Critical Essays on Educational Theory and Feminist Politics* (London: Routledge).

Bernstein, B. (1971) 'On the Classification and Framing of Educational Knowledge', in M. F. D. Young (ed.), *Knowledge and Control* (London: Collier), pp. 47–69.

Bernstein, B. (1995) *Pedagogy, Symbolic Control and Identity: Theory, Research and Critique* (London: Taylor & Francis).

Bernstein, B. (2003) *Class, Codes and Control* (4 vols) (London: Routledge).

Bourdieu, P. (1974) 'The School as a Conservative Force', in J. Eggleston (ed.), *Contemporary Research in the Sociology of Education* (London: Methuen), pp. 32–46.

Bourdieu, P. (1997) 'The Forms of Capital', in A. H. Halsey et al. (eds), *Education: Culture, Economy, Society* (Oxford: Oxford University Press), pp. 46–58.

Bowles, S. and H. Gintis (1976) *Schooling in Capitalist America: Educational Reform and the Contradictions of Economic Life* (London: Routledge & Kegan Paul).

Collins, R. (1984) *The Credential Society* (New York: Academic Press).

Connell, R. W., D. J. Ashenden, S. Kessler and G. W. Dowsett (1982) *Making the Difference: Schools, Families and Social Division* (Sydney: Allen & Unwin).

Dale, R. (1989) *The State and Education Policy* (Milton Keynes: Open University Press).

Dale, R. (2000a) 'Social Class and Education in Aotearoa/New Zealand', in J. Marshall, E. Coxon, K. Jenkins and A. Jones (eds), *Politics, Policy, Pedagogy: Education in Aotearoa/New Zealand* (Palmerston North: Dunmore), pp. 107–37.

Dale, R. (2000b) 'Globalisation and Education: Demonstrating "A Common World Educational Culture" or Locating "A Globally Structured Educational Agenda?"', *Educational Theory* 50(4), pp. 427–49.

Dale, R. (2001) 'Shaping Sociology of Education over 50 Years', in J. Demaine (ed.), *Sociology of Education Today* (Basingstoke: Palgrave Macmillan), pp. 5–29.

Dale, R. (2005) 'Globalisation, Knowledge Economy and Comparative Education', *Comparative Education* 41(2), pp. 117–49.

Dale, R. and S. Robertson (2004) 'Interview with Boaventura de Sousa Santos', *Globalisation, Societies and Education* 2(2), pp. 1–24.

Drori, G. S. (2003) *Science in the Modern World Polity: Institutionalization and Globalization* (Stanford, CA: Stanford University Press).

Flude, M. (1974) 'Sociological Accounts of Differential Educational

Attainment', in M. Flude and J. Ahier (eds), *Educability, Schools and Ideology* (London: Croom Helm), pp. 15–52.

Ianelli, C. and L. Paterson (2005) *Briefing No. 35: Does Education Promote Social Mobility?* (Centre for Educational Sociology, University of Edinburgh).

Jessop, B. (1990) *State Theory: Putting the Capitalist State in Its Place* (University Park, PA: Pennsylvania State University).

Karabel, J. and A. H. Halsey (1977) 'Educational Research: a Review and an Interpretation', in J. Karabel and A. H. Halsey (eds), *Power and Ideology in Education* (New York: Oxford University Press), pp. 1–85.

Meyer, J. W . (1986) 'Types of Explanation in the Sociology of Education', in J. Richardson (ed.), *Handbook for Theory and Research in the Sociology of Education* (New York: Greenwood Press), pp. 341–59.

Meyer, J. (2001) 'Globalization, National Culture, and the Future of World Polity', Wei Lon Lecture, The Chinese University of Hong Kong, 28 November 2001, available at: http://sociology.berkeley. edu/faculty/evans/evans_pdf

Meyer, J. W., A. Benavot and D. Kamens (1992a) *School Knowledge for the Masses: World Models and National Primary Curricular Categories in the Twentieth Century* (Brighton: Falmer).

Meyer, J. W., F. Ramirez and Y. Soysal (1992b) 'World Expansion of Mass Education, 1870–1980', *Sociology of Education* 65(2), pp. 128–49.

Murphy, R. (1988) *Social Closure: The Theory of Monopolization and Exclusion* (Oxford: Clarendon Press).

Parsons, T. (1959) 'The School Class as a Social System: Some of its Functions in American Society', *Harvard Educational Review* 29(4), pp. 297–318.

Robertson, S. L. (1999) 'Teachers' Work, Restructuring and Post-Fordism: Constructing the New Professionalism', in J. Marshall and M. Peters (eds), *Education Policy* (Cheltenham, UK: Edward Elgar), pp. 236–67.

Shavit, Y. and H. Blossfeld (eds) (1993) *Persistent Inequalities: A Comparative Study of Educational Attainment in Thirteen Countries* (Boulder, CO: Westview Press).

Tyack, D. and W. Tobin (1994) 'The Grammar of Schooling: Why Has It Been so Hard to Change?', *American Educational Research Journal* 31(3), pp. 453–79.

Willis, P. (1979) *Learning to Labour* (London: Saxon House).

FEELING: EMOTIONS · BELIEVING: RELIGION · **EDUCATING** · STRAYING: DEVIANCE ·
MEDIATING: TECHNOLOGY · INFORMING: MEDIA · RELATING: FAMILY · BELONGING: COMMUNITY · FINISHING

14   315

DOING RESEARCH ▪ MODERNIZING ▪ WORKING ▪ CONSUMING ▪ TRADING ▪ STRATIFYING: CLASS ▪ ORGANIZING ▪ POWERING: POLITICIZING ▪ GENDERING ▪ SEXUALIZING ▪ BEING: IDENTITY ▪ FEELING: EMOTIONS ▪ BELIEVING: RELIGION ▪ EDUCATING ▪ STRAYING: DEVIANCE ▪ MEDIATING: TECHNOLOGY ▪ INFORMING: MEDIA ▪ RELATING: FAMILY ▪ BELONGING: COMMUNITY ▪ FINISHING

15 straying: deviance

Michael Lloyd

KEY
POINTS
- The sociology of deviance has traditionally relied on norms as a key definitional feature of its inquiry. This reliance needs serious examination because the relationship between deviance and straying needs to be seen as complex and heterogeneous.

- The study of deviance will almost invariably involve lay–expert interactions. In this, we need to be alert to the looping effect of interactive kinds, i.e., the way that people are aware of what they are called, hence changing their self-awareness and behaviour, in turn making deviance a dynamic process rather than a social fact.

- Sharyn Anleu Roach draws our attention to five key questions surrounding norms: whose norms; how do some norms become official; why are some more important than others; does visibility make a difference; can there be deviance without breaking norms?

Introduction

Pick up any standard sociology textbook and chances are you will find a definition of deviance much like the following: 'non-conformity to a given norm, or set of norms, which are accepted by a significant number of people in a community or society' (Giddens, 1989, p. 118). Definitions like this have been around for some time. Three decades prior to Giddens you can find, for example, an encyclopaedia of the social sciences entry on deviance defining it as 'behaviour that violates the normative rules, understandings, or expectations of social systems' (Cohen, 1968, p. 148). While the wording is slightly different, there is clear agreement that deviance is about not conforming to, or violating, norms. To put it another way, deviance is a form of straying. 'Straying' is a term used in everyday talk so we can do without a definition, but we should note that sometimes an instance of straying may get someone into trouble (perhaps turning into 'deviance'); other times it does not. Consequently, the relationship between straying and deviance needs to be seen as a complex one, the intricacies of which will be introduced in this chapter.

One response to complexity is to simplify, and this could be done with our relationship between straying and deviance by simply inserting an arrow between the two: straying → deviance, where the arrow indicates that straying leads to deviance (much like the notion that soft-drug use leads to hard-drug use). While an over-simplification, this representation does draw our attention to several factors. For one, it adds a useful time-bound dimension to our understanding of deviance: for there to be a straying, there must first exist common patterns or well-established pathways. Obviously, norms are very well-established patterns, and as our definitions above indicate, sociologists typically take norms to be a fundamental feature of social systems or societies. The 'acceptance' of norms does not stem from some kind of democratic vote or social survey, rather it comes from the fact that we are born into a pre-existing order that comes ready-made with a large stock of norms and rules that we must learn if we are to participate as competent members of society. In Émile Durkheim's famous words, norms are a 'social fact', they exhibit 'the power of external coercion', capable of being exercised upon individuals, where 'the presence of this power is in turn recognisable because of the existence of some pre-determined sanction' (Durkheim, 1982/1895, pp. 56–7).

Following on from Durkheim, questions about how normative orders form, and how specific norms work, have occupied sociologists for many years. In a useful discussion Sharyn Roach Anleu (1991) summarizes five key questions surrounding norms. First, whose norms? In complex societies there simply may not be a consensus regarding norms; instead, there will be many conflicting and competing norms, hence dissensus may be more frequent than consensus in determining the relevant rules to apply to any particular behaviour. Second, how do some norms become official or legal? It is very uncommon for laws or rules to have universal application; hence again consensus does not exist, so is it the case that economically and politically powerful individuals and groups will be more successful in codifying their norms into laws? Three, why are some norms more important than others? The violation of some norms provokes more serious sanctions than others, so does this suggest, in contrast to the first two points, that some norms could be equally important to all sectors of society? Four, does visibility make a difference? Despite the fact that everybody breaks norms, not everyone is sanctioned or accused of deviant behaviour. Factors such as gender, ethnicity and appearance all affect visibility and hence may lead to a greater chance of drawing official sanctioning action (see 'Introduction: On Being Sociological'). Five, can there be deviance without breaking norms? Some people may be defined as deviant because of physical or other characteristics even though they have not consciously broken any rules.

The existence of these diverse questions about norms is one reason why the sociology of deviance is full of debate and competing theories, and has even led one commentator (Sumner, 1994) to seriously claim that the field reached a dead-end by the late 1970s. Disagreements aside, sociologists are united in arguing that deviance must be treated as a form of social action. A fundamental insight here is that deviance is a 'social construction', that is, it does not exist out there in the world independent of human action. This point was stated with great clarity in Becker's influential labelling theory of deviance: 'The deviant is one to whom that label has successfully been applied; deviant behaviour is behaviour that people so label' (Becker, 1963, p. 9). Or, as Georges Canguilhem puts it in his analyses of 'normality': 'We have to reserve the designation "monster" for organic beings only. There are no mineral monsters. There are no mechanical monsters' (Canguilhem, 2005, p. 187). So, both normality and deviance are the result of active, human, sense-making work – in short, they are constructed.

There is little dissent from this general constructionist tenet; however, there is less certainty about how empirical data could be gathered on this social construction process (for a general discussion of difficulties with constructionism, see Hacking, 1999). Hence, there are many critiques of the study of deviance based on consideration of empirical detail, something often found lacking. David Francis and Stephen Hester (2004), for example, discuss Erving Goffman's important concept of civil inattention – the norm of interacting with strangers using mutual non-engagement – and question the tendency of sociologists to simply stipulate that normative pressures are operative in any social situation. They argue that 'normative explanations fail to elucidate the methods by which persons recognize the situated relevance of such rules or norms. ... Given that there are occasions when strangers can and do talk to one another in public places, how do members of society analyse their circumstances so as to find that disattention is the appropriate course of action here and now?' (Francis and Hester, 2004, p. 86). In other words, we need to know exactly when, how and why norms are applied.

A form of explanation that Francis and Hester are critical of is a socialization model of deviance. Basically, the socialization model holds that members of a society are socialized into knowledge of what is right, wrong, normal, and so on. Consequently, in studying any social situation sociologists tend to assume that everyone acts upon their knowledge of a core group of norms that will make the situation orderly and simultaneously preserve individuals' 'face'. In turn, this socialization model tends to be based on a cognitive model of individual action (on cognitive models see Edwards, 1997). Ultimately, when pressed, there is an assumption that people have 'norms in their head', as it were. If norms are taken to be in people's heads, there tends to follow a naïve assumption that we can get them out, by, for example, doing interview studies. All we have to do is to ask the right questions about what it is that people know, and they will tell us. However, as some classic sociological work shows, what people know cannot always be put into words (Winch, 1958; Garfinkel, 1967); moreover, what people can say will itself conform to normative expectations. For example, an interview study of sexual practices could not just assume that men would give the same response to a male interviewer as they would to a female interviewer (see Grenz, 2005). If this is not trouble enough, the cognitive model suffers from an awkward infinite regress: if it is argued that we 'know' when to apply norms and rules, this knowledge itself will be more or less norm- or rule-like; hence we need to stipulate norms or rules for looking up the original norms or rules, putting us in a hopelessly circular position of endlessly 'looking up' rules and norms (see Coulter, 1991).

Obviously, the last thing we want to do is to stray off the straight and narrow path and find ourselves going in endless circles. Perhaps one way to avoid this in our understanding of deviance is to consider some examples of straying in action. While there is a great deal more literature in the sociology of deviance that could be reviewed, it may be that by considering some examples we can clarify the flexible and dynamic relationship between straying and deviance. To this end, two cases are presented below. The first involves an important turning point in the life of the famed New Zealand writer Janet Frame; the second involves the battles of a gambler called 'Steel Balls'. These two cases are very different; however, common elements in both will be drawn out. The goal in considering these cases will be to shift our relationship between straying and deviance from a one-way to a two-way arrow: from straying → deviance, to straying ↔ deviance. This small distinction indicates a world of difference.

Frame walks out

For some time before her death in 2004, Janet Frame was known as one of New Zealand's greatest literary talents. She was internationally recognized for novels like *Owls Do Cry* and *The Carpathians*, not to mention her short stories and poetry, and her well-read autobiographical trilogy, *To the Is-Land*, *An Angel at My Table* and *The Envoy from Mirror City* (see King, 2000). Through the autobiography and other biographical work (King, 2000; Evans, 1977) the details of Frame's life have been well chronicled. As a result, it is widely known that her life was marked by a significant encounter with mental illness, discussed here as an interesting example of the flexible relationship between straying and deviance.

Frame's encounter with mental illness is connected with a key event in her early adulthood. She had just turned 21 (the year is 1945), had left home, and was training to be a primary school teacher. As part of her accreditation as a teacher she had to be observed by an inspector, teaching in front of a class. She had to pass through this test to get her 'ticket', modern New Zealand slang for a trade union membership card (Orsman, 1999) or a completed apprenticeship. At this time, that is, towards the end of the Second World War, the social effects of the Great Depression of the 1930s were still unfolding, hence 'getting a ticket' was a prize – as near as one could get to secure employment for life. Therefore, how Frame reacted to the inspection was a significant straying: when faced with this judgement, she turned and walked out of the classroom, passing up the chance to enter a 'normal' profession and the secure everyday life it promised.

The chapter in Michael King's biography of Frame that covers this event is titled 'An Unravelling', suggesting that this is where Frame's life came apart. In King's biography this unravelling is connected with Frame's infatuation with a young psychology lecturer. King notes:

> The student Money was about to counsel in September 1945 would provide precisely the kinds of problems he would find interesting – and, for a 24-year-old psychologist with no clinical training or experience, challengingly and hazardously complicated. Frame came to Money's office in the attic of one of the university's old ivy-covered professorial houses on 19 September. She told him that she had walked out of her classroom at Arthur Street the previous week 'as the inspector walked in'. This was in part a consequence of her deep fear of being judged; but it was related, she said, to the fact that she was even more unconfident than usual because Money had passed her in the street the previous day without recognising her ... Frame also told Money of her 'deep devotion to literature' and indicated it was in that direction that she would prefer to make a career. She had no wish to return to teaching, but had told her headmaster by telephone that she would produce a medical certificate to explain her sudden departure from school and continuing absence. (King, 2000, pp. 65–6)

In contrast, when Janet Frame tells the story herself, it takes the form of an epiphany, a significant turning point:

> And now the year was passing quickly with the school inspector's crucial final visit soon to be faced. Inevitably, one bright morning of daffodils and flowering currant and a shine on the leaves of the bush along Queen's Drive where I walked to school each morning, of a hint of warm gold in the sharp lemon-coloured sunlight, I arrived at school to find that it was the Day of Inspection, and at midmorning the inspector and the headmaster came to my classroom. I greeted them amiably in my practised teacherly fashion, standing at the side of the room near the display of paintings while the inspector talked to the class before he settled down to watch my performance as a teacher. I waited. Then I said to the inspector, 'Will you excuse me a moment please?'
> 'Certainly, Miss Frame.'
> I walked out of the room and out of the school, knowing I would never return. (Frame, 1984, p. 63)

The two versions of this straying offer quite different emphases. In the first, the walkout is taken as another instance of Frame's inability to face the regularity demanded by institutions, and, when coupled with an infatuation that was not reciprocated, leads to an unravelling. In the second, Frame's agency is emphasized: she knew that teaching was a stopgap measure; her real desire was for the 'other' world of poetry and literature. Despite these differences, both are agreed about what happened thereafter: Frame makes a suicide attempt, is admitted to a mental hospital, where, after a period of close observation, she is diagnosed with 'incipient schizophrenia'.

These brief details are sufficient to make some interesting points about the relationship between straying and deviance. In many ways these revolve around attempts to distinguish between cause and consequence. Frame is participating in the normal world by training to be a schoolteacher, where to be certified as competent she must face a kind of examination. We can think of this as providing a range of clear, normative options. If she fronts up to the examination, the preferred result is a pass, which then leads to a teaching career; but even a failure in the examination is not a stop to this career. In this event, the preferred, normative response is to do remedial work and then be re-examined, hopefully to pass at a second try. Likewise, the option that Frame takes – the walkout – has a means of redress: to apologize, admit to nerves, and to ask to face the examination again. However, Frame takes the most limiting option, the most significant straying. She does not apologize, does not ask to be re-examined, but simply disappears from the world of teaching.

Clearly, these are events portraying a familiar world. Our world is one of judgements, and related assumptions about normal courses of action in response to such judgements. We all know that to get on in the world we have to face examinations, front up to them, and press on. That much is clear, but what Frame's case nicely highlights is the great difficulty in disentangling cause and consequence. On the one hand, there are those who will say that Frame was obviously suffering from a mental illness, and this *caused* her inability to face up to her teaching examination. From this, a chain of events is set in process that leads to the 'correct' discovery of her mental illness. We could call this a 'realist' model of mental illness/deviance, as it suggests that a pre-existent 'reality' has been discovered. On the other hand, there are those who will say that Frame's diagnosis as mentally ill was the *consequence* of her inability to face judgement. We

FEELING: EMOTIONS • BELIEVING: RELIGION • EDUCATING • **STRAYING: DEVIANCE** • MEDIATING: TECHNOLOGY • INFORMING: MEDIA • RELATING: FAMILY • BELONGING: COMMUNITY • FINISHING

15   323

could call this a 'relativist' model of mental illness/deviance, as it suggests that the intelligibility of real events is relative to social factors and requires active constructive work. Referring to our terms 'straying' and 'deviance', the key issue is again that of the relationship between the two: did Frame stray because she really was deviant (i.e. mentally ill) all along, or was the straying – her inability to face examination and judgement – an important first step towards a social designation of deviance? Sociologists need to be honest here and admit that we currently have no way of providing an agreed-upon answer to such a question. We cannot disentangle cause from consequence (this might be one reason for Sumner's claim that the sociology of deviance is hopelessly fragmented).

That said, those who tend to favour a 'realist' point of view on mental illness/deviance will find other details of Frame's case somewhat hard to accommodate. As is well known, after seven years in and out of mental hospital, including over 200 applications of electroconvulsive therapy, Frame was about to receive a more extreme treatment: a pre-frontal lobotomy. What saved her from this treatment was the timely publication of a collection of her short stories, which then won an esteemed literary prize. While still a patient in a mental hospital, questions were raised about whether someone so obviously talented should be lobotomized. Subsequently, Frame left New Zealand and voluntarily admitted herself to the Maudsley Hospital in London, where, after intense examination, she was told that 'I had never suffered from schizophrenia ... I should never have been admitted to a mental hospital. Any problems I now experienced were mostly a direct result of my stay in hospital' (King, 2000, p. 186). This retraction of the label 'schizophrenic' was obviously welcome, but also brought its own problems. Frame's comments about this are striking: 'The loss was great ... Schizophrenia, as a psychosis, had been an accomplishment, removing ordinary responsibility from the sufferer. I was bereaved. I was ashamed. How could I ask for help directly when there was "nothing wrong with me"?' (King, 2000, pp. 186–7).

Of course, Frame did go on from this situation of uncertainty to establish herself as a major author; her epiphany led to a successful career. But her encounter with mental illness indelibly marked her life as well as her writing, which often played mischievously with the relations between reality, truth and language (Oettli-van Delden, 2003).

A gambler called 'Steel Balls': in or out of control?

The case of Steel Balls, like that of Janet Frame, involves a person entangled with a medical category but, unlike the latter, this person is still alive. During the late 1990s a man called Graham Bruton became famous for his gambling with a state-owned legal sports betting agency. Grant (2000) highlights some of the key features of the Steel Balls story: he won nearly $500,000 over a six-month period in 1998 and became an 'expert' on gambling advice, with weekly columns in two daily newspapers (Grant, 2000, pp. 317–18). There are many media reports of 'fearless' betting, of a gambler who apparently knew no vulnerability, *and* was very successful in his betting. Through such bravura gambling activities Graham Bruton was transformed into the public figure of his betting alias, 'Steel Balls'.

Initially, Bruton was happy about, and profited from, this transformation. But later, when betting failures occurred, he seemed to want to distance himself from Steel Balls. Between 2002 and 2004 his fortunes plummeted. Conway (2002, p. 1) reports that 'his dream of destroying the bookies with a single plunge has given way to a nightmare': a tavern owner accepted a $20,000 credit bet from Bruton; he lost the bet, but could not come up with the money and 'bolted' to Thailand. It has been claimed that shortly after that, Bruton owned up to a destructive addiction. 'I do have a sickness. Gambling has ruined my life,' he said then. Through friends he comments about his betting that it is small scale and indicates sincere reform: '"I am an absolute minnow," he said. ... He again insisted that he was a reformed gambler, firmly in control, who wanted nothing more than to spend $100 or $200 a week' (Conway, 2004, p. 2).

These brief details tell an interesting story of the relationship between a person and a publicly known nickname, and the framing of their activities. This framing ranges from the pleasurable straying of placing bets, to the out-of-control deviance of a 'pathological gambler'. The story is complicated by the issue of persona: we have a real person whose life is superimposed with a nickname, the exploits associated with the latter approaching mythic proportions, at least in gambling circles. Just as there is a flexible relationship between straying and deviance, there is a flexible relationship between Graham Bruton and Steel Balls. In the good times, being Steel Balls is a useful asset; in the bad times, it is Steel Balls who is acknowledged to be a 'pathological gambler'. When life reaches a more stable state (he is able to pay off his debts due to success with a co-owned racehorse), Graham Bruton strives to cast off his alter ego and present himself as a seeker of pleasurable straying – he wants to pursue a 'healthier', more sustainable level of gambling.

As sociological scholarship has pointed out, gambling is something of an enigma, combining, in Gerda Reith's apt phrase, 'pathology and profit' (Reith, 2003, p. 9). It is now a global player in the economies of North America, Europe and Australasia, creating vast profits for corporations and contributing massive tax revenue to state and federal governments (see Curtis, 2002; Reith, 2003). At the same time, it is equally clear that gambling cannot throw off the taint of being a deviant activity. In short, profit from gambling is still regarded as ill-gotten gain, or at least not to be compared with hard work and striving in the more traditional economy. In her impressive survey of the field, Reith comments that for those who do not condone play, gambling is regarded as 'fundamentally problematic' and 'variously sinful, wasteful, criminal and pathological' (Reith, 1999, p. 3).

It is the term 'pathological' that should particularly take our attention here. As Canguilhem's classic work (Canguilhem, 1989/1966) shows, the distinction between the normal and the pathological was a key construction of medical thought, beginning at least as early as the 1600s. At about the end of the nineteenth century, the medical profession refined this distinction further by postulating a state of 'addiction' – a disease of the will – in the process creating the new identity of the 'addict' (Reith, 2004). The involvement of gambling in this history is very clear. As Reith puts it, 'The pathological gambler is perhaps one of the most successful creations of this medical discourse; a distinct "type" of person who was "made up" through an association of statistical surveys, medical questionnaires and academic research at the same time that commercial gambling developed into a mass consumer activity during the 1980s' (Reith, 2004, p. 292). During this period, pathological gambling appears in the third edition (1980) of the *Diagnostic and Statistical Manual of Mental Disorders* (DSM) as a disorder of impulse control, but is then revised towards an addiction model in the DSM III revised (see Castelliani, 2000). It should be noted that there is a wealth of sociological discussions of the 'medicalization of deviance', a key work being Conrad and Schneider's *Deviance and Medicalisation* (1980). Castelliani (2000), amongst others, has applied this argument to pathological gambling (but see Lloyd, 2002). More recently, the DSM itself has come in for concerted sociological critique, most famously from Kutchins and Kirk (1992, 1997).

Concretely, out of this large-scale historical process, it is real individuals, like Graham Bruton, who find themselves faced with the category 'pathological gambler'. Just as the real individual Janet Frame is changed by her encounter with medical knowledge and institutions, Graham Bruton confronts the power of 'pathological gambler' as a medically sanctioned and constructed category. And exactly comparable to the case of Frame, we have the problem of disentangling cause and consequence, of choosing between realist and relativist arguments. The former view would have it that with the development of technologically speeded-up forms of gambling, Graham Bruton's addiction, his underlying reality, comes out. He gains notoriety for his gambling, and this in turn seems to feed his desire for increasingly risky bets. When, as almost always happens, his betting fails, he seeks help and seems willing to accept the label of 'pathological gambler', that is, a deviant identity. But is this realist view as clear cut as it seems? At the same time that some forms of his gambling fail, others continue to be successful: his racehorse ownership seems to be a very successful business. Does it make sense to call someone 'pathological' who can run racehorses for many years? Bruton seems aware of this 'relativist' response. In effect, he claims the right to use his financial success in this sphere to continue his other gambling that he finds so 'pleasurable'. However, to continue with this 'straying' he now has to provide evidence that he is a reformed pathological gambler. In doing so, he faces the problem of the self-fulfilling nature of medical categories. The statement that he just wants to return to a low level of gambling is easily interpreted, by the betting agency and gambling counsellors, as the wily cunning of someone who knows what has to be said and done so that he can desperately return to his gambling 'fix'.

Those who tend to favour a realist view on gambling will find some of the academic research on its supposed pathological nature very puzzling. Abbott et al.'s longitudinal study (1999) recruited a group of gamblers and re-studied them seven years later. At the re-study period, less than a quarter of the 1991 'current pathological gamblers' fitted their original categorization. This change seems to have occurred without treatment,

FEELING: EMOTIONS ▪ BELIEVING: RELIGION ▪ EDUCATING ▪ **STRAYING: DEVIANCE** ▪
MEDIATING: TECHNOLOGY ▪ INFORMING: MEDIA ▪ RELATING: FAMILY ▪ BELONGING: COMMUNITY ▪ FINISHING

15   327

presenting a challenging finding to the conventional wisdom that pathological gambling is a supposedly chronic, life-long disorder. Perhaps Graham Bruton fits this category of those once labelled 'pathological gambler' who have somehow moved beyond their previous problems?

Conclusion: beyond normative dopes

In being called Steel Balls, Bruton has available one name and one metaphorical description of himself, thus opening up a complex range of lay–expert interactions he might be involved in. Does he accept the Steel Balls nickname and its implications for the kind of gambler he is supposed to be? Given public knowledge of who he is, does he 'play to the public' every time he stakes a major bet? Should Graham Bruton accept expert advice and agree that as Steel Balls he is a pathological gambler? Just as Janet Frame battled with her categorization as 'schizophrenic', Graham Bruton cannot will away the category of 'pathological gambler'. However, a key thing to reflect upon here is that Graham Bruton, the real individual who places the Steel Balls bets, is a sentient, intelligent, reflective being, just like all the rest of us. Once aware that he is known as Steel Balls, does he *become* Steel Balls, does he indulge in a certain style of betting as 'action under that name'? (On this term, see Lloyd, 2005.) If so, is this a good or bad thing? If Graham Bruton/Steel Balls is adjudged to be a pathological gambler, whose fault, or whose 'failure of will', is that?

These questions are about what Ian Hacking has called the looping effect of human (or interactive) kinds:

> If H is a human kind and A is a person, then calling A H may make us treat A differently ... We may reward or jail, instruct or abduct. But it also makes a difference to A to know that A is an H, precisely because there is so often a moral connotation to a human kind. Perhaps A does not want to be an H! Thinking of me as an H changes how I think of me. ... Even if it does not make a difference to A it makes a difference to how people feel about A – how they relate to A – so that A's social ambience changes. (Hacking, 1995, p. 368)

Two key things that Hacking introduces here are, firstly, the prevalence of moral connotations around what people are called, and, secondly, the fact that humans are self-aware, thus the term 'interactive kinds'. This term needs to be distinguished from what Hacking calls 'indifferent kinds', where natural science furnishes the best examples of the latter. For example, physicists have a classification of basic particles called 'quarks', which are not aware, even if people do things to them in particle accelerators. Human knowledge does affect quarks, but not because they become aware of what we know about them, hence the choice of 'indifferent' (Hacking, 1999, p. 105).

Further, the notion of interactive kinds helps to focus our understanding of deviance upon action, awareness and agency. Importantly, this incorporates the self and the social:

> The awareness may be personal, but more commonly is an awareness shared and developed within a group of people, embedded in practices and institutions to which they are assigned in virtue of the way they are classified. We are especially concerned with classifications that, when known by people or by those around them, and put to work in institutions, change the way in which individuals experience themselves – and may even lead people to evolve their feelings and behaviour in part because they are so classified. Such kinds (of people and their behaviour) are interactive kinds. (Hacking, 1999, p. 104)

Using terms such as 'schizophrenic' and 'pathological gambler' on self-aware people, within social and institutional contexts, leads to changes in consciousness and social practice; it makes and moulds kinds of people. In many ways this brings us full circle back to the classic 'labelling perspective' on deviance (Becker, 1963). However, to avoid revisiting the critiques of that perspective (see Sumner, 1994; Downes and Rock, 1995, pp. 202–8), I would suggest that Hacking's emphasis on making and moulding is more nuanced. It is consistent with the reversible arrow view promoted here, that is, straying ↔ deviance. Simply, we need to know more about the interactions people have with relatively official discourses that wish to name them as Xs and Ys, and know more about the flexibility of, and resistance to, such categorizations of personal type. As Hacking has recently framed a key social science question, we need to ask: 'How is the space of possible and actual action determined not just by physical and social barriers and opportunities, but also by the ways in which we

FEELING: EMOTIONS • BELIEVING: RELIGION • EDUCATING • **STRAYING: DEVIANCE** •
MEDIATING: TECHNOLOGY • INFORMING: MEDIA • RELATING: FAMILY • BELONGING: COMMUNITY • FINISHING

15   329

conceptualize and realize who we are and what we may be, in this here and now?' (Hacking, 2004, p. 287). Are we just straying, or are we really deviant? What is the connection between the two? As I hope to have shown above, it may be that there are no hard and fast answers to such questions: every particular case will have its own detail, and it will pay us to give careful scrutiny to particulars rather than assume that any case can be explained through knowledge of general social processes.

We began with definitions of deviance that centred upon the violation of norms. Straying from a normal literature review approach, we considered two cases that highlighted the potential for straying to be connected to deviance, but never in a hard and fast manner. If attention is paid to this discussion, the careful reader will note that there was little identification of the norms that were broken, although nods in this direction were made. Perhaps our understanding of how norms work could learn from Harold Garfinkel's (1967) identification of the 'documentary method of interpretation', uncovered in his study of jury decision making. In brief, he found that the verdict came before the deliberation – the jurors began with the outcome and then worked back to fill in the reasons for it. Could it be that violation, as an event, is known before we identify the norm that supposedly pre-dates the violating act? Others have reached similar conclusions. Canguilhem, a philosopher who influenced Michel Foucault, strongly argued in his important work *The Normal and the Pathological* (Canguilhem, 1989/1966), that 'the abnormal, while logically second, is existentially first' (Rose, 1998, p. 163). Canguilhem used the term 'normative' not as a kind of rule or strongly held value, but to refer to human adaptation to physiological and social constraints: to be normative is to be capable of pursuing new norms of life. Moreover, it is fair to say that without deviance there could be no social change. To that end, Janet Frame's walkout on the teaching inspector can be understood to break norms, but it can also be seen as normative, that is, by not taking the preferred option of facing up to judgement, she puts in train the possibility of new norms in her life. Similarly, Steel Balls challenges conventional thinking about gambling: he does admit, at times, to being a pathological gambler, but he maintains that there is a level of gambling he wishes to sustain; he too wishes to put new norms in his life. Perhaps one reason why Colin Sumner (1994) has argued that the sociology of deviance has turned from a corpus into a corpse is because it has focused far too much on norms at the expense of normativity. By seeing the relationship between straying and deviance, and between norms and normativity, as a flexible interactive process, there may be the possibility for new life in the sociological study of deviance.

Suggestions for further reading

Downes, D. and P. Rock (1995) *Understanding Deviance*, 3rd edn (Oxford: Oxford University Press).

Ferrell, J. and N. Websdale (1999) *Making Trouble: Cultural Constructions of Crime, Deviance, and Control* (New York: Aldine de Gruyter).

Hillyard, P., C. Pantazis, S. Tombs and D. Gordon (2004) *Beyond Criminology: Taking Harm Seriously* (London: Pluto).

Sumner, C. (1994) *The Sociology of Deviance: An Obituary* (Buckingham: Open University Press).

Bibliography

Abbott, M., M. Williams and R. Volberg (1999) *Seven Years On: A Follow-up Study of Frequent and Problem Gamblers Living in the Community* (Wellington: Department of Internal Affairs).

Becker, H. (1963) *Outsiders* (New York: Free Press).

Canguilhem, G. (1989/1966) *The Normal and the Pathological* (New York: Zone Books).

Canguilhem, G. (2005) 'Monstrosity and the Monstrous', in M. Fraser and M. Greco (eds), *The Body: A Reader* (London: Routledge).

Castelliani, B. (2000) *Pathological Gambling: The Making of a Medical Problem* (New York: State University of New York Press).

Cohen, A. (1968) 'Deviant Behaviour', in *International Encyclopaedia of the Social Sciences*, ed. D. Sills (New York: Macmillan).

Conrad, P. and J. Schneider (1980) *Deviance and Medicalisation: From Badness to Sickness* (St Louis, MO: Mosby).

Conway, M. (2002) 'Beaten Favourite', *The Press* (26 January 2002), p. 1.

Conway, M. (2004) 'High-profile Punter Beats TAB Ban', *The Press* (22 May 2004), pp. 1–2.

Coulter, J. (1991) 'Cognition: Cognition in an Ethnomethodological Mode', in G. Button (ed.), *Ethnomethodology and the Human Sciences* (Cambridge: Cambridge University Press).

Currie, S. (1999) 'Daredevil Punter to Reveal His Secrets', *The Press* (17 February 1999), p. 1.

Curtis, B. (ed.) (2002) *Gambling in New Zealand* (Palmerston North: Dunmore).

Downes, D. and P. Rock (1995) *Understanding Deviance*, 3rd edn (Oxford: Oxford University Press).

Durkheim, E. (1982/1895) *The Rules of Sociological Method* (London: Macmillan).

Edwards, D. (1997) *Discourse and Cognition* (London: Sage).

Evans, P. (1977) *Janet Frame* (Boston, MA: Twayne).

Ferrell, J. and N. Websdale (1999) *Making Trouble: Cultural Constructions of Crime, Deviance, and Control* (New York: Aldine de Gruyter).

Frame, J. (1984) *An Angel at My Table. An Autobiography*, vol. 2 (Auckland: Hutchinson).

Francis, D. and S. Hester (2004) *An Invitation to Ethnomethodology* (London: Sage).

Garfinkel, H. (1967) *Studies in Ethnomethodology* (Englewood Cliffs, NJ: Prentice-Hall).

Giddens, A. (1989) *Sociology* (Oxford: Polity Press).

Grant, D. (2000) *Two over Three on Goodtime Sugar: The New Zealand TAB turns 50* (Wellington: Victoria University Press).

Grenz, S. (2005) 'Intersections of Sex and Power in Research on Prostitution', *Signs* 30, pp. 2091–113.

Hacking, I. (1995) 'The Looping Effects of Human Kinds', in D. Sperber (ed.), *Causal Cognition: A Multidisciplinary Debate* (Oxford: Clarendon).

Hacking, I. (1999) *The Social Construction of What?* (Cambridge, MA: Harvard University Press).

Hacking, I. (2004) 'Between Michel Foucault and Erving Goffman: Between Discourse in the Abstract and Face-to-face Interaction', *Economy and Society* 33(3), pp. 277–302.

Hillyard, P., C. Pantazis, S. Tombs and D. Gordon (2004) *Beyond Criminology: Taking Harm Seriously* (London: Pluto).

King, M. (2000) *Wrestling with the Angel: A Life of Janet Frame* (Auckland: Viking).

Kutchins, H. and S. A. Kirk (1992) *The Selling of the DSM* (New York: Aldine de Gruyter).

Kutchins, H. and S. A. Kirk (1997) *Making Us Crazy: DSM, the Psychiatric Bible and the Creation of Mental Disorders* (New York: Free Press).

Lloyd, M. (2002) 'Sociological Reflections: Problem Gambling and Its Medicalisation', in B. Curtis (ed.), *Gambling in New Zealand* (Palmerston North: Dunmore).

Lloyd, M. (2005) 'A Gambler Called "Steel Balls"', *Addiction Research and Theory* 13(6), pp. 555–62.

Oettli-van Delden, S. (2003) *Surfaces of Strangeness: Janet Frame and the Rhetoric of Madness* (Wellington: Victoria University Press).

Orsman, H. (1999) *A Dictionary of Modern New Zealand Slang* (Auckland: Oxford University Press).

Reith, G. (1999) *The Age of Chance: Gambling in Western Culture* (London: Routledge).

Reith, G. (2003) *Gambling: Who Wins? Who Loses?* (New York: Prometheus Books).

Reith, G. (2004) 'Consumption and Its Discontents: Addiction, Identity and the Problems of Freedom', *British Journal of Sociology* 55(2), pp. 283–300.

Roach Anleu, S. (1991) *Deviance, Conformity and Control* (Melbourne: Longman Cheshire).

Rose, N. (1998) 'Life, Reason and History: Reading Georges Canguilhem Today', *Economy and Society,* 27(2/3), pp. 154–70.

Sumner, C. (1994) *The Sociology of Deviance: An Obituary* (Buckingham: Open University Press).

Winch, P. (1958) *The Idea of a Social Science and Its Relation to Philosophy* (London: Routledge and Kegan Paul).

16 mediating: technology

Steve Matthewman

KEY
POINTS
▪ Technology dominates our world, yet we habitually ignore this fact.

▪ Technology is an aspect of human culture: it is socially shaped and socially shaping.

▪ New technologies lead to new perceptions; some would say to new environments.

▪ Artefacts should be considered in terms of socio-technical systems.

▪ The best technology does not necessarily win: the role of social interests is decisive.

▪ Technologies have unintended consequences: we can never completely predict the ends to which technologies will be put.

▪ Technologies act as objects and metaphors.

▪ When thinking about technology it is often fruitful to think in terms of relationships.

▪ To understand technology is to understand ourselves.

Technology, modernity and speed

Sociology seeks to understand the structure and meaning of human action in modern society. Modernity is characterized by change. And technology, as Albert H. Teich (1993, p. iv) asserts, is its primary motor. As well as affecting the *pace* of social life, technologies affect its *patterns*. Daily life takes place within complex socio-technical systems that frame everything we do. Few of our activities are done alone. Technologies always seem to intrude. This has led theorists to argue that contemporary society is marked by mediated action (Bauman, 1991, p. 210). This holds even when we are trying to *be* alone. *New York Times* journalist Kate Zernike makes such a case when reflecting on her Manhattan existence. Apartment life is noisy. So much so that Zernike felt compelled to buy a Tranquil Moments Plus sound machine. The artificially generated wave sounds drown out the washing machine upstairs. On commutes to work, and while there, noise-cancelling headphones are used. Her email is filtered; her air is filtered. Tivo lets her remove commercials from her television viewing, while caller ID allows her to filter those she will talk to from those she will ignore. When you add to the list ATMs, self-serve booths on subways and at airports, plus the slew of online services now available, you realize that you are able to filter practically all human interaction (Zernike, 2004). Life is mediated. Increasingly, technologies are replacing people. We have relationships with and through things. Note that neither technology nor mechanization is a new development. The novelty lies in their total domination of social life. 'Everywhere we remain unfree and chained to technology', wrote Martin Heidegger (1977, p. 4) 'whether we passionately affirm or deny it.'

Strangely, despite technology's ubiquity, sociologists tend to 'deny it'. It is one of the great paradoxes of technology: the more pervasive a thing becomes, the more likely it is to escape our attention. Marshall McLuhan (1969, p. 22) famously compared us to fish that fail to see our water. For social theorists, as for everyone else, the material becomes invisible. This invisibility speaks volumes of its power and ubiquity. We only tend to notice things when they stop working. This oversight has prompted Bruno Latour (1992) to declare technology the 'missing masses' of sociological theory. In this chapter we will return these masses to their proper place, and examine the significance of technology in our world.

It is hard for us to imagine how radically (and rapidly) science and technology remade the world. In the early nineteenth century, science was a speculative endeavour with minimal social impact. When François Arago appeared before the French Chamber of Deputies to plead for funds, the question was 'Why?' What had science ever done for humanity? Arago's sole example of a technology that had made a difference was the lightning rod (Williams, 1978, p. 360). Refrigeration, steam power, the power printing press, the telegraph and scientific medicine changed all that. So great were the changes that by the 1890s America's Chief Patent Officer offered his resignation. There was simply nothing left to invent. Historian John Lukacs asks us to consider the period from the American Civil War up to the First World War: in the West life expectancy leapt by a third, infant mortality was quartered, living in pain became a rare exception rather than an expected development, mass education and – through it – mass literacy flowered, and the home comforts of heating, electricity and plumbing were extended to almost everyone. Lukacs (1985, p. 306) concluded that 'living conditions, for large numbers of people, changed more radically during the fifty years before 1914 than at any other time in recorded history before or after'. Small wonder, then, that sociologists speak of a 'great transition' from traditional to modern society (see Chapter 2, 'Modernizing'). This is as true for communications as it is living conditions. Napoleon could travel from the Seine to the Tiber no faster and no differently than Julius Caesar two millennia earlier. A century on, the Paris to Rome journey could be completed in 24 hours in a sleeping car. Marc Bloch declared that 'contemporary civilization differs in one particularly distinctive feature from those which preceded it: speed' (quoted in Virilio, 2003). Trains, steam ships, automobiles, aircraft, radio, telegraph, the telephone – these were all invented and used before 1914 (Lukacs, 1985, p. 306). Collectively, they changed the way in which we experience the world.

Paul Virilio (2000, p. 35) elucidates Bloch's observation. For him, 'it is of paramount importance to analyse acceleration as a major political phenomenon, a phenomenon without which no understanding of history, and especially history-that-is-in-the-making since the 18th century is possible'. In characterizing modernity, he notes three revolutions in speed and their exemplary technologies:

1 Transportation – movement *across* territory (enshrined in the engine: steam → internal combustion → jet → rocket).
2 Transmission – movement *independent* of territory (Marconi → Edison → radio → television → electronics).
3 Transplantation – *inwards* movement of technology. Miniaturization

and invasion of the human body (cardiac stimulator, memory implants, the 'biomachine').

Virilio (2003) adds that we can understand neither our history nor our technology without coming to terms with a related phenomenon: the accident. For when we invent a new technology we also invent the possibility of unintended and unfortunate outcomes. The invention of the ship creates the shipwreck; the invention of the airplane the plane crash. Discovery begets catastrophe. The proliferation of disaster has created conditions of deep unease. The twentieth century was marked by mass-produced disasters, with signal events like the sinking of the unsinkable *Titanic* (1912) and the meltdown of Chernobyl's nuclear reactor (1986), which had been celebrated under the title of 'Total safety' in the previous month's edition of *Soviet Life*. Industrial accidents – whether on land, water or in the atmosphere – continue, and these are compounded by new post-industrial accidents in genetic and information technology. As we move into the twenty-first century, such events move us towards what Virilio calls the generalized accident. This condition is symbolized by the attacks on the World Trade Center on 11 September 2001:

> Indeed, not to use weapons, not military instruments, but simple vehicles of air transport to destroy buildings, while being prepared to perish in the operation, is to set up a fatal confusion between the attack and the accident and to use the 'quality' of the deliberate accident to the detriment of the quality of the aeroplane and the 'quantity' of innocent lives sacrificed, thus exceeding all limits previously set by religious or philosophical ethics. (Virilio, 2003).

Give way: strollers yield to cruisers

This chapter looks at technology through one of those pre-1914 artefacts that John Lukacs mentioned: the automobile. The reasons for doing so are simple. It is hard to think of a technology that has spread more rapidly or changed the world more fully than this.

In the late nineteenth century, before cars were invented, it made sense to privilege pedestrians. Large capital cities concentrated diverse groups of people in shared social spaces. Much was made of the stroller or *flâneur*.

For some, like Walter Benjamin (1999), the *flâneur* was the quintessential figure of modernity. This man of leisure would feel the rhythm of the city but never be ruled by its pace. He could mingle in the crowd, lose himself in the masses, experience privacy in public. In so doing this premier urban figure read and observed the metropolitan scene, decoding the city's many spectacles. For the great new cityscapes, with their open boulevards, pavement cafés, parks and arcades, provided new ways of seeing and being seen.

Social theorists have continued to fixate on *flânerie*, while the sights, sounds and consequences of the automobile 'are seen as largely irrelevant to deciphering the nature of contemporary life' (Urry, 2000, p. 2). Is the boulevard still the best place to view the world? Surely these days it is the cruiser rather than the stroller that typifies modern experience. Benjamin's head was always in the nineteenth century, but even he was forced to concede that the railways of his native Berlin had had their day and that 'car horns dominate the orchestra of cities' (1979, p. 179). Though they tend to be the dominant form of noise pollution in most cities, it is not only through their clatter that cars make their presence felt. Cities are lit with cars in mind, and increasingly built around them too. American construction is predicated on 'the developer's first law'. Simply stated, Americans will not walk more than 600 feet. The space required for parking upon arrival is one and a half times that required for the people themselves, regardless of whether we are talking retail or office space (Garreau, 1992, pp. 117, 120). Consequently, cars monopolize public space. It is estimated that a quarter of the land in London and almost a half of the land in Los Angeles is car-only territory (Urry, 2000, p. 5). 'Car-travel,' writes Urry (2000, p. 5) 'interrupts the taskscapes of others (pedestrians, children going to school, postmen, garbage collectors, farmers, animals and so on), whose daily routines are obstacles to the high-speed traffic cutting mercilessly through slower-moving pathways and dwellings.' Should we be surprised that many drivers act as if they *do* own the road? 'And which driver is not tempted,' asked Theodor Adorno (1974, p. 40) 'merely by the power of his engine, to wipe out the vermin of the street, pedestrians, children, and cyclists?' As the saying goes, if you don't like the way that I drive, stay off the pavement.

Just as the *flâneur* saw things differently in the new metropolitan environment, new technologies help us see the world afresh. 'Each new technology – new environment – is a reprogramming of sensory life' (McLuhan, 1969, p. 33). Steam trains enclosed people and cut them off from their surroundings. Seer and seen no longer occupied the same place. The intimacy between traveller and location, such as the *flâneur* had, was no more. People saw views *through* trains. Trains transformed landscape into something different: geographic space. The metaphor of train as projectile loomed large throughout the nineteenth century. Travelling at hitherto unknown speeds, depth perception was lost. The foreground disappeared, but a new panoramic sensibility came into being. People could see the big picture, and take in the ever-changing vistas (Schivelbusch, 1986, pp. 53, 61–4). Sigfried Giedion states that, thanks to revolutions in modern science and modern art, twentieth-century life has a 'space–time' perception all of its own. And it is the car that has concretized the vision of the arts and sciences. 'The space–time feeling of our period can seldom be felt so keenly as when driving, the wheel under one's hand, up and down hills, beneath overpasses, up ramps, and over giant bridges' (1982, pp. 826, 831), he writes. Indeed, '[t]oday we must deal with the city from a new aspect, dictated by the advent of the automobile, based on technical considerations, and belonging to the artistic vision of our period...' (Giedion, 1982, p. 822).

So let us see the car, and see it sociologically.

Automobility and meaning

> The only element of culture, the only mobile element: the car.
>
> Jean Baudrillard, *America*

Sociology, like the car, allows for new ways of seeing. In Peter Berger's (1968, pp. 32–3) famous words, '[t]he fascination of sociology lies in the fact that its perspective makes us see in a new light the very world in which we have lived all our lives'. Implicit within the sociological enterprise is the discipline's 'first wisdom' that 'things are not what they seem' (Berger, 1968, p. 34). Sociologists are equally sceptical of official pronouncements and plain common sense. Instead of searching for a single simple answer, they recognize that 'social reality turns out to have many layers of meaning' (ibid.). Fortunately for us, John Urry (2000) has already articulated many meanings of the automobile.

In Urry's discussion 'automobility' is used in preference to the car. This denotes both the movement of motor vehicles and the interactions of person, machine and traffic system. Cars are not static when used, and they have no meaning without us. We need, therefore, to be thinking about a powerful *relationship*. Automobility, he says, 'is a complex amalgam of interlocking machines, social practices and especially ways of inhabiting not a stationary home but a mobile, semi-privatized and hugely dangerous auto-mobile capsule' (Urry, 2000, p. 4). Urry urges us to see automobility as a central component of contemporary life: it is the premier object of production; the second most significant article of consumption; a commanding socio-technical assemblage; the commonest form of personal mobility; a culture in its own right and consequently an important source of status; and the biggest cause of environmental resource depletion. Let us discuss each of these points in turn.

The processes by which cars are produced provided the paradigm for twentieth-century industry. Automobile manufacturers have been 'iconic', to use Urry's word. It was the car industry that gave us Fordism, that low-trust factory system based on a fixed and hierarchical division of labour in which head is separated from hand. Labour is specialized and production is standardized through assembly line practices (see Chapter 3, 'Working' and Chapter 5, 'Trading'). When this American mass-manufacturing model ran into difficulty, it was a Japanese automobile manufacturer that provided the new model for success, hence the term 'Toyotaism'. Toyotaism stressed just-in-time production methods, avoiding warehousing costs by responding to market demand. Toyotaism is based on fluid hierarchies and openness to communication and participation. It stresses 'corporate citizenship' through jobs for life. In comparison to the Fordist model, it provides for a high-trust, horizontally organized workplace, with wide autonomy for production units and individual workers (Boyer and Freyssenet, 2002). We should remember that the automobile industry is paradigmatic for good reason: in America the production, maintenance, selling and servicing of automobiles is responsible for anywhere between one-sixth and one-fifth of the nation's economic activity (Bryson, 1995, p. 197). Globally, motor manufacturing is the premier industrial employer (Roberts, 2003).

FEELING: EMOTIONS • BELIEVING: RELIGION • EDUCATING • STRAYING: DEVIANCE •
MEDIATING: TECHNOLOGY • INFORMING: MEDIA • RELATING: FAMILY • BELONGING: COMMUNITY • FINISHING

16   341

After houses, cars are the most expensive things that we buy. Henry Ford famously stated that the customer could have any colour car he wanted so long as it was black. But as soon as General Motors began releasing yearly models the race was on to keep up with the Joneses. Cars have been important status symbols ever since. They signify such things as wealth and importance, and serve as proxies for sexual prowess. We give our cars names and affection, often loving them more than our family members. They are vehicles of desire. 'The average man hardly cares for any living being with the intensity and persistence he shows for his automobile. The machine that is adored is no longer dead matter but becomes something like a human being' wrote Herbert Marcuse (1995, p. 128). All of this comes at a price. Cars ushered in new financing techniques. The words and phrases 'instalment plan', 'time payments', 'one-third down' and 'buy now, pay later' were first heard in connection with the car (Bryson, 1995, p. 202).

New technologies create new environments (McLuhan, 1969, p. 31). Cars are no different. They form part of a massive 'machinic complex'. 'The motor car's environment creates roads and surfaces. It doesn't simply occupy a space. It creates its own space' (McLuhan, 1968, p. 334). To do this requires the existence of many things: the producers and purchasers of cars listed above; car sellers; parts suppliers; mechanics; panel beaters; petroleum refiners, distributors and sellers; road designers, builders and repairers; hotels, motels and roadside eateries; retail and leisure centres; advertising and marketing; town planning, governance and policing. Edward Tenner (1996, pp. 262–3) attributes the political strength of the automobile to this diversity of stakeholders. Motoring's benefits were not restricted to the big car makers and the oil cartels. Untold small businesses, like haulage companies, petrol station owners and moteliers, were also beneficiaries. Since the production and use of objects (in our case the car) always requires people (drivers, engineers, insurers, mechanics, police, roading contractors) and other objects (lighting, safety barriers, roads, signage) in combination, now is as good a time as any to remind ourselves that artefacts should be thought of as *socio-technical systems*.

The socio-technical system that is the car happens to be the leading form of 'quasi-private' mobility. This privatized form of transportation dominates public mobilities. We have already noted the car's dominion over the pedestrian. Max Horkheimer and Theodor Adorno (1972, pp. 221–2) also mourn the passing of rail travel: 'Railroads have given way to private automobiles, which reduce acquaintanceships made during journeys to contacts with hitchhikers – which may even be dangerous. Men travel on rubber tires in complete isolation from each other.' Ray Bradbury also condemns the car's alienating effects: 'You go through your house into the garage, drive alone to an underground parking place at your office, take the elevator to your cubbyhole and drive home at night without so much as waving at a fellow-being' (quoted in McLuhan and Nevitt, 1972, p. 246). In the USA this process was assisted by General Motors. In 1932 they purchased America's tramways, and promptly closed them down (Roberts, 2003). Herein lies another lesson for the student of technology. Technological triumphs are always more than a matter of mechanical efficiency. The best technology does not always win; *its fortunes are shaped by social interests.*

We have already noted the car's effects on human relationships; what about its effects on our relationship with the physical environment? The road-building programme that commenced in the United States in 1952 was the biggest-ever public works project. This literally paved the way for suburbia and a new American dream. Cars took people out of the cities and into the suburbs. Great distances began to separate where people live from where they work, where they sleep from where they eat and play. What happens during the journeys between? Sounds and smells are filtered out. Motorways in particular are built with minimum distractions in mind. Thus landscape is experienced as a form of estrangement. 'Freeways ... shift our vision into extreme long shot and confuse the nearby sensory field with a blur of speed, wind, and noise, pushing us to seek refuge in the sounds of our car stereos or silences of our daydreams' (Shaw and Prelinger, 1998, p. 2). Cognition is no longer necessary. Maps and signage tell us where to go, what to look at, what to buy and what to think. Our cars will tell us if we are travelling too close or too fast. 'Business, technics, human needs and nature are welded together into one rational and expedient mechanism' (Marcuse, 1995, p. 127). Spontaneity and feeling are sacrificed. Paul Virilio (1995, p. 85) condemns this 'pathology of movement' in which we go 'between *being there* and *no longer being there*'. He regards such journeys as 'states bordering on sensory deprivation'. Spare a thought for those displaced by mass road-building projects. They too go from 'being there' to 'no longer being there'. Marshall Berman (1988) documents the effects of the Cross-Bronx Expressway on his beloved neighbourhood. At a stroke 60,000 people were exiled, and an entire town and way of life went with it. 'Indeed,' he tells us, 'when the construction was done, the real ruin of the Bronx had just begun'.

> Miles of streets alongside the road were choked with dust and fumes and deafening noise ... all through the day and night. At the same time, the construction had destroyed many commercial blocks, cut others off from most of their customers and left the storekeepers not only close to bankruptcy but, in their enforced isolation, increasingly vulnerable to crime ... Thus depopulated, economically depleted, emotionally shattered – the Bronx was ripe for all the dreaded spirals of urban blight. (Berman, 1988, p. 293)

Despite automobility's ability to sever self from community Urry (2000, p. 2) notes that it is the pre-eminent means by which we measure quality of life. Automobility has given us a rich array of cultural signs, symbols and images. The literature he cites stretches from E. M. Forster to J. G. Ballard. Eyerman and Löfgren (1995) chart America's post-war infatuation with the automobile, where car ownership extended to even the poorest social strata. Movement became a measure of hope and American culture became car culture. In Baudrillard's assessment, '[a]ll you need to know about American society can be gleaned from an anthropology of its driving behaviour. That behaviour tells you much more than you could ever learn from its political ideas' (1988, p. 54). Americans live 'the whole of life as a drive-in' (Baudrillard, 1988, p. 66). Books, films, television programmes and popular music reflect this. John Steinbeck's *The Grapes of Wrath* (1939) and Jack Kerouac's *On the Road* (1957) are twentieth-century classics. No great action flick is worthy of the title without a car chase, and driving has spawned a film genre of its own – the road movie. This includes such greats as: *The Hitch-Hiker* (1953), *Bonny and Clyde* (1967), *Easy Rider* (1969), *Badlands* (1973), *Paris, Texas* (1984), and *Thelma and Louise* (1991), to name but a few. Often the vehicles on screen are the most important actors: think of the Caped Crusader's Batmobile, the Dukes of Hazzard's General Lee, Michael 'Knight Rider' Knight's KITT, Chitty Chitty Bang Bang, Herbie. And what else could the first rock and roll record be about? Jackie Brenston and the Delta Cats' 'Rocket 88' was written by Ike Turner and produced by Sam Phillips. It is a tribute to the Oldsmobile Rocket 88, a model first introduced in 1949. Legend has it that Turner and his band were playing clubs in America's South when B. B. King arranged a recording session for them with Phillips in Memphis. Lyrics were reportedly written en route. The recording is also notable for its pioneering use of distorted 'fuzz' guitar. This was said to be the result of amplifier damage sustained while travelling Highway 61 to the session in Memphis. This was not the first popular song about the Oldsmobile, and it would not be the last. 'In My Merry Oldsmobile' came out in 1905, while rap group Public Enemy's debut album contained 'You're Gonna Get Yours', a tribute to the Oldsmobile 98 – 'The ultimate Home Boy car'. As Henri Lefebvre observed, people realize themselves through their vehicles. 'They deploy qualities which lie fallow elsewhere; daring, virility, mastery of self, energy, and even sexuality (or so they say) would all be part of this relationship with the car' (Lefebvre, 2002, p. 212). Nowhere is this more apparent than in the domain of popular culture. In 'Little Deuce Coupe' the Beach Boys even made gearing and clutch components the height of cool.

Popular culture is a good site for exploring the pleasures of the automobile – it is less willing to entertain its costs. The last level of meaning that Urry directed our attention to was that of car as consumer of scarce resources. This relates not only to the production and manufacture of motor vehicles, but the networks required to sustain a system of automobility and the pollution that results. Let us examine the downside of this technology.

Axles of evil

Peter Berger (1968, p. 51) tells us how sociologists understand history. It is something more than the triumph of collective will or the rule of great ideas. A recurring motif in early sociologist Max Weber's sociology is the *unintended consequences* of human activity. For instance, in *The Protestant Ethic and the Spirit of Capitalism* (1930) Weber noted the linkages between religious and economic practice. In particular, Calvin's doctrine of predestination led people to act ascetically in all aspects of life, especially economic life. This, he argued, gave rise to the ethos of capitalism, something that the founders of the Calvinist Reformation never envisaged (see Chapter 13, 'Believing: Religion'). 'In other words, Weber's work ... gives us a vivid picture of the *irony* of human actions' (Berger, 1968, p. 52). This disjuncture between intention and outcome presents itself with technology as with everything else. When the British Royal Commission on the Automobile convened in 1908, the biggest problem that they foresaw with the new technology was dust from unsealed roads (Collingridge, 1980, pp. 16–17). No one realized that it would supercharge teenage sexuality, destroy the inner city, kill and maim more people than firearms or give us a range of other ailments such as gridlock and road rage. Edward Tenner (1996, p. 7) calls the unforeseen negative aspects of technology their 'revenge effects'.

Although it is too late for us in our car-saturated world to look at the coming of the automobile and its revenge effects, we have plenty of documentary evidence of the disruption its introduction visited upon society. Robert and Helen Lynd's *Middletown* studies tell us of the unintended consequences of car ownership in Muncie, Indiana. Through it we can see how the many levels of automobility's meaning identified by John Urry mesh in a single case study. Their first book looked at middle America through its work and home life, its child-rearing practices, its leisure patterns, its religious observances and its community activities. It became sociology's first ever bestseller. Among their many discoveries was that 'Middletown', like the rest of America, had become Motortown.

The Lynds (1929, p. 260) noted how the automobile democratized leisure. Leisure became an expectation, the norm rather than the occasional luxury. Vacations increased in frequency and spontaneity. People could go at the drop of a hat, and they could venture farther. No more Sundays spent on the porch. Meal patterns were altered accordingly, as long lunches with the extended family yielded to quick bites on the run. Naturally this impacted upon other pursuits. Walking for pleasure became 'practically extinct' (Lynd and Lynd, 1929, p. 260), while gardening became ever rarer. Lawns had to give way to driveways and garages, and as the automobile came to rival the home itself as the premier status symbol, residential sections became smaller. Cars led to second mortgages and the collapse of traditional saving practices. Rival retail industries complained that the automobiles were hogging consumer spending (Lynd and Lynd, 1929, pp. 95, 255, 153).

Although some noted that cars brought the family together, the car's 'decentralizing' tendencies were more commonly observed (Lynd and Lynd, 1929, p. 257). Indeed, this seems to be one of the car's most profound sociological effects: it shifted the balance of power from collective to individual modes of organization (Garreau, 1992, p. 107). Cars were significant sources of intergenerational conflict. In surveys, Middletown boys rated it as their fifth most likely source of parental friction, while girls rated it their fourth (Lynd and Lynd, 1929, p. 522). The desirability of cars made them the targets of theft; speeding was a problem; and, in the words of one juvenile court judge: 'the automobile has become a house of prostitution on wheels' (quoted in Lynd and Lynd, 1929, p. 14). Thirty girls had been charged with 'sex crimes' in the year up to 1 September 1924. Nineteen committed their offence in a car. 'Here again,' the Lynds wrote, 'the automobile appears to some as the "enemy" of the home and society' (1929, p. 258). This theme was reiterated by working men, who worried that anyone with a car could head into town and undermine local unionized labour. Their fear was an overcrowded labour market. Precisely the reverse fear afflicted the churches. Nearly all felt that their flocks were deserting them. One pastor diagnosed 'automobilitis' as the cause of his empty pews. In the end, preachers began reducing their Sunday sermons in an effort to compete (Lynd and Lynd, 1929, pp. 254, 259, 350).

In their follow-up study of Middletown, which continues the history of the town up until 1936, it is fair to say that the Lynds find the same, only more so. Now the automobile is identified as a leading agent of secularization. It made the weekly Sunday exodus from town possible. Such was the dominance of cars that children no longer played in the streets or even on the sidewalks. And such was the centrality of cars that the Great Depression hardly put a dint in usage. Car ownership changed less than the rates for marriage, divorce and birth, or the consumption of clothing or jewellery or 'most other measurable things both large and small' (Lynd and Lynd, 1937, pp. 266–7).

With the rate of car ownership constantly increasing, automobile technology has thrown up other ironies. These days, surely one of the biggest ironies of the car is that it is used for its convenience. We use them because they are a quicker mode of transportation than foot or pedal power. Yet when Ivan Illich did the maths in 1974 he found the following:

> The typical American spends over 1,600 hours a year ... in his car. This includes the time spent behind the wheel, moving or stopped, the hours of work needed to pay for it and for gasoline, tires, tolls, insurance, fines, and taxes ... For this American it takes 1,600 hours to cover a year a total of 6,000 miles, four miles per hour. This is just as fast as a pedestrian and slower than a bicycle. (Quoted in Tenner, 1996, p. 264)

This message is yet to sink in. The 2000 American census showed that more people than ever drive alone to work (76 per cent) and that their commutes are taking longer. Only 5 per cent of the population use public transportation and a meagre 3 per cent walk to work (Anon., 2002). Traffic congestion is a growing problem the world over, and the annual dollar cost of this to a single American city – Atlanta – was estimated at US$1.9 billion in wasted time and fuel (Sloan, 2003).

Mass automobility also results in pollution. Thus the *Exxon Valdez* had an 'accident' and covered Prince William Sound with crude oil. '"Normalcy", Cockburn (1995, p. 163) wryly concludes, 'would have been for the ship to proceed to Long Beach, California, and unload its crude, which, duly refined, would then have been vented through car exhaust pipes over Los Angeles.' These emissions include carbon dioxide, which is associated with global warming and crop loss, and carbon monoxide, which pollutes the air and causes cancers; nitrogen oxide is linked to acid rain. And while our personal air might be better inside the vehicle thanks to air conditioning, their effect on the environment is certainly for the worse. Such devices are the single largest source of chlorofluorocarbons (CFCs). These destroy the protective capacities of the planet by eating away at the ozone layer. Cars also emit ozone. Around half of all US cities do not meet Environmental Protection Agency standards for ozone, which is linked to human disease and crop loss. The millions of cars that are on the road are major users of limited oil resources. We should also think about where all of the old oil goes, what happens to the millions of discarded tyres each year and the tons of lead from dead car batteries.

As sociologists, we should ask which groups of people bear the costs of automobility. Ian Roberts states that it is the young rather than the old, the poor rather than the rich, the people of the South rather than the North, the pedestrian rather than the driver:

> Car dependence is a global public health issue of which gasoline wars are only one facet. Every day about 3,000 people die and 30,000 people are seriously injured on the world's roads in traffic crashes. More than 85% of deaths are in low and middle-income countries, with pedestrians, cyclists and bus passengers bearing most of the burden. Most of the victims will never own a car, and many are children. (Roberts, 2003)

This is also a good time to remind ourselves of the perils of technological prediction. The British Royal Commission on the Automobile foresaw a dust problem. Twelve years earlier, upon recording a verdict of accidental death for the world's first car crash victim, Coroner Percy Morrison hoped that 'such a thing would never happen again' (Anon., 2005). That fateful 'one-off' is now accepted as a fact of life. The personal trouble of a century ago is now a public issue: 1.2 million people die on the world's roads annually, and perhaps 50 million more are maimed (World Health Organization, 2004).

Conclusion

Dazzled by the new Citroën D.S. 19, Roland Barthes – a man who would later fall victim to a Parisian laundry truck – wrote: 'I think that cars today are almost the exact equivalent of the great Gothic cathedrals: I mean the supreme creation of an era, conceived with passion by unknown artists, and consumed in image if not in usage by a whole population which appropriates them as a purely magical object' (2000, p. 88). The final words are telling: in the popular imagination technologies are mysterious. 'All our technologies in the Western world,' McLuhan confirmed, 'are built on the assumption that they have complete immunity from inspection' (1968, p. 335). Sociologists should not show such awe and reverence. When immunity is lifted we see that technology operates in profoundly important ways: as object and metaphor, as network and system, as environment and culture. Our social actions are constrained and enabled

FEELING: EMOTIONS • BELIEVING: RELIGION • EDUCATING • STRAYING: DEVIANCE •
MEDIATING: TECHNOLOGY • INFORMING: MEDIA • RELATING: FAMILY • BELONGING: COMMUNITY • FINISHING

16   349

by technology. We have relationships through it. And, as Barthes would doubtless agree, we have relationships *with* it. In order to understand technology we must understand all of these operations, just as we must be mindful of issues of ownership, access and control. Technology 'does not form an independent system, like the universe: it exists as an element in human culture and it promises well or ill as the social groups that exploit it promise well or ill' (Mumford, 1962, p. 6).

Technologies are human products. They are designed, made and marketed by people. It is true that technology frames our world, but it is itself socially shaped. Embedded within technologies are rafts of social, cultural, economic, political, even military goals. These goals may conflict. John Law and Wiebe E. Bijker remind us that:

> The idea of a 'pure' technology is nonsense. Technologies always embody compromise. Politics, economics, theories of the strength of materials, notions about what is beautiful or worthwhile, professional preferences, prejudices and skills, design tools, available raw materials, theories about the behavior of the natural environment – all of these are thrown into the melting pot whenever an artefact is designed or built... (1992, p. 3)

Therefore, when we think of technology we should think of contingency: '*They might have been otherwise...*'

Contingency has relevance beyond the points of design and production. Consider adaptation. While all technologies are planned with specific things in mind, unintended consequences cannot be anticipated, nor can all applications be legislated (think of hackers). In many instances sophisticated cultures of use develop around a technology, and these may fracture along the familiar sociological lines of class, age, gender, ethnicity, nationality and sexuality. 'Technologies are never neutral; they are always embedded in and generated by a cultural context, and the most important cultural context is that of use' (Pinch and Trocco, 2002, p. 309). In sum, it is sociologically necessary to know what technology does to us and what we do with and through it. Only through such understandings can we understand ourselves (Mumford, 1962, p. 6).

Suggestions for further reading

Bijker, W. E. (1995) *Of Bicycles, Bakelites, and Bulbs: Toward a Theory of Sociotechnical Change* (Cambridge, MA: MIT Press).

Hughes, T. P. (2004) *Human-Built World: How to Think About Technology and Culture* (Chicago, IL: University of Chicago Press).

Pinch, T. and F. Trocco (2002) *Analog Days: The Invention and the Impact of the Moog Synthesiser* (Cambridge, MA: Harvard University Press).

Wajcman, J. (2004) *TechnoFeminism* (Cambridge: Polity Press).

Bibliography

Adorno, T. (1974) *Minima Moralia: Reflections from Damaged Life*, trans. E. F. N. Jephcott (London: New Left Books).

Anon. (2002) 'Americans Get Behind the Wheel Alone', *USA Today*. Available: http://www.usatoday.com/news/nation/census/2002-08-20-driving_x.htm [accessed: 2/2/2005].

Anon. (2005) 'Bridget Driscoll', *Wikipedia*. Available: http://en.wikipedia.org/wiki/Bridget_Driscoll [accessed 15/11/2005].

Barthes, R. (2000/1957) 'The New Citroën', *Mythologies* (London: Vintage), pp. 88–90.

Baudrillard, J. (1988) *America* (London and New York: Verso).

Bauman, Z. (1991) *Modernity and Ambivalence* (Cambridge: Polity Press).

Benjamin, W. (1999/1955) 'On Some Motifs in Baudelaire', *Illuminations*, trans. Harry Zorn (London: Pimlico), pp. 152–96.

Benjamin, W. (1979) 'A Berlin Chronicle', *One-Way Street and Other Writings*, trans. Edmund Jephcott and Kingsley Shorter (London: New Left Books), pp. 293–346.

Berger, P. L. (1968) *Invitation to Sociology: A Humanistic Perspective* (Harmondsworth: Penguin).

Berman, M. (1988) *All that is Solid Melts into Air: The Experience of Modernity* (New York: Penguin).

Boyer, R. and M. Freyssenet (2002) *The Productive Models: The Conditions of Profitability* (Basingstoke: Palgrave Macmillan).

Bryson, B. (1995) *Made in America* (London: Minerva).

Cockburn, A. (1995) *The Golden Age is in Us* (London and New York: Verso).

Collingridge, D. (1980) *The Social Control of Technology* (New York: St Martin's Press).

Eyerman, R. and O. Löfgren (1995) 'Romancing the Road: Road Movies and Images of Mobility', *Theory, Culture and Society* 12, pp. 53–79.

Garreau, J. (1992) *Edge City: Life on the New Frontier* (New York: Anchor Books).

Giedion, S. (1982) *Space, Time and Architecture: The Growth of a New Tradition*, 5th edn (Cambridge, MA: Harvard University Press).

Heidegger, M. (1977) 'The Question Concerning Technology', *The Question Concerning Technology and Other Essays* (New York: Harper & Row), pp. 1–35.

Hess, D. J. (1995) *Science and Technology in a Multicultural World: The Cultural Politics of Facts and Artifacts* (New York: Columbia University Press).

Horkheimer, M. and T. W. Adorno (1972) *Dialectic of Enlightenment*, trans. John Cumming (New York: Herder & Herder).

Latour, B. (1992) 'Where are the Missing Masses? The Sociology of a Few Mundane Artefacts', in W. E. Bijker and J. Law (eds), *Shaping Technology/Building Society: Studies in Sociotechnical Change* (Cambridge, MA and London: The MIT Press), pp. 225–58.

Law, J. and W. E. Bijker (eds) (1992) *Shaping Technology/Building Society: Studies in Sociotechnical Change* (Cambridge, MA: MIT Press).

Lefebvre, H. (2002) *Critique of Everyday Life: Foundations for a Sociology of Everyday*, vol. 2, trans. John Moore (London and New York: Verso).

Lukacs, J. (1985) *Historical Consciousness* (New York: Schoken).

Lynd, R. S. and H. M. Lynd (1929) *Middletown: A Study in American Culture* (New York: Harcourt, Brace).

Lynd, R. S. and H. M. Lynd (1937) *Middletown in Transition: A Study in Cultural Conflict* (New York: Harcourt, Brace).

McLuhan, M. (1968) in G. E. Stearn (ed.), *McLuhan Hot & Cool* (Harmondsworth: Penguin).

McLuhan, M. (1969) *Counterblast* (London: Rapp & Whiting).

McLuhan, M. and B. Nevitt (1972) *Take Today: The Executive as Dropout* (New York: Harcourt, Brace, Jovanovich).

Marcuse, H. (1995) 'Some Social Implications of Modern Technology', in D. McQuire (ed.), *Readings in Contemporary Social Theory: From Modernity to Postmodernity* (Englewood Cliffs, NJ: Prentice Hall), pp. 124–33.

Mumford, L. (1962) *Technics and Civilization* (London: Routledge & Kegan Paul).

Pinch, T. and F. Trocco (2002) *Analog Days: The Invention and the Impact of the Moog Synthesiser* (Cambridge, MA: Harvard University Press).

Roberts, I. (2003) 'Car Wars', *Guardian*, 18 January 2003. Available: http://www.guardian.co.uk/comment/story/0,,877203,00.html [accessed 3/2/2005].

DOING RESEARCH • MODERNIZING • WORKING • CONSUMING • TRADING • STRATIFYING: CLASS •
GOVERNING: POWER • RACIALIZING • GENDERING • SEXUALIZING • BEING: IDENTITY •

Schivelbusch, W. (1986) *The Railway Journey: The Industrialization of Time and Space in the Nineteenth Century* (Berkeley and Los Angeles, CA: University of California Press).

Shaw, M. and R. Prelinger (1998) 'Manifest Congestion', *Bad Subjects: Political Education for Everyday Life* 40, pp. 1–8. Avaliable: http://eserver.org/bs/40/shaw-prelinger.html [accessed 20/07/04].

Sloan, S. (2003) 'Traffic Jams Cost Metro Atlanta $1.9 Billion a Year', *Atlanta Business Chronicle*, 29 May 2003. Available: http://www.bizjournals.com/atlanta/stories/2003/05/26/daily19.html [accessed 4/2/2005].

Teich, A. H. (1993) *Technology and the Future* (New York: St Martin's Press).

Tenner, E. (1996) *Why Things Bite Back: Technology and the Revenge Effect* (London: Fourth Estate).

Urry, J. (2000) 'Inhabiting the Car', Unesco International Conference, Universidade Candido Mendes, Rio de Janeiro, Brazil, May 2000. Available: http://www.comp.lancs.ac.uk/sociology/papers/urry-inhabiting-the-car.pdf [accessed 30/4/2004].

Virilio, P. (1995) *The Art of the Motor*, trans. Julie Rose (Minneapolis and London: University of Minnesota Press).

Virilio, P. (2000) 'From Modernism to Hypermodernism and Beyond: an Interview with Paul Virilio', in John Armitage (ed.), *Paul Virilio: From Modernism to Hypermodernism and Beyond* (Sage: London), pp. 25–55.

Virilio, P. (2003) 'Foreword', *Fondation Cartier*, trans. Chris Turner. Available: http://www.onoci.net/virilio/pages_uk/virilio/all_avertissement.php [accessed 27/1/05].

Weber, M. (1930) *The Protestant Ethic and the Spirit of Capitalism*, trans. Talcott Parsons (London: Unwin University Books).

Williams, L. P. (1978) *Album of Science: The Nineteenth Century* (New York: Charles Scribner's Sons).

World Health Organization (2004) 'Road Safety: a Public health Issue', 29 March 2004. Available: http://www.who.int/features/2004/road_safety/en/ [accessed 15/10/2005].

Zernike, K. (2004) 'First, Your Water was Filtered: Now It's Your Life', *The New York Times*, 21 March 2004. Available: nytimes.com

FEELING: EMOTIONS • BELIEVING: RELIGION • EDUCATING • STRAYING: DEVIANCE •
MEDIATING: TECHNOLOGY • INFORMING: MEDIA • RELATING: FAMILY • BELONGING: COMMUNITY • FINISHING

16   353

17 informing: media

Aaron Norgrove

KEY POINTS

- Sociologists examine the role of the media in constructing reality and informing the individual of their existence within that reality.
- Many sociologists see the media as a set of institutions that convey ideologically infused messages to large populations on behalf of powerful social groups.
- Sociologists debate whether the relationship between the media and the audience produces passive or active consumers; many think the reality lies somewhere between these two extremes.
- Semiology allows us to analyse how culturally embedded meanings are encoded in the signs that constitute media texts, and the processes by which they are decoded by the audience.
- Some post-modernists claim that 'reality' has been supplanted by simulations, which are themselves the 'new' reality as experienced by individuals. Mediated images then assume equal status with the reality (itself now but a simulation) they purport to represent.
- News production is socially constructed, deeply rooted in the workings of particular media institutions rather than a reflection of what is objectively newsworthy.
- There is widespread acceptance that changes in government policy in Western nations over recent decades has entailed, on the one hand, increasing deregulation and the loosening of controls on ownership of media institutions, and, on the other, a concentration of ownership of media institutions into fewer and fewer hands.
- Focusing solely on media effects, content or production, obscures understanding of the relationships between these three domains.

- An accurate portrayal of the media in contemporary society should as much as possible consider the various dynamics inherent at each level, and consider the different methods and theories as partners in the process of sociological interpretation.

Introduction

> Neither the life of an individual nor the history of a society can be understood without understanding both. Yet men do not usually define the troubles they endure in terms of historical change and institutional contradiction. ... The sociological imagination enables its possessor to understand the larger historical scene in terms of its meaning for the inner life and the external career of a variety of individuals. ... We have come to know that every individual lives, from one generation to the next, in some society; that he lives out a biography, and that he lives it out within some historical sequence. (Mills, 1959, p. 3)

Writing in 1959, C. Wright Mills was concerned with what he saw as the central task of the discipline of sociology: the ability to offer the individual a set of tools and ideas that would enable them to interpret their existence in the world, understand their location within social groups and their historical foundations, and ultimately inform them of the underlying reasons for, and culturally embedded meaning of, that existence. In the almost half-century since the publication of his book *The Sociological Imagination*, one could argue that this task of informing the individual, and the mass of individuals known as society, has increasingly been usurped by the set of institutions and practices that are captured by the umbrella term 'the media'. Understandably, as witnesses to the shift from processes of industrialization and capitalism that dominated the social identities of modernity, to the increasing role of the media in producing and distributing cultural experiences in post-modern times, sociologists have themselves become increasingly concerned with the role of the media in constructing reality and informing the individual of their existence within that reality.

Instead of an overview of 'sociology of the media' research, this chapter will look at a selection of tools that are used to examine how different kinds of media can be experienced. Just as the media offer us interpretations of the world, this chapter will provide a lens through which the media may be examined and understood. Various interpretations of media output attribute differing levels of interpretive power to the individual media consumer, as a member of the wider audience. In some cases, the audience is seen as *passive* – a mass of spectators who are manipulated by the owners of media institutions as they pursue their own ends. At the other extreme, audiences are seen as *active* force, who can select from media images and texts and reinterpret them according to their own wants and needs.

Two central concepts underlie most, if not all, sociological research on media. The first is the notion of 'the media' itself. Obviously it is made up of a wide array of different types of publication, from print, such as newspapers and magazines, to the primarily image-based forms of television and film. There are also the various 'new media', such as the internet, mobile phones and computer games. Despite their different forms, they share a common characteristic – the capacity to deliver ideas, information and/or entertainment for large-scale public consumption. In recognition of this diversity of form but similarity of purpose, Trowler (2001, p. 1) defines the media as 'the methods and organizations used by specialist social groups to convey messages to large, socially mixed and widely dispersed groups'.

In highlighting the role of *specialist* social groups, Trowler hints at the second concept that underpins sociological research on the media: that of ideology. In simple terms, an ideology can be defined as a set of ideas and discourses that serve to structure and interpret the world, and are in some way linked to the interests of a particular social group. There is disagreement over whether the media reinforce or resist the ideologies of (in particular) dominant social groups in a society, or are in fact neutral. Nevertheless, whether in the context of media effects on audiences, media content in textual and image form, or the patterns of ownership of media institutions, sociologists are implicitly or explicitly concerned with the extent to which some social groups are more able than others to influence the wider society. With this in mind we will now look in detail at these media domains, highlighting the place of ideology in each.

Media effects: are we passive or active?

Of all the areas of media research discussed here, questions about cultural effects on audiences are the most likely to provoke debate and generate concern in the public domain. This is particularly true when issues of censorship are involved. The decision to ban the computer game *Manhunter* in New Zealand, the outcry over Janet Jackson's partially naked breast during the Superbowl in the United States, subsequent tightening of codes governing television content, and the regular panics over the accessibility of pornography on the internet are simply the latest political expressions of a long-standing suspicion. It is widely believed that the media are able to influence the actions of the intended audience in some way, whether it be violence, offensive language or sexuality. Leaders of some Christian churches, for example, have at times tried to restrict the availability of the Bible, for fear that general public access would erode their own authority. The 1950s saw fears that Elvis Presley's seductive body movements, if seen on television, would turn teenagers to criminal deviance. On the other hand, regulations governing the availability of media can also, over time, be loosened, as was the case when hard-core pornography was, in 2002, permitted to be sold in the United Kingdom for the first time. Age restrictions have also been lowered on particular films if they are deemed of 'educational value' despite representations of violence and/or sexuality.

Approaches to media effects that view the audience as a *passive* mass of spectators are often referred to as 'hypodermic needle' or 'silver bullet' models (Schramm and Porter, 1982). Broadly speaking, passive audience research tends to emanate from two distinct camps: the Marxist-influenced Frankfurt School theorists such as Theodor Adorno, Max Horkheimer and Jürgen Habermas, and various researchers in the field of literary criticism. Adorno and Horkheimer in particular were concerned with the role of the media in developing a 'false consciousness' amongst the working class as audience members. They detailed how television and related entertainments were a conduit for capitalist ideology, and how such ideas obscured the underlying reality of class struggle and capitalist exploitation (Adorno and Horkheimer, 1969; Adorno, 1971) (see Chapter 6, 'Stratifying: Class'). Literary critics, such as Frank Leavis (1962), were more concerned with the erosion of 'high culture', typified in Shakespeare, Mozart and the like; by the spread of 'mass culture', especially through the 'lies and deceit' of advertising and commercialized media systems that debased human emotion and confused value with the possession of material goods – a process that is irresistible to the average media consumer.

In response to these overly deterministic models, a number of researchers have conducted investigations into how media consumers are able to construct meaning for themselves as members of an *active* audience. Fiske points out:

> A homogeneous, externally produced culture cannot be sold ready-made to the masses: culture simply does not work like that. Nor do the people behave or live like the masses, an aggregation of alienated, one-dimensional persons whose only consciousness is false, whose only relationship to the system that enslaves them is one of unwitting (if not willing) dupes. Popular culture is made by the people, not produced by the culture industry. All the culture industries can do is produce a repertoire of texts or cultural resources for the various formations of the people to use or reject in the ongoing process of producing their popular culture. (1989, p. 23)

Michel de Certeau (1990) was an early advocate of the active character of audiences and greatly influenced Fiske. He demonstrated that people do their utmost to find, or read, texts in ways that are meaningful to them. He contrasted the strategies used by the dominant elites who produced media and texts with the *tactics* of everyday people to resist and subvert those texts. He coined the notion of 'textual poaching' to describe this struggle. Accordingly, researchers have tended to focus on the strategies of resistance used by readers, from Janice Radway's investigations of the sense of 'escape' from daily life enjoyed by readers of romantic fiction (Radway, 1987), the possibility of resisting patriarchal ideologies in the music of Madonna (Fiske, 1989), to the conversation networks surrounding television soaps that reinterpret plot-lines in terms of the community's own needs (Tursi, 1996).

In actuality, neither of these two extremes capture the complexities of both the encoding and decoding of meaning that accompany the production and consumption of media. Stuart Hall (1980), for example, suggests that a preferred reading for a text may exist, where various techniques (the cropping of photographs, editing of news footage and so on) are used by media producers to influence the perceptions of the audience. The distinction can therefore be made between *open* and *closed* texts, where it is recognized that all texts are open to a variety of interpretations, but in a closed text there is one reading intended by the producer. The emergence of digital media and technology has also opened new pathways for the interactivity of audience and media content, and the extent to which the consumer is able to manipulate media products. This is particularly evident in the convergence of computer gaming, as both a social practice and an act of media consumption, and the use of the internet as a communication and distribution tool. This convergence has led to the emergence of a significant number of 'virtual communities' that are formed on the basis of a common interest in particular computer games from *The Sims* through to *Doom 3*, where members digitally manipulate the content of the original game and offer the fruits of their labour, usually for free, for others to download, critique and 'patch' their own copy of the game (see Chapter 19, 'Belonging: Community').

Beyond this, it is, however, apparent that media content is able to influence the beliefs that people hold: research into the effects of Hollywood movies on historical knowledge in Britain found that some 10 per cent of people thought Adolf Hitler and Winston Churchill were fictional characters, 57 and 27 per cent respectively thought King Arthur and Robin Hood actually existed, 32 per cent thought the Cold War never took place, and 6 per cent thought the Martian invasion in H. G. Wells's *War of the Worlds* took place (Milmo, 2004). Given the impact that the media can have on people's beliefs, then, semiologists and post-modernists have preferred to focus on the meaning inherent in the content of the media rather than the relative passivity or activity of audience reception.

Media content: what does it mean?

Semiology and post-modernism should not be seen as the only means of analysing media content from a sociological perspective. Content analysis, for example, is a predominantly quantitative accounting of pre-selected themes and ideas as expressed in media texts – for instance, the number of violent images in a children's cartoon show or how frequently the words 'freedom' and 'democracy' appear in political speeches. Max Weber used content analysis as early as 1910 to examine the press coverage of political issues in Germany, whilst Harold Laswell undertook similar studies in the 1930s and 1940s to examine the message content of American wartime propaganda. As image-based communications have superseded print media, content analysis has expanded to include the use of specific representations in television and film media. Rimm (1995) sought to quantify the number of pornographic images in circulation in cyberspace, a study that made it to the front cover of *Time Magazine* (3 July 1995).

There are five steps in content analysis: Coding, Categorizing, Classifying, Comparing and Concluding. Coding is the basic tool, where the unit of analysis is selected (such as a specific word or words) and then counted in the selected text. Categorizing is the process by which meaningful descriptive categories are selected into which the basic units can be grouped (for example, images that may be described as 'pornographic' as opposed to 'erotica'). Classifying involves the use of independent subjects to test the reliability of the categories, ensuring that there is agreement between the researcher and others as to the applicability of the categories. Comparing occurs between terms in the same text (for example, the use of conflict versus conciliatory references in a speech) or between texts (for example, the frequency with which women appear as domestic labourers in advertising from the 1950s compared with the present day, or with official statistics on the number of women who classify themselves as domestic labourers). The final and perhaps most contentious step is concluding the theoretical relevance of the content and the context within which it appears, such as the stereotyping of gender, ethnicity and sexuality in the mass media and the relationship with wider social relations and dominant ideologies.

A number of problems have been identified with content analysis when it is used in isolation from other methods, especially in terms of the more qualitative steps of categorizing and concluding. How do we get an 'objective standard' by which to measure the basic units of analysis? Further, we cannot assume audience consensus on the importance of such categories. Nor can we simply assume that frequency is a proxy for significance.

FEELING: EMOTIONS · BELIEVING: RELIGION · EDUCATING · STRAYING: DEVIANCE ·
MEDIATING: TECHNOLOGY · **INFORMING: MEDIA** · RELATING: FAMILY · BELONGING: COMMUNITY · FINISHING

17   361

Here, the main focus will be on semiology and post-modernism, which, in fact, correspond roughly with the active/passive audience split already described. Where semiology ascribes the power and ability to decode meaning to the individual 'expert' (for example, the sociologist), post-modernism suggests that this process has been dispersed throughout the audience as a whole. In addition, both perspectives treat media content as a product of wider social relations and are therefore able to account for the influence (or otherwise) of ideology in practices of encoding and decoding meaning.

Semiology

Semiology is a quite complex method for understanding media content. It is based on the ideas of Swiss linguist Ferdinand de Saussure, who describes it as 'a science which studies the life of signs at the heart of social life' (de Saussure, 1971, p. 33). For semiologists, media such as pop songs, billboard advertisements, television sitcoms, news reports and video games can be seen as texts, composed of verbal and non-verbal signs which are then read, sometimes in conflicting ways, by their respective audiences. Thus semiology is effectively the study of meaning production – or signification – and the task of the semiologist is to uncover the culturally specific systems of meaning that are hidden within the circulation of value-laden signs in the media. These semiologists use an extensive and particular vocabulary to break down and analyse both the signs and the process of meaning production.

Saussure assumes that there is no necessary relationship between the circulation of linguistic signs and the various 'things in the real world' to which they refer. On one level, this may seem counterintuitive: linguistic signs such as George Bush, Robbie Williams, the Tower of London, all refer to specific 'real world' people and entities. However, this apparently simple relationship begins to break down when we consider signs such as 'man', 'woman', 'dog', 'city' and so on. Which 'man' or which 'dog' in the 'real world' are being referred to? In this case, Saussure de-emphasizes the relationship between the sign and their 'real world' referents, suggesting instead that a linguistic sign should be seen as the relationship between a sound image and a concept that the sound image refers to (such as a culturally accepted concept of what a 'man' is). For Saussure, then, a sign can be seen to be made up of two parts: the 'signifier', or form of the sign (the printed or spoken word, the image of a woman); and the 'signified', or concept, that is conjured by the signifier. The notion of the sign therefore can be expanded to include non-linguistic signs and their meanings, as shown in Figure 1.

Figure 1 **The structure of the sign**

SIGN = SIGNIFIER (word/ image) + SIGNIFIED (concept)

Both the word 'car' and the image → The concept of a 'car'

Saussure takes this arbitrariness of signs one step further: if the meanings of signs are the result of conventions arrived at by those who communicate the signs (the wider culture), then it is reasonable to expect that the values and ideologies prevalent in the culture are themselves embedded in the chains of signification. So, although the act of reading a specific text (a news bulletin, a movie, a pop song) is an active process of decoding meaning according to principles of cultural convention, this process is also to some extent culturally conditioned – there is a dominant, preferred reading that is itself a product of cultural convention. As Fiske points out:

> 'reality' is always encoded, or rather the only way we can perceive and make sense of reality is by the codes of our culture. There may be an objective, empiricist reality out there, but there is no universal, objective way of perceiving and making sense of it. What passes for reality in any culture is the product of the culture's codes, so 'reality' is always already encoded, it is never 'raw'. (1987, pp. 4–5)

This process of encoding reality according to culturally specific meanings is taken a step further in the work of Roland Barthes (1957), who breaks the sign down further into denotation and connotation, or first and second orders of signification. The denotation of a sign is the literal, taken-for-granted meaning – in this case, a car. The connotation of a sign is the activation of meanings that are culturally embedded. Of course, connotations are not fixed for each and every member of society – the image of a car may connote transportation to some people, and social status among others. The important point to remember is that for many signs there is a culturally accepted connotation, and various techniques are used to produce and enhance the transmission of specific meanings (for example, lighting and camera angles in advertising). In the case of the car, the connotations may be individual liberty and affluence. And it is this second order of signification that Barthes refers to as myth – especially in cases where the connotation is so widely accepted as to become the literal meaning of the sign itself such that the sign is the signifier of specific cultural values.

The third order of signification is concerned with the ideological import of such meanings – the manner in which specific connotations are used to structure and organize a society and therefore the meanings that are attached to particular signs. Thus in the case of the car, the third order of signification might be concerned with property relations that value individual freedom and the use of property to convey one's social status to others. For Barthes, many signs in modern society are imbued with the myths, or ideologies, of the capitalist classes, such that the connotations that are coupled with specific signs reflect the values of these classes in such a way as to make them appear natural, taken-for-granted, commonsense meanings: their function is to legitimize existing class relationships. This is particularly true of advertising, where it is not just a product that is being sold but also a particular lifestyle, especially where celebrity endorsements are concerned (see Chapter 4, 'Consuming'). As will be seen in the final section of this chapter, many sociologists argue that there is a clear relationship between the content of media that is consumed (whether news, advertising or entertainment) and the patterns of ownership that characterize the companies involved in the production and distribution of the media.

Post-modernism

A more recent approach to understanding media content is the range of theories and ideas that have come to be labelled 'post-modernism'. Put simply, post-modernism is the 'incredulity towards metanarratives' characteristic of modernity (Lyotard, 1984). The grand projects of the

Enlightenment (liberalism, Marxism, socialism, nationalism and so on) have, it is argued, failed in their promise to emancipate humanity through scientific rationality and political and economic progress, culminating in the death and destruction of the Nazi death camps (Lyotard, 1988) (see Chapter 2, 'Modernizing'). In contrast to the singular totalities promised by these sets of beliefs (mythologies, in Barthes' schema), post-modernists hold that the world is comprised of multiple realities (possibly as many realities as there are people to experience them), and those realities are increasingly experienced as and through the exponential production of signs in the media (Smart, 1993). The semiological relationship in the media between the signifier as word/image and the signified as some 'reality' has broken down, leading Strinati to conclude:

> The mass media ... were once thought of as holding up a mirror to, and thereby reflecting, a wider social reality. Now that reality is only definable in terms of the surface reflections of that mirror. It is no longer a question of distortion since the term implies that there is a reality, outside the surface simulations of the media, which can be distorted, and this is precisely what is at issue. (1992, p. 224)

Given this breakdown in any widespread and generalized consensus over meaning, it is also argued that the projects of interpretation and critique characteristic of 'modern' institutions, such as sociology and political economy, have themselves become irrelevant. The 'death of the social', understood as a unified consensus on the meanings of cultural conventions, renders sociology impotent, a relic of the past and just one domain of meaning production among many – and no more important than any other (Baudrillard, 1983).

Perhaps the most well-known exponent of post-modern approaches to understanding the media is French sociologist Jean Baudrillard. According to Baudrillard, contemporary consumer society is so saturated by mediated signs that any distinction between the imaginary and the real is abolished – a state of affairs he calls *hyper-reality*, where existence is experienced as a complex web of representations, or *simulacra*, that refer not to some external reality but only to other representations. Hyper-reality is, for Baudrillard, the culmination of the Third Order of simulacra (see Table 9), where total simulation and reproduction has supplanted any relationship between the real and the copy, where imitation, duplication

FEELING: EMOTIONS • BELIEVING: RELIGION • EDUCATING • STRAYING: DEVIANCE •
MEDIATING: TECHNOLOGY • **INFORMING: MEDIA** • RELATING: FAMILY • BELONGING: COMMUNITY • FINISHING

365

and parody no longer make sense as the models themselves are the new 'real' (Baudrillard, 1994). Where once we may have gone to a corner shop and purchased a bottle of apple, grape or orange juice (flavours that are 'copies' of 'real' flavours, or First Order Simulacra), we are now bombarded with a bewildering choice of drinks that have no 'real world' flavour equivalents, from wild ice zest berry to double fudge mocha.

Table 9 **The Orders of Simulacra (simulacra are copies of things that no longer have an original, or never had one to begin with)**

Order	Explanation	Example
First Order	The relationship between the meaning of a sign and a copy, or counterfeit, is seen as natural, albeit wrapped in relations of power.	Clothing styles are used as signifiers of a person's class position. Counterfeiting is possible, but there remains a natural referent between the original and the copy – or the clothing style, and the social class it refers to.
Second Order	The birth of the Industrial Revolution resulted in the ability to reproduce goods and signs in large numbers as copies of an original form.	The mass production of clothing means the natural relationship between a clothing style and the social class it signifies breaks down. There exists the ability to produce and reproduce an infinite series of identical beings.
Third Order	The advent of hyper-reality, where the relationship between a sign and its referent break down completely, to the point where signs exist only as copies, referring to other copies, which in turn refer to other copies, and so on ...	Clothing now has no reference to things such as class position and, if anything, clothing styles refer only to other clothing styles. Also the recycling of elements of clothing styles from previous decades to produce a new 'form', albeit one that is itself a copy of previous forms and so on.

Examples of hyper-reality from the media are endless, with Baudrillard pointing to the television coverage of the First Gulf War (1991) as the prime example. Baudrillard predicted at the onset of hostilities that the war would not actually happen (Baudrillard, 1991). Furthermore, following the end of the war, he argued that he was correct and that no war had taken place. He argued that instead a 'copy war' had replaced a real war in which people fight and are killed. The copy war was beamed to televisions around the world and acted rather like a video game. As a result the USA was experiencing the illusion of war in which almost none of its citizens had actually participated in combat (Baudrillard, 1995).

Other examples of hyper-reality include the delivery of flowers from 'fans' to soap stars who are about to get married or have 'died' on the show; staged events in 'reality' shows such as *Survivor*; the practice of 'touching up' photographs of models and celebrities in magazines; the fact that television news does not just 'report' the news but also 'produces' the news by virtue of selecting and reporting a particular event. In the video game *America's Army*, released for free by the US Army, players can 'train' for particular roles in the military with the aim of enlisting for the real army. At the same time, in actual military training video simulations are increasingly used and new technologies are developed to fight actual battles between unmanned vehicles transmitted digitally to operators sitting in front of computer screens. The key element of all these examples is this: that 'reality' has been supplanted by simulations, which are themselves the 'new' reality as experienced by individuals, where mediated images assume equal status with the reality (itself now but a simulation) they purport to represent.

Media production: who made it?

Although all forms of media can be seen as a 'product', to be sold and consumed much as any other commodity, the term 'media production' is most often associated with two specific areas of sociological analysis: first, the manner in which particular events are selected, edited and produced as news, and, second, the patterns of ownership characteristic of contemporary media companies. In relation to news production, sociologists are interested in the extent to which media institutions, such as news disseminating organizations, set agendas and serve as gatekeepers. Clearly, the operational practices and work relationships within media organizations function to shape public opinion, through what and how they report as a news event, and what they leave out. Criteria known as 'news values' influence the inclusion and exclusion of particular events from the news headlines. These include the frequency, threshold, unambiguity and meaningfulness of the event being reported, and tend to be predicated on capacity to convey information in terms of predominant cultural norms and values. They privilege events involving powerful groups that share a cultural proximity to the target audience (Galtung and Ruge, 1973).

Stuart Hall (1973) suggests that such criteria indicate the extent to which news production is socially constructed, deeply rooted in the workings of particular media institutions rather than a reflection of what is objectively newsworthy. Different modes of delivering news (press, television, radio) may have different decision-making processes according to time and space constraints, but despite the need for diversity, in a competitive business environment there tends to be broad consensus across media as to what events are considered and covered as 'news'. As Fowler (1991) indicates, journalists from competing organizations will invariably make use of the same government and official sources, attend broadly similar types of events, and report on press statements that are issued by individuals and groups seeking publicity for a particular cause, if they fit the news value criteria. Target demographics may influence the inclusion and/or extent of coverage of a story in some publications and not others, for example, but major events such as the attack on the World Trade Center in 2001 will attract almost universal coverage.

If it is accepted that the process of selecting news events is socially constructed, there still exists a range of views on the ideological impact of news values. Does the process of news selection and production act to reinforce or resist dominant ideologies, or does it simply reproduce what the public, as consumers of news products, wish to hear? The competing perspectives on this issue tend to mirror the binary opposition already described in relation to media effects, especially the extent to which the public is viewed as a passive spectator or active participant in the news production process. Similarly, a sociologist's theoretical position on the relationships between ideology and news will reflect his/her position on the other aspect of media production mentioned above: namely the patterns of media ownership that have developed over recent decades. It is therefore useful to reflect on these developments for a moment and consider several theoretical approaches to their import in terms of news production.

There is widespread acceptance that changes in government policy in Western nations over recent decades has entailed, on the one hand, increasing deregulation and the loosening of controls on ownership of media institutions, and, on the other, a concentration of ownership of media institutions into fewer and fewer hands (Doyle, 2002). Most spectacular was the 2001 merger of America Online (AOL) and Time Warner, producing the world's biggest media company. As shown in Table 10, the Time Warner conglomerate has interests in a diverse range of media institutions, from television to film to internet productions, and reflects a pattern evident in other large companies such as Disney, News Corp, Bertelsmann and Viacom. In most cases there are high degrees of vertical and horizontal integration, with the same parent company owning the institutions responsible for the publication, distribution and delivery of media content.

Table 10 **Holdings of Time Warner**

Television & radio	Press	Publishing	Film	Internet	Other
14 companies, including the CNN group of stations and HBO	Time, *Fortune* and 33 other magazine titles	24 book brands and 52 record labels	29 operations from Poland to Brazil, and multiplex cinemas in 12 countries	AOL US and AOL Int. in 14 countries with 27 million subscribers, plus 8 other online ventures, including Netscape and Winamp	4 sports teams, Warner Brothers theme parks and related retail stores in 30 countries

Source: MediaChannel.org and CJR.org (*Who Owns What?*)

Such trends can also be seen in the emergence and development of the internet as a source of information and a conduit for the delivery of media products. Early cyber-utopians such as Nicholas Negropontes and George Gilders suggested that the so-called 'digital revolution' would lead to the withering or elimination of the traditional media giants. They thought that the increasing internet access combined with the development of user-oriented software, making it possible for anyone to produce entertainment or information-oriented media, would 'level' the playing field of media production. Indeed, there is evidence that the internet has become an important source of information, challenging the television as the primary news source as well as providing the consumer with more 'control' (Mandese, 2004). However, as McChesney (2000) suggests, the content of internet media is not immune to the trends and patterns of ownership that accompanied the development of the pre-digital commercial media world. Whilst the internet may enable the emergence of some new commercial entities (for example, the transformation of Google from a simple search engine to a significant corporate player), the previous decade has, if anything, seen the incorporation and co-option of digital communications by the traditional media giants. Far from replacing other sources of communication and information, the combination of corporate power and government policy will ensure that the 'digital revolution' will do little to change the identity and nature of existing powerful groups.

Why do sociologists find media ownership patterns important? Gillian Doyle (2002) suggests two reasons: first, because concentration of ownership in *any* industry can lead to the abuse of political power, and the exclusion and marginalization of some social groups (for example women, ethnic and religious groups) from participation in the public domain. She also argues that in democratic societies individuals must have access to a range of viewpoints so that they can make informed decisions. The selection, editing and delivery of particular events as news may privilege the perspective of some social groups over others and limit available opinions. The extent to which these two processes are related to patterns of media ownership, however, depends on the theoretical standpoint of the author. These can be identified as instrumentalist, pluralist and hegemonic perspectives.

Instrumentalist perspectives
Associated with the Marxist-influenced work of Louis Althusser and Ralph Milliband, this approach is similar to the hypodermic needle model of audience effects, described earlier, in that the audience is seen as a passive conduit for ideological messages. For these theorists, the media are part of an ideological state apparatus, together with religious institutions, and legal and education systems. Their function is to legitimate the ideology of the ruling class, maintain the class structure of capitalism and marginalize

alternative perspectives. Because the vast majority of media institutions are owned by members of this class, the content of the media will necessarily present the world-views and beliefs that perpetuate a class-based system of privilege for the few, whilst sustaining the myth that individual endeavour and responsibility are the key to overcoming hardship. The media are also supportive of the capitalist system to the extent that the content (news stories, television programmes, films etc.) are peripheral to the real task of the media: the delivery of advertising to the consumer. A classic example is the television quiz show, where particular forms of knowledge are privileged, individual capabilities are rewarded especially in terms of risk taking and luck, and prizes are invariably material goods or cash (Fiske, 1987).

Pluralist perspectives

At the other end of the spectrum, and emphasizing the role of an active audience in the production of media content, the pluralist perspective conceives of society as made up of a number of different competing interest groups that struggle for prominence through the media. Who actually owns the media is almost irrelevant in terms of media content, as it is ultimately the consumer who is sovereign and who determines the nature of media output. The media simply produces, and reproduces, that which the consumer demands, and if there are no viewers or readers then a media venture will fail. Because different newspapers present different political perspectives it is obvious that the media does not speak with one voice; each caters to its target market. Pluralists also argue that standardized 'women's' magazines outsell feminist-influenced publications because the latter do not correlate with the majority of women's experiences (Jones and Jones, 1999).

Hegemonic perspectives

This model rejects both interpretations of audience as passive spectators or active readers. Although influenced by Marxist thought, the approach suggests that ideological control can only exist where there is active consent on behalf of the media's audience rather than direct ideological manipulation of that audience. Hegemony, as the moral and philosophical leadership of a ruling class, is not a one-way process but a continual

FEELING: EMOTIONS · BELIEVING: RELIGION · EDUCATING · STRAYING: DEVIANCE · MEDIATING: TECHNOLOGY · **INFORMING: MEDIA** · RELATING: FAMILY · BELONGING: COMMUNITY · FINISHING

17   371

struggle over meaning, and one that cannot be won by force or coercion alone. In the case of media ownership, it would be rare for the owner to have total and direct control over programme and news content; this is more the task of editors and journalists. As Fowler (1991) suggests, ideological influence is more likely to be the result of editorial and journalistic interpretations of events as news, and of reporting practices that replicate formal, bureaucratic language and rely on 'experts' from the political, bureaucratic and academic domains as sources of interpretation and opinion. This effectively privileges the perspectives of particular social groups and marginalizes the discourses and 'ways of speaking' of the vast majority of the population.

Trowler (2001) notes that the social organization of capitalism and the place of media institutions within those relations may sideline certain 'left-wing' or alternative perspectives. Since the existence of most media depends on advertising revenue, it is not surprising that publications hostile to capitalism are unable to compete. It is not, as pluralists might suggest, that their ideas are not 'popular' or 'in demand' but rather that the financial structures of capitalism enable or inhibit particular types of media production. Finally, Jones and Jones (1999) use the example of apartheid in South Africa to show how the audience is not simply a passive conduit for ideological messages, but actively engaged in the negotiations over the acceptance or rejection of dominant ideologies. Whilst the media, under white control, played an important role in the legitimation of a society divided by skin colour, the dismantling of the apartheid system under Nelson Mandela has seen a shift in the dominant perspectives expressed through the media. The central point here is that even dominant ideologies remain contestable, and to a certain extent open to negotiation within the media and its audience.

Conclusion

The process of locating oneself in the social relations that enable, and are enabled by, the cultural institutions we identify as the media is an important, and essential, first step towards understanding, from a sociological perspective, the unique impact of this domain. It is possible to analyse the use of particular images or words in news reports – the use, for example, of the word 'terrorist' to describe groups who may be opposed to the dominant ideologies of the country of broadcast while other groups are described as 'freedom fighters'. A relationship can also be seen between the content of news productions, the institutional relations of the company that produce them, and wider political influences. In the wake of 11 September, for example, CBS news anchor Dan Rather suggested that his role involved:

> a form of self-censorship. It starts with a feeling of patriotism within oneself. It carries through with a certain knowledge that the country as a whole … felt and continues to feel this surge of patriotism within themselves. And one finds oneself saying: 'I know the right question, but you know what? This is not exactly the right time to ask it.'

It is important to remember that each of the research perspectives described here have issues and problems associated with them and that none of them is intended to explain, single-handed, the complex and richly varied phenomenon they explore. The use of post-modern analysis or semiotics in isolation, for example, would only provide a partial account of the media at the beginning of the twenty-first century. Similarly, to rely solely on theories of media effects, or content, or production will obscure the significant connections between these three domains. An accurate portrayal of the media in contemporary society requires understanding of the dynamics inherent in each level. These different methods and theories should be seen not as competing accounts in a struggle for meaning but rather as complementary to the project of sociological understanding.

Suggestions for further reading

Adorno, T. (1990) 'Culture Industry Reconsidered', in *The Culture Industry: Selected Essays on Mass Culture* (London: Routledge), pp. 85–92.

Golding, P. and G. Murdock (1997) 'Ideology and the Mass Media: the

FEELING: EMOTIONS · BELIEVING: RELIGION · EDUCATING · STRAYING: DEVIANCE · MEDIATING: TECHNOLOGY · **INFORMING: MEDIA** · RELATING: FAMILY · BELONGING: COMMUNITY · FINISHING

17   373

Question of Determination', in P. Golding and G. Murdock (eds), *The Political Economy of the Media* (Cheltenham: International Library of Studies in Media and Culture), pp. 476–506.

Jenkins, H. (2000) 'The Cultural Logic of Media Convergence', *International Journal of Cultural Studies* 7(1), pp. 33–43.

Windschuttle, K. (1998) *The Poverty of Media Theory*. Available: http://www.sydneyline.com [accessed 17/01/2006].

Bibliography

Adorno, T. W. (1971) *The Culture Industry: Selected Essays on Mass Culture* (London: Routledge).

Adorno T. W. and M. Horkheimer (1969) *Dialectic of Enlightenment* (New York: Social Studies Association).

Barthes, R. (1957) *Mythologies* (Paris: Editions du Seuil).

Baudrillard, J. (1983) *Fatal Strategies* (Paris: Editions Galilée).

Baudrillard, J. (1991) 'The Gulf War Will Not Take Place', *Liberation*, 4 January 1991.

Baudrillard, J. (1994) *Simulacra and Simulation* (Ann Arbor, MI: University of Michigan).

Baudrillard, J. (1995) *The Gulf War Did Not Take Place* (Bloomington, IN: Indiana University Press).

Berger, A. A. (2003) *Media and Society: A Critical Perspective* (Lanham, MD: Rowman and Littlefield).

Boyd-Barrett, O. and C. Newbold (1995) *Approaches to Media: A Reader* (London: Arnold).

de Certeau, M. (1990) *The Invention of Everyday Life* (Paris: Editions Gallimard).

Doyle, G. (2002) *Media Ownership* (London: Sage).

Fiske, J. (1987) *Television Culture* (London: Methuen).

Fiske, J. (1989) *Understanding Popular Culture* (London: Unwin Hyman).

Fowler, R. (1991) *Language in the News: Discourse and Ideology in the Press* (London: Routledge).

Galtung, J. and M. Ruge (1973) 'Structuring and Selecting News', in S. Cohen and J. Young (eds), *The Manufacture of News: Social Problems, Deviance and the Mass Media* (London: Constable).

Hall, S. (1973) 'Encoding and Decoding in the Television Discourse', *Culture and Education* 25 (Council of Europe, Strasburg).

Hall, S. (1980) 'Encoding/Decoding', in S. Hall, D. Hobson, A. Lowe and P. Willis (eds), *Culture, Media, Language* (London: Hutchinson).

Jones, M. and E. Jones (1999) *Mass Media* (Basingstoke: Macmillan).

Leavis, F. R. (1962) *Two Cultures? The Significance of C. P. Snow* (London: Chatto).

Lyotard, J. F. (1984) *The Postmodern Condition: A Report on Knowledge* (Manchester: Manchester University Press).

Lyotard, J. F. (1988) *The Postmodern Explained to Children* (Paris: Editions Galilée).

McChesney, R. (2000) 'So Much for the Magic of Technology and the Free Market', in A. Herman and T. Swiss (eds), *The World Wide Web and Contemporary Cultural Theory* (New York: Routledge).

Media Moguls. http://www.mediachannel.org/ownership/chart.shtml, 2005 [accessed 31/1/05].

Mandese, J. (2004) 'TV's Still the "Greatest", but Digital Technology is Altering Media Preferences'. http://www.mediapost.com/dtls_dsp_news.cfm?newsID=277407, 2004, [accessed 4/8/05].

Mills, C. W. (1959) *The Sociological Imagination* (London: Oxford University Press).

Milmo, C. (2004) '1066 and All That: How Hollywood is Giving Britain a False Sense of History', *Independent*, 5 April 2004.

Radway, J. (1987) *Reading the Romance: Women, Patriarchy and Popular Literature* (London: Verso).

Rather, D. (2002) 'Veteran CBS News Anchor Dan Rather speaks out on BBC Newsnight tonight'. http://www.bbc.co.uk/pressoffice/pressreleases/stories/2002/, [accessed 1/11/06].

Rimm, M. (1995) 'Marketing Pornography on the Information Superhighway: A Survey of 917,410 Images, Descriptions, Short Stories, and Animations Downloaded 8.5 Million Times by Consumers in over 2000 Cities in Forty Countries, Provinces, and Territories', *Georgetown Law Journal* 83(5), pp. 1849–934.

de Saussure, F. (1971) *Course in General Linguistics* (Paris: Payot).

Schramm W. and W. E. Porter (1982) *Men, Women, Messages and Media* (New York: Harper and Row).

Smart, B. (1993) *Postmodernity* (London: Routledge).

Strinati, D. (1992) 'Postmodernism and Popular Culture', *Sociology Review*, April 1992.

Trowler, P. (2001) *Investigating Mass Media* (London: Collins Educational).

Tursi, R. (1996) 'Hey, Mr. Spelling, Look What We've Done to Your 90210! – An Ethnographic Study of the Audience of Beverley Hills 90210'. http://collection.nlc-bnc.ca/100/202/300/mediatribe/mtribe94/bh90210.html, 1996 [accessed 31/1/05].

Who Owns What? http://www.cjr.org/tools/owners, 2005 [accessed 31/1/05].

FEELING: EMOTIONS • BELIEVING: RELIGION • EDUCATING • STRAYING: DEVIANCE •
MEDIATING: TECHNOLOGY • **INFORMING: MEDIA** • RELATING: FAMILY • BELONGING: COMMUNITY • FINISHING

17 375

18 relating: family

Rhonda Shaw

KEY
POINTS
- Changes in society affect how we construct and manage arrangements for family life and intimacy.

- Families take many shapes and forms; there is no unchanging and universal version.

- The nuclear family – mother and father married to each other plus their children – which Talcott Parsons described, and which is dominant in much American sociology, is increasingly replaced by other forms of family life.

- Families can be warm and supportive; they can also be oppressive, destructive and harmful to their members.

- Family life generally rests on inequalities between parents, children and siblings. Marxist sociology makes this especially clear.

- Technological and medical developments have expanded the possibilities of biological and social parenthood.

Does the family exist?

For sociologists, the family is not a stable or unchanging universal phenomenon. Some sociologists would go so far as to say that the family, as an entity, does not exist. Many would assert that we cannot understand changes to family life and intimacy without taking into account important institutional and social changes elsewhere in society, and these changes are occurring all the time (see Chapter 9, 'Gendering'). Certainly findings from empirical studies of family life over the last quarter of the twentieth century, which have documented significant changes to family life and relationships in Western societies, highlight the dynamism of contemporary family life. In so doing, they have shown how dominant myths about the family – promulgated by the media and by politicians – often bear little resemblance to reality. Such approaches follow Peter Berger's advice to look 'for levels of reality other than those given in the official interpretations of society' (Swain, 1994, p. 11). They go beyond commonsense assumptions about what we might think a family is, and how we've been taught to think about families, as well as taking us beyond institutionalized definitions of how to define a family.

More than one introduction to the sociology of the family has quoted from Philip Larkin's (1974) downbeat version of family life in which he describes how parents hand on their own faults, give you some extra new ones, and generally do to you just what their parents did to them. So, in an ever-repeating cycle, the families of Larkin's gloomy vision hand on deeply sedimented misery that 'deepens like a coastal shelf'.

Part of the sociological interest of this poem lies in its image of family as an immutable object. Larkin sees it as an entity or social fact that exists prior to the birth of new family members. This notion of the family as unchanging and always there highlights how, for many people, family life expresses and symbolizes order in society (Cameron, 1990). As a social grouping and institution, the family reproduces the kind of order people feel they need to anchor them to the world and to give them a sense of place relative to those things around them that are constantly changing. Many are therefore deeply disturbed when they perceive that changes to the constitution of the family or to its meaning are taking place. They then tend to assume that the family is breaking down, and worry that any collapse of family also threatens social stability and even society, as they understand it.

Another way in which the family symbolizes order is also implied in Larkin's poem. That is, the idea that family life anchors us temporally in the world. That is to say, the family grounds us in time in a way that orders our sense of who we are and our place in the scheme of things. Larkin demonstrates this by drawing on the geological metaphor sociologists themselves often use to explain the course of historical time – the coastal shelf that is formed by layers and layers of sediment being built up over different, consecutive time periods. For him, layers of family life stretch back to become ossified and hardened into unmoveable bedrock. This makes the family so *deep* historically that it is literally a static structure and metaphysical entity in its own right. Certainly the family can be viewed as a social fact that exists prior to the birth of new family members. It pre-exists us and, for better or worse, it will exist into the future with or without us (if we follow Larkin's advice). For many people, though, this anchoring to the past and to ancestors, as well as to the future, through children, is crucial to their sense of wellbeing.

As well as providing temporal order, the family also shapes or determines the lives of family members in irrevocable and fixed ways, and so reproduces certain sets of social relations and ways of behaving and interacting over time. For Larkin, the social relations the family reproduces are fundamentally damaging, and cannot possibly be transformed or changed, so the picture he paints of the family is very grim indeed. In sum, the poet is saying that the family is an institution that changes very little over time, but few contemporary sociologists of the family would agree.

Two sides of family life

Larkin's verse is sociologically relevant because it expresses and exposes what sociologists, until recently, mostly ignored – the dual or double life of the family (see Bittman and Pixley, 1997). It foregrounds questions of what the family is, and what it should be. In terms of wellbeing, family is a site of intimacy and disclosure of personal feelings and closeness to others, but also an institution that reproduces a whole host of inequalities and not so loving, unethical, and sometimes violent behaviours.

We often think of family relationships as made up of intimate interactions that confirm the importance of emotional bonds, ties and closeness to others. This ideology about familial closeness and bonding is tied to the thesis of affective individualism, which describes a series of changes to social life in the Western world during the eighteenth century. The gradual separation of work from home, which led to the privatization of the family, meant that marriage ties were formed on the basis of romantic attraction rather than economic or political necessity. Correspondingly, child rearing became increasingly centred on the needs of the child and the parent–child relationship, and children were less seen as economic resources or production units within the household itself. But, in Larkin's poem, the family portrait is one where there is little or no expectation of such emotional tenderness or affection.

Family life *can* be enriching and fulfilling, but it can also be based on relationships that are oppressive, destructive and harmful to family members. Or, as Larkin suggests, the family is a miserable institution that we are better off without. Even if we do not entirely agree with this perspective, one key point to be gleaned from Larkin's account is that physical proximity is not synonymous with intimacy. At the very least, familial conflict might include the minor disputes and quibbles of sibling rivalry as well as a generational hierarchy where children 'do what they are told' because mum or dad says so.

Ritual celebrations, too, can demonstrate the patterned enactment of family inequalities. For people who celebrate Christmas, 25 December is a day when family members may gather together through a sense of obligation and duty rather than by choice or desire. As a result, 'old and new tensions lurk just below the surface' (Bittman and Pixley, 1997, p. 24) and are often subtlety manifested through the giving and receiving of gifts. This is because although the perfect present can symbolize an enduring bond between giver and recipient, gift-giving rituals are often enforced enactments of how to do family that are designed to express and display affection which may actually not exist. The conflicts that ritual celebrations like Christmas can present for family members can be about positioning within the family, and may involve assumptions about gender, age, social roles and perceived status.

Although the quality of family life can be said to have improved in the last hundred years, family environments can still be dangerous, especially for women and children. This oppressive dimension of family life, which includes domestic violence, incest and the sexual abuse of children, also reveals the deeply unequal power relations that underpin families. On the one hand, there is an expectation and desire that families will fulfil our human need for intimacy, but family life can also be exploitative because it is permeated by inequalities that stem from gender imbalances and generational differences. In short, the family is not the most democratic institution in most societies (see Chapter 7, 'Governing: Power'). The sociological theory that in its typifications of family life best illustrates this point is known as structural functionalism.

Talcott Parsons and the nuclear family

Structural functionalism formed the basis of one of the most dominant perspectives on the sociology of the family in the Anglophone world up until the 1970s, and persists into the twenty-first century. This tradition of thinking about the family has been dominated by North American sociologists who based their theories on the model they knew best – the North American middle-class, nuclear family. The nuclear family has been defined in various ways, but for structural functionalists the following definition is considered foundational. In this paradigm of thinking, the nuclear family is a 'social group characterized by common residence, economic co-operation, and reproduction. It includes adults of both sexes, at least two of whom maintain a socially approved sexual relationship, and one or more children, own or adopted, of the sexually cohabiting adults' (Murdock cited in Gittins, 1985, p. 60). Not surprisingly, this definition is also the image against which many sociologists, who do not subscribe to the structural functionalist tradition of thinking that deploys it, define themselves.

This typical family contains a father, a mother and 2.2 dependent children. Structural functionalists basically believe that the family has a biological basis, which is rooted in kin relations. They also believe the family fulfils a number of basic social functions as an institution – hence the name 'functionalism'. These functions – the socialization of children, the stabilization of adult personalities, the regulation of sexuality, and the provision of food, warmth and shelter – are thought to be tasks that family presumably fulfils in all societies.

Probably the most influential sociologist in this tradition was Talcott Parsons, who describes a nuclear family made up of a sexually involved man and woman, with their offspring, who are joined by blood, marriage or adoption. The man and woman have sex for reproductive and pro-creative purposes, and raise their children together in a shared common residence (Parsons and Bales, 1955). Hand in hand with this version of the family come traditional ideologies about the roles of men and women and the needs of children. Structural functionalists famously claim that family members in modern societies share a division of labour in which men and women perform different tasks. This differentiation of roles and tasks has occurred with the onset of industrialization and modernization and is the most effective arrangement for industrial capitalist societies: it assumes a public role for men and a private one for women (see Chapter 2, 'Modernizing'). The tasks that make up this division of labour, while different, are thought to be equitably distributed and (presumably) complementary. Women are primarily charged with taking care of the home, emotional life, and the 'affective/expressive roles' that families need to function efficiently in the modern world. In contrast, men have 'instrumental' roles, which take them outside the home to earn money and provide the material goods necessary for family survival and optimum wellbeing. In short, Dad goes out to work in the public sphere or domain, and, because Dad is the breadwinner, Mum is obliged to provide him with a number of services *gratis*. She must, for instance, ensure he has clean clothes, dinner on the table in the evening when he gets home from work, and sexual services – all in return for her upkeep.

In the present day this may seem a quite unreal (even caricatured) picture of the family, but the image has been both powerful and pervasive. Sociologists now also recognize that because Parsons was actually describing the North American middle-class family he knew and understood, his model is also an ethnocentric one. Both his image of the nuclear family and Murdock's definition of it fail to accommodate a whole host of different family arrangements. In the real world there are many exceptions to Parsons's ideal family type and to the rule that Murdock's normative definition prescribes. But there is also, in the real world, a tendency for policy makers to plan as though the ideal-type nuclear family predominated in their societies.

Research evidence from many countries now demonstrates that Parsons's model was never appropriate for the majority of working-class families where both parents were, of economic necessity, performing paid labour in industrial processes or in other people's houses and businesses. Nor does it represent the numerous women who, since the 1970s and with access to education and to professional and managerial jobs, choose to enter the paid workforce. For example, in Australia the change has been from around 12 per cent of women doing paid work in 1948 to 50 per cent in 2000. There were some assumptions that this change would be reflected in the gender division of labour within households, but expectations that changed circumstances would see women doing less domestic work and men more have not eventuated. A Sydney time-use study between 1987 and 1992 showed that women still did 70 per cent of unpaid household labour, and that even when men were working fewer paid hours they did not pick up any extra household work (Bittman and Pixley, 1997). Under a splendidly evocative chapter heading – 'Mars and Venus Scrub the Toilet' – Susan Maushart sums up the Australian experience.

> In all this voluminous research, there is really only one variable that explained much at all. In fact it explained everything. If you want to know who does what around the house in any particular marriage, it was conclusively demonstrated, you need look no further than gender. (2001, p. 84)

In Parsons's terms, many women are now performing both sides of the labour division and they work what Arlie Hochschild describes as a 'second shift' in their homes (Hochschild and Machung 2003).

Nor is an assumption that families everywhere always live together necessarily accurate. There are many cross-cultural, global examples where co-residence or co-habitation and family membership or practices do not necessarily coincide. In the Dominican Republic, for example, families may live in separate households, and although these groups appear to resemble nuclear family arrangements, they are in fact extended family groupings of people living within close proximity to one another (Leeder, 2004). Another example, from New Zealand society, is the Maori practice of *whangai*. *Whangai*, which literally means to feed or nurture, occurs where adults other than birth parents or grandparents are also the 'primary' caregivers or guardians of children. It may mean that the child goes to live in a different residence, for a short or long period, with an elder or senior relative (Durie-Hall, 1993).

While such situations reflect the cultural diversity of family life, there are also numerous examples that reflect the organizational or situational diversity of family life in contemporary society. The concepts 'cultural diversity' and 'situational diversity' are borrowed from the work of David

FEELING: EMOTIONS • BELIEVING: RELIGION • EDUCATING • STRAYING: DEVIANCE •
MEDIATING: TECHNOLOGY • INFORMING: MEDIA • **RELATING: FAMILY** • BELONGING: COMMUNITY • FINISHING

18 383

Cheal (2002, p. 19) on family life. Cultural diversity refers to the different ideals underpinning different family practices of people from different cultural and ethnic groups. Situational diversity, which is synonymous with the concept of organizational diversity (Rapoport and Rapoport, 1982), occurs where people share similar family values, but organize and practise family life differently due to work patterns and attitudes toward marriage. Rapoport and Rapoport (1982) also make reference to social class diversity, life cycle diversity and family life-course diversity within the range of family types. For example, changes in the nature of work patterns and employment opportunities in contemporary post-industrial societies have meant that some families do not co-habit or reside, or only form households for periods of time. Children sent to boarding school, says British sociologist Diana Gittins, 'may spend little more than a third of the year residing with their parents' (1985, p. 61). Another set of family arrangements where co-residence and familial ties do not seamlessly coincide are those where the father, or one of the partners, has to travel abroad frequently so that they are only resident for short periods of time. These may involve, for example, migrants whose business interests remain in their country of origin, migrant workers, engineers on overseas projects, diplomats, academic researchers, merchant bankers, naval officers, and many other situations.

Other similar kinds of arrangement, called commuter marriages, also exist where partners live in different cities due to work commitments and travel to be with one another in the weekends. In such cases, where children are involved, they tend to stay with one person as the primary caregiver. Although these lone-parenting arrangements may be temporary situations, travel is often a feature of the work lives of professional or dual-career couples and their families. So, while dual-career couples and their families might fit some of the criteria that make them a nuclear family in the conventional sense, they still don't fit the cereal-packet image, presented to us by the media, of a breadwinner dad, stay-at-home mum, and 2.2 smiling kids living contentedly in the suburbs in a home with backyard section and white picket fence (Leach, 1967).

More recently, social researchers have documented the emergence of 'satellite' or 'multi-local' families (Ho, 2003). These exist where partners have jobs some distance away from one another and may maintain a second household where one of them lives during the week. Family members may, therefore, be separated by hundreds or thousands of kilometres. Despite distance, and much like extended families, as Elaine Leeder shows in her book *The Family in Global Perspective* (2004), 'there is intimate, ongoing economic and psychological interaction. ... money is sent home to the family, regular phone calls maintain the emotional bonds, and visits take place back and forth frequently' (2004, p. 27).

Physical proximity, to reiterate, does not always define a family, nor does physical distance indicate an absence of love, affection or intimacy. While family members may live together in one household, this isn't always the case. At the same time, persons living together in one household may or may not be a family. They may not be related by blood, marriage or kinship ties. Furthermore, while love and affection may be hallmarks of modern familial relationships, biogenetic or conjugal connection may also be the basis of quite conventional family groupings (see Chapter 12, 'Feeling: Emotions').

If the nuclear family is in part simulation, or a figment of dominant cultural imagination, then we not only need to ask what an effective definition of 'family' would look like, but also which sociological perspectives are best equipped to understand and explain the multi-faceted nature of family life in contemporary society.

Other sociological ways of understanding family life

Clearly, the poetic view of the family that began this chapter is partial and from a particular point of view. Not everyone's experiences of family life correspond to Larkin's. There are a variety of ways to view and 'do' family. In contrast to Larkin's image, and in contrast to the image of family life promulgated by structural functionalism, many sociologists would say, as Gittins (1985, p. 4) points out, that there is no one clear-cut model as to what a family 'is' and what a family 'does' (see Bernardes, 1993; Cheal, 1993; Morgan, 1996). Correspondingly, sociologists have a variety of approaches to the study of families. Some focus on macro-concerns involving the family as an institution in conjunction with other social, political and economic institutions (e.g. Engels, 1972; Zaretsky, 1976). Others, such as

Bernardes (1997) and Delphy and Leonard (1992), explore so-called middle-range or micro-concerns. Of pivotal importance to these scholars is what happens inside or within families and between individuals in terms of their interactions and exchanges with one another. These two broad approaches can be broken down further into a number of different perspectives on the study of families, each with its own theoretical traditions and research paradigms. Marxist, developmental and structural functionalist approaches to family life fall under the rubric of macro-sociology, whereas feminist and interactionist approaches, for example, tend to take a micro-sociological view of family formation. Many introductory texts on the study of families discuss these different perspectives (see, for example, Leeder, 2004 and Steel and Kidd, 2001).

Marxist approaches

Much of the initial impetus for Marxist work on family life derives from the writings of Karl Marx and his friend and collaborator Frederick Engels. Very schematically, Engels argued that the form of family life changes as the mode of production changes. So, as one way of organizing the production of food, goods and services shifts and gives way to another, the structure or nature of the family changes to accommodate it (see Chapter 6, 'Stratifying: Class'). According to Engels, the supposedly now ubiquitous nuclear family did not always exist. When property was collectively owned and sexuality was not closely regulated, task sharing within family arrangements was rather more egalitarian than the division of labour within the patriarchal nuclear family. As Engels stated in *The Origin of the Family, Private Property and the State* (1884/1972), it was only with the domestication of animals and development of private property, which led to the control of women's sexuality, that the monogamous nuclear family emerged. The overthrow of mother-right, as Engels put it, and women's subordination and economic dependence on men, can thus be traced back to monogamous marriage, which provided men with a means to ensure that their property would be inherited by their sons.

The crux of the Marxist argument is that families perpetuate the class structure, as well as perpetuating the social dominance of men over women, thereby benefiting the ruling class. While orthodox Marxists are primarily interested in the relationships between the family and the structural conditions of society at large, Marxist feminists emphasize that the domestic labour that wives and children perform in the family is essential to ensure the continued reproduction of capitalism. Domestic labour has to be undertaken in the home by wives, mothers and sisters in order to reproduce family members and their labour power. If domestic services such as housework were not provided through women's unpaid labour then men's wages or salaries would have to be high enough to absorb the costs of purchasing these services in the marketplace. For Marxists, then, the way the nuclear family is constituted has direct benefits or pay-offs for capitalism. In other words, the structural features of the nuclear family support capitalist commodity production and capitalist ideology encourages people to want to reproduce normative family arrangements (see Chapter 3, 'Working').

Feminist approaches

Feminist scholars reject the structural functionalist idea that the family exists as a bounded unit prior to its interaction with other social institutions or structures like production relations, or even femininity and masculinity constructs. Nor do they admire its suggested nostalgia for a particular kind of imaginary family; that is, the 1950s cereal-packet family. According to Stevi Jackson (1999, pp. 165–6), families are in fact constituted by a complex set of relationships and practices, and because no member of the same family experiences family life in the same way, the interests of all family members will be relatively divergent. What this means is that various individuals will experience family life differently in ways affected by their positioning in the family. The latter will condition how much or how little power they are able to exercise in the family and how much benefit they gain from family life.

Rather than assume a harmoniously balanced division of labour within the household, with each member performing his or her tasks and chores reciprocally and symmetrically, feminist sociologists argue that the division of labour and the tasks that women in particular have to perform in the family are not very equitable at all. Indeed, the asymmetrical nature of the household division of labour has prompted feminist sociologists to claim that the family is a site of inequality, in which men receive greater material benefits than women.

FEELING: EMOTIONS • BELIEVING: RELIGION • EDUCATING • STRAYING: DEVIANCE • MEDIATING: TECHNOLOGY • INFORMING: MEDIA • **RELATING: FAMILY** • BELONGING: COMMUNITY • FINISHING

18   387

Radical and materialist feminists, for example, view the family as the main site of women's oppression. In their book *Familiar Exploitation: A New Analysis of Marriage in Contemporary Western Societies* (1992), Christine Delphy and Diana Leonard describe the nuclear family as an economic system, which has historically been headed by men who have made key decisions about how to allocate family income. Even when women engage in work in the paid labour force, their jobs tend to be regarded as secondary in the family, and women often have little decision-making autonomy.

Additionally, despite entering the workforce in greater numbers and holding down full-time paid jobs, studies of the division of labour within families show that women still do more housework than men. This is to say nothing of affective work. And even though some men have taken on a greater role in terms of housework contribution, women spend more time looking after the children. Although shifts are occurring in fatherhood and contemporary men's relationships with their children, evidence from time-use surveys shows that when women complete their household and child-caring tasks for the day, they have less leisure time than men. This is because women are constantly 'on call', even when the children are asleep. Because women are more likely to have to care for children, the sick and the elderly, they are less able to participate with men on an equal footing in the paid workforce.

In short, feminist sociologists argue that women are systematically disadvantaged in families. Not only does women's housework and domestic labour go unrecognized, it is also unrewarded. As Delphy and Leonard say, the unpaidness of housework depends 'on the fact that the tasks which comprise it are performed within a particular relationship, one where the people who usually do the work do not own the products of their practical, emotional, sexual and reproductive labour' (1992, p. 84).

Micro-sociological traditions

Perhaps one of the most significant breakthroughs in recent years for sociologists who study families has to do with a shift in focus from discussing the composition of family structures and how to draw boundaries around 'the family', to an emphasis on micro-sociological concerns. In contrast to macro-sociological approaches to the family, which stress the interplay of social institutions and broad societal processes, micro-sociological perspectives focus on the interactions of family members and how individuals construct and experience family life.

These sociologists are interested in the sorts of relationships that people have with one another within families and households, and how people negotiate and renegotiate changes to family formation. All these are important factors to consider, given the rise of marriage dissolution and recoupling in the West, as well as how people negotiate their relationships with one another when they are involved in adoption processes or assisted reproductive strategies such as surrogate pregnancy arrangements. They may also be interested in looking at changes to behaviours between members of the family group due to changes in the life course: for instance, how a person experiences parenthood or how childhood is experienced within the family. In such cases, sociologists look at the meanings that people attach to their relationships with one another in families and how patterns of caring and intimacy operate within familial arrangements and households.

Doing family

Increasingly, then, sociologists have rejected a view of the family as a static structure or timeless monolithic entity. Instead, they have tended to characterize family life and familial arrangements, especially in contemporary societies, as dynamic, fluid and open-ended social groupings and relationships (Gittins, 1985, p. 4). This has produced a shift of focus from defining the boundaries of family in terms of blood kin and conjugal roles and duties, to understanding how different participants in family groupings 'practise' family life (Morgan, 1996). In so doing, these sociologists emphasize how individuals actively 'do' (create and experience) family, rather than describing the structure and functions of family life. While the meaning and significance of these practices, as well as the practices themselves, vary culturally and historically, the concrete activities that family members engage in – like eating meals together, or doing the gardening – may or may not reveal the quality of people's felt relations to one another. In short, sociologists, as well as taking account of the practices that family members engage in, now also consider their differential moral and emotional investments in those practices (see Morgan, 1996).

The family, much like gender, is both a series of practices and an institution. Family is constituted through actions and interactions, and is reiterated in particular contexts, sites and locations. This is effectively demonstrated, as Bernardes (1997, pp. 91–2) points out, in the ways in which some families construct or achieve a sense of belonging through the public display of photographs, or by keeping photographic albums as a historical record of family life. Decisions about who gets included in these collections are clear symbolic indicators as to perceptions of family membership. It is this blurring of the boundaries between what we take the family to be or official normative definitions of the family, and how we *live* and *experience* family life that increasingly interest many contemporary sociologists.

Diverse family types

It should now be clear that one of the reasons the poet Philip Larkin is so discontented with the family, as he paints it, is that the relationships we have with members of our families are not voluntary. Family membership, which is traditionally rooted in kinship relations, is often based upon obligations and duties. We are born into families that precede us and we cannot choose our parents (or ancestors). In contrast, membership in social groups of friends or peers, and even in political parties, is much more voluntary. But this is not always the case.

Sociologists (for example Stacey, 1996 and Weeks, 2002) have recently compared notions of the normal or typical family based on blood kin with quite diverse and fluid forms of household that include non-marital, heterosexual partnerships, de facto marriages, same-sex partnerships, single-parent families, blended and extended family arrangements, as well as numerous combinations of these types. In some of these groupings, especially those that are not officially recognized by the state or ideologically sanctioned by religious institutions, people choose to call themselves family. Although their relationships may fall outside the bounds of conventional understandings of what a family is or should look like, these people often pretend they are kin (i.e. related by blood or marriage). Sociologists refer to these families as 'fictive kin' (Gittins, 1985, p. 65; Leeder, 2004, p. 25), 'elective families', or 'families of choice' (Weeks, 2002). They signal the emergence of highly individualistic, purportedly democratic forms of relationship that have begun to replace older ideas about familial intimacy and obligation with new ideas about 'plastic' sexuality, companionship, and open and diffuse relationships (Giddens, 1992; Weeks, 2002).

As well as being defined by choice – because families often include kith and friends as kin or relatives – and due to changes in marital trends, these newer kinds of familial arrangement also deconstruct or debunk the idea that the family is an objective entity that must be defined in terms of a 'heterosexual conjugal unit based on marriage and co-residence' (Jackson, 1999). This suggests that although all family types may share some qualitative aspects about the depth and significance of relationships and attitudes toward care and belonging, they are incredibly diverse.

Whether families are more diverse today than they were in the past is clearly debatable. However, the speed with which families change and the conditions under which they are reconstituted has greatly accelerated. Given the proliferation of family types and formations in the world today, sociologists try to be very precise about what kind of family they are discussing when they disseminate the results of their research to the public and to other social and political institutions. They will therefore refer to a variety of hyphenated family forms such as extended families, nuclear families, lone-parent families, symmetrical families, blended families, families of choice, and so on (Baker, 2001).

Although the meanings attached to relationship breakdown in contemporary social life remain contested, divorce is more socially acceptable than it once was. However, increasing divorce rates have not led to a corresponding decline in marriage or in cohabitation rates overall. Marriage, especially remarriage, remains popular, and cohabitation, which often leads to marriage in any case, is increasing. Accompanying these trends, we have seen a rise in blended and reconstituted families made up of children and biological and step-parents, as well as the proportion of family households headed by a lone parent. Sole-parenthood is mainly the

FEELING: EMOTIONS • BELIEVING: RELIGION • EDUCATING • STRAYING: DEVIANCE •
MEDIATING: TECHNOLOGY • INFORMING: MEDIA • **RELATING: FAMILY** • BELONGING: COMMUNITY • FINISHING

18   391

lot of women, and whilst some women decide to become single parents (especially in Scandinavian countries, where single mothers are paid a living wage), lone parenting is largely the result of separation or divorce rather than choice. Because a lone parent's ability to engage in paid work or to undertake further education is often compromised by child-care and domestic responsibilities, lone-parent families are typically poorer than other family types.

The question of children

The cultural and organizational diversity of families is reflected in the range of different and sometimes conflicting theories offering explanations of family life. Certainly, sociologists are clear that the dominant image of the cereal-packet family that circulates in popular culture and in the Western cultural imagination bears little resemblance to the reality of familial life as it is lived in the contemporary world. Not only does this image conflate a moral and ideological norm with empirical reality, but those who believe the nuclear family is an ideal-typical construct perceive as a stable structure what is actually the interplay of several political, economic, technological and historical factors.

Today, there are many factors that have a significant impact on the ways we organize, structure and live family life in contemporary Western society. Some of these relate to political economy and shifting employment patterns, such as more flexible hours of work and more and more jobs that are part-time and casual; changes in gender relations and sexuality; increased and shifting expectations of what we want from life; and last, but not least, changes to reproductive options.

I mentioned earlier that for many people, identifying as a member of a family or as part of a family anchors people in time and gives them a strong sense of who they are. Clearly, everyone can be located within some form of kinship arrangement – even hybrid or cyborg creatures in science fiction films have at least one parent, albeit usually a father figure. However, it is not necessarily the case that everyone has children.

In fact, since the late nineteenth century, and particularly since the 1960s, fertility rates in the Western world have been falling, and these patterns have had profound demographic consequences. The total fertility rate is the average number of children a woman has during her lifetime of childbearing years. As Marshall (2005, p. 225) has noted, United Nations figures put the total average world fertility rate at 2.7 from 1995 to 2000, yet this figure was around five births per woman in the 1970s. In Russia, the figure is now around 2.6 children per woman (Abbott et al., 2005, p. 166); in Australia, fertility rates dropped to 1.73 in 2001, which is below the replacement level of 2.1 children per woman for the population; and in Italy and Spain the figure for the same period was estimated at 1.3. During the 1990s, the total fertility rate in New Zealand was 2.0.

In addition, recent research indicates that somewhere between 14 and 25 per cent of the total female population of childbearing age in countries such as New Zealand, Australia and Canada will have no children at all (Baker, 2001; Marshall, 2005). Some of these women will be faced with fertility issues and will seek treatment at fertility clinics. Most, however, will choose not to procreate. With increased availability of reliable contraception and the attendant uncoupling of sexuality from reproduction, more and more people are making lifestyle decisions not to have children.

Numerous reasons are given for the broad pattern of declining overall fertility patterns around the world. These are linked to the economic costs and emotional burdens of raising children; overpopulation; the loss of adult autonomy; complications associated with changes to relationship patterns; and also women's increased financial independence and work-force participation.

Technological and medical advances are worth noting in the context of these changes. Improved contraceptive methods, such as the availability of the Pill in the 1960s in Western countries, are often said to be a major cause of decreased fertility. Although few children proportionately are born per annum to men and women who have used assisted reproductive technologies, their existence may also have contributed to changing attitudes around fertility behaviour. Certainly, such technologies have contributed to the flexibility of family formation and have enabled infertile couples and single persons to have children and thus create families where they would otherwise have been unable to do so. Indeed, since the late twentieth century and the development of in vitro fertilization technology and the birth of the world's first 'test-tube baby', Louise Brown, in the UK in 1978, it has been possible for a child to have up to five parents: that is, a child's parents could include an ovarian egg donor, sperm donor, gestating mother, social mother and social father. In such cases, biogenetic or biological parenting is separated from social parenting, and this fragmentation results in a number of different persons all engaging in different strategies to facilitate the reproductive process from conception to birth and beyond (to say nothing of the techno-medics who manipulate these processes). Aside from these biological aspects, in some jurisdictions it is becoming legally and socially possible for all those persons listed above to have a relationship with the child in one way or another if offspring of these arrangements choose to do so (see Law Commission, 2005).

This example shows that the boundaries around the ideological cereal-packet family, whose existence has always been questionable outside its Western countries of origin, are becoming ever more permeable; and part of this permeability is due to technological and medical developments. As a consequence of these, as well as other personal, historical, economic and political factors, sociologists now recognize a much wider network of relationships that make up family life in the twenty-first century.

Families, old and new

Certainly, ways of doing family are constantly changing. American sociologist Judith Stacey (1996) suggests that we might be in the midst of what she calls the 'postmodern family condition'. Whether or not we agree with Stacey's choice of language to describe contemporary family arrangements, her observation has resonances for those who recognize the cultural and situational diversity of familial life. Stacey's remarks about the so-called post-modern family are relevant in this respect and provide a neat summation to this chapter.

> The postmodern family condition is not a new model of family life equivalent to that of the modern family; it is not the next stage in an orderly progression of stage in family history; rather the postmodern family condition signals the moment in history when our belief in a logical progression of stages has broken down. ...

> [t]he postmodern family condition incorporates both experimental and nostalgic dimensions as it lurches forward and backward into an uncertain future. (Stacey, 1996, pp. 7–8)

Generally speaking, then, family formations are made up of a mixture of both old and new, and incorporate beliefs about kin that stem from traditional values. Conventional ways of doing family are often tempered with pragmatism and, on occasion, innovative technological and social practices. Essentially, older, more traditional, forms of kinship relations persist and proliferate alongside newly emerging, ostensibly more democratic and open-ended family forms. For sociologists, this is not a situation to bemoan, but an aspect of our social and cultural history that should be carefully observed, documented and critically analysed for what it tells us about the ways human beings live their lives in connection to those closely related to them.

Suggestions for further reading

Jackson, S. (1999) 'Families, Households and Domestic Life', in S. Taylor (ed.), *Sociology: Issues and Debates* (Basingstoke: Macmillan), pp. 158–79.

Silva, E. and C. Smart (eds) (1999) *The New Family?* (London: Sage).

Therborn, G. (2004) *Between Sex and Power: Family in the World, 1900–2000* (London: Routledge).

Weeks, J. (2002) 'Elective Families: Lesbian and Gay Life Experiments', in A. Carling, S. Duncan and R. Edwards (eds), *Analysing Families: Morality and Rationality in Policy and Practice* (London: Routledge, 2002).

Bibliography

Abbott, P., C. Wallace and M. Tyler (2005) *An Introduction to Sociology: Feminist Perspectives*, 3rd edn (London: Routledge).

Baker, M. (2001) *Families, Labour and Love: Family Diversity in a Changing World* (Sydney: Allen & Unwin).

Bernardes, J. (1993) 'Responsibilities in Studying Postmodern Families', *Journal of Family Issues* 14(1), pp. 35–49.

Bernardes, J. (1997) *Family Studies: An Introduction* (London: Routledge).

Bittman, M. and J. Pixley (1997) *The Double Life of the Family: Myth, Hope and Experience* (Sydney: Allen & Unwin).

Cameron, J. (1990) *Why Have Children?* (Christchurch: University of Canterbury Press).

Cheal, D. (1993) 'Unity and Difference in Postmodern Families', *Journal of Family Issues* 14(1), pp. 5–19.

Cheal, D. (2002) *Sociology of Family Life* (Basingstoke: Palgrave).

Delphy, C. and D. Leonard (1992) *Familiar Exploitation: A New Analysis of Marriage in Contemporary Western Societies* (Cambridge: Polity Press).

Durie-Hall, D. (1993) 'Whanau, Hapu, Iwi', in S. Coney (ed.), *Standing in the Sunshine* (Auckland: Penguin Books), pp. 68–9.

Engels, F. (1972) *The Origin of the Family, Private Property, and the State* (New York: Pathfinder Press).

Giddens, A. (1992) *The Transformation of Intimacy: Sexuality, Love and Eroticism in Modern Societies* (Stanford, CA: Stanford University Press).

Gittins, D. (1985) *The Family in Question: Changing Households and Familiar Ideologies* (Basingstoke: Macmillan).

Ho, E. (2003) 'Reluctant Exiles or Roaming Transnationals? The Hong Kong Chinese in New Zealand', in M. Ip (ed.), *Unfolding History, Evolving Identity: The Chinese in New Zealand* (Auckland: Auckland University Press), pp. 165–84.

Hochschild, A. with A. Machung (2003) *The Second Shift* (New York: Penguin Books).

Jackson, S. (1999) 'Families, Household and Domestic Life', in S. Taylor (ed.), *Sociology: Issues and Debates* (Basingstoke: Macmillan), pp. 158–79.

New Zealand Law Commission (2005) New Issues in Legal Parenthood: Report 88. Wellington: New Zealand. (http://www.lawcom.govt.nz)

Leach, E. (1967) *A Runaway World?* (London: BBC Publications).

Leeder, E. (2004) *The Family in Global Perspective: A Gendered Journey* (Thousand Oaks, CA: Sage).

Marshall, H. (2005) 'Fertility: Changing Pressures and Choices', in M. Poole (ed.), *Family: Changing Families, Changing Times* (Sydney: Allen & Unwin), pp. 223–42.

Maushart, S. (2001) *Wifework: What Marriage Really Means for Women* (Melbourne: Text Publishing).

Morgan, D. (1996) *Family Connections: An Introduction to Family Studies* (Cambridge: Polity Press).

Parsons, T. and R. Bales (1955) *Family, Socialization and Interaction Process* (New York: Free Press).

Stacey, J. (1996) *In the Name of the Family: Rethinking Family Values in the Postmodern Age* (Boston, MA: Beacon Press).

Steel, E. and W. Kidd (2001) *The Family* (Basingstoke: Palgrave Macmillan).

Swain, D. (1994) 'Family', in P. Spoonley, D. Pearson and I. Shirley (eds), *New Zealand Society: A Sociological Introduction*, 2nd edn (Palmerston North: Dunmore Press), pp. 11–25.

Weeks, J. (2002) 'Elective Families: Lesbian and Gay Life Experiments', in A. Carling, S. Duncan and R. Edwards (eds), *Analysing Families: Morality and Rationality in Policy and Practice* (London: Routledge).

Zaretsky, E. (1976) *Capitalism, the Family and Personal Life* (London: Pluto Press).

FEELING: EMOTIONS • BELIEVING: RELIGION • EDUCATING • STRAYING: DEVIANCE • MEDIATING: TECHNOLOGY • INFORMING: MEDIA • **RELATING: FAMILY** • BELONGING: COMMUNITY • FINISHING

18   397

belonging: community

Douglas Hoey

KEY
POINTS

- Community is a core sociological category like family or nation.

- 'Communities' refers to associations of people. 'Community' refers to the shared feelings that bond these people together.

- 'Community' as a term signifying natural social bonds between people has a long history. It has been seen to be unquestionably a good thing and this has led to the word having utopian associations.

- Community, however, is not always positive, having elements of exclusion within it.

- Community was originally seen by sociology as a feature of the pre-modern world. The task of sociology was to study the associations that were replacing community.

- Community studies have produced a great deal of useful information on how people live and interact together. However, the imprecision of the term has led some to call for its abandonment; one preferred alternative is 'networks'.

- Community has returned as an important sociological term through its use within social policy and the rise of electronic communities.

Introduction

We all live in communities. Some we are born into; others we join, help sustain or leave as life progresses. In this sense they remain, like family, one of the basic components of society. Yet when I first encountered sociology the term seemed to have slipped out of the discourse. Its use as a meaningful conceptual term was in abeyance. As an undergraduate new to the discipline, it was difficult to locate much information on the topic in introductory texts. Anthony Giddens's *Sociology* (1993) was the set text and it contained five entries on community in the index, these being: community care, community charge, community divorce, community service work orders and community supervision. From these definitions it can be seen that community had little meaning of its own and had become an adjunct to other areas of concern, in this case deviance and social intervention. It appears to have become one of the victims of the crisis in sociology that Alvin Gouldner (1970, p. 439) warned of, its demise as a radical discipline to become simply part of the effort 'to help clean up the vomit of modern society'. What is particularly interesting within the Giddens text is that community's curative remedies for social ills are simply taken for granted. The understanding of community that is expressed – a salve to apply to the wounds of society – was captured by Raymond Williams (1983). For Williams, community had two aspects: 'on the one hand the sense of direct common concern; on the other hand the materialization of various forms of common organization'. However, this interpretation is not the most important aspect of the word. It is the attached positive associations that stand out. 'Community can be the warmly persuasive word to describe an existing set of relationships, or the warmly persuasive word to describe an alternative set of relationships. What is most important, perhaps, is that unlike all other terms of social organization (state, nation, society, etc.) it seems never to be used unfavourably, and never to be given a positive opposing or distinguishing term' (Williams, 1983, p. 76).

Yet by the end of the decade even these interpretations appeared to have gone. In the text used in the first institution I taught in, *Introductory Sociology* (Bilton et al., 1997), only the reference to community charge was left. This was a euphemism for Margaret Thatcher's infamous poll tax. Perhaps this is one of the contributions to the marginalization of community – its association with a regressive tax and other neo-liberal panaceas such as the withdrawal of custodial care for the mentally ill. The healing powers of community proved of little use to those involved in social work when, as under-staffed and under-trained people, they were asked to apply it to the abrasions caused by economic restructuring. Like many desirable things, community was hard to find when most needed.

Community, however, did not disappear as a concept. Community was on the way back. Or at least one particular understanding of the term was reappearing and, as will be shown in this chapter, it was joined with others until, as in the words of Tom Morten (2001), 'Community has become a cult, an object of warm-and-fuzzy ritual worship for politicians of all stripes, academics and the rapidly expanding new class of social commentators. Nobody can get enough of the C-word.' There are a number of reasons for this. The main one is that within sociology the term is constantly reinvented, because, as R. A. Nisbet once wrote, community is 'the most fundamental and far reaching of sociology's unit-ideas' (1966, p. 47). In other words, its importance and usefulness as an essential concept to the discipline make it unlikely to be ever completely abandoned. Another reason is the adoption of the term within social policy discourse. The appearance of Third Way political parties has seen a merging of neo-liberal economic priorities with social democratic concerns about the social cost they entail. Community is resurrected because theoretically it can provide social welfare without requiring too much government intervention. However, community operates outside the realms of cost/benefit considerations and in practice this translates into not requiring too much cost or responsibility. The rise of computers and computer networks provides the third reason. Within cyberspace the term is used to denote online interaction and what is perceived as the creation of 'new social spaces in which to meet and interact with one another' (Kollock and Smith, 1999, p. 3). Here, community is rediscovered as electronic glue to reconnect an atomized society.

To understand community and its constant reinvention it is therefore necessary to trace the historic use of the term within sociology. To understand all the implications impacted within the word it is, however, necessary to go even deeper than this. Community may have become the aloe vera of social interaction, the ginseng tea of social stability, but the positive associations that the term conjures up have ancient roots. The feel-good factor associated with communities is a consequence of the early theorizing on the subject within sociology and this in turn draws from older resonances within the term. It will be argued that although community can mean all things to all people it does not mean that the term has to be abandoned, merely that we should be aware of this lack of precision. Whenever we encounter the word we should ask ourselves: in which sense is community being used? To follow our own advice and to understand how community can at once be so universally understood and at the same time so indefinable, this chapter will do a number of things. First, the unquestioned beneficence of the word will be examined by separating the denotative and connotative aspects. This will show that there is a distinction between *communities* and *community* and it is the failure to realize this difference that has led to much of the confusion about the term. Second, the historical use of the term within sociology will be traced to show how it has been used as a conceptual tool. Finally, we will ask how useful these applications are in understanding the current phenomenon of virtual communities.

Defining community

Norbert Elias wrote: 'The key problem with which one is confronted by the variety of contemporary community studies is straightforward and relatively simple. The figurations of people which are investigated today under the name "community" vary a great deal' (1974, p. ix). The indecisiveness about who the term denotes is compounded by the lack of precision in the term's meaning. This has had its effect on social theory's having some ambivalence towards the term. While some (Bell and Newby, 1974) propose to abandon the term because of its vagueness, others suggest that 'we should celebrate the richness in "community" as a metaphor' (Carter, 1997, p. 8). It would seem that because of its lack of a clear and agreed definition it has the flexibility that is simultaneously its main advantage and drawback.

When it comes to attempting a definition it is useful to keep in mind that the word can be used in either a denotative or connotative manner. Dictionary.com provides us with a number of definitions to illustrate this point:

1 (a) A group of people living in the same locality and under the same government. (b) The district or locality in which such a group lives.

2 (a) A group of people having common interests: *the scientific community*; *the international business community*. (b) A group viewed as forming a distinct segment of society: *the gay community*; *the community of colour.*
3 (a) Similarity or identity: a community of interests. (b) Sharing, participation and fellowship.
4 Society as a whole; the public.

We see that community refers to definitions of social groups and does so through connecting them by *locality* or *common interest*. This is the denotative aspect. It can refer to society as a whole, the community, or to one of the smaller groups – the student community, the hip hop community, the local community – that make up society. This definition is easily understood because there is common understanding about what is being referred to. Nevertheless this spatial definition of community has come under challenge by the increased mobility and atomization that marks contemporary living. This is what has led some to advocate that the term be abandoned and substituted with *networks*. The connotative aspects – those ideas associated with a term beyond its literal meaning – give community its other meaning, which is the sense of belonging that connects us to *others* in society. It is these connotations that give community the aspects of always being positive because it refers to something that is at the very centre of what sustains us as social beings. This includes 'all forms of relationship which are characterized by a high degree of personal intimacy, emotional depth, moral commitment, social cohesion, and continuity in time' (Nisbet, 1966, p. 47).

The denotative aspects of the word are ones of *definition*. They mark out territories and define social groups. This definition can be very loose and is often conflated with the connotative aspects of the term to serve as a claim to legitimacy as well as defining a category. This can be illustrated by looking at some of the uses of community. A look at current news reports sees talk of both the *community of nations* and the *business community*. Here the term is descriptive and is used to group together individual people or organizations by the aspect they have in common. Yet it can be seen that the connotative aspect of the word, that of positive goodness, is also being attached to these groups. It acts as a claim to legitimacy in placing them within the orbit of our own experiences of the world. This can be seen if the term 'community' is dropped and another definition of these groups is offered. Instead of the community of nations we might more accurately refer to a fractious collection of often antagonistic nation states, or instead of the business community we could speak of a cabal of the rapaciously self-interested. If the origins of these positive connotations attached to community are traced then it is found that they are very old. Eugene Kamenka informs us that 'it has a rich and important pre-history in the Christian concept of community in the ideal of being brothers and sisters of Christ' (1982, p. vii). Community in this sense is an ideal. It is like justice in that it is something that we seek to attain. It is, in the terminology of post-structuralism, something that is becoming. As Jacques Derrida would say, we seek to create the conditions for it to arrive. Derrida (1992) wrote that justice was a concept that was yet to come. It is an ideal and as such does not exist here in this life. As an ideal it is something that we constantly strive towards. The ideal nature that applies to justice also applies for community. As Zygmunt Bauman puts it, 'community stands for the kind of world which is not, regrettably, available to us – but which we would dearly wish to inhabit and which we hope to repossess' (2001, p. 3). As has been shown, this ideal or even utopian aspect of the word underlies many of its common uses even when it is not specifically referred to. And, as we will see, it is also an unacknowledged concern of much of the sociological investigation of community. It is the feeling that community is being lost that drives us to seek it out. If it has gone then we seek to find what it was; and if we can understand it then can it be reconstituted? These are the motivations behind much investigation into the term. Despite the problems with definition and its lack of usefulness as a sociological term the sociology of community does exist. It seems that this lack of precision has not been a hindrance to the proliferation of community studies. As previously noted, Carter suggests it may be this lack of precision that has contributed to this. Investigators have been able to construct their own meaning for the term. It is therefore through the construction of the term that meaning is derived, and, through tracing the history of its use, that the many meanings and nuances that have attached themselves to the word can be understood.

Gemeinschaft and gesellschaft

Sociologies abound nowadays; a look at courses offered by any departmental handbook show sociologies studying subjects ranging from religion and emotions to food and violence. There seems to be no area that does not have a sociology that investigates it. The subject matter is seemingly endless and the entire world of collective behaviour lies before the researcher, begging for examination and explanation. As Terry Eagleton comments, 'In the old days, rock music was a distraction from your studies; now it may be what you are studying. Intellectual matters are no longer an ivory tower affair, but belong to the world of media and shopping malls' (2003, p. 3). This diversity, however, has not always been the case. The classic sociologists had a much more focused idea of the discipline's subject matter. They wrote in response to the epochal shifts in the organization of society that were happening around them. Sociology grew out of a response to what Karl Polanyi (1944) termed the 'great transformation'. Their main concern was that the breakdown of pre-modern social organizations would leave people without the sense of belonging that traditional ways of living provided. Georg Simmel explained this transformation as follows: 'In the Middle Ages a person was a member bound to a community or an estate, to a feudal association or a guild. His personality was merged with real or local interest groups, and the latter in turn drew their character from the people who directly supported them. This uniformity was destroyed by modernity' (1991, p. 17). The fear was that the destruction of traditional ways of life would leave people without a means of establishing and maintaining the moral codes that sustain social order. Such concerns run through the works of the classic sociologists Karl Marx, Max Weber, Emile Durkheim, Ferdinand Tönnies and Georg Simmel. Although they addressed modernity in different ways and with varying degrees of optimism and pessimism, all perceived it as a great dislocation that heralded new ways of living. Sociology, then, is a response to this change in the way groups of people live in, and relate to, the world around them (see Chapter 2, 'Modernizing').

For Karl Marx (1982, p. 25) it was a fundamental change in the economic structure of society, a change from one mode of production (feudalism) to another (capitalism) which 'has put an end to all feudal, patriarchal, idyllic

FEELING: EMOTIONS • BELIEVING: RELIGION • EDUCATING • STRAYING: DEVIANCE •
MEDIATING: TECHNOLOGY • INFORMING: MEDIA • RELATING: FAMILY • **BELONGING: COMMUNITY** • FINISHING

19   405

relations. It has piteously torn asunder the motley feudal ties that bound man to his "natural superiors," and has left no other nexus between man and man than naked self interest' (1982, p. 25). The Industrial Revolution changed production and economics, and the very way people lived. 'All fixed, fast frozen relations, with their train of ancient and venerable prejudices and opinions, are swept away' (Marx, 1982, p. 27). Marx was ultimately optimistic. He saw the destruction of old ways of living as offering the possibility of a new, more equitable, social organization – first, socialism and ultimately the return of community in communism. Capitalism may be exploitative and class-ridden, but its revolutionary overthrow would result in an egalitarian society in which goods and services would be distributed according to social need. For Durkheim (1984) this change was from one form of social organization to another, what he counter-intuitively termed mechanical and organic society. What had been a natural outgrowth of social interaction within mechanical (traditional) societies became solidified into institutions within organic (modern) ones. Max Weber (1968) also noted the rise of these new institutions of state politics and bureaucracy. The organizational complexity of industrialization and urbanization was accompanied by the bureaucracies of administration and the expert institutions of health, education and justice. For sociology the subject matter was to be this new phenomenon that had not been seen before. These new structures of social regulation were to be the sites of sociological investigation – not community, but what was arising to replace it. This new phenomenon was society.

It was Ferdinand Tönnies who defined this area of study and who separated community (gemeinschaft), which he defined as 'All intimate, private and exclusive living together', from society (gesellschaft), which was the 'mere coexistence of people' (1967, p. 7). For Tönnies, gemeinschaft 'is the lasting and genuine form of living together ... Gesellschaft is transitory and superficial' (1967, p. 8). Gemeinschaft should be understood as a living organism. It is stronger in rural areas than in urban. It is based on kinship but extends further to neighbourhood and friendship. There are communities of physical life and communities of mental life. Above all, according to Tönnies, community was something that came naturally and was commonly understood. This gives insights into the nature of community and also points to its fragility. Community is a naturally occurring understanding of belonging and therefore is a naturally occurring understanding of who does not belong. It is also vulnerable to the development of individualism, the official ideology of modern capitalist society. Capitalist society is based on the private ownership of property and the means of production. This means that people who are conscious of themselves as individuals are necessary to perform the tasks of ownership. Here is the driving force behind individualism but, once it comes into being, the naturally occurring sense of community is destroyed. Community is the antithesis of the individual. *As community collapses identity appears* (see Chapter 4, 'Consuming', and Chapter 11, 'Being: Identity'). Modernity has been the experience of being cast out of the 'warm circle of belonging' into the cold calculation of individualism. The search to understand contemporary society, which is the origin of the discipline of sociology, has led to the conclusion that: 'the gravest and most painful testimony of the modern world, the one that possibly involves all other testimonies to which this epoch must answer ... is the testimony of the dissolution, the dislocation, or the conflagration of community' (Nancy, 1991, p. 1).

Tönnies' definition of community may differ from some of those in common use but it is important because it is the technical definition used by sociology. Not that the other connotations of the word disappear; they remain attached to the term as an unspoken supplement. From Tönnies we derive the important characteristics of the word that inform much of the subsequent research into the topic. These are the separation of community from association. Although associations abound in society, from the official and vocational to the informal and casual, they differ from communities in that participants 'remain nevertheless independent of one another and devoid of mutual familiar relationships' (Tönnies, 1967, p. 10). As Robert M. MacIver puts it, 'a community is a focus of social life, the common living of social beings; an association is an organization of social life, definitely established for the pursuit of one or more common interests' (1970, p. 31). The difference is clear: associations are constructed; communities occur naturally. Furthermore, communities are of two types: physical and mental. As Benedict Anderson (1983) pointed out, communities are not only lived in, they are also largely *imagined*. This is the feature that lets a sense of community be sustained beyond face-to-face encounters and shared locality. Unspoken in Tönnies' definitions is the

FEELING: EMOTIONS • BELIEVING: RELIGION • EDUCATING • STRAYING: DEVIANCE •
MEDIATING: TECHNOLOGY • INFORMING: MEDIA • RELATING: FAMILY • **BELONGING: COMMUNITY** • FINISHING

19   407

assumption that communities are superior to associations. Their passing signals the end of a better, more moral and human age. Tönnies was not the only one to think this. He was merely expressing a widely held view. Indeed, as George Mosse notes: 'The longing for community has been one of the driving forces of modern history' (1982, p. 27).

However, the sense of community that we either long to arrive or mourn in its passing has ambivalence to it. Although community refers to a naturally occurring sense of belonging and inclusion, it also has an element of *exclusion* about it. Community speaks of 'Us' but to have such a concept a 'Them' is required. Community needs an 'Other' to construct itself against. Historically, people lived in small groups separated from each other by the lack of the sort of communication devices that we take for granted nowadays. 'For those who considered the next town or the next city block alien territory ... deeply felt loyalties served both as a defence against outsiders and as a means of identification within' (Wiebe, 1967, p. 27). This partisanship of locality still exists and can be found expressed through support of bounded groups that extends from local sports teams to nations. However, one of the hallmarks of modernity is this compression of distance and difference. Immigration, roads, the railway, the press and national institutions of government and administration all seemed to threaten this solidarity as the boundaries of the local disappeared. Community under threat becomes reactive and is not such a positive thing if you do not belong to it. The utopian aspect of the term – that the good life is only attained through community and, moreover, *our* community – suggests perfection, that is, a oneness of agreement. This is the totalitarian aspect of community. The neo-Nazi *Stormfront* website gives an example of this when it speaks approvingly of gemeinschaft: 'America has fallen into the mode of contractual agreements and self-interest society, termed in German as gesellschaft. The older traditions consisting of kinship, blood lineage, and mutually assisted community are labelled part of Gemeinschaft. Stormfront is therefore logically defined as a community' (Volkssturm, 2001). This plays on the definition of community Tönnies offers, located in blood. The more intensely community is felt, the more it becomes exclusionary to those who are not included. Although the above passage refers to community with its connotations of inclusion, it is clear, if unspoken, that the focus is also on those who do not belong. This sinister side of community has as long a history as the positive connotations of the term.

Sigmund Freud gives an illustration of the double nature of community. On the one hand, he acknowledges its fundamental part in allowing us to live together: 'Communal life becomes possible only when a majority comes together that is stronger than any individual ... The replacement of the power of the individual by that of the community is the decisive step towards civilization' (Freud, 1961, p. 41). Here he points to the inherent antagonism between individualism and community. Communities cannot exist until individual interests are subsumed into those of the collective. There is also another antagonism between those who are within the communities and those who are not, once this bond is established: 'After St Paul had made universal brotherly love the foundation of his Christian community, the extreme intolerance towards those left outside it was the inevitable consequence.' Here community arrives and its antagonism is not to the individual but collective others. It may be worth noting at this point that the two great totalitarian movements of the twentieth century were based on claims of community. Fascism has its promise of a community of blood while communism, named after the very word, has its promise of the good life inherent in the term. While both may have delivered their promise, to some they are more likely to be remembered for the murderous practices engaged in towards those not included. Although modernity may promise to deliver us from some of the stultifying aspects of traditional communities, it also has shown that it can replace these within something more sinister. An example of this is when Susan Sontag (2001, p. 27) informs us of the case of Walter Benjamin, who 'hailed the irony that allows individuals to assert the right to lead lives independent of the community as "the most European of all accomplishments", and observed that it had "completely deserted Germany"'. The irony may be deeper and darker – it was Nazis who filled this vacuum, proclaiming a *volkish* community bound by blood, who hounded him to his death.

Community studies

The abundance of meaning and nuance that community contains means that its application in research has led to a plethora of types of community

FEELING: EMOTIONS • BELIEVING: RELIGION • EDUCATING • STRAYING: DEVIANCE •
MEDIATING: TECHNOLOGY • INFORMING: MEDIA • RELATING: FAMILY • **BELONGING: COMMUNITY** • FINISHING

409

studies. That said, Tönnies' classic definitions of the characteristics of community still provide a useful template to examine the history of community studies and the concerns raised within it. One of these is a romantic and nostalgic understanding of community when it is seen as what has been lost by modern society. These are the unspoken and natural bonds of attachment that people felt for each other before they were subjected to the cash nexus and forced into the social relations of capitalism. These investigations are combined with the definition of community as a bounded space and tend to focus on community as delimited areas – whether in the new industrial cities, where it plays the role of integration, or the small town and village, where community can be found as a remnant of the pre-modern age. Although they may have been instigated by a search for community, these studies provide a wealth of information and data on the working of communities.

Drawing on Durkheim's detail of a shift within modernity from mechanical to organic society, Robert Park (1925, 1952) developed an analysis, based on Chicago, of communities within modern cities. For Park and his associates, who collectively became known as the Chicago School, society was akin to a living organism that always sought stability. Here they are drawing on Durkheim's functionalist concept of society. Each part of the social structure was an element of a whole that worked to maintain the survival and integrity of this whole. This approach followed Tönnies in that community was a naturally occurring phenomenon and the source of social integration. Community was a functioning part of society, the most basic that assimilated new arrivals into the body of the city. This is the origin of the American concept of the city as a melting pot. Common residence was thought to provide the solidarity and shared interests that marked out communities. Community is defined here as a spatial and physical phenomenon, synonymous with neighbourhood. This has been one of the most productive fields of community studies and includes such classic studies as W. Lloyd Warner's *Yankee City* (1963) and the Lynds' *Middletown* (1956) series, which focused on small-town America as a microcosm of a larger whole.

Whereas the Chicago School used community as a functional part of urban integration, others used it to study small rural societies. The assumption was that these communities retained certain qualities that had been lost by those who had left the country for the city. If community was to be understood, it needed to be examined in its natural habitat: the rural village. This underpinned the investigations into rural communities that were carried out as anthropological studies. Typical of this approach was the folkways approach to peasant societies; within the United States this was led by Robert Redfield (1960) with his study of pre-European societies. Another focus was the European village as a remnant of folkways guiding social cohesion, such as A. D. Rees's *Life in a Welsh Countryside* (1950), W. M. Williams's *The Sociology of an English Village* or J. Galtung's (1971) study of Sicilian villages, *Members of Two Worlds*. These investigations are now regarded as the classical works within community studies. They provide a wealth of detail and sociological data as well as important developments and innovations in the way groups of people can be studied. They also provide the discipline with many questions and problems.

Criticisms of the Chicago School approach can be made. Is locality enough? Does such spatial determinism really work? Is rural life really that simple? Are people in neighbourhoods really that homogenous? What are the boundaries of community and where does the rural end and the urban begin? Work such as Redfield's (1960) seems to rely too heavily on a romantic nostalgia and Warner's or the Lynds' studies of America seem to have as their purpose justification of the status quo. These questions, combined with the passing of the functionalist paradigm, are what led the classic collection on the topic (Bell and Newby, 1974) to argue for the term's rejection. However, community has too much history, meaning and usefulness to be simply cast aside like last year's fashion.

Community rediscovered

At the beginning of this chapter it was suggested that community had largely ceased to be a meaningful sociological concept. There are two factors that have, however, brought the concept of community back into the limelight. The first is a political definition that accompanies the so-called 'third way' that replaced neo-liberalism as the political orthodoxy in the 1990s. The ravages of neo-liberalism on society forced it to adopt a more user-friendly interface. Here, the economic strictures of the ideology are softened so as to be made more palatable; the search for community returns but is based on the assumption that it will be achieved through involving communities. The Third Way tries to meld social democratic concerns for equality and social justice with neo-liberal beliefs in the primacy of the market in providing social and economic solutions. When it comes to those living in poverty the solution is not sought in reformation of the economic system but in the reformation of the poor by reintroducing them into strong communities. This manifested itself in Europe during the late twentieth century with a focus on social inclusion. This view is derived from the work of Rene Lenoir (1974), who introduced the term 'social exclusion' to account for those in poverty. This concept was seized upon by Western democracies and deprivation was addressed through inclusion into strengthened communities. This is what Tom Morten comments on when he says nobody can get enough of the C-word. The curative power of community is rediscovered and is sought within communities. But what sort of communities are to perform this task? As Tuula Helne points out, the excluded are feared in contemporary society for their disruptive potential and 'spontaneous community formation by the excluded would, then, not be welcomed by everyone. To the extent they are expected to join any community, it is the collective social community' (Helne, 2004, p. 14). Membership of this community relies on being in paid employment. This type of community was identified by British Prime Minister Tony Blair as being brought into being by 'social entrepreneurs ... the policeman who turns young people away from crime, the person who sets up a leisure centre, the local church leaders who galvanize the community to improve schools and build health centres' (Blair, 1997). These people were to be helped by co-ordinating with what Blair sees as the agencies of community: 'schools, police, probation, youth service, social services, the courts, the Employment Service and Benefits Agency, TECs, health authorities and GPs, local authorities, City Challenge initiatives, English partnerships, careers services'. Here we see community being co-opted into the state and also an attempt to apply the characteristics of individualism, self-help and personal responsibility to community. The success of this strategy may be judged by a report from the Office of National Statistics (2004) showing the increasing social disparity that accompanies its application.

Virtual communities

Running parallel to the interest in community generated by neo-liberalism was the rise of the internet and the advent of virtual communities. Tönnies had noted the mental aspect of community and Benedict Anderson had furthered this by pointing out imagination's role in their creation and sustenance. The internet and its killer application, the World Wide Web, introduced the most imagined of all communities, the *virtual* community. The internet became a focus for community and displays all the hopes, fears and interpretations that have been traditionally attached to community. Critiques of online communities (Ronnell, 2001) concentrate on the lack of face-to-face interaction and ask whether computer-mediated interaction can have the same qualities. This seems to ignore the fact that the telephone, the letter and the telegraph have long sustained communities rather than destroyed them. The same can apply to those who see the internet as re-establishing community in fragmented societies. The positive interpretations of these see them as communities of the global village. Marshall McLuhan (1994, p. 9) wrote that the message of electricity 'eliminates time and space factors in human association'. This is seen as the return of community through the electronic village. Once again, the best way to evaluate these claims is through examining the history of the use of the term within the contexts in which they arose.

Steven Levy (1994) details how the early development of the internet within United States military and university circles was accompanied by an informal growth of personal communication systems. The original purpose of the internet was to co-ordinate research in large scientific endeavours that were being carried out at various university and military sites. Features such as email, user groups, list serves and multi-user games were developed unofficially by the engineers working on these projects. This resulted in the Usenet system that pre-dated the World Wide Web. Within the universities those attracted to the new departments of computer science at MIT, Stanford and Berkeley tended to come from maths and engineering. They brought with them a number of attitudes and traditions. One was a general nerdiness, which explains the first Usenet group's dedication to the space opera *Star Trek*. A more important tradition, however, was that of the free exchange of information, which underpins other online communities such as the open source movement or the practice of file sharing. The development of personal computers (PCs) in the late 1970s increased the number of people able to connect to the growing internet, and online communities extended out of institutions into more informal sites such as bulletin boards, and Internet Relay Chat (IRC). This has continued with the advent of fan sites, blogs and personal websites dedicated to any subject imaginable, all of which have the potential to grow communities.

Communit*ies* will appear spontaneously whenever people interact, but it seems that when they appear, the search for the utopian Communit*y* soon follows. Howard Rheingold defined virtual communities as 'social aggregations that emerge from the Net when people carry on those public discussions long enough, with sufficient human feeling, to form webs of personal relationships' (1993, p. 5). Rheingold was a prominent member of the pioneering web community the WELL, which in 1985 grew out of remnants of the 1960s counter-culture. Its various founding members had links to such iconic 1960s structures as *The Whole Earth Catalogue*, Ken Kesey's Merry Pranksters and the famous hippie commune The Farm. The vision of the WELL was an online community imbued with an ethic of freedom of thought and expression, an expression of the counter-cultural zeitgeist freed into cyberspace and unhindered by the hard realities that 1960s utopian movements had foundered on. However, experience was to show that online communities were quick to take on the characteristics of those in the material world. The WELL began to perceive itself as a group mind but found, like traditional communities, that unity also encourages exclusion. If the WELL was the model of communities that were to follow, it was also the first to encounter this problem. As John Seabrook testifies, 'although the WELL was rooted in the idea of social equality, in practice it tended to promote something like the opposite of that ideal – it divided people into insiders and outsiders. This phenomenon was by no means unique to the WELL, but could be observed in many other sites across the Net where virtual communities formed' (1997, p. 197). Julian Dibble's (1993) classic account of the growth of an online community, *A Rape in Cyberspace*, found that the internet is not a place where the non-virtual world can be escaped. He also found that community has its downside. Human feelings are not always positive or personal relationships affirmative. Anyone who has been 'flamed' on a user group or has encountered a troll (a poster whose sole intent is to annoy and disrupt) on a blog discussion can attest to that.

A distinction can also be made between communities that rise spontaneously and communities that are purposely set up on the internet to become communities. There are web rings of support that cover most areas of interest. There is also the development of commercial communities. A look at the wrapper on a chocolate bar or the can containing an energy drink will show that most products nowadays are launched with an accompanying website. If these links are followed one is encouraged to become part of the community built around the product. This is unlikely to become the future of community because such endeavours lack the robustness and the power to sustain meaningful and supportive social interaction necessary in true community. Here again is the use of community to establish legitimacy. The collapse of the dot com boom at the end of the twentieth century also saw the demise of some of the wilder claims that were being made for the internet. A new sense of maturity and sober assessment seems to have developed. While it is true that technologies add new potentials for social interaction, existing social phenomena such as community are quick to inhabit these new areas. By their nature, however, they do not solve the contradictions of community and instead just add another layer of complexity to the term.

Conclusion

Community may be an infuriatingly imprecise term at times but it is unlikely to be abandoned. It remains the indefinable thing that sustains free human association and, as such, it will always be part of the discourse of sociology. Communities are an intrinsic part of social life but they contain all the contradictions, joys and dangers that social life brings. Problems arise when either a larger community is sought in communities or communities are assumed capable of delivering community. The imprecision of the term is not likely to be resolved, as communities will always have the promise of community, an ideal retaining a sense that it is necessary for us to lead the good life. If only we could achieve community

FEELING: EMOTIONS • BELIEVING: RELIGION • EDUCATING • STRAYING: DEVIANCE •
MEDIATING: TECHNOLOGY • INFORMING: MEDIA • RELATING: FAMILY • **BELONGING: COMMUNITY** • FINISHING

19   415

then all social problems would be solved. It is this aspect that is played upon by those who use the term to claim legitimacy or mask other projects. The processes and disruptions that first drew the attention of sociologists to community continue, and the pull between community and individualism remains one of the defining features of being modern. Community haunts us as either something we have lost or as something we aspire towards but never can reach. Although we draw sustenance and support from communities as the only truly reliable source of support in modernity, we can also thrill to the feeling of promise and excitement that comes from escaping them. We are left juggling identity and community, not happy to be subsumed by sameness yet wary of being too individual and left alone.

Suggestions for further reading

Bauman, Z. (2001) *Community* (Cambridge: Polity Press).

Bell, C. and H. Newby (eds) (1974) *The Sociology of Communities* (London: Frank Cass); this remains the best collection on the sociology of community both for an overview of the work undertaken on community and for identifying the debates and problems within the subject.

Bruhn, J. G. (2005) *The Sociology of Community Connections* (New York: Springer).

Delanty, G. (2003) *Community* (London: Routledge).

Kollock, P. and Smith, M. A. (eds) (1999) 'Communities in Cyberspace', in *Communities in Cyberspace* (London and New York: Routledge).

Bibliography

Anderson, B. (1983) *Imagined Communities: Reflections on the Origin and Spread of Nationalism* (London: Verso).

Bauman, Z. (2001) *Community* (Cambridge: Polity Press).

Bell, C. and H. Newby (eds) (1974) *The Sociology of Communities* (London: Frank Cass).

Bilton, T., K. Bonnett, P. Jones, D. Skinner, M. Stanworth and A. Webster (1997) *Introductory Sociology* (London: Macmillan).

Blair, T. (1997) *The Will to Win*, speech by the Prime Minister on Monday, 2 June 1997, at the Aylesbury Estate, Southwark. Available online at http://www.socialexclusionunit.gov.uk/downloaddoc.asp?id=59 [accessed 30/10/05].

Carter, I. (1997) 'Foreword' to Claudia Bell (ed.), *Community Issues in New Zealand* (Palmerston North: Dunmore), pp. 7–8.

Derrida, J. (1992) 'Force of Law: The "Mystical Foundation of Authority"', in D. Cornell, M. Resenfeld and D. Carlson (eds), *Deconstruction and the Possibility of Justice* (New York: Routledge), pp. 3–67.

Dibble, J. (1993) 'A Rape in Cyberspace', *The Village Voice* (23 December 1993). Available online at http://www.caida.org/outreach/iec/courses/ife97/articles/arics.html [accessed 22/10/04].

Durkheim, E. (1984) *The Division of Labor in Society*, trans. W. D. Halls (New York: Free Press).

Eagleton, T. (2003) *After Theory* (London: Allen Lane).

Elias, N. (1974) 'Towards a Theory of Communities', in C. Bell and H. Newby (eds), *The Sociology of Communities* (London: Frank Cass), pp. ix–xli.

Freud, S. (1961) *Civilization and Its Discontents*, trans. and ed. James Strachey (New York: W. W. Norton).

Galtung, J. (1971) *Members of Two Worlds: A Development Study of Three Villages in Western Sicily* (New York: Columbia University Press).

Giddens, A. (1993) *Sociology*, 2nd edn (Oxford: Polity Press).

Gouldner, A. (1970) *The Coming Crisis of Western Sociology* (New York: Basic Books).

Helne, T. (2004) 'Exclusion in 17 Paradoxes', Paper presented at the ESPAnet Annual Conference, Oxford, 9–11 September 2004.

Kamenka, E. (1982) 'Introduction', in E. Kamenka (ed.), *Community as a Social Ideal* (London: Edward Arnold), pp. 2–12.

Kollock, P. and M. Smith (1999) 'Communities in Cyberpace', in P. Kollock and M. Smith (eds), *Communities in Cyberspace* (London and New York: Routledge), pp. 29–59.

Lenoir, R. (1974) *Les exclus: Un Français Sur Dix* (Paris: Editions du Seuil).

Levy, S. (1994) *Hackers: Heroes of the Computer Revolution* (New York: Dell).

Lynd, R. and H. Lynd (1956) *Middletown: A Study in American Culture* (New York: Harvest Books).

MacIver, R. (1970) *On Community, Society and Power* (Chicago and London: University of Chicago Press).

FEELING: EMOTIONS • BELIEVING: RELIGION • EDUCATING • STRAYING: DEVIANCE • MEDIATING: TECHNOLOGY • INFORMING: MEDIA • RELATING: FAMILY • **BELONGING: COMMUNITY** • FINISHING

19   417

McLuhan, M. (1994) *Understanding Media* (Cambridge, MA: MIT Press).

Marx, K. (1982) 'The Communist Manifesto', in Emile Burns (ed.), *The Marxist Reader* (New York: Avenel), pp. 22–36.

Morten, T. (2001) quoted in K. Gibson and J. Cameron, 'Transforming Communities: Towards a Research Agenda', *Urban Policy and Research* 19(1), pp. 7–24.

Mosse, G. (1982) 'Nationalism, Fascism and the Radical Right', in E. Kamenka (ed.), *Community as a Social Ideal* (London: Edward Arnold), pp. 27–43.

Nancy, J. (1991) *The Inoperative Community* (Minneapolis, MN: Minnesota University Press).

Nisbet, R. (1966) *The Sociological Tradition* (London: Heinemann).

Office of National Statistics (2004) *Income: Gaps in Wealth and Income Remain Large.* Available online at http://www.statistics.gov.uk/cci/nugget.asp?id=1005 [accessed 1/10/05].

Park, R. (1952) *Human Communities: The City and Human Ecology* (Glencoe, IL: Free Press).

Park, R., E. Burgess and D. McKenzie (1925) *The City* (Chicago, IL: University of Chicago Press).

Polanyi, K. (1944) *The Great Transformation: The Political and Economic Origins of Our Time* (Boston, MA: Beacon Press).

Redfield, R. (1960) *The Little Community and Peasant Society and Culture* (Chicago, IL: University of Chicago Press).

Rees, A. (1950) *Life in a Welsh Countryside* (Cardiff: Universality of Wales Press).

Rheingold, H. (1993) *The Virtual Community: Homesteading on the Electronic Frontier* (Reading, MA: Addison-Wesley).

Ronnell, A. (2001) 'A Disappearance of Community', in D. Trend (ed.), *Reading Digital Culture* (Oxford: Blackwell), pp. 286–93.

Seabrook, J. (1997) *Deeper: A Two-Year Odyssey in Cyberspace* (London and Boston: Faber and Faber).

Simmel, G. (1991) 'Money in Modern Culture', *Theory, Culture and Society* 8, pp. 17–31.

Sontag, S.(2001) 'Introduction', *Walter Benjamin: One-Way Street and Other Writings*, trans. Edmund Jephcott and Kingsley Shorter (London: NLB), p. 27.

Tönnies, F. (1967) *Community and Society* (Detroit: Michigan State University Press).

Volkssturm (2001) 'A Living Community', *Stormfront.Org*. Available online at http://www.stormfront.org/forum/showthread.php?t=127068 [accessed 12/10/04].

Warner, W. (1963) *Yankee City* (New Haven, CT: Yale University Press).

Weber, M. (1968) *Economy and Society: An Outline of Interpretive Sociology* (New York: Bedminster Press).

Wiebe, R. (1967) *The Search for Order, 1877–1920* (New York: Hill and Wang).

Williams, R. (1983) *Keywords: A Vocabulary of Culture and Society* (London: Fontana, Flamingo).

Williams, W. M. (1956) *The Sociology of an English Village, Gosforth* (London: Routledge & Kegan Paul).

FEELING: EMOTIONS • BELIEVING: RELIGION • EDUCATING • STRAYING: DEVIANCE • MEDIATING: TECHNOLOGY • INFORMING: MEDIA • RELATING: FAMILY • **BELONGING: COMMUNITY** • FINISHING

19   419

20 finishing

Steve Matthewman

KEY
POINTS
- Being sociological involves a particular state of mind, way of seeing and orientation to the world. The sociological imagination is as good a name as any for this state of being.

- A sociological state of mind is marked by scepticism towards all apparently 'natural' distributions and commonsense categories.

- Sociological naming can make visible what the powerful would prefer to hide and what the powerless struggle to know.

- The sociological imagination can sometimes reveal ways of transforming troubling situations.

As the many parts of this book came together it looked more and more like the map we wished to create for a new traveller in the world of sociology. We've tried to give you a sense of what it is to be sociological – a form of consciousness, a way of seeing and (returning to our opening comments on ethics) a responsible orientation to the world. Like any map, this collection of sociological insights, practices and imaginings offers directions. We hope you will use it to see your place in the world and how it relates to others (Smith, 1999, p. 66) and to navigate social life with greater clarity. Because we believe good sociology should be recognized and celebrated wherever it appears, we have, quite consciously, strayed into the territories of literature ('On Being Sociological'), economics ('Trading'), politics ('Governing: Power'), and what is known as Science, Technology, Society studies ('Mediating: Technology'). Because 'the social' is such an all-embracing category, any attempt at a comprehensive and truly meaningful representation of its key arrangements and connections must look beyond

421

the sometimes restrictive limitations of 'orthodox sociology'. Economics, politics and technological artefacts cut deeply into the business of everyday life, and literature reveals our inner world, making public these privately felt effects (Braudel, 1993, p. 428).

But we are also aware that maps are not without distortions – they reduce the three-dimensional world to two, and they fix things that are in flux (even continents drift). And, like all other mapmaking exercises, ours is also political and persuasive as well as simply instructive (Wood, 1992). Jorge Luis Borges' (1998, p. 325) cautionary tale 'On Exactitude in Science' is useful here. It concerns a fictive seventeenth-century empire in which cartography had attained such heights that the map of a province covered a city, and the map of the empire a province. Dissatisfied with the results, the Guild of Cartographers proceeded to a 1:1 scale. They produced a map of the empire the size of the empire. Of course, the perfect map also proves to be completely useless. Mapmakers are also deeply prone to significant omissions. In scaling down the social world – in putting it on paper, so to speak – we have similarly lost details, even entire provinces of sociology. It was simply impossible to cover everything we considered important, and tough decisions were made. We gave no space to playing – sport, tourism and leisure – just as we neglected bodies, medicine and death, although all of these are significant in contemporary social life and are the subjects of sociologists' attention. Nor, in a time when global migration flows have generated hugely diverse student audiences in many countries, could we be as global in the range of examples and case studies as we wanted. Again we remind the reader that sociology criticizes everything, and that includes its own terms of reference.

Many pages ago we began with insights and understandings from Avery Gordon, Roland Barthes and Robert Musil, among others. In closing, we return to these three scholars. Robert Musil reflects upon what it means to live, as we all do, in a well-ordered state, to detect what is *not* there. At this point in the story, an altercation has broken out in a Viennese street between (drunken) men of opposing political viewpoints. A policeman is within earshot:

> The policeman began by watching it over his shoulder, subsequently turning to face it and then coming closer; he attended as an

observer, like a protruding offshoot of the iron machinery of the state, which ends in buttons and other metal trim. There is always something ghostly about living constantly in a well-ordered state. You cannot step into the street or drink a glass of water or get on a streetcar without touching the balanced levers of a gigantic apparatus of laws and interrelations, setting them in motion or letting them maintain you in peaceful existence; one knows hardly any of these levers, which reach deep into the inner workings and, coming out the other side, lose themselves in a network whose structure has never yet been unraveled by anyone. So one denies their existence, just as the average citizen denies the air, maintaining that it is empty space. But all these things that one denied, these colorless, odorless, tasteless, weightless, and morally indefinable things such as water, air, space, money, and the passing of time, turn out in truth to be the most important things of all, and this gives life a spooky quality. (Musil, 1997, pp. 165–6)

One of Avery Gordon's most significant contributions to refining our understanding of sociology's potential for furthering the work of justice is her insistence that sociologists must name those 'indefinable things' which give shape to our existence and which cause us concern. It is our task to articulate, concretize, name and comprehend and, as Gordon puts it, 'to conjure up social life' (1997, p. 22). In the sense in which she is using the term, conjuring means identifying the levers, networks and connections that Musil evokes, to summon and seek out those very things, for 'the intricate web of connections that characterizes any event or problem *is the story*' (Gordon, 1997, p. 20). This is our domain; only sociology deals with this.

We engage in this process of showing the world 'as it is'. We do this to offer insights for those who might want to change it and because the powerful are loath to put words to their privilege. Roland Barthes (2000, p. 138) calls this phenomenon 'exnomination', the avoidance of naming. His own example takes as its model the French bourgeoisie. Despite being the most privileged strata of society, this dominant group operated through a culture of anonymity, universalizing their own norms and preferences, and dictating the terms on which everyone else relates to the world. In naming every group but their own the bourgeoisie were able to occupy their 'natural' place at the top of the order of things. For Barthes, exnomination is a practice that 'transforms the reality of the world into an image of the world, History into Nature' (2000, p. 141).

Gordon believes that in undertaking sociology's task 'we have made considerable representational reparations for past exclusions and silencings, making the previously unknown known, telling new stories, correcting the official records' (Gordon, 1997, p. 20). But the work is not complete, and it can never be. There are always networks to unravel. Nor can we only fixate on the ruling classes. Sociology cannot exonerate itself; we are not exempt from criticism. As sociologists reflecting on our disciplinary history, we can see a trail of classificatory schemes and 'scientific' findings that perpetuated old injustices and supported new ones. Many 'distributions' considered natural have been anything but: racial and gender inequalities are no longer seen as fixed consequences of physical attributes but as sociologically explainable consequences of structural inequalities and the operations of power. This our discipline knows, but what do we yet know of speciesism? What representational reparations have we made towards flora and fauna, much less machines? 'Time and time again,' John Law says,

> we have learned that a distribution that appears to be inscribed in the order of things could be otherwise; ... sociology knows something about the (formerly) 'natural' distributions of racism, sexism, class prejudice and ageism. But it knows little of speciesism: machines, animals and plants – still we confine these to a different place in the order of things. (Law, 1991, p. 17)

What sociology was is not what it now is, much less what it will become. Our introduction took inspiration from Peter Berger's (1966) sociological imaginings. Like him, we have taken sociology as a quest for comprehension and celebrated its ability to render the social world transparent and see it anew. We've enjoyed the pleasures inherent in that process of discovery. But our admiration of Berger's sociology stops short of some of the less pleasing characteristics of the sociology of the 1960s. Written in the time and place that it was, it may not be surprising that women only figure in Berger's book as distractions for – and significant others of – sociologists: being sociological also entailed being male. It is surely not even necessary to point out that this book has come into being in a world where such a proposition would be greeted with derisive disbelief by at least half of those studying it. But there was a time when sociology was done by men *not* women, by the middle class *not* the working class, and by Europeans *not* Others. Sociology applied to modern societies *not* traditional ones, and to heterosexuals *not* homosexuals. It was to be practised in the city *not* the country, and in the public sphere *not* the private. It was a nationally bounded enterprise *not* an open global one. Sociologists once feared to tread beyond the front doorstep, the city limits, passport control. That time was not so long ago. Now, these borders are routinely transgressed, and sociology is all the better for it. There are many more sacred barriers that need to be profaned, yet more 'natural' distributions that await critical attention.

Suggestions for further reading

Blackman, T. (2000) 'Complexity Theory', in Gary Browning et al. (eds), *Understanding Contemporary Society: Theories of the Present* (London: Sage), pp. 139–51.

Collins, R. (1999) 'The European Sociological Tradition and Twenty-first-Century World Sociology', in J. L. Abu-Lughod (ed.), *Sociology for the Twenty-first Century: Continuities and Cutting Edges* (Chicago and London: University of Chicago Press), pp. 26–42.

Gordon, A. F. (1997) *Ghostly Matters: Haunting and the Sociological Imagination* (Minneapolis and London: University of Minnesota Press).

Latour, B. (2000) 'When Things Strike Back: a Possible Contribution of "Science Studies" to the Social Sciences', *British Journal of Sociology* 51(1), pp. 107–23.

Smith, D. E. (1999) 'From Women's Standpoint to a Sociology for People', in J. L. Abu-Lughod (ed.), *Sociology for the Twenty-first Century: Continuities and Cutting Edges* (Chicago and London: University of Chicago Press), pp. 65–82.

Bibliography

Barthes, R. (2000) *Mythologies*, trans. Annette Lavers (London: Vintage).

Berger, P. L. (1966) *Invitation to Sociology: A Humanistic Perspective* (Harmondsworth: Penguin).

Borges, J. L. (1998) 'On Exactitude in Science', *Collected Fictions*, trans. Andrew Hurley (London: Penguin).

Braudel, F. (1993) *A History of Civilizations*, trans. Richard Mayne (New York: Penguin).

Gordon, A. F. (1997) *Ghostly Matters: Haunting and the Sociological Imagination* (Minneapolis and London: University of Minnesota Press).

Law, J. (1991) 'Introduction: Monsters, Machines and Sociotechnical Relations', *A Sociology of Monsters: Essays on Power, Technology, and Domination* (London and New York: Routledge), pp. 1–23.

Mullan, B. (ed.) (1987) *Sociologists on Sociology* (London: Croom Helm).

Musil, R. (1997/1978) *The Man without Qualities*, trans. Sophie Wilkins (London: Picador).

Smith, D. E. (1999) 'From Women's Standpoint to a Sociology for People', in J. L. Abu-Lughod (ed.), *Sociology for the Twenty-first Century: Continuities and Cutting Edges* (Chicago and London: University of Chicago Press), pp. 65–82.

Wood, D. (1992) *The Power of Maps* (New York: Guilford).

glossary

Aesthetic of consumption The social ideal associated with consumerism. This is a contested and emergent norm that reflects the growing importance placed on lifestyles and conspicuous consumption.

Blasé attitude A state of mind produced through the growth of big cities in the late nineteenth century in which individuals, through living in close contact with many others, become immune to urban stimulations and excitement and indifferent toward others. The term was first used by Georg Simmel.

Blended family Also called a reconstituted family. This family type brings together into one household two sets of children and two adults, at least one of whom is from a previous relationship.

Capillary power Description of power created by Michel Foucault. It sees power as located everywhere and produced in and through all forms of social relations.

Capital Refers to the resources associated with business; these include: money, technology and machinery, intellectual property, premises and land. Marxists argue that capital accumulation is the major driver for business and that profits are the basis of this growth.

Capitalism A society based on social relations of production in which the means of production are owned by capitalists who expropriate surplus-value from the labour of wage workers. Put more simply, a system in which 'capitalists' employ free wage workers in order to produce profit. Accordingly, labour markets are essential to capitalism.

Cases One of the major building blocks of sociological research (see **variables**). Research may range across a single case, for example participant observation at a sports stadium, or a great number of cases, for example the millions of forms sent out by government during census year. Cases represent the sites of study, both in terms of physical location (events at a place) and conceptually (the things different types of people do). Cases provide the examples, instances and types as the subject of research and its findings.

Celebrity In pure form the celebrity is someone who is famous for being famous. They are mass media creations who act as role models for consumption.

Charismatic leader A leader who rules through personal exceptional powers and qualities which form the basis of his/her authority. Such a person may be regarded as having divine or supernatural origin.

Citizenship Status as a member of a political community – usually a nation state – which carries rights and duties. When states control the right to citizenship, withholding acceptance as citizens marginalizes individuals and populations.

Class See **social class**.

Class consciousness Usually a reference to the subjective awareness by members of a class of the economic interests of that class – for example, working-class consciousness of wage exploitation.

Cold War The period between the 1950s and the beginning of the 1990s when the United States of America and the Union of Soviet Socialist Republics were in direct power confrontation through a competition for military superiority, although not actually at war.

Collective effervescence A shared social experience of emotion in a group engaged in ritual together – for example, religious ceremonies or gatherings, or public grieving for a well-known person. Émile Durkheim thought this experience was effective in binding members of a society together.

Collective sentiments Feelings that humans share and experience through social interaction, beliefs and values.

Colonialism Classically, political control of one place (city, region, country) by another. Today, usage has expanded through notions like informal empire to cover constraint exercised by one political unit over another, whether or not this takes the open form of political domination.

Commodification The transformation of relationships between people into goods and services of monetary value made available for sale in the market. For example, prostitution in both its legal and illegal forms represents the commodification of otherwise non-monetary intimate relations between people.

Community Used to denote 'natural' informal social bonds between people based on shared location, kinship, occupation or interests. Often used in opposition to the formal social institutions and systems of expertise that have grown out of modernity, such as the nation, the education system, health services and the military.

Competition It is important to distinguish 'perfect' from 'imperfect' competition. In perfect competition, there are a large enough number of buyers and sellers in a particular market such that no single buyer or seller can affect market prices. There is 'price competition'. Imperfect competition includes monopoly, one seller and oligopoly. In oligopoly, there are several sellers that dominate a market, there are barriers to entry and products are relatively similar. This is the situation of the large corporation and is the central feature of modern capitalist economies. There is no clear-cut theory of oligopolies, but it is agreed that because large corporations are interdependent, they reject potentially fatal price competition and engage in non-price competition, for example, in efforts at product differentiation. Prices in such markets are often fixed by a leading producer and are stable.

Consumer ethic Conduct based on a private consumer (rather than a public citizen) model. An individualized rather than collective orientation to life, irrespective of the issues confronted. This is the shopper mentality writ large – the social world as shopping mall in which everything is seen as a personal purchasing decision. Topics like health, education and politics are approached as products in a supermarket aisle.

Consumer society One in which a vast range of goods and services are offered, the means to consume them are widely available, and the desire to do so is socially encouraged. Such societies are based on capitalist economics, mass production, the extension of credit and mass advertising.

Control In the sociology of work, refers to the ongoing struggle for managerial direction over work and workers. This drive seeks to encompass all aspects of work and production so as to maximize efficiency and profits and to erode the oppositional capacity of workers. Arguably, control is also exercised by monopoly capital in the realm of consumption, in which workers manifest as active or passive consumers.

Cost/benefit analysis Broadly, in cost/benefit analysis, the total expected 'costs' are subtracted from total expected 'benefits' of alternative choices in order to choose the best option. This involves, critically, quantitative measures. Thus, a fundamental assumption of neoclassical price theory is the idea that decisions are rational in the sense that actors seek to maximize 'utilities', or 'satisfactions', subjectively determined. It is further assumed that these can be arranged in order of preference and weighed against 'costs'.

Culture industries A term coined by Theodor Adorno and Max Horkheimer, who were concerned by the rationalization and standardization of contemporary cultural production. They argued that cultural entities were being turned into commodities and culture itself into an industry. The media served to manipulate the masses into passivity by cultivating the false needs of consumption (to be satisfied by capitalism) and by marginalizing the true needs of freedom, creativity and happiness as exemplified in the high arts. Thanks to the culture industries, high art loses its autonomy and low art its rebelliousness.

Definition of the situation Created by W. I. Thomas, a sociologist of the

Chicago School, this phrase draws attention to the socially constructed nature of social reality and the fact that this is a social not individual process. This concept is implicit in and underpins phenomenological and ethno-methodological approaches and deconstructionist analysis.

Demand curve Graphical representations of the amounts of goods consumers are willing and able to buy at various prices.

Dependent (uneven) development A distortion of economic development which typically involves unequal exchanges, and the production and exploitation of resources for export. On the theory of *comparative advantage*, there should be no unequal exchanges, but unfortunately the conditions set out by the theory do not and cannot exist.

Desacralization An aspect of the secularization process where there is a decline in the significance of things religious as well as a devaluation of non-scientific explanations for natural and social phenomena.

Deviance Non-conformity to norms that act as a dominant currency for shaping what should or should not be done in social life. This may be viewed positively, neutrally or negatively and treated correspondingly via reward, indifference or sanction.

Dialectic A mode of thinking that sees contradictions as the source of greater understandings in the form of thesis, antithesis, synthesis.

Disciplinary powers A range of techniques of power that do not rely on coercion or force but are constituted through disciplinary knowledge and operate as ways of controlling and training individuals who willingly co-operate in disciplinary practices.

Disenchantment The development of a consumer society is associated with disenchantment of both workers and consumers. This perspective draws from Max Weber's vision of modernity. On the one hand, workers are increasingly constrained in the forms of resistance available to them. On the other, consumers confront crass commercialism. In sum, the citizens of today's society find their means of expression channelled through large-scale bureaucracies (advertising agencies, big business, institutions of state and government, banks and other credit providers).

Division of labour Breaking up a particular task (whether making something or administering something) into a larger number of smaller units, with each more modest task performed by specialized workers. This brings dramatic productivity gains, but at the risk – Émile Durkheim urged – of threatening to reduce social cohesion.

Doing family The ways people construct or create their families by engaging in different sorts of practices (e.g., how people organize meal-times together or how they create a sense of family history).

Double life of the family The idea that family life is not always harmonious and does not always benefit its members, but can be conflict-ridden and dangerous.

Education All societies educate their young; however, education in modern societies is formalized, institutionalized, nationalized and compulsory. Further, modern education rests on the allocation of status on the basis of individual *achievement* rather than the pre-modern allocation of privilege on the basis of the father's place in the social order – what is known as *ascription*.

Efficiency A distribution of goods or a scheme of production is inefficient when there are ways of doing still better for some individuals without doing any worse for others. Thus, an efficient allocation of resources is that allocation which maximizes output. But an efficient allocation need not be *socially optimal* – for example, if it requires the destruction of the natural environment.

Elasticity of demand Relative change of demand as a function of price.

Emotional labour Appropriate feelings produced in the course of employment at the employer's direction as a required part of the job. These are particularly characteristic of service industries, for example airline cabin crew, shop salespeople, and hospitality industry workers.

Emotions In sociology this term describes the feelings that are experienced and expressed with social effects, that is, those that people describe in words, communicate to each other, and which influence their collective and individual actions.

The Enlightenment A collection of eighteenth-century European philosophies broadly committed to progress, the perfectibility of humans and the pursuit of freedom. Enlightenment philosophers championed reason and science against dogma, superstition and (sometimes) religion. Such tenets heavily influenced early sociology, and it is often argued that Enlightenment thinkers set the model of the secular intellectual. Later (post-modern) sociologists questioned the universality of their pronouncements as well as the extent to which we can speak of 'progress' after a century of world wars, genocides, environmental degradations and the like.

Epistemology A philosophical term that refers to the nature, sources and range of knowledge.

Essentialism The idea (in contrast to **social construction**) that most of our social behaviour is innate and unchangeable. In its crudest form it is the 'This is human nature' argument; in its more sophisticated form it acknowledges that evolutionary heritage is responsible for certain social traits and patterns.

Ethics Moral issues relating to right and wrong.

Ethnicity Categorization of groups on the basis of shared culture, sometimes claimed positively as a source of identity. Also, as the 'new racism', used as a ground for discrimination especially in the multicultural societies produced through global movement of peoples.

Ethnocentrism Using one's own culture as the benchmark against which all others are judged and finding all others lacking by comparison with one's own. Refusing to approach the values, beliefs and practices of other cultures on their own terms.

Eurocentrism A form of ethnocentrism which takes European culture and values as the most desirable form. It is often associated with the export of European norms to the rest of the world through the empire-building activities of European nations in the eighteenth and nineteenth centuries.

Extended family Consisting of a nuclear family plus one or more other relatives living together in the same household or in close proximity.

Externalities Roughly, externalities are side-effects, spill-over costs or benefits for third parties. Polluting smoke from a steel mill is a negative externality. Thus the (real) costs of producing steel are not included in the supply schedule and social utility is not optimized.

Faith In a religious context faith is an acceptance of the beliefs and principles of a religion as well as an expression of loyalty to that religion. Faith can be seen as the living trust and confidence in a god's or gods' concern with human affairs.

Family of choice A non-traditional family arrangement chosen and created by people who want to establish long-term, caring and supportive relationships with one another.

Fordism The system of mass production introduced by Henry Ford. This involved the introduction of the assembly line and machine pacing in the manufacture of Model T automobiles. More broadly, Fordism refers to an approach to mass production that relies on specialized technologies, standardization and the elimination of craft work.

Free market In uncritical general use, a condition where there is little or no government interference. But since markets require rules, and governments have a huge role in establishing these, 'a free market' is a market constituted so that *entrepreneurial* actors are not hindered by laws or regulations aimed to protect employees, consumers, the environment, or public goods not provided by the market. This is defended in the name of 'efficiency'.

Free-rider problem Individuals may well see benefits in some action, but if each believes that the others will do it, nobody acts. Thus, in a perfectly competitive market, firms have a common interest in a higher price for the industry's product, but it is in the interest of each firm that the other firms pay the cost – in terms of the necessary reduction in output – needed to obtain a higher price. Indeed, 'the only thing that keeps prices from falling in accordance with the process ... is outside intervention. Government price supports, tariffs, cartel agreement, and the like may keep the firms in a competitive market from acting contrary to their interest'.

Functionalism Represents a recurring perspective within sociology that understands social processes or institutions primarily in terms of their assumed contribution to the operation of society. Functionalism presumes a normative consensus and tends to deny the operation of structural inequalities (e.g., in class, gender, race) and of contested meanings or definitions of given situations.

Fundamentalism A religious movement or point of view characterized by a return to what they define as the fundamental principles of the religion, by rigid adherence to those principles, and often by intolerance of other views and an opposition to secularism. It has especially come to refer to any religious enclave that intentionally resists identification with the larger religious group in which it originally arose, on the basis that fundamental principles upon which the larger religious group is supposedly founded have become corrupt or displaced by alternative principles hostile to its identity.

Gemeinschaft Term used by Ferdinand Tönnies to denote traditional community: authentic, tight-knit, 'naturally' occurring and usually rural. He contrasted this with the **gesellschaft** of modern society.

Gender Gender is typically used in contrast to the biological term 'sex' to show the socially constructed aspects of masculine and feminine identities. Gender norms (what is considered appropriately feminine and masculine) change across contexts, cultures and time.

Gender performance The idea that we perform our femininity and masculinity in the presence of others, much like actors perform their characters on stage in a theatre. Erving Goffman suggested that gender performances involve a 'front stage' zone, where we appear publicly, and a private 'back stage' zone where we prepare ourselves for our public appearances.

Gender roles Socially shaped and shared expectations about which activities, attributes, behaviours and spheres of action are suitable for men and women. The term was developed within sociology during the 1940s as women's increasing labour-force participation challenged traditional ideas about the activities best suited to each gender.

Generalized accident A term coined by Paul Virilio to describe the era we are moving into. Virilio argues that the invention of a new technology is simultaneously the invention of its accident – for example, the ship begets the shipwreck. Our condition is one of deep unease created by the accumulated calamities of scientific and technological 'progress' thus far – and because of scientific revolutions in all fields (genetics and information technology particularly) – and those still to come.

Gesellschaft The term Ferdinand Tönnies used to denote associations of interest in modern society. Unlike the communities of old, there are no deep 'natural' underlying bonds between participants – for example, the business community.

Globalization Often used as a synonym for the worldwide spread of neo-liberal economic policies or for Americanization, it more accurately refers to flows of people, finance, commodities, images and ideas beyond the borders of nation states. These flows are by no means recent. Processes of globalization are uneven and they do not form a coherent whole.

Hegemonic masculinity The form of masculinity dominant in a given place at a given time. Not necessarily adhered to in practice by all or even most men, it represents the most legitimate or ideal form of masculinity. Social and economic changes cause the character of hegemonic masculinity to shift over time, sometimes quite markedly.

Hegemony Dominant monopolization of meaning. Term popularized by Antonio Gramsci to explain the mechanism of the apparent consent of the oppressed to their oppression.

Heteronormativity The concept that heterosexuality is the 'normal' form of human sexual behaviour and that any others are therefore abnormal or less legitimate.

Homosexuality The term, invented in the late nineteenth century, to describe sexual activity between two people of the same biological sex. It was originally used as a political tool that claimed homosexuals were a naturally occurring category of human being and therefore deserved to be treated equally.

Hyper-reality According to Baudrillard, contemporary consumer society is so saturated by mediated signs that any distinction between the imaginary and the real is abolished – a state of affairs he calls 'hyper-reality'. Existence is experienced as a complex web of representations, or *simulacra*, that refer not to some external reality but only to other representations.

Identity The sense of self acquired by individuals through socialization and interaction with others.

Identity politics Debates and actions around the unequal distribution of power in societies on the basis of membership of a social category or group defined by identifiable characteristics, e.g., gender, race, religion, sexuality, disability.

Ideological processes Social arrangements which enable ideologies to be effective.

Ideology Shared ideas, beliefs and discourses in a social system that attempt to structure and interpret the world where there are structural inequalities. Ideologies legitimate the position of those in power and thereby further their interests and perpetuate their dominance.

Imagined community Term coined by Benedict Anderson to describe the kind of ideological attachment that connects citizens and states and to explain how national loyalty works.

Impression management Strategies for presenting the most strategically useful version of 'the self' in particular social situations.

Interaction Social action that occurs in a situation of the recognizable co-presence of at least two persons.

International division of labour The organization of production and distribution on an ever-wider scale, leading (for those enthused by this notion) to nations or regions reaping the greatest possible economic and social benefit by specializing in producing commodities for which they enjoy comparative advantage. Critics see this process as a disguised form of colonialism, since today's global international division of labour is articulated and controlled by transnational corporations registered in advanced capitalist countries.

International shadow powers Networks of goods and services, some illegal, that operate outside formal state and legal channels.

Kinship Historically, kinship refers to people who are related by blood, marriage or adoption.

Market A market is a social institution in which people voluntarily exchange commodities (goods, resources, services) and where co-ordination of those exchanges is accomplished via a system of prices. Market economies, which may be capitalist or socialist, contrast to *command economies*, in which planning replaces the system of prices. The planner is presumed to have all the relevant information needed to co-ordinate, allocate and distribute rationally.

McDonaldization The extension of principles of mass production and managerial control into the realms of service work and consumption. As a result, the modern world more and more comes to resemble a fast-food restaurant in which standardization, limited choice and surveillance are norms.

Medicalization of deviance A generally observable trend in which various arms of the medical profession increasingly get to diagnose, categorize and treat what is considered deviant behaviour. This reflects a broad shift in Western approaches to deviance from punishing the body to curing the mind.

Modernization The process of becoming modern, as an individual or as society. Initially defined with close reference to Great Britain, the first modern society; but the success of many non-Western societies (led by Japan) in modernizing has forced sociologists to acknowledge that routes to the modern world are less limited than this.

Modernism A set of Western high cultural practices roughly dated between 1880 and 1940, which, while differing in detail from one domain to another – from the visual arts and literature to art, music and architecture – shared some common ground in openly celebrating the nature of the medium being used. Modernism stands in a complicated and contested relationship to modernity, not least because many artists who were labelled as modernists employed their own versions of the **traditional–modern dichotomy** to denounce and reject much – or for some, all – previous art.

Modernity The condition of being modern. Though definitions abound and differ in detail, each usually contains some mix drawn from the following list: capitalist industrialization; novel forms of urbanization and urbanism; bureaucracy as the dominant organizational form; extensive divisions of labour; cosmopolitanism; global extension of trade networks and exploitation of raw materials; active citizenship and the reasoning subject.

Monopoly capital The result of the drive by businesses for profits and to accumulate capital. Monopoly capitals are very large businesses that typically operate across global markets. These businesses often have the capacity to transcend the laws of competition associated with markets and can even be bigger than the national governments which may try to regulate them. Because of their size and global reach monopoly capital intensifies the drive for control over the areas of production and consumption.

Neo-liberalism A resuscitation of the laissez-faire liberalism of the late nineteenth century that calls for privatization, free markets, free trade and the withdrawal of social safety nets. Neo-liberals believe that unregulated markets can provide solutions to both economic and social problems. Although against state intervention in the economy, they promote globalization through the support of transnational enterprises.

Network society A term coined by Manuel Castells to describe the contemporary world situation where the globalization of economic activity and culture undermines the autonomy and independent capacity of individual nation states.

New media A term used to describe the increasing prevalence of computer technologies, the internet, gaming and mobile phone devices as means for the delivery of media content. The prefix 'new' is used to dissociate these technologies from traditional media forms such as print and television, due to their relative novelty and the levels of interactivity between producer and user.

New racism Using cultural differences of ethnicity to further racism in a different guise. The result is still prejudice, discrimination and social inequality.

New religious movements A new religious movement appears as a religious, ethical or spiritual grouping that has not yet been recognized as a mainstream denomination or church. These new religious bodies may be in a relatively high state of tension with the wider society, especially when they are seen to have a novel belief system.

Norms A constellation of values that shapes social life; a common pattern. Most commonly realized only when they are breached.

Nuclear family A family composed of parents and their dependent children.

Ontological security Ronald Laing's term. It means being secure in one's own being. More broadly, it could be said to be the state of knowing one's self and one's place in the world.

Ontology The study of being, of existence. This has strong relevance for thinking about reality.

The 'other' Usually written in quotation marks, it describes the situation of minorities who are marginalized by definition of being 'other' to the dominant and mainstream knowledge, culture or '**race**'.

Path dependence Originally applied to formal systems, in path dependence a particular actual outcome depends upon the choices or outcomes of events intermediate between the initial conditions and the outcome in question. Different intermediate choices lead to different outcomes. In history, of course, there are no initial conditions, and all outcomes depend upon choices that actually preceded the outcome in question

Pathology The branch of medicine concerned with the cause, origin and nature of disease. For sociology, it could equally be rendered as path-ology, i.e. the study of how we go astray and the consequences of straying and deviance.

Patriarchy Traditionally used to refer to the rule of older men over younger men, women and children, the term now refers to male dominance over women more generally. Sylvia Walby suggests that patriarchy is manifest through the operation of six social structures: paid work, household labour, culture, sexuality, violence and the state.

Phenomenology In sociology a method of inquiry that focuses on individual experience as a way of understanding how everyday social life is constructed.

Pluralist power A theory that in democratic societies a number of interest groups complete to have their point of view accepted in political decision making and so no single group is able to dominate. This was developed as a counter to C. Wright Mill's concept of elite power.

Positivism A philosophical doctrine whose sociological origins begin with Auguste Comte. Positivists see science as the supreme knowledge form. They believe that there is a single universal scientific method, and that sociologists should emulate this to search for laws that structure the social world. Observable entities based on direct sensory experience are all that counts; metaphysical notions are to be dispatched. Consequently, positivist research has tended towards quantitative data sets and precisely expressed theories.

Post-emotional society A description of contemporary Western societies, which are described as having lost touch with 'real' feelings as individuals experience mainly second-hand, pseudo-emotions delivered through the media. In such a society people are said to have lost the capacity for spontaneous (and therefore authentic) emotional responses.

Post-modernism The culture of the post-modern. It usually denotes the collapse of distinctions between high (elite) culture and low (popular) culture, with heavy emphasis on irony, pastiche and kitsch.

Post-modernity The condition of being post-modern. In the realm of economics it denotes the shift to a service-based (post-industrial) information economy, and the move towards niche marketing. In politics it speaks to the collapse of mass parties (such as of Labour) and the increasing salience of single-issue politics (gay rights, greens). Philosophically, it refers to relativist thinking: the doubt that such a thing as a universal truth exists. Allied to this is the rejection of Enlightenment beliefs in human progress through the application of reason and science. Jean-François Lyotard summed up the post-modern mind-set in the phrase: 'incredulity towards metanarratives'. Debate rages as to whether or not we truly are post-modern: some argue that post-modernity is simply a critical self-aware phase within modernity; yet others, that we are in a qualitatively different world from what we have recognized as modern. The latter argument seems to be falling from favour.

Power A central concept in sociology. Max Weber's classic definition treats it as the capacity of individuals to achieve their aims. It is an important element in all human relationships and is a key dimension in analyses of social inequalities of class, race and gender. Some sociologists distinguish between legitimate power (authority) and illegitimate power.

Power elite A term introduced by C. Wright Mills to describe the overlapping set of ruling interests – military, industrial and political – that govern in many modern democratic societies.

Profane The profane belongs to the realm of the mundane, everyday world. It involves those aspects of social reality that are routine and secular.

Qualitative research Has a focus on a single or a few cases and uses many variables to describe and explain these examples. Participant observation is the classic form of qualitative research. This type of research is characterized by the use of notes, texts and detailed writings to provide rich accounts of relatively narrowly defined areas of study.

Quantitative research Has a focus on many cases and uses few variables. The survey is the classic form of quantitative research. This type of research is commonly associated with the use of numbers, in particular statistical formulae. Numbers are used in this way because of their capacity to condense data as an aid to the study of broadly defined areas of social life.

Race Categorization, without scientific support, which claims to distinguish human groups on the basis of physical characteristics and, sometimes, associated social traits. The grounds on which claims of racial superiority and inferiority are made.

Racialization The process through which ideas and beliefs about 'race' shape social relationships and cast political and economic inequality in terms of racial or ethnic identity. In short, the mechanism by which 'race' is translated into action and becomes an effective social category.

Recalcitrant worker The defiant, non-compliant and strike-prone worker was the focus of sociology in the 1950s, 1960s and 1970s. The recalcitrant worker was seen simultaneously as a threat to capitalism and as an agent for progressive change. The capacity of workers to resist monopoly capitalism and to impose an alternative polity has lessened in recent decades.

Religion Religion is the social institution that revolves around the area of life people regard as sacred. It consists of any socially organized pattern of beliefs and practices concerning ultimate meaning that assumes the existence of god or gods. The sociology of religion is the study of the behaviour and institutions of groups influenced by religious beliefs.

Resacralization A return to and search for sacred, spiritual or symbolic aspects of everyday life. This is often seen as a response to secularization and **desacralization** processes.

Resistance The capacity of workers and consumers to actively oppose managerial and corporate initiatives.

Retail therapy The relief of personal troubles through purchases. Even though these troubles may be the result of public, institutional and structural issues, they are 'resolved' by individual consumption acts.

Revenge effects A phrase used by Edward Tenner to denote the unintended (and frequently negative) consequences of a technology.

Role A collection of attributes and expected behaviours associated with specified social relationships and positions that individuals are expected to perform. Frequently used in sociology in association with a theatrical metaphor of social life.

Sacred The sacred is extraordinary and awe-inspiring, beyond the **profane** realm; it evokes an attitude of reverence. For Émile Durkheim nothing is inherently sacred or profane but rather it become such after being defined and labelled by individuals and groups.

Secularization The process by which religious thinking, practice and institutions lose social significance.

Self Sense of individual personhood originally defined by psychologists and subsequently adopted and developed in sociology to explain how and why individuals experience themselves as social beings.

Sex/gender distinction Developed in the 1970s, this separates the biological attributes that make a person male or female (sex) from the social aspects of masculinity and femininity that we express as boys, girls, men and women (gender). The distinction has lost ground within sociology, given the difficulty of fully separating biology (nature) from society (nurture).

Sexuality The social patterning of sexual expression and behaviour. Different societies at different times have regulated sexual behaviour in different ways. All societies have privileged some forms of sexuality over others.

Signifier/signified For Ferdinand de Saussure, a sign can be seen to be made up of two parts: the *signifier*, or form of the sign (the printed or spoken word, the image of a woman); and the *signified*, or concept that is conjured by the signifier.

Social class A fundamental form of social stratification grounded in economics. Mainstream sociology defines class in terms of relations of distribution; radical sociology defines class in terms of relations of exchange; and Marxist sociology defines class in terms of relations of production.

Social constructionist explanations Contrast with **essentialist** explanations. They assume that the phenomenon being explained is produced in society and through the social interactions of many individuals.

Social democratic A political philosophy that pursues social and economic equality through state intervention.

Social dynamics The working of social processes to produce particular outcomes.

Social inequality Disparities in status, income, life chances and so on between different social groupings (for instance, classes, ethnic groups). The definition, measurement and policy implications of social inequality depend upon its imputed cause – distributional, exchange-based or production-based relations – over which there is considerable debate.

Social justice Refers to ongoing struggles to eliminate or ameliorate the multitudinous inequalities in society. Many of the struggles for social justice are organized as the struggle for rights and equity (e.g., gay rights, women's rights, human rights).

Social movements A concept of a solidarity association on the basis of opposition to one or several forms of inequality, for example the women's movement, the indigenous people's movement, gay liberation. The World Social Forum has come to be known as the 'movement of movements'.

Social reproduction Refers to the familial, institutional and cultural mechanisms by which the social structure is continued, inequalities and all. Education is a central element in the process of social reproduction.

Social status A Weberian concept that defines status as social prestige, compared to class as ownership of economic assets, and power as the exercise of political force.

Sociological imagination C. Wright Mill's term. He urged that all social scientists should exercise the sociological imagination, by which he meant the ability to trace the links between biography (the individual) and history (culture), those things that connect the intimate environment of milieu with the broader one of social structure.

Sociology The study of group life in (modern) society. Sociology traces the (often hidden) relations between the private and the public; the individual and the collective; the personal and the systemic; the specific and the general.

Socio-technical system A combination of people and technology within a physical environment. This broadens our thinking from simply the thing itself to what, who and how the thing is used. Scholars note that technologies are used differently at different times and in different places. Thus attention is drawn to issues such as relevant social groups, power, culture and context.

Sovereign power The monopolistic capacity of the nation state as sole authority to make law and war.

The state Term used to describe the foundation and apparatus of political governance. It usually describes government institutions within a defined territory called the 'nation state', which hold the monopoly of law making within that territory and war making outside it. State formation is a key point in the history of societies because the centralization of power that results allows more complex social arrangements to develop.

Stigma Associated with a notion of socially undesirable, 'spoiled' identity which may originate in the social situation (convicted criminal) or physiological condition (physical or mental disability) of an individual.

Straying Leaving an established path (see **pathology**), going slightly off-course.

Supply curve A graphical representation of the amounts of a good a supplier is willing and able to supply at various prices.

Symmetrical family A nuclear family form in which parents have an egalitarian relationship and share interests, tasks, responsibilities and child care.

Technological determinism The idea that technology is the driver of history and the main cause of social change.

Technology Typically thought of as physical devices which help us do things. Sociologists tend to move beyond thinking about technology as mere artefacts to also thinking about their design, their use and their overall impact within a socio-technical system.

Theory From the Greek 'to look at'. The point of theory in sociology is to help us organize and make sense of aspects of the social world. Theory, then, is tied to comprehension and explanation. Frequently theories contain generalizable propositions.

Third Way A centrist political theory that presents itself as an alternative to both socialism and free market capitalism. It seeks to merge the concerns of the old left with equality into neo-liberal beliefs in the efficacy of market solutions. Critics point out that it works in favour of corporate interests and is really just neo-liberalism in another form.

Totem A totem is a plant, animal or object which is the symbol of a social group, particularly a clan or tribe. The totem is seen as **sacred**.

Totemism A system of religious belief which attributes divine properties to a particular type of plant, animal or object.

Traditional–modern dichotomy A term to capture classical sociologists' efforts to understand modernization. Though different writers inflected this dichotomy differently, they shared a profound sense that modernization brought qualitative change to the societies they inhabited, turning their known social worlds upside down.

Transactions cost Any cost incurred in making an economic exchange which is not included in producing the commodity to be exchanged. These include search and information costs; the costs of coming to an acceptable agreement with the other party to the transaction, including drawing up contracts; and the costs of making sure the other party sticks to the terms of the contract.

Urbanization The processes through which an increasing proportion of a national population lives and works in towns and cities. This marks a shift from a rural, agriculturally based society to an urban, industrial one.

Variables One of the major building blocks of sociological research (see **cases**). Research may focus on few or a great number of variables (see **qualitative research** and **quantitative research**). Variables provide the mechanisms for describing and explaining the case or cases under scrutiny. Variables provide the aspects, dimensions and features of analysis or comparison. For example, a survey on youth attitudes towards alcohol might include variables on age, gender, educational attainment, weekly alcohol consumption, place of residence and income.

Virtual community Unlike communities of old that were place-based and involved face-to-face contact, these are associations of people that have formed through the spread of electronic communications networks – for example, web rings, blogs and hacker communities. They are often seen as confirmation of Marshall McLuhan's prediction of the emergence of the 'global village'.

Work Has at least two aspects, paid and unpaid. Paid work is the core of social life insofar as it produces all the commodities (goods and services) of capitalist societies. Paid work, or production, has tended to be seen as the wellspring of technological and social innovation. Feminists have argued that unpaid work, in particular the domestic labour undertaken by women, is equally important to the reproduction of social life.

Work ethic A social ideal that is ascetic in nature, fostering savings and accumulation of wealth. The work ethic is associated with the rise of capitalism (Weber called it the 'Protestant ethic') and the operation of a society that values work over leisure and production over consumption.

Xenophobia A passionate dislike of foreigners simply because they are perceived as '**other**' (and therefore threatening) to members of one's own nation.

index

and nuclear family 387
postwar growth 121
and religion 282, 346
in terms of circulation 125
transformation of work 116–17
virtual 124
Carbado, D. 203
Caribbean Cricket Club (Leeds) 188
Carrington, B. 188
cars 5, 113, 115, 338–45
alienating effects of 343
creation of new environments 342
effect on our relationship with the
physical environment 343
infatuation with by Americans 344
monopolization of public space 339
negative impacts of 345–9
and pollution 348
and popular culture 344–5
production of 341
road fatalities 349
and secularization 347
as status symbols 342
Carter, Ian x, 2, 47–63, 404
cases 29–36, 37–8, 41, 427
Castelliani, B. 326–7
Castells, Manuel 3, 161, 163, 174
category error 88
Catholic Church
and sexuality 216–17
celebrity 100–1, 160, 427–8
censorship 358
Certeau, Michel de 78, 359
Chandler, A. 112
charismatic leader 155–6, 428
Chavez 144, 145
Cheal, David 383–4
Chechnya 179
Chernobyl 338
Chicago School 410–11
children
and family 392–4
China 112, 262

Christian Church
and sexuality 216, 227
Christian fundamentalism 289
Christmas 380
Chryssides, George 289
cities
and cars 339
communities within 410
and emotions 255, 256
see also urbanisation
citizenship 174, 180, 181, 428
civil inattention 96, 319
Civil Rights Act (1964) 243
Civil Rights Movement 242–3
Civil Rights Voting Act (1965) 243
Clark, T.J. 58
class see social class
class consciousness 134, 136, 137, 139,
428
Coca-Cola 98
Cockburn, A. 348
coffee drinking 91–3
cohabitation 391
Cold War 159, 428
collective effervescence 268, 428
collective identity 242–6
collective sentiments 268, 428
Collins, Randall 300
colonialism 428
demise of 178, 179
colonization 13
Columbine High School killings (1999)
267–8
commodification 110, 428
commodity fetishism 134, 136
communication codes 303
communications systems 174
communism 409
community 5, 399–416, 428
and associations 407–8
connotative and denotative aspects
403–4
defining 402–4

and coastal shelf metaphor 378–9
diverse types of 390–2
'doing' 389–90, 394, 395, 430–1
double life of 379–80, 431
feminist approaches 387–8
as immutable object 378
Marxist approaches 386–7
micro-sociological approaches 388–9
nuclear 266, 377, 381–5, 386, 388, 392, 437
post-modern 394–5
replacing of nuclear family with other forms of 377, 383-5
reproduction of social relations 379
and ritual celebrations 380
'satellite' 384–5
and structural functionalism 381, 382, 385
symbolization of order in society 378
unequal power relations within 380, 387
family of choice 391, 432
Fascism
and community 409
fashion 96, 98
feminism/feminists 61, 69, 166
and family 387–8
'feminization of poverty' 143
Fenton, S. 177, 181, 182
Fenwick, P. 197
Ferguson, Adam 51, 54
fertility rates 392–3
feudalism 116
Feuerbach, Ludwig 11, 279
First World War 60
Fiske, J. 359, 363
Flanagan, Richard
Gould's Book of Fish 9
flâneur (stroller) 338–9
folkways approach 411
football clubs 100
Ford, Henry 74, 75, 120, 121, 342
Fordism 67, 74–5, 341, 432

Fordist-Keynesian system 120–2
Foreman, George 29, 34–5
Foucault, Michel 3, 55, 75, 235, 242, 246
Discipline and Punish 164
History of Sexuality 224–5
on power 149, 163–7, 427
foundation myths 48
Fowler, R. 368, 372
Frame, Janet 321–4, 327, 328, 330
framing of research 36–9
France 180
bourgeoisie 423
Francis, David and Hester, Stephen 319, 320
Frankfurt School 136, 358
free market 107, 111, 112, 117, 432
free-rider problem 114, 432–3
French Revolution 17, 47, 51, 52, 53, 60
Freud, Sigmund 409
Civilization and Its Discontents 103
Fricke, Ron 18
Friedan, Betty 197
Friedman, Thomas 123
functionalism 381, 382, 385, 433
fundamentalism 289–91, 433
Fundamentalist Project 290

G
Gabriel, Y. 76, 79
Galanter, Marc 289
Galtung, J. 411
gambling 326–7
pathological 325–8
and Steel Balls case 325–8
Gandhi, Mahatma 155
Garfinkel, Harold 204, 205–6, 330
Gates, Bill 125, 126, 127
'gay gene' 223
Gay Liberation movement 225, 226, 243
gay marriage 228
gay masculinities 203
gemeinschaft 406, 408, 433
gender 3, 26, 142, 193–208, 433

Mosse, George 408
multiculturalism 14
multitude 132, 141, 143
Mumford, Lewis 74
Murdoch, Rupert 128
Murji, K. and Solomos, J. 187
Musil, Robert 422–3
  The Man without Qualities 11–12
Myrdal, Alva 196

N
NAFTA (North American Free Trade
    Agreement) 175
Nairn, T. 189
Napoleon 155
nation state 161, 163, 178, 179, 183
national identity 176, 179–80, 188
nationalism/nationality 3, 145, 171, 174,
    177–81, 185, 189
Native American cultures 221
nature
  and culture 61
  gendered 206
Nazis 60, 409
Negri, T. 143
Negroponte, Nicholas 369
neo-liberalism 4, 122, 123, 295, 305–6,
    411, 436
neo-Marxists/Marxism 135–6, 138,
    299–300
neo-Weberians 136–8
network society 161, 174, 436
networks 399, 403
New Deal 121
New Haven (Connecticut) 157
new management systems 76
new media 357, 436
new racism 183, 436–7
new religious movements 289, 437
new social movements 233
  and identity politics 242–6
New World
  European discovery of 17

New Zealand 3, 48, 62–3, 131, 142, 152,
    188, 393; *see also* Maori
News Corp 369
news production 355, 367–8
Newton, Isaac 54
Nietzsche, Friedrich 285–6
  The Gay Science 285
Niketown 127
Nisbet, R.A. 401
Nordstrom, Carolyn 161, 162
Norgrove, Aaron x, 355–73
norms 318–20, 330, 437
nuclear family 266, 377, 381–5, 386, 388,
    392, 437

O
Oakley, Ann 26
objectivity/subjectivity paradigm 26
Oklahoma City bombing (1995) 267
Oldsmobile 345
online communities *see* virtual
    communities
ontological security 437
ontology 437
organized crime 149, 161–2
Osborne, P. and Sandford, S. 172
'other' 171, 437

P
Pakistanis 182
Palestine question 278
Panopticon 75–6
Papua New Guinea 215
parenthetic statements 36
Park, Robert 410
Parkin, Frank 137, 155
Parsons, Talcott 5, 56, 377
  and nuclear family 381–3
  'The School Class as a Social System'
    300
  The Structure of Social Action 56
pastiche personality 235
PATCO 122

definition 26–7
differences between 42
framing of 36–9
and goals of sociological inquiry
	39–42
numbers and words 27–8
queer theory 214, 224–7

R
race 3, 141–3, 171–90, 439
	based on colour differentiation 181
	and class 142–3
	as social/cultural constructs 171, 173,
		182–3, 189
	sociological analysis of 183 7
	see also ethnicity
race relations 173
racialization 172, 173, 186, 187–9, 439
racism 173, 174–7, 182, 183, 186, 190
radicalism 55
Radway, Janice 359
Ragin, C. 5, 29, 37, 39
Rapoport and Rapoport 384
Rather, Dan 373
rationalization 54, 60
Rattansi, A. 187
Reagan, President Ronald 122
Real Madrid 100
reality
	encoding 363
	supplanting of by simulations 355, 367
reason 55
	and emotions 253, 254
recalcitrant worker 67, 72, 76, 79, 83, 439
Redfield, Robert 411
Rees, A.D. 411
Reformation 17
refugees 174, 176
Reichl, Ruth 234
Reith, Gerda 326
religion 4, 88, 145, 178, 275–91, 439
	as basic element of human
		experience 275–6

and capitalism 282, 346
classical sociology of 278–82
continuing relevance of 276, 282, 286
and death of God 285–6
defining 276–7
and fundamentalism 289–91, 433
importance of understanding 278
and legal codes 275, 276
and modernity 285, 286, 287, 288–9
resurgence of 289–90
and science 275, 286, 287
and secularization thesis 275, 283–4,
	285, 286–7, 291, 347, 440
and sexuality 214–15, 216
as social phenomenon 275, 277
sociology of today 282–4
Remington, R.A. 185
Renaissance 17
resacralization 291, 439
research 2, 25–43
	cases and variables 29–36
	deductive and inductive strategies 36
	developing of theories 40–1
	differences between quantitative and
		qualitative 42
	framing of 36–9
	and giving voice 41
	and goals of sociological inquiry
		39–42
	and identifying patterns 39, 41
	interpreting events 41
	making predictions 39–40
	Muhammad Ali example 29–36, 42
	qualitative–quantitative 2, 25–39,
		438–9
	testing theories 40
resistance 71–9, 439
resource depletion 61
retail merchandizing 127
retail therapy 87, 95, 439
revenge 262–4
revenge effects 346, 439
revenue classes 137, 138, 139, 146